TRANSATLANTIC PARTNERS

TRANSATLANTIC PARTNERS

Canadian Approaches to the European Union

Evan H. Potter

PUBLISHED FOR CARLETON UNIVERSITY
BY McGILL-QUEEN'S UNIVERSITY PRESS,
MONTREAL & KINGSTON, LONDON, ITHACA

ISBN 0-88629-348-0 (cloth)
ISBN 0-88629-346-4 (paperback)

Printed and bound in Canada

Canadian Cataloguing-in-Publication Data

Potter, Evan H. (Harold), 1964-
Transatlantic partners : Canadian approaches to the European Union

Includes bibliographical references.
ISBN 0-88629-348-0 (bound). —
ISBN 0-88629-346-4 (pbk.)

1. Canada—Relations—European Union countries. 2. European countries—Relations—Canada. I. Title.

FC244.E9P68 1999   303.48'271041   C98-900901-7
F1029.5.E9P68 1999

Cover Design: Steven Takach
Interior: Mayhew & Associates Graphic Communications, Richmond, Ont., in association with Marie Tappin.

Canadä

McGill-Queen's University Press acknowledges the financial support of the Government of Canada through the Book Publishing Industry Development Program (BPIDP) for our publishing activities. We also acknowledge the support of the Canada Council for the Arts for our publishing program.

For my parents
and
Lisa, Janet, and Louise

CONTENTS

FIGURES

TABLES

PREFACE

The present work began as a doctoral dissertation at the London School of Economics. A generous fellowship from the Canadian Department of Foreign Affairs and International Trade (DFAIT) enabled me to spend a most fruitful academic year in 1991-92 as the Norman Robertson Research Fellow in the Economic Planning section of the Department's Policy Planning Staff. There I found a suitable and rewarding environment to undertake the research papers that make up the core of this dissertation and to interview officials who had made and were making Canada's policy toward the European Community. In the fall of 1992, I was invited to gain another perspective on the decision making process by working in the Office of Multilateral Trade Negotiations at DFAIT, where I examined bilateral Canada-EC relations in the context of Canada's multilateral trade relations. In 1997, a familiarization tour of the EU, made possible by the European Union Visitors' Program, allowed me the opportunity to update and revise the text.

I owe debts of gratitude to numerous Canadian academics interested in Canadian foreign policy and/or the European Union. In the Canadian public service, I am especially grateful for the assistance of two officials: Michael Hart, who was director of the Economic Planning unit on the Policy Planning Staff during the period of my Fellowship and who was instrumental in giving me access to senior DFAIT officials; and Howard Balloch, who was director-general of the Policy Planning Staff and who, along with Mr. Hart, had created the Fellowship program to permit junior academics to gain a fuller understanding of the Canadian foreign policy process. I would also like to acknowledge the administrative support provided to me by the Professional Association of Foreign Service Officers (PAFSO) during 1993-96. PAFSO provided a collegial environment in which to carry out my research during those years. Special thanks go to Donald Mackay, Colin Robertson, Debra Hulley, Barbara Topp, and Susan Courville.

Finally, I deeply appreciate the valuable support of the Delegation of the European Communities in Ottawa and Carleton University Press. Jennifer Strickland of the Press generously helped me. Of course, I bear responsibility for all errors and/or omissions.

Evan H. Potter
Ottawa, July 1999

ACRONYMS

ACP - African, Caribbean, and Pacific states
BRITE - Basic Research in Industrial Technologies for Europe
BCNI - Business Council on National Issues
CCC - Canadian Chamber of Commerce
CAP - Common Agricultural Policy
CCP - Common Commercial Policy
CEE - Central and Eastern Europe
CEN - European Committee for Standardization
CENELEC - European Committee for Electrotechnical Standardization
CFCs - Chlorofluorocarbons
CFDI - Canadian Foreign Direct Investment
CBI - Confederation of British Industries
COFI - Council of Forest Industries of British Columbia
CPD - EC Construction Products Division
CSCE - Conference on Security and Cooperation in Europe
CUFTA - Canada-U.S. Free Trade Agreement
EC - European Community
ECB - European Central Bank
ECSC - European Coal and Steel Community
Ecu - European currency unit
EEA - European Environmental Agency / also, European Economic Area
EEC - European Economic Community
EEIGs - European Economic Interest Groupings
EFTA - European Free Trade Association
EMI - European Monetary Institute
EMS - European Monetary System
EMU - European Monetary Union
EPC - European Political Cooperation
EPU - European Political Union
ESA - European Standards Association
ESDI - European Security Defence Identity
ESPRIT - European Strategic Program for Research and Development in Information Technologies
ETSI - European Telecommunications Standards Institute
Euratom - European Atomic Energy Community
EUREKA - The European Research Coordination Agency
EAITC - External Affairs and International Trade Canada
FDI - foreign direct investment
G-7 - Group of Seven (United States, Japan, Germany, United

Kingdom, France, Italy, and Canada)
G-24 - Group of 24
GATT - General Agreement on Tariffs and Trade
GBP - Generalized System of Preferences
GDP - Gross domestic product
GNP - Gross national product
ISO - International Standards Organization
ITO - International Trade Organization
JCC - Joint Cooperation Committee
JESSI - Joint European Submicron Silicon Initiative
MFA - Multifibre Agreement
MFN - most favoured nation
MNEs - Multinational enterprises
MRAs - Mutual Recognition Agreements
MTN - Multilateral Trade Negotiations
MTO - Multilateral Trade Organization
NAFO - Northwest Atlantic Fisheries Organization
NAFTA - North American Free Trade Agreement
NATO - North Atlantic Treaty Organization
OECD - Organization for Economic Cooperation and Development
OEEC - Organization for European Economic Cooperation
OSCE - Organization for Security and Cooperation in Europe
PTT - Post, Telephone, and Telegraph
QRs - Quantitative restrictions
R&D - Research and development (see also S&T)
S&T - Science and Technology (see also R&D)
SBD - Second banking directive
SCEAIT - Standing Committee on External Affairs and International Trade (House of Commons, Canada)
SCFA - Standing Committee on Foreign Affairs (Senate, Canada)
SEA - Single European Act
SEM - Single European Market
SMEs - Small and medium-sized enterprises
TAD - Transatlantic Declaration
TAFTA - Transatlantic Free Trade Agreement
TCs - Technical committees
TOEP - Technology Opportunities in Europe
TRIMs - trade-related investment measures
VERs - voluntary export restraints
WEU - Western European Union
WTO - World Trade Organization

TABLE 1.1: CANADA-EU RELATIONS: THE BALANCE SHEET

Aspect of Relationship	Centripetal Forces	Centrifugal Forces
Civilization	common Judeo-Christian heritage	different political cultures
Historical Experiences	wartime and postwar cohesion	end to postwar cohesion with collapse of communist regimes in Central and Eastern Europe starting in 1989 and then the Soviet Union in 1991, closing of all Canadian military bases in Germany in 1994; Canada's "psychic link" with Western Europe eroding as "special relationship" with the U.K. becomes more tenuous as Canada evolves into a "nation of the Americas" and the U.K. incrementally begins to define itself more and more as "European" nation; growing proportion of Canadians of Asian descent, diluting ethnic ties.
Political-Economic Systems	pluralist democracies, mixed capitalist, developed economies; mutual commitment to human rights and good governance around the world.	EU states more corporatist in outlook; mixed pluralist political-economic systems allow special interest groups as producers to demand protectionist action by the state that when taken can disrupt overall ties.
Strategic Security	collective self-defence through sister organization, NATO; had equal stake in the defence of Western democracies against threat from Soviet Union; the mutuality of interests in managing the emerging, post-Cold War cooperative security issues such as drug interdiction, terrorism, refugee flows, environmental security, proliferation of weapons of mass destruction, etc.	the collapse of Soviet Union and the disbanding of the Warsaw Pact have resulted in the disappearance of a "transcendental, value-driven" reason for Canada to have an active in European security; the uncertain missions of NATO and the CSCE—the primary "pillars" in Canada's European policy framework—in the post-Cold War world are reducing Canadian influence in European eyes; the European desire to establish independent Common Foreign and Defence Policy through European Security and Defence Identity, the re-invigorated West European Union, and the Franco-German corps.

Aspect of Relationship	Centripetal Forces	Centrifugal Forces
Interdependence	because the EU in aggregate represents Canada's second largest trade partner after the U.S., there are relatively close trade investment ties; the fact of two cultures—English and the French—has led to close political relations with the U.K. and France; the issuance of the EC-Canada Transatlantic Declaration (TAD) has meant closer political links with the Community; a series of growing bilateral Mutual Recognition Agreements and Memoranda of Understanding were completed or under negotiation on issues such as standards and certification, Science and Technology, customs, competition policy, and fisheries; Canada and the EU consult and have common interests on a number of international issues such as the progress in the rebuilding of the Eastern European economies, Third World debt alleviation, and sustainable development.	asymmetric economic and political relations, i.e., any changes in bilateral relations have greater impact on Canada; lack of interest on both sides—and especially in Washington—to enshrine interdependence and individual bilateral issues in a broader Canada-EU free trade agreement or transatlantic treaty to create "Atlantic Community"; pull of faster Asia Pacific region for Canada and the pull the deepening and widening agenda of the Community.
International Trade	common stake in liberal world trade order.	Canada more vulnerable than EU to neoprotectionism; politicization of EU-U.S. trade conflicts could lead to Canada being "side-swiped"; international regime on investment more important for Canada than the EU.
Bilateral Trade	EU dependence on Canadian resource exports, especially forestry products and minerals and metals; Canadian dependence on EU exports of finished goods.	Canadian merchandise trade deficit with EU; greater intra-North American and intra-EU trade and steady erosion of EU as market for Canadian exports; "EU 1992" will present only niche markets for certain Canadian industries; creation of pan-European market—to include EFTA nations through the EEA and the expansion of the EU to 15 member states plus the push to the eastern half of Europe through "association"

Aspect of Relationship	Centripetal Forces	Centrifugal Forces
		agreements—means Canada may become only a residual supplier to EU market since its export mix is heavily resource-dependent.
Bilateral Investment	heavy dependence on each other's investment markets, with EU second-largest source of inward foreign direct investment into Canada after the U.S.; total joint investment stock at end of 1996 exceeded $70 billion.	barriers to trade in services and investment, especially at the level of the individual member states; NAFTA has more extensive investment provisions than does "EC 1992"; indication that height of Canadian investment occurred by a small number of Canadian MNEs in run-up to "1992" and that the coming years will see a steady decrease in annual Canadian FDI to the EU.
Domestic Conditions	Growing interdependence means that domestic conditions such as labour standards, interprovincial barriers, social policy, and the environment have increasing international dimensions.	The EU's and Canada's respective attentions to domestic economic downturns characterized by high unemployment rates and, in Canada's case, a dangerously large national debt and deficit, have meant that domestic economic issues are superseding "foreign" issues on the national agenda; on the political side, since the rejection of the Meech Lake and Charlottetown accords, Canada is also facing constitutional turmoil over the question of Quebec.
Leadership	politically strong leaders capable of balancing bilateral relations so that no one dispute poisons broader relations; the Transatlantic Declaration provides bilateral political forum, for political resolution to irritants—such as Atlantic fisheries and plant health issues on the Canadian side and environmental practices and beverage appellations on the EU side.	weak leaders susceptible to producer group protection calls; less capable of providing balance to overall relationship as each side means less to the other in political and economic terms.

Aspect of Relationship	Centripetal Forces	Centrifugal Forces
International System	members of numerous multilateral organizations and groupings of states as full members or observers.	changes in the international system from one of bipolarity to multinodal and increasing interdependence complicates bilateral relations; increased political and economic stature of EU and reduced U.S. hegemony means Canada may lose ability to "free-ride" on U.S. interests against Europeans; EU more worried about stability in the East and Russia than Canada's unique interests within what to the EU is usually "one" North American "pillar."
Foreign Policy	broad accord on long-term Western goals such as assistance to Central and Eastern Europe and the states of the former Soviet Union; mutual sensitivities to the emerging "cooperative security" issues such as illegal migrations, sustainable development, AIDS, and human rights (to include women's rights).	trend toward EU foreign policy independent of, and conflicting with, U.S. may mean that Canada will have to choose to side with one or the other and, given its increasing economic ties with the U.S., this may mean that Ottawa's foreign policy is more closely aligned with that of Washington; lack of mechanism to coordinate foreign policy outside NATO, NACC, and EU institutional constraints, the TAD may not act as the best instrument to systematize bilateral relations.

Source: Author's observations based on categories used to define EC-U.S. relations as developed by Roy H. Ginsberg, "U.S.-EC Relations," in Juliet Lodge, ed. *The European Community and the Challenge of the Future* (London, Pinter, 1989), Table 14.1, 258-59.

I

SETTING THE STAGE FOR CANADA-EU RELATIONS

"Small powers always expect more than they can get."
— A.E. Ritchie[1]

CANADA'S RELATIONS WITH EUROPE and its response to European integration has traditionally been supported by "three pillars," namely, the North Atlantic Treaty Organization (NATO), the Organization for Security and Cooperation in Europe (OSCE),[2] and the European Union (EU).[3] During the period from 1985 to 1996, the process of integration accelerated markedly as shown in three key areas of interest for Canada: economic, political, and security relations. While each "pillar" deals to some extent with these key areas, the European Union had by the early 1990s carved out a greater role for itself in all three domains.[4] Indeed, the EU showed the potential to one day supplant NATO as Canada's "first pillar" in Europe.

Although this study provides a broad historical perspective on Canada-EU relations, it concentrates on the time period between 1989 and June 1997. This period includes the second term of the Conservative government led by Prime Minister Brian Mulroney (1989-93) and the first term of the Liberal government led by Jean Chrétien (1993-97). It was during this period that Eastern and Western Europe, in particular the European Union, again occupied a central place on the Canadian foreign policy agenda. This period also highlights the redefinition of Canada-EU relations within the changing context of post-Cold War transatlanticism. The book concludes by exploring the implications of the Chrétien government's interest in a transatlantic free trade zone. It is not, however, an analysis of European integration, nor of Canada's place in the Union's external relations. On the latter point, some sense of Ottawa's relative importance to decision makers in Brussels is discernible from this study's description of European reactions to Canada's transatlantic policy initiatives. However, the primary purpose of this work is to examine both the process and substance of Canada's approach toward the Union.

In light of the essentially economic nature of bilateral Canada-EU relations since the beginning of Canada's diplomatic recognition of the Common Market in 1959, security will be dealt with in an economic and political context. Aspects of transatlantic security relations are already well covered in the Canadian and European defence policy literature.[5] Finally, the nomenclature of the EU (known as the European Community or EC until 1993), Canadian, and other institutions will follow what was used at the time of reference.

Two fundamental questions are posed. First, given the pace of global economic integration and the creation of a Single European Market (SEM) on January 1, 1993, have Canadian policy responses to European integration been driven primarily by Canadian industry or have they been state-led? Secondly, what does an analysis of this bilateral relationship reveal about the foreign policy choices and capabilities of a middle power such as Canada in a post-Cold War international system characterized by both globalization and regionalism? In particular, is Canada well or badly positioned to further its interests, bilaterally, multilaterally, or within the Triad (i.e., the trading blocs of North America, Europe, Japan)? This examination of Canada-EU relations in the context of changing transatlanticism offers a test of whether a middle power such as Canada has the potential to exert more, rather than less, influence in the post-Cold War era.

What little has been written about Canada-EC/EU relations over the last three decades has been grouped around particular issues. In the mid-1970s, there was a burst of scholarly work on the "Third Option" policy of diversifying Canada's external relations away from the United States and, later, on examinations of the 1976 "Framework Agreement for commercial and economic cooperation between the European Communities and Canada," hereafter referred to as the Framework Agreement or the EC-Canada Framework Agreement. Since the early

1980s, however, the bilateral relationship has been woefully underresearched with regard to both the policy process and the economic and political/security dimensions of bilateral relations. For instance, has Ottawa's response to the creation of the SEM hindered or promoted Canada's economic and commercial interests in Europe? And to what extent did the 1990 EC-Canada Transatlantic Declaration (TAD) give voice to a renewed transatlantic alliance and more balanced bilateral political links between Ottawa and the European Commission?

This study addresses this deficiency in three ways. First, its perspective combines the political, economic, and, since the early 1990s, the nascent security strands of Ottawa's approach to the EU. Second, this book represents the first comprehensive analysis of Canada's relations with the Union in almost a decade. Third, this study offers a two-pronged extension of the debate on the future of transatlantic relations: by including the EU as a legitimate institutional player, and by adding a Canadian perspective on the EU to a field of literature which has been devoted almost exclusively to discussing transatlanticism in the context of NATO, the CSCE/OSCE, and U.S.-EU relations. The Canada-EC partnership was largely forgotten during most of the 1980s on both sides of the Atlantic. It was only with the overlapping developments of the completion of the Canada-U.S. Free Trade Agreement (CUFTA) followed by negotiations to create a North American trade bloc, the momentum of the Single Market, and the collapse of communism in Eastern Europe and the Soviet Union starting in 1989, that the EU was once again firmly on the Canadian foreign policy agenda and Canada briefly rated somewhat more attention than Brazil in the Community's external relations.

This book also highlights the five major determinants of Canada-EU relations. In a seminal article in 1991, Charles Pentland wrote that the "twin themes of access and architecture" were always the foundation of Canada's policy approach to European integration.[6] By "access" he meant access for Canadian exports and investment into the integrating markets of the EU characterized by a common commercial policy and the Common Agricultural Policy (CAP). The term "architecture" referred to the scope and institutional design of Europe, the evolving roles of the Commission, the European Parliament, and Council of Ministers as well as the EC's relations to other European institutions, taking into account Canada's place in the transatlantic framework. Access and architecture are together the first two determinants of Canada's approach to, and observation of, the process of European integration.

To Pentland's "twin themes," this study adds three more major determinants. The third is the ebb and flow of the tide of Canada-U.S. and EU-U.S. relations. That is, Canada's reaction to the evolution of European integration cannot be fully understood unless it is put into the broader context of the evolving pattern of bilateral Canada-U.S. relations, and Ottawa's historic need to achieve diversification in its foreign relations through counterweights to both Britain and the United States.[7] Washington's role as the primary international interlocutor of both Ottawa and Brussels makes an appreciation of EU-U.S. relations integral to understanding the evolution of Canada-EU relations.

A fourth determinant comprises the various images that bureaucratic, political, and business elites in Canada have of the European Union. Historically, bilateral relations have been state- or, more specifically, bureaucratically-led on both sides, with little political or business support at a high level.

The final major determinant of Canada's approach to European integration is a perennial concern among Canadian analysts and decision makers that West European politicians, Commission officials, and American presidents (such as John F. Kennedy), and secretaries of state (such as Henry Kissinger and his "Year of Europe"), have tended to bury Canada's diplomatic identity under a "North American" rubric representing a so-called "two-pillars" image of the Atlantic world. Thus, while the Canadian government approaches Europe from a "three-pillars" framework, Western Europe and the United States tend to subsume Canada under a "two-pillars" image of transatlantic relations.

But beyond the importance of adding to a body of research, why is a comprehensive examination of Canada's approach to the EU worthy of study at this time? Put quite simply, the official end of the Cold War in November 1990 also appeared to mark the end of the need for an Atlanticist orientation in Canada's foreign policy. Actually, Canada's disengagement from Europe preceded the end of the Cold War by at least a decade and had at its roots the domestic consensus surrounding Canada's declining economic competitiveness, highlighted by world recessions in the early 1970s, the late 1970s, and again in the early 1980s. This consensus was, however, overshadowed at the time by the continuing exigencies of Cold War alliance structures. It was only with the rapprochement of the U.S. and the Soviet Union, dating from Mikhail Gorbachev's ascension to power in 1985, that Canada in its actions, as opposed to its declaratory policy, became openly less and less an Atlantic and European nation. At the same time, the European

Community, embodying Western Europe, was itself undergoing a process of sometimes wrenching change as it pursued political, economic, and monetary integration and acted as a magnet for both members of the European Free Trade Association (EFTA) and the former Communist nations of Eastern Europe. The question then remains whether there are sufficient bilateral economic interests at stake and whether there is sufficient political will on both sides that Canada-EU relations may be strengthened for the new millennium.

CANADA AS A "EUROPEAN" NATION

Chapters 2 to 5 of this book offer an historical overview of the evolution of Canada's interests in, and approach to, European integration in the decade following the War, through the Treaty of Rome that created a common market among the "original six" member states, until 1991. The discussion moves chronologically from Ottawa's reaction to Western Europe's attempts to rebuild its shattered economies in the late 1940s and 1950s; to a focus on market access issues in the 1960s; to the architecture of the EC institutions in the 1970s as Canadian and Commission interests converged; to a period of mutual neglect in the 1980s; and finally to a period of intense activity in 1989-91 as Canada rethought its approach to the European Community in the context of trying to carve out a niche for itself in the reconfiguration of overall transatlantic relations.

For most of its history, Canada has viewed itself as a European nation. A graph of its relations with Europe in terms of peaks and troughs would indicate that in the period from Confederation in 1867 to the signing of the Statute of Westminster in 1931, its national interests to a greater or lesser extent mirrored those of the United Kingdom. Thereafter, with the ever greater pull of north-south economic integration, London's influence on Canadian affairs waned as relations with Washington began to take precedence. From 1948 until 1984, the nature of Canada's policy toward Europe can, in large measure, be ascertained by looking at the degree to which Europe figured in the foreign policy priorities of successive prime ministers. Louis St. Laurent, both as Secretary of State for External Affairs and as Prime Minister, was a strong supporter of the reconstruction of a war-ravaged continent through Canada's leadership in the creation of multilateral security and economic forums, namely, the General Agreement on Tariffs and Trade (GATT) and NATO. Prime Minister John Diefenbaker's stubborn Anglophilism during the late 1950s and early 1960s, symbolized by, among other issues, his desire to diversify a significant portion of Canada's trade away from the U.S. and to the U.K., not surprisingly drove a wedge in Canada-U.S. relations. Lester Pearson, in his successive roles as Canada's senior diplomat, Secretary of State for External Affairs, and finally Prime Minister, believed strongly in a "North Atlantic Community" in which Europe could be used to balance the influence of the United States.[8] Pierre Trudeau's dilettantism in the late 1960s and desire for a less NATO-centric foreign policy led to the first serious questioning of Canada's European vocation.[9] His government's subsequent attempt to create a more "independent" and "nationalist" foreign policy in the early to mid-1970s instead created a peak in Canada's relations with Western Europe and, in particular, with the Community.

After 1984, the interplay of a trend and two events marked the beginnings of a serious rethinking of Canada's foreign policy orientation toward Europe, the EU, and its commitment to the Atlantic community in general. The trend toward an increasingly global economy, starting in the 1960s but gaining significant momentum by the 1980s, coincided with a Conservative government in Canada, led by Brian Mulroney, the first postwar Canadian prime minister to promote publicly Canada's proximity to the United States. It was also accompanied by the collapse of communist regimes in Central and Eastern Europe and the Soviet Union in the late 1980s and early 1990s.

Under the leadership of Prime Minister Mulroney, Canada became committed to fuller economic integration and political involvement in the Americas through a number of major policy initiatives. These included signing the CUFTA in 1988, joining the Organization of American States (OAS) in 1990, ratifying the North American Free Trade Agreement (NAFTA) in 1993, and increasing the prospect for further hemispheric integration through the NAFTA's accession clause. There also emerged a strong sense that Canada could not afford to be left out of the economically dynamic Asia Pacific region, prompting aggressive Canadian support of multilateral economic and security forums, such as Asia Pacific Economic Cooperation.[10]

In aggregate, then, these initiatives created a strong incentive for a profound change in Canada's traditional Eurocentric foreign policy orientation. Indeed, the decade from 1983 to 1993 saw Canada become more and more a "nation of the Americas."[11] In the words of John Halstead, Canada's former ambassador to NATO and astute observer of the evolution of Atlanticism, it appeared that by the early 1990s the Canadian dilemma had become how to "reconcile an Atlanticist foreign policy with a continentalist economic policy and a defence policy increasingly limited to territorial defence and peacekeeping."[12] Canada was clearly on the cusp of a new type of partnership with Europe.

Changing Canadian Leverage in Transatlantic Relations

Chapters 2 to 5 will show that the underlying challenge in Canada's approach to the EU was always how to gain satisfactory leverage. As a member of NATO, to which the original six EU member states also belonged, Canada was able to use its security role in Europe as a subtle but effective lever in its bilateral relations with the member states and, by extension, in its bilateral relations with the Union. This lever never approximated direct linkage. Canada had no such power. Issues in the transatlantic complexity were rarely driven in a tit-for-tat manner. Indeed, given the broad distribution of power within the transatlantic community, it has always been difficult to predict the outcomes of specific disputes or tensions and to disentangle the links on the fluctuating transatlantic agenda of political, security, and economic concerns.

In the transformed geopolitics of the late 1980s and early 1990s, however, issues of partnership, procedures, and leverage, had new salience for policy makers on both sides of the Atlantic. The removal of major structural features such as the Cold War, and the difficulties in completing the Uruguay Round, created a situation in which the broad, traditional expectations and images of Europe held by Canadian decision makers were no longer sustainable. The notion of "linkage" became more important in the 1990s because notions of economic partnership and security alliance could no longer be consigned to separate boxes.[13]

How did this affect Canada-EU relations? As envisioned by its founders, the EU had indeed evolved well beyond its mandate as a customs union into other spheres of competence as a result of revisions to the founding treaties in the Single European Act (SEA) and the Maastricht Treaty on European Union. In addition to full economic integration, by the early 1990s, foreign, security, and defence policy were also seen as legitimate objectives in the drive toward political union. The EU's decisions began to affect Canadian interests beyond the traditional areas of external and internal trade, agriculture, fisheries, and atomic energy, spreading to, *inter alia*, the "high" politics of sanctions on South Africa, East-West relations, aid to Central and Eastern Europe, population migrations, and the environment. That evolution made Canada's dual-track approach within its "three-pillar" European policy framework, that is, relegating its participation in the OSCE and NATO exclusively to the security track and its relations with the EU exclusively to the economic track, an increasingly untenable way to organize its transatlantic relations by the end of the 1980s. How to set the foundation for redefined bilateral Canada-EU relations in face of the end of the Cold War and the prospect of European economic, political, and monetary integration was thus a cause for reflection and action in Ottawa.

However, the challenge for Canadian decision makers was not necessarily to *increase* the number of diplomatic contacts with the West Europeans but rather to *systematize* relations with the increasingly important EU pillar of Canada's European policy framework. The West Europeans were, after all, allies, and occasionally adversaries, in most of Canada's international economic and political activities. In addition to NATO and the OSCE, Canada met with its European counterparts in the Group of Seven (G-7), the Commonwealth, La Francophonie, the Northwest Atlantic Fisheries Organization (NAFO), the Organization for Economic Cooperation and Development, peacekeeping missions, development assistance, international financial institutions such as the World Bank and the International Monetary Fund, and participatory or observer functions within social and economic bodies such as the UN Economic Commission for Europe (UNECE), the European Bank for Reconstruction and Development (EBRD), and the Council of Europe. Indeed, in Europe itself, the only distinctly European institutions that Canada did not have a formal role in were the EU and the Western European Union (WEU).

It could be argued that, given this level of contact, transatlantic relations were in fact over-institutionalized, a situation that was accentuated by bureaucratic impulses to create ever more talking shops. This book will explore how Canada reacted to the institutional density in Europe and whether such a conglomeration of overlapping mandates helped or hindered Canada's European role.

Furthermore, within the structural context of EU-Canadian relations, there were a number of privileged bilateral relationships between Ottawa and the national capitals of the member states. The most obvious but not the only one was that between Canada and the U.K. Another was the Canada-France relationship, strengthened in the

1980s through La Francophonie after a deterioration in the 1970s with Canada's perception of French interference in Quebec. Finally, in light of German unification and Bonn's support of a continuing Canadian presence in Europe, it would appear that the Ottawa-Bonn axis also increased in importance in the context of Canada's bilateral relations with the EU.

Yet, by the end of the 1980s these numerous contacts proved insufficient in the eyes of Canadian policy makers to protect Canada's European interests. In particular, the EU's post-1989 role in the coordination of Group of 24 (G-24) aid to Eastern Europe and the former USSR heightened its profile in the eyes of Canadian policy makers. And, as mentioned, the EU's push beyond full economic integration toward political and monetary integration highlighted the fact that Canada could no longer afford to keep separate economic and political "tracks" in its approach to transatlantic relations. As a result, the Canadian government decided that the twin institutional mechanisms of its privileged relationship with the EU—the Framework Agreement and the 1988 special access to European Political Cooperation (EPC)—were necessary but not sufficient to maintain Canadian interests in Western Europe. For this reason, Chapter 5 examines the Canadian attempt to infuse political energy into Canada-EC relations through the TAD.

CANADIAN RESPONSES TO THE SEM AND TRANSATLANTIC FREE TRADE

In contrast to the broad historical treatment in the first part of this book, Chapters 6-8 concentrate in detail on the impact of the SEM on Canada's economic interests and the changing structure of the transatlantic economic relationship in the 1990s. It does so by applying the implications of the SEM for Canadian suppliers (Chapter 6) in directly affected industries such as financial services and telecommunications, as well as in forestry products, although the latter industry was affected less directly by the creation of a SEM. Nevertheless, forestry products remained the major source of revenue in Canada's export trade with the Union. Chapter 7 then examines the state of Canada-EU economic relations to the end of 1996, probing trade and investment patterns before and after the creation of the SEM.

Although the TAD was significant in that it highlighted the growing *political* role of the EU in North American eyes, the key challenge posed by the EU to Canada was its growing weight as a trading entity, resulting from the deepening of integration through the so-called "1992" program and the effective widening of its approach to market liberalization to include the EFTA member states, the countries of Central and Eastern Europe (CEE), and some Mediterranean nations. If the primary effect on Canada of the EU's establishment in 1957 was discrimination against Canada in those areas where the EU developed common policies (e.g., the Common External Tariff and the CAP), then the considerable concern 30 years later in Canadian government and business circles over effects of the EU's "deepening" and "widening" processes on Canadian market access is not surprising.

To answer how the above processes conditioned Canadian responses to European economic integration, Chapters 6-8 highlight how the domestic debate on Canada's declining international competitiveness—a motivating force for securing a free trade agreement with the United States—was central in prompting Canadian policy makers to take the lead in seeking more secure access to the Western European market. What were the differences in Canada's response to North American and European integration? A number of Canadian analysts (Rugman, Eden and Molot, Doern and Tomlin)[14] have asserted that sustained pressure from both the Canadian and American business communities led the Canadian government to seek a free trade agreement with the United States, a deal that in subsequent years led to significant increases in bilateral trade and investment flows. In the case of the Canadian response to the SEM, this study will evaluate the relative involvements of the state and private sector actors and suggest that in the period leading up to the SEM exactly the reverse occurred; there was a distinctly muted response from Canada's private sector but very activist state involvement. First the "third option" and then the Framework Agreement point to the historical precedents for state-led Canadian responses to Western Europe's expanding economic clout. However, a consensus began to form in Canada by the late 1970s that the state-led approach to securing increased access to Western European markets had failed to produce any significant gains, a claim that is only partially true and will be discussed. A decade later, during a major advance in the Community's program to create an economic union, a development that would once again present both challenges and opportunities for Canada-EU commercial relations, there was still the question whether an Ottawa-based response would once more lead to both unreal expectations and ultimately disappointment.

Chapter 8 examines the structural sources of changing transatlantic economic relations in the early 1990s. In particular the following general areas are examined:

1) The impact on Canada-EC relations of radical structural change affecting Europe and the United States. In particular, the fact that between 1983 and 1993 the respective economic weights of the EC and the U.S. had changed in the international system.

2) The replacement of military and ideological rivalry with economic rivalry. The immediate post-Cold War period accentuated rather than diminished transatlantic economic friction. In an era of greater interdependence, this was bound to heighten the importance of market-access issues in Canada-EU relations.

The repositioning of Europe, Japan, and the U.S. in the global political economy had important policy and institutional implications for Canada during the Mulroney government's almost decade-long tenure. Four major interrelated processes significantly influenced Canada-EU relations during this period: the SEM, the CUFTA, the NAFTA and the Uruguay Round of multilateral trade negotiations under the GATT.

The international configuration of economic power must decisively influence any meaningful Canadian and, indeed, North American initiative to improve transatlantic relations. This is because the management of transatlantic trade and economic issues will prove critical as economic security becomes a paramount national interest. In this context, Chapter 8 compares an array of new economic frameworks within which Ottawa contemplated managing its bilateral relations with Brussels, including the prospects for a transatlantic free trade agreement (TAFTA). The look ahead to the future or next stage in Canada-EU relations draws from the experience of having a 17-year-old Framework Agreement, the lessons of closer EFTA-EU ties, the limits to greater transatlantic integration given the level of North American integration, and, most importantly, the political will for closer relations in Ottawa and in Brussels at the Commission and Community presidency level.

ADJUSTING TO THE POST-COLD WAR SYSTEM: CANADA AND THE EU

Chapter 9 examines the loss of Canada's Atlanticist influence and Ottawa's attempt to gain a toehold on pillar three, soft security issues under the Maastricht Treaty. Chapter 10 shows the qualitative change in the nature of Canada-EU disputes by the mid-1990s as transatlantic frictions, whether over the fisheries, leg-hold fur traps, or the Helms-Burton Act, pointed to clusters of entangled problems rather than the unidimensional disputes of the past. Not only were the old rules of the EU's comportment in transatlantic relations changing, but Ottawa also faced the certainly that the Union would enlarge, which would further dilute Canada's ability to use its special relationships with the U.K., France, and Germany to influence EU decision making.

A central theme of these chapters is that, perhaps more than any other Western industrialized state, Canada has had to make a number of major adjustments to its post-Cold War foreign policy priorities. Although every state has been affected by an increasingly multipolar world in which economic and political power is more diffuse, diplomacy is based increasingly on economic rather than ideological rivalry, and new regional groupings are coming into prominence, some states have been affected more than others.[15] Canada in the post-Second World War period has used the leverage of an "internationalist" foreign policy based on mediation, multilateralism, and coalition building to project an influence that is greater than its relative size would indicate. This has prompted scholars, practitioners, and other observers to label Canada as the quintessential "middle power."[16] Given Canada's high dependence on trade (more than a third of its Gross Domestic Product [GDP] by 1996), over the past 45 years, successive Canadian governments have relied on and advocated a "rules-based multilateralism" in a variety of U.S.-led international economic forums such as the GATT/WTO to achieve this additional leverage.[17] On the security and political fronts, Ottawa has favoured a more cohesive Western Europe, nested in and reinforcing the U.S.-dominated NATO, with Canada benefitting from an active American presence in Europe.

However, with the disintegration of the Soviet Union and the relative decline of the United States, other actors such as Western Europe through the EU, Japan, and the Newly Industrializing Economies (NIEs) of Asia Pacific have assumed new roles and increased influence on the international stage. By the late 1980s, Canada existed in a world where the sources of economic tension—or, as Sylvia Ostry has described it, "systems friction"—were at least as powerful as the forces driving economic integration. For a middle-sized, open economy caught between the twin realities of diminishing relative power, exemplified by steady declines in its slice of the global economic pie coupled with the loss of its traditional mediation role in East-West relations, and growing global interests, these trends were, to say the least, unsettling. Thus in the early 1990s, to use Wolfers' terms, not only were Canada's "possession" and "milieu" objectives being tested, but also the means by which it pursued them.[18]

And just as Canada's position in the international system was changing, so was Europe's. Indicative of the speed and the breadth of change that have swept across Europe since 1985, but particularly since 1989, were the movement to complete the SEM, the at times painful absorption of a united Germany, the attempt to create a European Monetary Union by the end of the 1990s, the strengthening of resolve toward political union, the establishment of a European Economic Area (EEA), the movement toward a common foreign and security policy, and the emergence of a European defence identity that challenged the traditional institutions of the Atlantic alliance. In short, there was an emergent pan-Europeanism. The European Union either created, or was directly affected by, the above events and processes. More subtle, perhaps, was the EU's growing influence outside Europe as a dialogue partner with numerous groupings of states, and through its independent voice in international organizations, most notably in the UN, the G-7, the GATT, the Quadrilateral Group, and at the OECD, where it has observer status.[19] For these reasons, by the mid-1990s the EU as an institution had become the dominant force in Europe and an increasingly important global actor as well. The respective evolutions of Canada and the EU during this period thus forms the context of Chapter 9 and 10's examination of bilateral relations in the post-Cold War era.

ANALYTIC FRAMEWORK FOR STUDYING CANADA-EU RELATIONS

The analytical framework underlying this study presupposes five major sets of variables that shaped bilateral Canada-EU relations during the period under examination (see centripetal and centrifugal forces in Table 1.1). The first is systemic, characterized by increased globalization and the impact of the end of the Cold War on the

European security architecture; the second is domestic, with the completion of the CUFTA and declining economic competitiveness in Canada; third is organizational (for example, "bureaucratic politics"); fourth is sociological, concerning the impact of values and perceptions among officials, politicians, and business leaders in Europe, the United States, and Canada; and finally policy, including Canada's foreign policy objectives and decisions and their implementation in the European Community. Of course, overlaying the above variables is the question of national interests. This study must answer the question of what specific policies were part of Canada's European framework in the 1980s and 1990s and to what extent the policies were consistent with national goals. Secondly, with regard to the choice of policies, the questions would be somewhat different. For example: who were the key actors? What were their policy preferences? What were their respective bargaining resources? And what was the relative importance of domestic and external factors in the policy making process? Finally, whose interests were reflected in policy outcomes and why?

To explain why relations did not become more market-driven requires a decision making analysis; that is, an examination of the relative importance of systemic, state, and societal forces in Canadian foreign-policy making. This study therefore invokes the bureaucratic politics paradigm as its particular conceptual lens. It supports the statist approach to Canadian foreign policy, which asserts that government actors in Canada are able to translate their preferences into public policies with a fair degree of autonomy from society.[20]

In the conclusion, we return to two themes introduced in this chapter and illustrated throughout the study. The first is historical. The history of postwar transatlantic relations highlights the remarkable similarities between the debates on the appropriate transatlantic institutional structure that took place within the Canadian government in the period leading up to the creation of NATO (September 1947-April 1949),[21] and those more than 40 years later (mid 1989-91) concerning Canada's foreign policy role in Europe during the post-Cold War period.[22] Indeed, as this study's analysis of post-TAD transatlantic policy options suggests, the policy debate surrounding the negotiations of the NATO Treaty may actually hold lessons for the ability of Canada in the post-Cold War period to influence the creation and/or reconfiguration of transatlantic institutions. But perhaps this study's most important contribution is that it confirms what Lester Pearson always recognized, namely, that the United States is the "key to any progress toward an Atlantic alliance" and by definition the "key" in the calculus of the Commission, the EU member states, and Canadian policy makers as they modulate their approaches to each other.[23]

The second theme is theoretical and has implications for the wider study of Canadian foreign policy. The analysis of Canadian-EU relations in this volume supports those theorists who assert that Canadian foreign policy is a largely state-led affair. This is in conformity with the majority of work in the field but the idea of an autonomous state actor has been challenged by some theorists writing about the evolution of the CUFTA. Our research accepts the idea that North American free trade has largely been defined by business interests and contrasts it with the private sector's indifference and resistance to Ottawa's initiatives in European relations. This study also makes use of, and adds credence to, the theory of bureaucratic politics by highlighting the importance of the personal interests of successive prime ministers and structural and personnel changes inside External Affairs and International Trade Canada (EAITC), the Cabinet, and the Prime Minister's Office (PMO). It is impossible to understand the direction of Canadian policy in this sphere without reference to these complex and interrelated conditions.

NOTES

1. As cited in J.L. Granatstein and Robert Bothwell, *Pirouette: Pierre Trudeau and Canadian Foreign Policy* (Toronto: University of Toronto Press, 1990), 172 and ftn. 89. Ritchie was among the original elite corps who constituted Canada's first foreign service (after the Statute of Westminster in 1931). He rose to become Under-Secretary of State for External Affairs.
2. The Organization for Security and Cooperation in Europe (OSCE) was known as the Conference on Security and Cooperation in Europe (CSCE).
3. The European Coal and Steel Community (ECSC), Euratom, and the European Economic Community (EEC) were formally amalgamated July 1, 1967 to become the European Community (EC). The EC became the European Union after ratification of the Maastricht Treaty on November 1, 1993. For a useful review of the rise of the EC, see John Pinder, *European Community* (London: Royal Institute of International Affairs, 1989), esp. ch. 1.
4. The 15 member states are: Germany, France, the United Kingdom, Italy, the Netherlands, Spain, Belgium, Denmark, Portugal, Ireland, Greece, Luxembourg, Austria, Sweden, and Finland. The latter three countries joined as of January 1, 1995, and are included in this study's statistical analysis.

5. The best regular source for Canadian views on European security is the periodical *Canadian Defence Quarterly.* See also, the most up-to-date research bibliography on Canada's defence and security literature in David B. Dewitt and David Leyton-Brown, eds., *Canada's International Security Policy* (Scarborough, ON: Prentice-Hall, 1995), Appendix.
6. Charles Pentland, "Europe 1992 and the Canadian Response," in Fen Osler Hampson and Christopher J. Maule, eds., *Canada Among Nations, 1990-1991: After the Cold War* (Ottawa: Carleton University Press, 1991), 126.
7. For an excellent historical discussion of the importance of diversification in Canada's foreign policy in the context of Canada's relations with Europe, see Panayotis Soldatos, "En guise d'introduction: Le Canada devant la diversification et le continentalisme libre-échangiste," in A.P. Donneur and P. Soldatos, eds., *Le Canada à l'ère de l'après-Guerre Froide et des blocs régionaux* (Toronto: Captus Press, 1993), esp. 1-3; see also, Donald Barry, "The United States and the Development of the Canada-European Community Contractual Link Relationship," *American Review of Canadian Studies*, vol. 10 (Spring, 1980): 63-74.
8. According to an acclaimed biography of Lester B. Pearson by John English, Pearson believed "that Canada's identity depended upon the nourishment that flowed from its links to Europe and that without such links the economic and political sinews of Canadian nationhood would shrivel." John English, *The Worldly Years: The Life of Lester Pearson*, vol. 2 (Toronto: Alfred A. Knopf, 1992), 110. For an equally profound treatment of Pearson's thinking on the North Atlantic community, see John Holmes, *The Shaping of Peace: Canada and the Search for World Order, 1943-1957*, vol. 2 (Toronto: University of Toronto Press, 1982), ch. 5. And for Pearson's "Atlantic Vision" in his own words see Lester B. Pearson, *Mike: The Memoirs of the Right Honourable Lester B. Pearson* (Toronto: University of Toronto Press, 1972), ch. 3.
9. The best treatment of Trudeau's "Europe" policy from the late 1960s to the early 1970s can be found in Peter C. Dobell, *Canada's Search for New Roles: Foreign Policy in the Trudeau Era* (Oxford: Oxford University Press, 1972); and Peter C. Dobell, *Canada in World Affairs*, vol. 17, 1971-73 (Toronto: Canadian Institute of International Affairs, 1985), ch. 8. On a reappraisal of the Third Option, see Panayotis Soldatos in Paul Painchaud, ed., *From Mackenzie King to Pierre Trudeau: Forty Years of Canadian Diplomacy, 1945-1985* (St. Foy, QC: Presses de l'université Laval, 1985); and Granatstein and Bothwell, *Pirouette*, 111-72.
10. See, for example, Lawrence Woods, *Asia-Pacific Diplomacy: Nongovernmental Organizations and International Relations* (Vancouver: University of British Columbia Press, 1993).

11. A phrase coined by Michael Hart in his chapter entitled, "Canada Discovers its Vocation as a Nation of the Americas," in Hampson and Maule, *Canada Among Nations 1990-91*, 83-108.
12. John Halstead, "Atlantic Community or Continental Drift?," *Journal of European Integration* 16, 2 (Spring 1993): 158.
13. Michael Smith and Stephen Woolcock, *The U.S. and the European Community in a Transformed World* (London: Royal Institute of International Affairs, 1992), 7.
14. Lorraine Eden and Maureen Appel Molot, unpublished paper on Canada-U.S.-Mexico free trade that was given to this author in October 1991; Tomlin and Doern (1991), Rugman (1991). Only Michael Hart, a Canadian official who participated in the negotiations leading up to the CUFTA, has argued that both the motivations for and the process of the free trade agreement was preponderantly influenced by a small number of trade policy officials. In his view, although the Canadian business community was consulted by government, it was almost tangential to the process of achieving the final agreement. See Michael Hart, with Bill Dymond and Colin Robertson, *Decision at Midnight: Inside the Canada-U.S. Free Trade Negotiations* (Vancouver: University of British Columbia Press, 1994).
15. A "multipolar" rather than "multinodal" world is referred to here because there will continue to be economic competition, although now among a greater number of regional groupings. Multimodality would not be appropriate in this instance since it de-emphasized competition.
16. A classic exposition of why Canada adopted an internationalist foreign policy is found in Holmes, *The Shaping of Peace*, vol. 2.
17. For an excellent historical examination of multilateralism in Canadian foreign policy, see Tom Keating, *Canada and the World Order: The Multilateralist Tradition in Canadian Foreign Policy* (Toronto: McClelland & Stewart, 1993).
18. According to Wolfers, possession goals are a means of preserving or enhancing a country's possessions or natural resources; milieu goals are aimed at influencing the nature of the international environment beyond a country's borders. Arnold Wolfers, *Discord and Collaboration: Essays on International Politics* (Baltimore, MD: Johns Hopkins University Press, 1962), ch. 5, 67-80.
19. The G-7 has been a prestigious forum for the discussion of macroeconomic policy since 1975 and, since 1980, international political issues as well. It is important to note that the G-7 summits are made up of no less than four EU member states (Germany, France, U.K., Italy) plus the president of the Commission to represent the interests of the smaller Community members. The Quadrilateral Group includes the EU, U.S., Canada, and Japan. The EU also is a dialogue partner of the following groups of countries: ACP states (69), Andean Pact, Arab

League, ASEAN, Contadora, Central America, Council of Europe, EFTA, Front Line states, G-8, GCC, Mediterranean states, and SELA. See Table 5-1 in Christopher Hill, "The Foreign Policy of the European Community," *Foreign Policy in World Politics*, Roy Macridis, ed., (Englewood Cliffs, NJ: Prentice-Hall, 1992), 127. With Canada's own affinity for "dialoguing" with as many groups of countries as possible there is considerable overlap between the Canadian and EU dialogue partners (e.g., at the annual ASEAN post-ministerial conference, former Front Line states, Contadora, ACP states).

20. On this statist approach, see Kim R. Nossal, "Analyzing the Domestic Sources of Canadian Foreign Policy," *International Journal*, 39 (1983-84): 1-22.
21. Pearson considered September 1947 as marking the beginning of the North Atlantic Alliance. See, Pearson, *Mike*, 41.
22. This has been noted in Robert O. Keohane, Joseph S. Nye, and Stanley Hoffman, eds., *After the Cold War: International Institutions and State Strategies in Europe, 1989-1991* (Cambridge: Harvard University Press, 1993), 16-19.
23. Pearson, *Mike*, 49.

II

FROM NATO TO NAFTA: THE RISE AND FALL OF CANADA'S EUROPEAN PROFILE

"We do not know (indeed Europe does not know) how far or how fast its experiment in integration will take it, or what form it will assume on arrival.... Canada is not seeking preferential treatment or special advantage ... but only a guarantee of fair treatment at the hands of an economic unit rapidly becoming the most powerful in the world."

— Pierre Elliot Trudeau, Mansion House, London, March 1975[1]

THE ANALYSIS OF CANADA'S reaction to the process of European integration would be incomplete without a review of the major forces and alliances shaping Canadian foreign policy in the early postwar years and during the building of the European Economic Community between 1951 and 1957. Most diplomats and academic observers would agree that the hallmarks of Canadian foreign policy in these years can be epitomized by Secretary of State for External Affairs Louis St. Laurent's "Gray Lecture," which was delivered at the University of Toronto in 1947.[2] At the centre of foreign policy considerations during his tenure was the contention that "the security of this country lies in the development of a firm structure of international organization."[3] St. Laurent saw the construction of strong international organizations and the development of international law as the key to global peace and Canadian prosperity.[4]

During this period, Canada was instrumental in the creation of both the United Nations and NATO. A central objective of Canadian foreign policy makers was to strike a balance between the world's former great power, the U.K., and the United States. Canada's relations with the rest of Europe and ties with the Commonwealth were clearly subordinate to its links with the Anglo-American alliance.[5] Although Ottawa was intent on buffering the fall of the U.K.'s power in the Western hemisphere, there was none of the zeal displayed before 1945.

CANADIAN REACTION TO THE CREATION OF THE EC

In 1948, with the beginnings of the Cold War in Europe, European reconstruction was the highest priority on Canada's foreign policy agenda. Canada's Lester Pearson, then Under-Secretary of State for External Affairs, was one of the most fervent advocates of the "embryo of an Atlantic community which would be the successor to the 'North Atlantic' triangle of the 1930s and 1940s, in which Canada had enjoyed close and counterbalancing ties with both Britain and the United States."[6] Notable Canadian diplomats such as Pearson and Escott Reid saw NATO as a unique mechanism for promoting transatlantic cooperation and understanding beyond a strictly military and political role, in effect creating an "Atlantic Union." This idea was embodied in the Canadian-authored Article 2 of the North Atlantic Treaty and elaborated in the 1956 Report of the "Three Wise Men," which included Pearson.[7] Canada did not eventually find adequate support for the concept of a broader Union, with dissenters in Canada and among Canada's allies noting the number of existing transatlantic economic mechanisms (United Nations Economic Commission for Europe, Organization for European Economic Cooperation—OEEC) and arguing against the need to create new ones.

For Canada, the North Atlantic proposal offered something more than bilateral alliances with its two most important partners. According to Canadian diplomatic historian, John English, Prime Minister Mackenzie King had apparently been "suspicious" of bilateral alliances with the U.K. and, in May 1948, rejected the option of a bilateral free trade agreement with the United States. For Norman Robertson, then a high-ranking Canadian diplomat, NATO thus provided "a providential solution for so many of [Canada's] problems": how to assure American commitment to European defence, how to avoid a bilateral Canadian-American commitment, and how to escape being "orphaned" by a purely American-European entente.[8] These three objectives would prove to be the basis of all successive approaches to Europe by Canadian governments, whether Liberal or Conservative.

Muirhead, in his rich and detailed study, *The Development of Postwar Canadian Trade Policy: The Failure of the Anglo-European Option*, concludes that Canada "failed miserably" to position itself as a predominantly Atlantic nation by developing trade relations with the United Kingdom and continental Western Europe between 1947 and 1957. In the same way that Canada's commitment to NATO was seen as a key pillar of its foreign policy, trade with the U.K. in particular was regarded as critical to Canadian prosperity and as an important counterweight to growing trade with the United Sates. He writes that, by 1950, Canadian policy makers had not yet abandoned "all hope of ever re-establishing the old North Atlantic triangle, though the prospects of doing so seemed bleak," and that Canada was settling "more comfortably into a continental role."[9] His study reveals that necessities and not preferences determined Canadian policy outcomes and that "Canadian policy was multilateral by preference, bilateral by necessity, and manifestly continental by default."[10] His study is also noteworthy in that, as Cutler points out, it reveals the "limits placed on policy autonomy by the desire in Ottawa to appease both London and Washington" and shows how the external determinants of Canada's foreign economic policy loom large in policy outcomes in the late 1940 and 1950s.[11]

Historically, Canada had to be wary of closer European economic cooperation, a caution that had its origins in the Great Depression of the 1930s. In terms of general support for the principle of European integration, in the early 1950s, it was not an issue in which Ottawa was actively engaged. The Department of External Affairs, for example, decided not to recommend that a delegation be accredited to the High Authority of the European Coal and Steel Community, feeling that Canada's interests did not justify such representation. Understandably, Canadian policy makers took a much more aggrieved position on regional groupings that threatened to keep Canada's products out of their markets, such as the Organization for European Economic Cooperation (OEEC), with its collective approach to currency convertibility and its deliberations concerning trade liberalizations.[12]

The Economic Effect on Canada of the EEC and EFTA

Muirhead contends that Canada remained relatively neutral during the early stages (for example, during the Messina conference of 1955) of what would later become the European Economic Community (EEC). Ottawa was in favour of the integration movement but opposed to the development of a discriminatory free trade area, and it wanted the integration process to evolve into a North Atlantic-wide free trade area that would breathe some life into the moribund Article 2 of the NATO Treaty.[13] By late 1956, although St. Laurent (now Prime Minister) indicated strong support for the principle of economic integration, the Canadian government became increasingly alarmed by the possibility of restricted trade, indeed more so by the prospect of a U.K.-led European Free trade Area[14] than by an EEC (since 15 percent of Canada's exports went to Britain and only 6 percent went to the countries comprising the EEC). There was also a concern among some Canadian mandarins about the political and military implications of European economic integration, a process that if "carried through steadfastly" could have seriously damaged the Atlantic Alliance and left a "stretched and strained" Canada as the United States and Europe drifted apart.[15]

What can be concluded from Canada's commitment to Europe from 1947 until the formation of the EEC? Muirhead notes a sense of "betrayal" and "disappointment" since, unlike the United States, Canada could do little to influence the course of European events during this period to better suit its interests. Although it had spent a better part of a decade attempting to convince the Europeans of the benefits of a multilateral and non-discriminatory trade, what had been created was in essence a regional bloc.[16] There was real concern about the discriminatory impact of the EEC on specific Canadian commodities such as wheat. More than 30 percent of Canada's total world sales of wheat were to the original six member states; in the case of flaxseed and polystyrene, the figure was more than 70 percent; as well, more than 10 percent of Canadian sales of barley, iron ore, nickel, tobacco, and aluminum went to EEC countries. With such significant proportions of Canada's world sales any adjustments or reorientation in European trade patterns had the potential to seriously disrupt Canada's agriculture and industry.[17]

In terms of a possible EFTA, despite the U.K. representing such a large market, for Canadian officials the saving grace was that each country was free to pursue its own commercial policy and set its own tariff rate on any product. As would be the case 40 years later when Ottawa calculated the economic cost to Canada of the European Economic Area's creation and the costs and benefits of transatlantic free trade, in the 1950s the primary Canadian concern with EFTA was not with the arrangement per se but precisely that it might merge with the Common Market and form a Europe-wide free trade zone with the more restrictive Common Market features. Canadian officials felt that such an arrangement would hit Canada especially hard in the areas of agriculture and fisheries.[18]

In short, Ottawa felt "betrayed" by its Atlantic partners in the mid-to-late 1950s. Canadian policy makers held that Canada did not receive a commensurate commercial return in Europe despite its heavy commitment to European security through NATO and the extension of financial assistance to its Western European allies through the OEEC. In other words, the European mind-set was not acknowledging a link between security, such as Canada's role in the liberation of Western Europe from Nazi occupation and its role in the Atlantic Alliance to counter the threat of Soviet domination, and economic components of the transatlantic relationship. Thus the only reliable market 12 years after the Second World War was the United States, which was the destination of 60 percent of Canadian exports and the source of 70 percent of Canada's imports, and which had exempted Canada from certain pieces of restrictive trade legislation and continued to purchase huge quantities of Canadian raw materials. While this created a dependency, Canada clearly had few other options.

By 1957, at the same time that the EEC was being formed, Canadians, witnessing the creation of a branch-plant economy as a result of enormous inflows of American investment, began to have considerable doubts about their economic relationship with the United States. The release of the Gordon Report in that year revealed the size of U.S. economic influence in Canada, which, many feared, posed a threat to Canadian sovereignty. This distrust of the U.S. would, at first glance, appear to have found understanding in the eyes of Canada's European allies since they too were receiving large amounts of U.S. investment. One could therefore assume that such an understanding would have buttressed Canada's political and economic links with Western Europe. Indeed, the official beginning of Canada's relationship with the newly formed EEC was in 1959 when Canada signed an agreement with the European Coal and Steel Community and its ambassador to Belgium was accredited to the EEC.

But while Canada forged new links with the new European economic bloc, it was also faced with the prospect of an erosion of its trade ties with Western Europe because the EEC's Common Commercial Policy and the CAP were now added to the factors that had traditionally impeded Canada's transatlantic trade, including transportation costs, communications, languages, customs, and consumer tastes.[19] Mirroring Canada's reaction to the creation of the Single Market 30 years later, Canadian decision makers in 1957 viewed the creation of a large preferential trading area as inevitably resulting in trade discrimination and trade diversion to the detriment of third countries in the short-term—no matter how much the new economies of scale resulted in trade growth.[20] Canada was left little choice in the matter of course, and would have to adapt its policies accordingly.

The formation of the EC was but one aspect of a fundamental and inexorable change in the structure of the international system in the late 1950s. Change was accompanied by the resurgence of Western Europe and Japan, the decline of Great Britain, and the spread of industrialization in the world, the result of the near monopoly of North American producers, and the gradual shift from a strictly bipolar world of military alliances to a more multipolar one based on regional trading blocs. There were other more direct indicators closer to home. As mentioned, Canada's economy was becoming more closely integrated with that of the United States. Finding themselves losing overseas market shares to more efficient competitors, Canadian exporters were increasingly inclined to focus on the more familiar American market.

One development in the early years of the Community, however, did provoke considerable concern in the Diefenbaker government, namely, the United Kingdom's unsuccessful first bid for EC membership in 1961.[21] The Canadian government drew pessimistic conclusions about both the economic and political consequences of British membership. At that time, Britain still took 17 percent of Canada's exports, as opposed to 57 percent to the United States and about 10 percent to the rest of Western Europe. In Prime Minister Diefenbaker's eyes, the cornerstone of Canada's trade policy was still Britain and the Commonwealth preferences.[22] For this reason, as Roseman points out, Diefenbaker saw the U.K.'s bid to join the EC as the worst of all possible scenarios, since the preferences would then be replaced by the common external tariff.[23] The estimated impact of Britain's accession and the consequent loss of preferences to Canada varied, running from a high of $900 million in exports being affected (since total exports to the U.K. at that time was approximately $1 billion and of those 95 percent were free of duty, with about half in a preferential position); to the estimate by the former president of the Canadian Exporters' Association of a direct loss of $400-500 million; and to the much more plausible estimate made by eminent Canadian economist, Harry Johnson, of between $55 to $70 million or less than 10 percent of total exports.[24]

In addition to fearing that Canadian exports, especially agricultural products which were a large proportion of Canada's exports,[25] would suffer drastically, the Diefenbaker government was concerned that Britain's role as *primus inter pares* within the Commonwealth would be ended, and even that North America's commitment to Western defence would be weakened.[26] Thus, Diefenbaker also opposed: (1) the U.K.'s forming a European Free Trade Area, and (2) London's offer of a Canada-U.K. free trade area as a response, apparently, to Diefenbaker's own calls in early 1957 for closer Canada-U.K. trade relations which he felt would lessen Canada's dependence on the U.S.[27] As a further measure of Ottawa's preoccupation with Britain's unsuccessful attempt to gain accession, during the Dillon Round of GATT negotiations between 1960 and 1962, the Diefenbaker government in fact entertained the possibility of applying to become an "associate member" of the EC.[28] This option was quickly dismissed by knowledgeable observers of transatlantic relations who understood that in the final analysis the aim of the Common Market was in fact political. By definition Canada could not be considered a "European" nation, although the Liberals seemed to support this strategy as they tried to forestall being left behind as the Americans pursued links of their own with the Common Market.[29]

If an associate membership was not an available option to Canada, then another strategy was to promote an Atlantic Community that would bind Canada, the United States, and the U.K. to the Common Market. Lester Pearson, who as the new Liberal leader in 1958 became the leader of the Official Opposition, was as suspicious as Diefenbaker of the increasing influence of the United States on Canadian life, but departed from the Conservative prime minister by warmly endorsing Britain's bid for membership in the Common Market. He believed that Britain within the EC would better strengthen a North Atlantic Community and thus better serve Canada's interests. Just a few days after he was elected leader, Pearson, in a speech, defined what would be the Liberal Party's view on Atlantic relations while in opposition:

> If then we do not wish to weaken the western coalition; and if, in Canada, we do not wish either to face the United States alone or become too dependent economically on it, then surely the best policy for us is to seek economic interdependence within the North Atlantic Community through freer trade.... For Canada, a North Atlantic area with the freest possible trade would certainly mean a much greater export market in the U.S.A. and in Europe; lower costs of production for many Canadian industries, and lower living costs, I would hope, for Canadian consumers.... There are undoubtedly certain industries that would have to receive special consideration in any such freer trade agreements, just as such consideration is being given in Europe to special economic situations in the negotiation of the free trade area there.... This is an appropriate time to push this proposal.... This is a challenging prospect and is surely worth serious and immediate consideration, negotiation and planning. Could there be a finer initiative for Canada? All this is, of course, long range policy.[30]

The Liberal criticism of the Conservative foreign policy was that rejecting closer relations with both the United States and the EEC amounted to a form of "plague on both your houses" and was thus a dangerous form of "economic isolationism" that ignored Canada's two leading markets.[31] The Liberals further asserted that the Diefenbaker government should have spent less time lobbying for Britain's continuing leadership of the Commonwealth and London's rejection of the Common Market, which Canada had no leverage to prevent, and more time doggedly pursuing an Atlantic Free Trade Area, which was consistent with both Canada's desire to promote "free trade in a free world" and the "only satisfactory solution to the problem of Western unity" in a world faced with a Soviet global threat.[32]

The Canadian private sector's perception of Canada's foreign interests in the early 1960s in many ways mirrored those of the politicians. Business leaders such as the then-president of the Canadian Pulp and Paper Association, R.W. Fowler, noted that while the single most important factor in Canada's trade policy was the development of the European Common Market, Canadians, in his view, could not look at European integration in isolation and would also have to "view European development in the context of the influence [it was] having on American thinking and policy." In short, it was the action in Europe and the reaction in the United States, and vice versa, that was of vital importance to Canadian trade, since Canadian economic policy was "caught in a vise" between these two forces on opposite sides of the Atlantic.[33]

This historical background shows that the concerns expressed by Canadian business people, politicians, and officials in the late 1950s about the impact of the EEC on Canada are both similar and different to the reactions 30 years later as the EC moved definitively toward economic union. Canadian business leaders in the 1980s, for example, did not share the previous generation's view of a unified European market as pivotal to Canada's national economic prosperity. In their eyes, Canada's trade policy priorities had shifted away from Europe. The reaction among Canadian politicians and officials (see Chapters 3, 4 and 5) in the late 1980s and early 1990s toward European economic union bore a striking similarity to the concerns expressed by officials and politicians a generation earlier. Certainly, both Canadian business and government feared the prospects of decreased Canadian access to European markets as a result of the parallel processes of "deepening" and "widening." But while the official Canadian reaction to the prospect of a Single Market may have rung the same notes as in 1960, the trade policy context could not have been more different by the 1980s. The Mulroney government had, after all, explicitly chosen the "continentalist" option. In the early 1960s, the Liberals had looked to an Atlantic free trade option but had realized that this was a non-starter given the Americans' lack of interest in joining regional trade blocs and the Europeans' (specifically the Commission's) repudiation of any such transatlantic alliance on the grounds that Europeanism was not reconcilable with Americanism as the United States was both a nation of the Atlantic *and* the Pacific.[34] In 1990, the Mulroney government's suggestion of an Atlantic free trade zone would be similarly rejected by the Americans and the Europeans. As the following chapters will show, although Canada was prepared to work with and within the post-Cold War transatlantic institutions and forces and to bend them to serve its interests, it was clearly no longer as likely to be crushed between the two powerful millstones on either side of the Atlantic.

THE 1960s: PARTIAL PARTNERS

During most of the 1960s rapid economic growth in Europe combined with successful tariff cuts of the Kennedy Round left few barriers for Canadian exports and investment (apart from agriculture) in the EC market.[35] By the late 1960s, however, confrontations between Canadian and EC negotiators at the GATT concerning the Community's Common Agriculture Policy highlighted Canada's inability to ensure adequate trade access through multilateral channels, and suggested the potential need for a more a direct bilateral link to the Community.[36] These bilateral problems coincided with a recurrence of Canadian fears of excessive dependence on the United States and with the election in 1968 of a decidedly nationalist Liberal government led by the charismatic Pierre Trudeau. By then the stage was set for Canadian politicians and senior officials (primarily Europeanists at the Department of External Affairs[37]) to push Canada's relations with Western Europe higher on the Canadian foreign policy agenda.[38]

The "STAFEUR" Report

A Eurocentric foreign policy was at first rejected by Trudeau. During the 1968 election campaign, Trudeau announced his intention to launch a "pragmatic and realistic" review of Canada's foreign policy which would embrace defence, economic, and aid policies. Trudeau committed his government to "take a hard look, in consultation with our allies, at our military role in NATO and [to] determine whether our present military commitment is still appropriate to the present situation in Europe." Perhaps most ominously Trudeau spoke of Canada's need

> not so much to go crusading abroad as to mobilize at home our aspirations.... Our paramount interest is to ensure the political survival of Canada as a federal and bilingual sovereign state. This means strengthening Canadian unity as a basically North American country.[39]

Consistent with this pledge, after his electoral victory Trudeau assigned the foreign policy review to External Affairs, the Treasury Board, the Privy Council Office, and the Department of Finance. Mitchell Sharp, his Secretary of State for External Affairs, had already authorized the creation of an interdepartmental Special Task Force on Europe (known as STAFEUR) in the spring of 1968. Its mandate included a major examination of Canadian relations with Europe, with a particular focus on NATO and Canada's role therein. The STAFEUR Report[40] was completed by the end of February 1969. Parts of the Report were included in a booklet on Europe, one of six in a series entitled *Foreign Policy for Canadians* (FPC), which was released in 1970 and represented the Trudeau government's redefinition of Canadian foreign policy.[41]

The 1969 STAFEUR Report was highly pro-Atlanticist in its outlook. In retrospect, the Report appears much more forward-looking in terms of Canada's relations with Western Europe than some of its writers could have imagined at the time. Many of its recommendations would have resonated with policy makers struggling to develop a Canadian response to post-1989 events in Europe. Officials at External Affairs concluded at the time that it was not in Canada's interests to loosen its ties with Europe, and that to do so would mean "having to pay an excessive price in political and possible economic terms."[42] The Report noted that Canada's interest in Europe was greater than in any other area except North America, given that all of Canada's major interests, political, military, economic, scientific, and cultural, converged in Europe.[43]

The Report was surprisingly prescient for a period in which East-West tensions were high as a result of American involvement in Vietnam, especially as it did not equate these ties with an *indefinite* Canadian military commitment to the continent. Instead, it foresaw the day when "political society" in Europe would resist communism, Germany would be in a state of "peaceful evolution," and "other [non-military] forms of Canadian presence" would have to be developed to maintain the transatlantic ties important to Canada.[44]

In keeping with a concern at the political level that Canada was becoming overly dependent on a North American outlook, the Report encouraged "additional organic links" with Western Europe through NATO and "other economic and political organizations." In the event of NATO becoming "unnecessary" or "transformed," these other links would remain and would serve Canadian objectives.[45] The Report was, no doubt, also influenced by having been written in the aftermath of the Warsaw Pact's invasion of Czechoslovakia. It argued strongly for Canadian membership in the North Atlantic alliance. Perhaps to account for Trudeau's skepticism about Canada's military commitment to Europe, it also advocated a continuing, albeit possibly smaller, military contribution to NATO as a symbol of Canada's stake in the defence of Europe.[46] The Report never went so far as attempting to estimate when Soviet hegemony in Eastern Europe would end or defining "other forms of presence" or "organic links." Nonetheless, as later chapters of this study will indicate, concerning the push for bilateral cooperation on various transnational challenges in the post-Cold War era, the STAFEUR Report was in many ways prophetic.

With regard to NATO, the Report considered its role was in peacekeeping functions for military stability and as an "important forum for the expression of Canadian views on a wide range of international issues and for the achievement of a number of Canadian political aims in Europe."[47] It acknowledged that a diminishing Western European dependence on American political and military leadership was probably inevitable in the long run. It also forecast, correctly, that an integrating Western Europe would be a "magnet" for EFTA nations.

On the progress of European integration, it is significant that the Report addresses *full* European union at a time when Europe had just completed the process of establishing a customs union, stating that such a union would work against Canadian interests not only by excluding Canada from Europe but also by excluding Canada from any Europe-United States dialogue. Furthermore, it would lead ultimately to a parallel trend toward continentalism in North America, within which Canada could expect increased integration with the United States. In this context, the Report referred to the "two-pillar" principle of Canada's relations with Europe, leaving Canada necessarily either entirely excluded or else included within the American "pillar."[48]

Canada wished to counter tendencies by Europeans as a group to bypass Canada in their dealings with the United States. Related to this concern was the painful recognition that Canada's objectives vis-à-vis Europe were absent from European preoccupations in their dealings with Canada. This great disparity between the historical importance of Europe for Canada and the political importance of Canada for Europe constitutes the single most persistent limiting factor affecting the range and scope of policy options available to Canada. It was, in the Report's words, "a sobering but seemingly inescapable fact of life."[49] It also reflected the Europeans' two-pillar image of transatlantic relations.

In preparing a blueprint for Canada's policy approach to the EC for the 1970s, however, Canadian officials were careful to describe this "two-pillar" theory as oversimplification: Canada would more likely face a process of Community building, albeit uneven in nature, with which Canada would have to come to terms.[50] In this realistic appraisal of the range of Canada's responses to evolving European integration, a positive spin was given even to concern that Britain's accession to the EC would have "short-run" commercial drawbacks for Canada. Unlike the Diefenbaker government's earlier misgivings about the deleterious impact of European integration on Canada's foreign trade, the Report saw disadvantages suffered by Canada as balanced by improved access to an enlarged and more open Europe. Canadian officials further speculated that, with Britain as a member state, Canadian interests would be "given greater weight."[51]

In summary, Canadian officials concluded that: (1) Canada had no hope of reversing the process of European integration, and its interest might not even be served in the attempt; and (2) it was "not clear" Canada's interest would be served if U.S. influence became "even more predominant."[52] The Canadian side was particularly concerned over European interest in greater autonomy and over the uncertainty of future U.S. policy toward Europe, leaving the environment no longer one of "counterbalancing interdependence" which Canadian officials had felt benefited them in the past, but rather one in which the prospects of an Atlantic community had diminished, to be replaced by political and economic bipolarization.[53] From this perspective, officials advocated that Canada "obtain" its historical "diversification" once again, seeing it still in the national interest. They described Canada as best achieving leverage by developing its multinational relations with Europe.

The language of the Report leaves no doubt that diversification would be a future goal. Reinvigorated Canada-Europe relations would act as a "counterweight" to the "relatively benevolent but overwhelming influence of the United States."[54] Canadian officials saw certain features of Europe's future configuration as coinciding with national interests. They recognized that: (1) Canada's security was intimately linked with Europe; (2) Europe was maintaining an interdependent relationship with North America while becoming increasingly self-reliant; (3) Europe would become united and outward-looking rather than fragmented and inward-looking; and (4) Europe would be prepared to enter into an active partnership with Canada in certain areas of mutual interests.

As we shall see in the following discussion, Trudeau at first ignored the recommendations of the STAFEUR Report and sought non-European counterweights to perceived U.S. influence. But when this approach failed, in stark contrast to successive American administrations, the Liberal government warmed up to the idea of closer relations with the European Community. Also indicated in this study is the possibility that the acrimony in Brussels-Washington relations during the 1960s and 1970s gave Canada an opportunity to present itself to the Europeans as a more cooperative and distinct partner in North America, thereby for a time rendering the "two-pillar" analogy false.

Diverging EC-U.S. Interests

In Chapter 1, it was stated that Canada's relations with Brussels are greatly affected by Washington's relations with Brussels. By the early 1960s, Washington had begun to lose its impact on the EC's integration. Ginsberg characterizes bilateral relations during the period from 1963 to 1970 as one that "gyrated between insensitivity and hostility" as the U.S. and the EC attempted to adjust to altering relative positions in the world.[55] American policy makers became progressively more skeptical about implications of European economic and political integration for a host of major reasons:[56] the EC's granting of tariff reductions on certain imports from close trading partners in the Mediterranean and Africa were regarded as highly discriminatory vis-à-vis American exports; the notorious chicken war of 1963 and 1964 caused by the CAP's devastating effect on U.S. market share of the EC poultry market; the EC's toughness in its negotiations with the United States during the Kennedy Round of multilateral trade negotiations; by EC member states' silence over, or condemnation of, involvement in Vietnam;[57] and the 1970 introduction of a foreign policy coordination system under the framework of ECP was seen by some U.S. decision makers as a threat to American leadership on foreign policy matters.[58] From an institutional perspective, the Nixon administration disregarded traditional U.S. support for EC bodies, preferring instead bilateral ties with member governments.

Thus by the early 1970s, the United States was becoming increasingly disillusioned with the impact of European integration on its interests. Then Secretary of State Henry Kissinger's "Year of Europe" initiative, instead of reconciling these transatlantic tensions, succeeded in exacerbating them: Europeans viewed the attempt by the United States to redirect development of EC foreign policy back to an Atlantic-based centre as "patronizing and clumsy."[59] Relations between Brussels and Washington stagnated even further as evidenced in the foreign policy differences between the EC and the U.S. on the Yom Kippur War, and are characterized by Ginsberg as moving in the 1970s between unilateral neglect and bilateral cooperation.[60] By contrast, Canada shared many common interests with the EC during these same years.

THE 1970s: TRUDEAU'S EUROPE POLICY

The early Trudeau years can be seen as a watershed in postwar Canadian foreign policy, leading some observers to characterize Canada as a "principal power" rather than a "middle power" during this period.[61] This development was somewhat ironic given Trudeau's shift away from Pearsonian internationalism to an initial skepticism toward the Commonwealth, given also his complaint that NATO had dictated Canada's external policies, and his advocacy of greater attention to domestic policies as opposed to European security.[62] Indeed, some analysts saw Trudeau as "bored" with the Western half of the European continent during the first few years of his government.[63] For instance, although Trudeau accepted greater political, economic, and cultural ties with Europe, he seemed to take greater interest in the diplomatic coup over relations with Beijing in which he granted Communist China diplomatic recognition ahead of the U.S., the well publicized visits by his ministers to Latin America, and his own travels to New Zealand, Australia, Japan, Malaysia, India, Pakistan, and the Soviet Union. These actions underlined Trudeau's conviction that Canada's foreign policy priorities entailed generating relationships well away from the North Atlantic.[64] This was also the message of the first book of the FPC in which the government stated that

> The predominance of transatlantic ties—with Britain, France and Western Europe generally (and new links with the Common Market)—will be adjusted to reflect a more evenly distributed policy emphasis, which envisages expanding activities in the Pacific Basin and Latin America.[65]

Ironically, this very strategy was to be adopted by the Mulroney-led Conservative government more than 20 years later. At the time, Trudeau's predecessor and mentor, the by-now-retired Lester Pearson, did not agree with his protegé's approach, seeing it as defining Canada's national interests too narrowly by not taking into account the significance of global security concerns.[66] Conservative foreign policy analysts of the period, such as Peyton Lyon, feared that a retreat from Europe could be equated with a retraction from the rest of the world—a matter that re-emerged two decades later as Canada debated its post-Cold War Europe policy.[67]

The Trudeau government quickly discovered, however, that despite its awareness of Canada's need for countervailing relations, there was a decreasing confidence that it could be established on the necessary scale beyond the Atlantic community. According to Peyton Lyon, although Canada's commitment to foreign aid increased substantially in the late 1960s, relations with developing countries proved too one sided to counterbalance Canada's dependence on its relations with the United States. Although trade with Japan was expanding greatly, Japan's interest in Canada did not extend far beyond a need for raw materials. It also lacked the defence, personal, historical, and cultural bonds Canada maintained with Europe. Finally, although the Canadian public showed some sympathy for Trudeau's overtures toward Moscow, large numbers objected to the notion that relations with the Soviet Union could ever approach the intimacy of those with Canada's southern neighbour.[68] After an extensive and sobering *tour d'horizon* in search of non-Atlantic sources of significant counterweight, Canada's political leaders returned to the bosom of "mother Europe."

Foreign Policy for Canadians and the "Third Option"

Trudeau's FPC sets out six policy themes for the direction of Canada's foreign policy in the 1970s: (1) fostering economic growth; (2) safeguarding sovereignty and independence; (3) working for peace and security; (4) promoting social justice; (5) enhancing the quality of life; and (6) assuring a harmonious natural environment.[69] The first goal, economic growth, would be accomplished through trade diversification among the rising industrial powers. Diversification in Canadian political and economic policy was seen as leading to the second goal, sovereignty and independence. Intensified relations with Western Europe during the 1970s were seen as fulfilling this second requirement.

Trends described in the FPC that would not fully take shape until the late 1980s and 1990s include the increasing importance in world affairs of transnational production[70] and the prediction of a "worldwide trend toward regionalism in one form or another."[71] The current shift toward world trading areas—the European Union, the Asia-Pacific region, and the Americas—is the manifestation of a trend predicted in Ottawa two decades ago.

By the end of 1970, Mitchell Sharp and his cabinet colleague, Jean-Luc Pepin, had become the first Canadian ministers to visit the headquarters of the European Commission. Federal officials in Ottawa were also becoming more inclined to disregard the anti-Atlanticist thrust of the first booklet in the FPC packet and to take their cues from the volume entitled *Europe*. As mentioned, this booklet was essentially a repackaging of the STAFEUR Report. In it, Europe once again was recognized as "the only area outside North America where the major themes of Canadian policy converge"[72] and specifically linked to Canada's quest for a counterweight: "The maintenance of an adequate measure of economic and political independence in the face of American power and influence is a problem Canada shares with the European nations."[73]

It also maintained that:

> The more the European countries combine their efforts, the more opportunities there will be for Canada to find rewarding forms of cooperation with them. It is not realistic to imagine that the present could be changed 90 degrees in direction ... but there would be much merit in seeking to develop at least some measure of countervailing influence.[74]

The political need in Canada for a "countervailing influence" resulted from increased public and official anxiety about Canada's overdependence on its so-called "special relationship" with the United States, a term that Sharp says

> recognized the extensive and close ties between the Canadian and U.S. economies, unmatched anywhere else in the world in relations between independent countries. Consequently, the effect of U.S. economic policies upon Canada was far greater than upon any other country.[75]

These fears in Canada, combined with an increase in East-West détente, ensured that the attraction of a separate strategy for relations with the European Community was growing ever stronger.

It is somewhat odd, however, that the Trudeau government's comprehensive review of Canadian foreign policy as laid out in the 1970 White Paper would be noticeably silent on the question of Canada-U.S. relations. Indeed, much surprise and confusion greeted the unveiling of the FPC booklets when none appeared on the subject of Canada's most important bilateral relationship and primary foreign policy interest.[76] This significant policy area was addressed in a separate paper two years later under Sharp's authorship in what was then the Department of External Affairs' semi-official periodical, *International Perspectives*. This Options paper presented three alternatives for Canada's relationship with the United States: (1) maintaining the status quo whereby relations would continue to be managed in an ad hoc fashion; (2) closer economic integration with the United States; and (3) more diversified multilateral ties.[77] Sharp's strategy, in addition to calling for a strengthening of Canadian identity through the promotion of Canadian culture, encouraged a more deliberate long-term approach to economic development. This involved an industrial strategy from which emerged the Foreign Investment Review Agency (FIRA) in 1975 and the National Energy Program (NEP) in 1980.

The Options paper, consistent with the conclusions of the STAFEUR report and the FPC's *Europe* booklet, was also a reaction to Canada's "vulnerability" to American policy actions, the most notable of which at the time was the Nixon administration's 10 percent surcharge in August 1971 on all manufactured goods entering the United States. With the U.S. market accounting for over 70 percent of Canada's international trade, this hit Canada particularly hard, especially since it was denied exemption from this particular measure.

These developments in turn put pressure on the "special relationship" that had existed since the end of the Second World War. This point was stressed in the subsequent Nixon Doctrine concerning "independent" relations between mature partners, forcing a consensus in the Canadian government on the need for redefining the Canada-U.S. bilateral relationship.[78] The Nixon Doctrine ultimately succeeded in forcing the Liberal government to put clear policy actions behind its rhetoric on rejecting closer ties with the United States. This development in effect nullified the first two options in the *International Perspectives* article. As a result, the so-called "Third Option" became the prevailing conceptual framework. Consequently, the biggest change in the direction of Canada's post-Second World War foreign policy came about less because of what the Canadian government said it was going to do than because of a U.S. government decision to bring its continuing foreign exchange crisis under control.

The Third Option was not confined to the EC. In addition to Europe, Sharp had mentioned diversifying relations to Japan and the Soviet Union. For practical reasons, however, the option took the explicit form of an attempt to build closer relations with the European Community. The Japanese market at the time was deemed too esoteric. The state-trading countries of Eastern Europe and the Soviet Union meanwhile were complex and difficult markets in which to do business.

Interestingly, in light of the STAFEUR report and the government's promulgation of foreign policy as an expression of national interests, the architects of the Third Option later claimed that they never intended it to divert trade away from the United States. Rather, as Sharp pointed out,

> We were not thinking in terms of substituting Europe for the United States as a trading partner.... We believe we can multiply our exchanges with other countries, particularly in Europe, with a view to promoting the cultural life and economic prosperity of Canadians without loosening in the process our vigorous ties with our southern neighbours.[79]

Or, in the words of Jeremy Kinsman, at the time a middle-ranking member of External Affairs's Commercial Policy Division:

> Diversification of our external economic relations is not an end in itself, but is a function of reduction of the vulnerability of the Canadian economy.... The EEC is an obviously important feature of the external dimension of Canadian industrial development.... Diversification does not mean a transfer of any of our economic activity from North America elsewhere. It can be seen more aptly as the development elsewhere of additional and strengthened ties.[80]

Ever since its inception, the Third Option has been hotly debated in Canadian academic and governmental circles: Was it ever a full-fledged policy? Was it just an "impulse," a "tactic," or a "strategy"? In Sharp's view, this Option was a "strategy" only approved by the Trudeau cabinet after "long and detailed discussion."[81] This was in stark contrast to the "Policy Framework" and the "Plan of Action" for Europe that would be adopted speedily by Mulroney's Conservative cabinet in 1990.

With the creation of FIRA and NEP, with the latter agency especially criticized by Western Canadians and foreign (primarily American) oil interests, it must be emphasized that the Third Option became largely a domestic economic, rather than a foreign, policy exercise to prevent closer integration with the United States. It did not have popular support, especially as it was initiated by a select group of mandarins and ministers who at the time had Trudeau's approval. Polls in the early 1970s indicated Canadian inclination to favour the status quo rather than closer relations with either the United States or Europe.[82]

Whatever its merits or failures, the Third Option did epitomize the direction of Canadian foreign policy for the better part of a decade after its introduction. During this period bilateral Canada-EC relations were institutionalized: "high levels," as annual meetings between senior Canadian and EC officials came to be known, were established in 1972. Canada also opened a diplomatic mission in Brussels in 1973 and the Commission established a delegation in Ottawa in 1976. It was in November 1972, after the creation of the "high levels" that the Canadian government delivered an *aide-memoire* to the European Commission exploring the possibility of a general agreement on trade and economic matters. In 1973, a Canadian Senate report called for the creation of a framework within which bilateral relations could be improved.[83] The European Commission, increasingly intent on exercising its own diplomatic role,[84] was receptive to Ottawa's overtures on formalizing and intensifying bilateral ties. It also saw Canada, particularly during the period of OPEC-induced economic crises in the early 1970s, as an alternative source of abundant raw materials, in particular uranium.

The process of formalizing bilateral relations reached its peak with the signing of the Framework Agreement on July 6, 1976. Known in Canada as the "contractual link," this agreement was implemented to promote increased commercial and economic links.[85] The parties established a Joint Cooperation Committee as part of the Framework's permanent structure, responsible for promoting and reviewing the various aspects of commercial and economic cooperation. It is noteworthy that the Framework Agreement left intact the competence of EC member states to undertake bilateral arrangements with Canada.[86]

As Granatstein notes, however, the process of securing an agreement from the Commission was not, for a number of reasons, a foregone conclusion. The Commission did not wish to be perceived as a political dwarf and thus sought a substantial foreign policy role. Dissatisfied with Canada's 1974 *aide-memoire* which had proposed a draft trade agreement to exchange MFN treatment on tariff and related charges, it advocated instead an agreement that "would also provide a framework for economic and commercial cooperation 'extending well beyond the field of classical trade policy.'"[87]

The negotiations culminating in the Framework Agreement could also well have been torpedoed as a result of public comments on Canada's commitment to NATO by Trudeau which challenged conventional wisdom. Trudeau's speculations about the continuing utility of

NATO and the support by some prominent members of his cabinet (especially Jean Marchand, Jean Pelletier, Donald MacDonald, and Eric Kierans) for a Canadian withdrawal from NATO, or, at the very least a return of Canadian troops from Europe, prompted unfavourable reactions from Canada's European allies.[88] Eventually a 50 percent reduction was approved in Canada's troop strength in Europe.

Sharp describes Canada's announcement that it would remain in NATO after a 1970 review of its commitment as a "mishandling" that would have "unfortunate repercussions *for years* [emphasis added] on relations between Canada and [its] allies in Europe."[89] The West Germans, in particular, saw such actions as jeopardizing their support for Canada's "privileged" economic link to the Community. This West German reaction clearly indicated European willingness at that time to draw an unambiguous link between closer trade or economic relations and Canada's security commitment to Europe.[90]

Given the German willingness to link support for the Framework Agreement to Canada's continued military commitment to Europe, it was, according to Granatstein, Trudeau's "close and confidential relationship" with West German Chancellor Helmut Schmidt that allowed Canada a foot in the door to Europe when the EC seemed at its most tendentious concerning Canadian overtures.[91] In fact, the cool reception to Trudeau's offer to establish the contractual link with the EC warmed somewhat when he undertook a modernization of the Canadian armed forces, which included the purchase of German Leopard tanks for the Canadian troops still committed to NATO.[92]

Thus, after "endless coordination," the European Commission recommended in 1975 that the Council of Ministers authorize the beginning of negotiations with Canada for a framework agreement.[93] Even then, however, there remained a problem with select member states. The French, for example, were distinctly cool to the idea of the Community expanding its competence through any such agreement with Canada. Deft Canadian diplomacy finally persuaded President Giscard d'Estaing of France that Canada's motivation for an agreement was "political," not simply "economic." Only then did the French acquiesce and vote for the Council of Ministers to begin negotiations.[94]

The Council of Ministers nonetheless stalled over a Danish complaint against non-discriminatory access to Canada's natural resources, particularly in light of Canada's two-price system for the oil of which Denmark was an importer. Only upon resolution of this issue was the agreement speedily finalized. Granatstein notes that:

> The successful conclusion of the agreement was a triumph for Canadian diplomacy and for Prime Minister Trudeau, whose visits to European leaders had tilted the balance from opposition to support for the Canadian initiative. To persist over four years, to persuade a reluctant and dubious European Community to expand its jurisdiction, and to essay a new direction was a tribute to the skill of the officers of the Department of External Affairs.... Moreover, the EC at the last seemed to be aware that Canada existed as an entity separate from the United States.[95]

Certainly, it was a "triumph" for Canadian diplomacy that it was selected the first industrial non-member state to have a privileged link with the EC. It was not the first North American state to do so, however, as Mexico had signed a Framework Agreement with the EC the year before.[96]

By the mid- to late-1970s, just as Canada was enhancing its institutional links with the Community, a combination of factors ensured that the constituency for the EC in Canada among federal officials, politicians, and the business community underwent severe attrition. A number of specific trends fed altering Canadian images of the EC. For example, the lack of market access provisions in the Framework Agreement, leaving no tax breaks, no export incentives, and no subsidies to encourage research and development, ensured at best an indifferent, and at worst a suspicious, Canadian business audience.[97]

When the increase in trade augured by the Agreement did not materialize, due in part to the onset of "Eurosclerosis," this served only to confirm business's suspicions and to feed perceptions at both political and business levels, though not yet at the bureaucratic level, that the Framework was of little practical use. On the political side, dismay arose over European inability to invigorate a common foreign policy through EPC.

The Third Option as a Trade Policy Failure

An examination of the Canadian economy provides additional reasons for the difficulty entailed in redirecting Canadian trade flows to Europe. A traditional characteristic of the Canadian private sector is its preoccupation with the domestic market. This concern stems from the earliest days of Canada's industrialization and the decision to pursue the strategy of import substitution industrialization (ISI), which Glenn Williams describes in *Not for Export.*[98] Williams points out that, "This domestic market approach was similarly applied in the case of export trade, whereby the private sector sang psalms of praise to the 'home market' while downgrading the importance of export sales."[99] The prevailing attitude appeared to be based on the perception of inferiority vis-à-vis other industrial states. Furthermore, the desire to fully occupy the domestic market precluded export sales except in the cases of surplus.[100]

A second result of the ISI strategy was the development of technological dependence. To expand domestic manufacturing, the use of foreign technology under licence combined with the establishment of branch plants was encouraged.[101] Such technology transfer offered Canadian manufacturers the advantage of exploiting innovations in relatively short order, without the time, expense, and risk incurred in developing their own technology. As Williams notes, however, little concern was given to the potential disadvantages of this technological dependence. ISI effectively created a branch-plant economy in Canada by encouraging foreign direct investment (FDI).

Unless governed by a world product mandate, branch plants will have constraints imposed on them by their parents. It is not surprising, therefore, that trade with the United States, the home of most parent companies, and hence the dominant investor, is the most active.[102] Throughout the post-Second World War period, but gaining momentum in the 1960s, the two economies had become more fully integrated with primarily raw and semi-processed materials flowing to the United States and capital goods and manufactured products flowing north. An understanding of these continental links is fundamental to an understanding of attempts to diversify Canada's trade relations.

Not surprisingly, under these circumstances the Canadian business sector developed close links to the United States, enhanced by common values, language, and traditions. The two countries became natural partners. Each regarded the other partner as its best customer while developing the largest bilateral trade relationship in the world. This natural state of affairs was seemingly threatened by attempts in the Canadian government to alter the relationship.[103] Business was from the outset more naturally skeptical of links with the EC.[104] The Liberal government was pursuing a strategy that not only did not provide any meaningful incentives, but went against the grain of an integrated North American economy and business culture. In other words, by the time of the Third Option there had been a continental outlook to business for at least 20 years in the Canadian corporate sector, an outlook resistant to change. It would appear that "Europeanist" bureaucrats at External Affairs were out of step with the business community on whose behalf they were attempting to foster closer relations with Europe.[105]

This "continentalist fact" goes a long way to explain the reluctance of Canadian business to turn its attention to Europe, a fact admitted in the Canadian government's 1983 Trade Policy Review (to be discussed in the next chapter). Following from our discussion about the state-centred approach to studying Canada's international relations, the fact that the Third Option's diversification strategy overrode the realities of Canada's natural trading patterns as long as it did is a testament to the power of the Canadian state in its relations with other domestic actors, in this instance the business community.

In sum, Canada's relations with the EC during its first two decades assumed a cyclical nature. The first concerted attempt to expand relations came as a result of concern over U.K. accession to the EC and overdependence on, and vulnerability to, the United States. The Framework Agreement represented the "foreign" dimension of the government's new policy direction under the Third Option.[106]

The recessions in the industrialized economies at the end of the 1970s, a Canadian economy characterized by a preponderance of American control, and a slowdown in the process of Community-building dictated a return to a highly conservative approach to trade relations in Canada. In the area of trade relations the primary actors, the business world and the politicians, did not maintain any sustained commitment to diversification.They were disappointed at the less than stellar commercial results of the Third Option. Neither of Sharp's successors, Allan MacEachen and Don Jamieson, shared the same commitment to diversification; Trudeau himself eventually lost interest.[107]

Ultimately, the political successes achieved by Canada in Europe were greatly overshadowed by the tendency to make the alleged "failure" of the Third Option synonymous with the "failure" of Canada's attempt to strengthen its relations with Western Europe.[108] By the early 1980s the Liberal government's continuing association with the Third Option was considered damaging in terms of public perceptions. Senior Canadian officials at External Affairs quietly declared the Third Option dead in 1983, although its so-called "failure" was to haunt the Ottawa-Brussels axis throughout most of the 1980s.[109] When Canada's political and business leaders eventually did agree on a new orientation for trade policy it would not be to the benefit of Canada-EC relations.

NOTES

1. Quoted by Andrew Griffith, "From a Trading Nation to a Nation of Traders," *Policy Planning Staff Papers* (Ottawa: Department of External Affairs and International Trade, 1992), Annex B.
2. James Rochlin, *Discovering the Americas: The Evolution of Canadian Foreign Policy Towards Latin America* (Vancouver: University of British Columbia Press, 1994), 34.
3. Prime Minister Louis St. Laurent, "The Foundations of Canadian Foreign Policy in World Affairs," [the Gray Lecture], University of Toronto, January 13, 1947. Cited in J.L. Granatstein, ed., *Canadian Foreign Policy: Historical Readings* (Toronto: Copp Clark Pitman, 1986), 28.
4. *Ibid.*, 32.
5. *Ibid.*, 25-32.
6. John Halstead, "Atlantic Community," 153; see also, John B. Brebner, *North Atlantic Triangle: The Interplay of Canada, the United States and Great Britain* (Toronto: McClelland & Stewart, 1966).
7. Perhaps the best treatment on Canada's role in the formation of NATO is in Escott Reid, *Time of Fear and Hope: Making of the North Atlantic Treaty 1947-49* (Toronto: McClelland & Stewart, 1977).
8. Quoted in John English, *The Worldly Years*, 15, from Robertson to Secretary of State for External Affairs, April 2, 1948, External Affairs Records, file 264(s); and Alex Danchev, "Taking the Pledge: Oliver Franks and the Negotiation of the North Atlantic Treaty," *Diplomatic History* 15, 2 (Spring 1991): 199-220.
9. B.W. Muirhead, *The Development of Postwar Canadian Trade Policy: The Failure of the Anglo-European Option* (Montreal: McGill-Queen's University Press, 1992), 46.
10. *Ibid.*, 15.
11. A. Claire Cutler, review of B.W. Muirhead, *The Development of Postwar Canadian Trade Policy*, in *International Journal* 49, 1 (Winter 1993-94): 160-61.
12. See Muirhead, *Postwar Canadian Trade*, ch. 4, "The Organization of European Economic Cooperation, Dollar Restrictions, and Canada, 1948-1957."
13. *Ibid.*, 164, 166-67.
14. A free trade treaty among the U.K., Austria, Denmark, Norway, Portugal, Sweden, and Switzerland was finally signed in November 1959.

15. Muirhead quoting A.F.W. Plumptre, then Assistant Deputy Minister of Finance, *Ibid.*, 170.
16. *Ibid*, 176.
17. *Ibid.*, 174-75.
18. *Ibid.*, 175-76.
19. See H.I. Macdonald, "The European Common Market," *Behind the Headlines* 18, 4 (Toronto: Canadian Institute of International Affairs, Nov. 1958); and H.I. Macdonald, "Canada's Foreign Economic Policy," *Behind the Headlines* 20, 4 (Nov. 1960).
20. See, for example, R.E. Caves, "Europe's Unification and Canada's Trade," *Canadian Journal of Economics and Political Science* 25, 3 (Aug. 1959): 249-58; Edward H. English, ed., *Canada and the New International Economy* (Toronto: University of Toronto Press, 1961).
21. R.A. Mathews, "Canada, Britain and the Common Market," *World Today* 18, 2, (Feb. 1962): 48-57, as cited in Daniel Roseman, "The Canadian-EC Framework for Economic Cooperation: From Dreams to Reality." Ph. D. dissertation, Institute universitaires des hautes études internationales, University of Geneva, Switzerland, 1983, 23. France twice, in 1963 and 1967, vetoed the U.K.'s bid to join the EC.
22. The Commonwealth preferences originated in the Ottawa Agreements of 1932, at the time when Britain still took over 30 percent of Canada's exports. They were intended to discriminate chiefly against American goods which were gaining ground in British and Canadian markets. They permitted 95 percent of Canada's exports to Britain to enter duty free and 60 percent of the U.K.'s exports to Canada to do the same. See Roseman, "Canada-EC Framework," 23; and R.A. Mathews, "Britain's Move into Europe: The Implications for Canada," *Behind the Headlines*, 31, 5-6 (Oct. 1972):3.
23. Roseman, "Canada-EC Framework," 23. He speculates that the second British bid for EC membership did not cause much alarm in Ottawa because a less Anglophile and more "continentalist" government under Lester B. Pearson was in power.
24. M. Wardell, "The Challenge to Canada: The Threat to Canadian Trade," in W.B. Cunningham, ed., *Canada, the Commonwealth, and the Common Market* (Montreal: McGill University Press, 1962), 98, 104.
25. H. Basil Robinson, *Diefenbaker's World: A Populist in Foreign Affairs* (Toronto: University of Toronto Press, 1989), 67.
26. Peyton V. Lyon, "The Quest for Counterweight: Canada and the European Economic Community," in Peter Stingelin, ed., *The European Community and the Outsiders* (Don Mills, ON: Longman, 1973), 50.
27. Maxwell Stamp Associates, *The Free Trade Area Option* (London: The Atlantic Trade Study, 1967), 28. This book states that the reason that

the Canada-U.K. free trade area proposal did not go forward was that "it was not seriously intended," containing few details. There was nothing really in it for Canada since Canada already enjoyed preferential entry into the U.K. market. As a result, according to this study, it had remained a "sensitive" point in Anglo-Canadian relations.

28. Canada, House of Commons, *Debates*, July 1, 1960, 5639.
29. M. Lamontagne, "Canada and the Common Market," in Cunningham, *Canada, the Commonwealth*, 33, 36.
30. Excerpts from Pearson's speech reprinted in *Ibid.*, 25.
31. *Ibid.*, 27-28.
32. *Ibid.*, 28.
33. R.M. Fowler, in Cunningham, *Canada, the Commonwealth*, 19.
34. According to R.B. Bell, who was the Assistant Director of Research at the Canadian Labour Congress, Walter Hallstein, the first president of the European Community had rejected the proposal of an EC-North American confederation in an article entitled "The Value of Atlantic Partnership": "No Atlantic government has been contemplated.... The source of the ideological strength of the European Community is Europeanism, whereas the United States is not only an Atlantic power, but also a Pacific power and an exponent of Americanism.... EEC quarters in Brussels are realistic enough not to think in terms of a confederate structure of the Atlantic area, desirable though it might be." Cited in *Ibid.*, 44-45. Hallstein, according to the above quotation, was making clear that the objective of economic integration in Europe was eventual political union, and not a transatlantic political or economic community. It is worth noting that, given this study's reference to the Europeans' two-pillar image of transatlantic relations, Hallstein did not refer explicitly to Canada. However, his notion of irreconcilability between nations and communities that define themselves differently—in this case the EEC and the U.S.—would have presumably applied to Canada as well, given its geographical location. In fact, 30 years later, when Canadian politicians promoted Canada's "Pacific," "Arctic," "North American," and "Atlantic" nationhoods, Hallstein's remarks may have been more on the mark for Canada than they were for the United States.
35. Pentland, "Europe 1992," 126.
36. E.E. Mahant, "Canada and the European Community: The New Policy," *International Affairs* 52, 4 (Oct. 1976): 551.
37. In his dissertation, Roseman was careful to distinguish between the Europeanists in External Affairs and other senior officials in the department who had significant input into the Third Option. This distinction has been confirmed. For example, Michel Dupuis, a high-ranking External Affairs official commenting ten years after the Third Option's unveiling, pointed out that although he was skeptical of its

impact, he was equally aware that given the Liberal government's nationalist rhetoric, of the three options it was the only one that was politically acceptable.

38. The animosity engendered by the Kennedy Round negotiations convinced a number of key officials at External Affairs (centred on John Halstead, head of the European Division in 1968, but then rising to become Assistant Under-Secretary in 1971) of the need to work out mechanisms for direct consultations with the EC to prevent these hostilities. The "Europeanists" at External Affairs met stiff opposition in other federal government departments such as Industry, Science and Technology, which delayed any immediate action that might have been taken. See Roseman, "Canada-EC Framework," 26, 28.
39. Office of the Prime Minister, *Press Release*, May 29, 1968, as cited in Granatstein and Bothwell, *Pirouette*, 14.
40. At the time there had been two previous major studies of European relations: "Eurocan: A Policy Planning Paper on Relations between Canada and Europe," November 10, 1965; and "Canada's Stake in Europe," May 30, 1967, by the Departmental Study Group on Europe. Cited in *Ibid.*, 387, note 42.
41. Government of Canada, *Foreign Policy for Canadians* (hereafter, FPC) (Ottawa: Queen's Printer, 1970).
42. Department of External Affairs, *STAFEUR Report* (Ottawa: 1969), 250.
43. *Ibid.*, 252.
44. *Ibid.*, 251.
45. *Ibid.*
46. Granatstein and Bothwell, *Pirouette*, 19, 388, note 74.
47. *Ibid.*, 251.
48. *Ibid.*, 252.
49. *Ibid.*, 257.
50. *Ibid.*, 253.
51. *Ibid.*, 253.
52. *Ibid.*, 254.
53. *Ibid.*, 257.
54. *Ibid.*, 255.
55. Ginsberg, "U.S.-EC Relations," in Lodge, *The European Community*, 265.
56. For a brief but incisive historical review of U.S. attitudes toward the EC see, Roy H. Ginsberg, *Foreign Policy Actions of the European Community: The Politics of Scale* (Boulder, CO: Lynne Rienner, 1989), 129-49; and Y. Devuyst, "European Community Integration and the United States: Toward a New Transatlantic Relationship," *Journal of European Integration* 14, 1 (1990): 6.
57. Ginsberg, "U.S.-EC Relations," 266.
58. This view was expressed clearly by Henry Kissinger when he commented that: "We cannot ignore the fact that Europe's economic

success and its transformation from a recipient of our aid to a strong competitor has produced a certain amount of friction." In H.A. Kissinger, "The Year of Europe," *Department of State Bulletin*, May 14, 1973.

59. Ginsberg, "U.S.-EC Relations," 268.
60. *Ibid.*, 266.
61. Rochlin, *Discovering the Americas*, 65.
62. Lyon, "The Quest for Counterweight," ftn. 14
63. *Ibid.*, 56.
64. *Ibid.*, 56.
65. *FPC*, 39
66. Quoted in Bothwell and Granatstein, *Pirouette*, 34.
67. Peyton Lyon, "A Review of the Review," *Journal of Canadian Studies* 5 (May 1970): 34.
68. Lyon, "The Quest for Counterweight," 57.
69. *FPC*, 14.
70. *Ibid.*, 24.
71. *Ibid.*, 28.
72. Quoted by Lyon in "The Quest for Counterweight," 57.
73. Europe, *FPC*, 14.
74. *Ibid.*, 27.
75. Mitchell Sharp, *Which Reminds Me ...* (Toronto: University of Toronto Press), 178.
76. In addition to Europe, the other booklets were on the Pacific, the United Nations, Latin America, and international development. Granatstein calls the *FPC* white paper "seriously flawed." See Granatstein and Bothwell, *Pirouette*, 33-35.
77. See Mitchell Sharp, "Canada-U.S. Relations: Options for the Future," *International Perspectives* (Autumn 1972, Special Issue): 1-21.
78. In his memoirs, *Which Reminds Me ...*, Sharp goes so far as to conclude that the Nixon Doctrine "killed" the "special relationship" (178-81). See also, Harald von Riekhoff, "The Third Option and Canadian Foreign Policy," in Brian Tomlin, ed., *Canadian Foreign Policy: Analysis and Trends* (Toronto: Methuen 1978).
79. M. Sharp, quoted in Daniel Roseman "Canada and the European Community," *Behind the Headlines* 32, 6 (Feb. 1974): 24.
80. Alan Gotlieb and Jeremy Kinsman, "Reviving the Third Option," *International Perspectives* (Jan./Feb. 1981): 2-5.
81. Sharp, *Which Reminds Me ...*, 185.
82. See Granatstein and Bothwell, *Pirouette*, 162-72.
83. See Canada, Parliament, Senate Standing Committee on Foreign Affairs, *Canadian Relations with the European Community* (Ottawa: Canadian Parliament, July 1973).

84. Pentland states that in 1970 a controversy arose between the Council and the Commission about the interpretation of Article 113 of the Treaty of Rome. The Council proved to be quite hesitant in allowing the Commission to expand its scope from limited foreign trade policies to more comprehensive foreign economic policies that would allow the Commission to negotiate foreign economic cooperation agreements. The 1976 Framework Agreement thus achieved this breakthrough for the Commission. See Charles Pentland, "Linkage Politics: Canada's Contract and the Development of the European Communities' External Relations," *International Journal* 32, 2 (1977): 229.
85. See Daniel Roseman, Ph.D. dissertation as an excellent analysis of the evolution of the institutional structure of the Framework Agreement, 1976-83. On the institutionalization of cooperation, see also Barry, "The U.S. and Development" (1980); and Lyon, "The Quest for Counterweight" (1973). Article 1 of the Framework Agreement provided for an extension of MFN status to the parties, in keeping with the rights and obligations under the GATT; Article 2 called for commercial cooperation as the parties agreed to "promote the development and diversification of their reciprocal commercial exchanges to the highest level"; Article 3 called for economic cooperation through industrial, scientific, and trade opportunities between the two parties; Article 4 called for the creation of a Joint Cooperation Committee to oversee the implementation and operation of the Agreement; and Article 5 provided for the operation of the Agreement in relation to other trade agreements.
86. Robert J. Boardman *et al.*, *The Canada-European Communities Framework Agreement: A Canadian Perspective* (Saskatoon, SK: Canadian Council for European Affairs, 1984), 15.
87. Granatstein and Bothwell, *Pirouette*, 165. Granatstein cites A.J. Easson, ed., *Canada and the European Communities: Selected Materials* (Kingston: Queen's University Press, 1979), 86ff. An official of the Wirtschaftsministerium, Bonn, said that, "We at meetings tried to impress on our Canadian visitors that their request was beneath Canada's dignity ... the substance was so slight. But the political interest of Canada was powerful." Confidential interview, *Ibid.*, 414, note 35.
88. Sharp, *Which Reminds Me ...*, 173.
89. *Ibid.*, 175.
90. Robert J. Boardman, "European Responses to Canada's Third Option Policy," in Marie Fleming, ed., *The European Community and Canada-EC Relations* (Ottawa: European Politics Group, 1979), 126.
91. Granatstein and Bothwell, *Pirouette*, 168.
92. See John Halstead, "Trudeau and Europe: Reflections of a Foreign Policy Adviser," *Journal of European Integration*, 12, 1 (Fall 1988): 37-50.

93. Granatstein and Bothwell, *Pirouette*, 168.
94. *Ibid.*, 169.
95. *Ibid.*, 170.
96. On the EC's relations with North America, including Mexico, see Evan H. Potter, "The Transatlantic Relationship in Flux," in Donald Barry and Gretchen Macmillan, eds., *Toward a North American Community* (New York: St. Martin's Press, 1995).
97. Daniel Roseman, "Canada-European Community Relations: An Agenda for Action," *Behind the Headlines* 46, 3 (Spring 1989), 6.
98. Glen Williams, *Not for Export: Toward a Political Economy of Canada's Arrested Industrialization* (Toronto: McClelland & Stewart, 1986). Williams points out that the ISI strategy was adopted with the first national policy of 1879. Under that policy, high tariffs were set to "protect existing Canadian industries, [and] to give manufacturers a chance to expand their operations or to establish a new plant or fill orders for goods which were formerly imported." Both government and manufacturers looked to the tariff as the means to secure/occupy the "home market," 18.
99. *Ibid.*, 19.
100. James Boyd, "Canada and the European Community." Masters Thesis, Carleton University, Ottawa, 1992, 25.
101. Williams notes the amendments to the Patent Act of 1872 opened the way for the import of foreign technology.
102. For a detailed review of the constraints imposed by foreign investment, see Government of Canada, *Foreign Direct Investment in Canada* (1972), the Gray Report. See also Wallace Clement's classic 1977 study on why change in the structure of North America's economy is so difficult. He points out that part of that resistance probably stems from having social links with the U.S. elite, combined with the fact that the Canadian elite is generally a small, close-knit group that, in the absence of new blood, may not be exposed to new ideas. See Wallace Clement, *Continental Corporate Power: Economic Elite Linkages between Canada and the United States* (Toronto: McClelland & Stewart, 1977).
103. Boyd, "Canada and the European Community," 29.
104. See "Business skeptical of EEC Link," *Globe and Mail*, June 11, 1976, 7. The skepticism was further noted in "How Canadians struggle with Europe's red tape," *Financial Post*, Nov. 12, 1977, 12-13. The article discusses the non-ferrous metals mission sponsored by the federal government earlier that year, noting that "some companies needed a lot of persuading before they agreed to participate."
105. This view was identified by Stephen Clarkson in an article in the *Globe and Mail* of December 13, 1976, 7, where it became apparent that the prevailing attitude was that Canada could not "afford to get tough with the Americans"; the status quo was the "only option."

106. Roseman, "Canada-EC Framework," 67. concludes that:
The Third Option was a declaratory policy which, as such, did not need to be converted into action. In the words of one of its authors: "the Third Option was not about diversification or counterweights ... it was a profession of faith in Canada." The Third Option could serve as a useful purpose as a symbol to the world of Canadians' determination to remain distinct from and independent of the United States; it was tarted up with talk of "a comprehensive, long-term strategy [etc.]," so that it would be taken seriously. If politically and pragmatically the government really had wanted to implement it, it would have had to follow-up with hard decisions, coherent policies—in short, an industrial strategy. But in the face of the continental business community's growing opposition by the early 1980s it no longer had the will.
107. See Boyd, "Canada and the European Community," 23, 46. Boyd, quoting Halstead, says that Jamieson in fact considered the contractual link as nonsense from the beginning. This view appears to be corroborated by Granatstein and Bothwell, *Pirouette*, 172.
108. See Alting von Geusau, "Between Superpowers: Challenges and Opportunities for Canadian-European Cooperation," in C.H.W. Remie and J.M. Lacroix, eds., *Canada on the Threshold of the 21st Century: European Reflections Upon the Future of Canada* (Amsterdam: John Benjamins, 1991).
109. Foreign Policy Advisors Group, "The Third Option: Retrospect and Prospect," Third Meeting, Feb. 3-4, 1983. Selected Documents (Ottawa: Department of External Affairs, 1983).

III
THE IMPACT OF CANADA-U.S. FREE TRADE ON CANADA-EC RELATIONS

A NEW ERA BEGAN in 1980. Vast changes occurred on the global landscape, as they did on the Canadian domestic scene. Against what the U.S. perceived to be a threatening international environment, the Reagan administration was elected with the hope of reasserting U.S. hegemony. In Canada, after the country's remarkably brief flirtation with the Progressive Conservative government led by Joe Clark from May 1979 to February 1980, the Trudeau government returned to power for the final four years of its almost uninterrupted 16-year tenure and, after losing the 1984 election, was replaced by a Conservative government led by Brian Mulroney which held power for the rest of the decade.

This is the context of Canada's relationship with the Community and Western Europe during the period 1980-89. After 1983, this decade was enormously important to the evolution of Canada's relationship with the United States, and far less important to the evolution of Canada's policy approach to European integration. The crisis of confidence of the European idea which had begun in the last years of the 1970s was carried over into the first half of the 1980s. This was an incentive for Canadian decision makers to focus more and more on relations with the United States.

With federal government officials and politicians still smarting from the Canadian business community's indifference to the objectives of the Third Option, with the pressure of a recession in 1981-82, and with the Republican administration in Washington threatening to inflict even worse damage on Canadian interests than the Nixon administration had 10 years earlier, first the Liberals and then the Progressive Conservatives undertook a fundamental review of Canada's trade policy, lasting until 1985.

In the early 1980s, the Canadian business community's unease had grown regarding the Trudeau government's determination to use trade policy, through the NEP, FIRA, and industrial policy, as a vehicle to change Canada's economic policy orientation. The business community was particularly concerned with how programs such as the NEP and the rumoured strengthening of FIRA were being perceived by their largest market, the U.S., since these federal initiatives were fundamentally at odds with the Reagan administration's commitment to the free-enterprise system and deregulation and had heightened the U.S. decision makers' awareness of foreign practices that might undermine U.S. business interests abroad.[1] The pressures of recession, which hit Canada harder than any other OECD country, combined with a nationalist lurch in Canadian energy and investment policies, convinced the traditionally cautious Canadian business community of the need for a change in Canada's commercial relations with the United States. Early in 1983, for example, the Canadian Chamber of Commerce had adopted a resolution asking the Trudeau government to join with industry and the provinces to explore the "benefits and adjustments required to facilitate a free trade agreement with the U.S. to be effective by 1987."[2]

THE CANADIAN FREE TRADE DEBATE

Under growing domestic and international pressure, the Liberal government initiated a trade policy review in 1982. The review was spearheaded by Derek Burney, who had become the director of the now-named Department of External Affairs and International Trade Canada's (EAITC) trade relations bureau in 1981 and would later become EAITC's second-highest official as Associate Under-Secretary of State for External Affairs. He was assisted by a small team of like-minded trade policy experts. Two prescriptive studies focusing on the roles of trade and trade policy in the Canadian economy resulted from the project: *A Review of Canadian Trade Policy* and *Canadian Trade Policy for the 1980s*.[3]

The review, released in August 1983, affirmed that Canada was strongly attached to the multilateral trading system. It was newsworthy because it became a vehicle for a full-scale debate on Canada-U.S. trade relations and the merits of a comprehensive Canada-United States trade agreement by calling for bilateral negotiations with the United States on a sectoral and functional basis. In the end, the U.S. did not show much interest in a sector-by-sector initiative.

On relations with Europe, the review appeared to pay lip-service to the importance of Western Europe to Canadian interests. It stated that an agreement needed: to match the close political and security ties; to blend longer-term European requirements with Canadian supply capability; to provide an effective counterweight to Canada's substantial dependence on economic relations with the U.S.; and to facilitate greater investment and technology exchanges both ways.[4] However, the review noted the limited chances for significantly improved terms of access to the EC given the lack of tariff arrangements favouring Canadian goods: "our terms of access are largely determined by GATT arrangements."[5]

Burney had become skeptical about multilateralism as the complete answer to Canada's trade policy in the early 1980s because, although GATT had served Canada well in the past, by this time it had become stalled. At the same time, not only had Canada-U.S. relations soured with the Liberal government's nationalist economic policies of the past decade, but Trudeau's "peace initiative" in his last months as prime minister in 1984, in which he tried to use personal diplomacy to mediate the differences of the increasingly antagonistic superpowers, proved to be at once ineffectual and irritating to Washington.[6] Burney, based on his consultations and analysis of Canada's trade position (see Tables 3.1 and 3.2), had concluded long before it became fashionable in political and bureaucratic circles that bilateral free trade with the United States was the only path to ensure Canada's prosperity.

He and his officials saw clearly the fundamental link between trade and domestic economic policy. His consultations with the Canadian private sector and academic community had demonstrated the strongly held view outside official Ottawa, especially among academic economists, that a successful trade performance required a competitive domestic economy and that government trade policy should concentrate in the first instance on promoting competitiveness.

The pro- and anti-free trade positions can perhaps be summarized best by looking at the positions of Richard Lipsey, a leading Canadian

TABLE 3.1: COMMODITY COMPOSITION (%) OF CANADIAN EXPORTS, 1960-84

Commodity	1960	1970	1980	1983	1984
Food and Beverage	18.8	11.4	11.1	11.6	9.7
Crude Materials	21.2	18.8	19.8	15.9	15.8
Fabricated Materials	51.9	35.8	39.8	33.3	32.0
Manufactured End Products	7.8	33.8	29.4	38.9	42.1
Special Transactions	0.3	0.2	0.3	0.3	0.4
Total	100	100	100	100	100

TABLE 3.2: DISTRIBUTION OF CANADIAN EXPORTS BY TRADING AREA, 1960-96 (%)

Importer	1960	1970	1980	1983	1984	1995	1996
United States	55.8	64.4	63.2	72.9	75.6	79.1	81.3
United Kingdom	17.4	9.0	4.3	2.8	2.2	1.5	1.5
Other Western European Countries	11.3	9.8	10.6	5.8	5.0	4.9	4.3
Japan	3.4	4.9	5.9	5.3	5.1	4.8	4.0
Other Asian Countries	2.2	2.9	4.0	4.4	3.8	3.0	2.6
Other	9.9	9.0	12.0	8.8	8.3	6.7	6.3
Total	100	100	100	100	100	100	100

Sources: Hart *et al.*, *Reconcilable Differences*, 14, 15, citing Richard R. Lipsey and Murray G. Smith, *Taking the Initiative: Canada's Trade Options in a Turbulent World* (Toronto: C.D. Howe Institute, 1985), 47. Also, Statistics Canada, *Canada's International Investment Position: Historical Statistics, 1926-91*, cat. 67-202 (Ottawa: 1993), 27.

trade policy expert and economist, and David Crane, a well-known journalist at the *Toronto Star*, a paper that was implacable in its opposition to free trade. Canada had come to a fork in the road in its post-World War II history: would it stick to the old policies or would it break out and start anew?

Lipsey contended that it was time to strike a new trading relationship with Canada's most important trading partner.[7] The argument was simple and straightforward enough. Canada's postwar wealth had been built on ready markets and the products of an abundant and low-cost resource base. But new competitors in developing countries, new technologies, substitute materials, and the increasingly higher costs of extraction had created the realization that Canada's resource base was no longer an assured source of wealth. This resource-based wealth could also no longer finance the maintenance of an inefficient manufacturing economy sheltered behind high tariff walls. Lipsey argued that small economies dependent on trade with larger economies need free, stable, and secure access to at least one large market in order to reap the benefits of specialization and long production runs that are available to industries in Europe, the United States, and Japan because of large domestic markets.

While in the 1960s, some economists had opted for a North Atlantic free trade area; in the 1970s a greater number had turned increasingly to a North American free trade area.[8] But their views ran counter to the lingering legacy of Canada's National Policy of high tariffs, started in 1879 by John A. MacDonald, that continued to dominate business and official circles.[9] In the 1980s, however, economists were finding the business community increasingly interested in more secure access to a large market and prepared to pay for this access by opening the Canadian market to U.S. competitors. Federal officials and Liberal politicians could no longer stand by in the face of further reduction in Canada's competitiveness, output, employment, and real incomes. By the mid-1980s, apart from Australia, Canada was the only advanced industrial country in the world that did not have secure access to a large market of a hundred million or more people. This lack of secure access to a large market threatened a deterioration of Canada's competitive trading position, resulting in higher costs for consumers and producers alike.[10]

On the other side were the nationalist forces represented by observers such as Crane, whose opposition to bilateral free trade was not economic but political.[11] He, like many other nationalists, felt that Canada-United States free trade would lead first to economic and then eventually political absorption by the United States. On the domestic front, this translated into fears that Canada's cultural sovereignty was at risk as well as social and economic programs that would have to be realigned and harmonized with the United States, or even eliminated. On the international front, this view was in harmony with Trudeau's *Foreign Policy for Canadians* and the Third Option, in that a free trade agreement with the United States would erode Canada's capacity to conduct an independent foreign policy.[12] Most worrisome from the nationalists' perspective was that Canada's other trading partners would regard it as even more of an appendage of the United States, thus reinforcing the "two-pillar" European view of transatlantic relations. For the nationalists, the assumption was that bilateralism and multilateralism were mutually exclusive rather than complementary as the pro-free traders argued, with the latter group pointing out that the GATT encompassed a series of bilateral agreements under which barriers to a great deal of cross-border trade had already been eliminated in the world's largest bilateral relationship.

But despite the strong argument for at least bilateral Canada-U.S. free trade made by Burney's team and academic economists, and despite growing support in the Canadian business community, in 1983 free trade was still a non-starter at the political level. Trudeau, whose "intellectual preference had always been to seek 'counterweights,'" understood both the importance of the U.S. relationship and its potential for restricting independent Canadian action.[13] He had surrounded himself with advisers who believed in government's ability to design industrial policies to spur greater competitiveness. But this is not to suggest that there was unanimity in the Liberal cabinet on the question of free trade. Well-known junior ministers such as Edward Lumley, who was one of the few Liberal ministers with any private-sector experience and who was minister for international trade, and other ministers such as Mark McGuigan and Gerald Regan, who held the external affairs and international trade portfolios respectively, were sympathetic to bilateral free trade with the United States. On the other side, not sympathetic to free trade, were more senior ministers with Trudeau's ear such as Allan MacEachen, twice Trudeau's Secretary of State for External Affairs, and Herb Gray, the "spiritual father" of the nationalism that had underpinned the economic policies of the Trudeau government in 1980-81.

No doubt reading the political signals, the senior levels of the federal bureaucracy were not prepared to, and indeed, philosophically unwilling to, support a bilateral free trade initiative. The arguments for free trade were thus rejected by the senior members of Burney's own department, where multilateralism was still the prevailing orthodoxy as it was in State, Commerce and USTR in the U.S., making him a "lone wolf."[14] As an example of the persistence of the Third Option in official thinking in his department, concurrent with the trade policy review, another group at EAITC under the direction of the Deputy Minister for Foreign Relations was reviewing the Canada-United States relationship more generally and, based on limited external consultations came to conclusions very much in the vein of Mitchell Sharp's 1972 paper.[15]

Three Options Again

The heterodoxy of free trade advocacy in official Ottawa circles did not prevent Burney and his small coterie of like-minded officers at EAITC from biding their time until the political winds changed, which happened once the Progressive Conservative party came to power in 1984. Although it had not been explicitly couched in sectoral free trade terms, the entire thrust of the recommendations to the Liberal government in the 1983 Review was now in the opposite direction of the Third Option described in the previous chapter.

Indeed, Michael Hart, a senior trade policy specialist at EAITC, who had been a member of the team working for Burney on the 1983 trade policy review, saw the debate surrounding the trade policy review and the actual report as again offering to the government three options, each with its own philosophical underpinnings. The first option revolved around an integrated industrial policy that would involve nationalizing some industries, raising barriers to some imports, and engaging in large-scale industrial subsidization in order to strengthen manufacturing. This approach, embraced by the left, had never met the test of office in Canada and was counter to the liberal ideology of comparative advantage and free markets, favouring "the mercantilist philosophy of engineered comparative advantage and mechanical calculations of national interest."[16] The second option was the status quo. Canada would continue to rely largely on the multilateral system but would, as opportunities arose, enter into special bilateral arrangements, such as the sectoral free trade option with the United States. This had been the policy of successive postwar Canadian governments, resulting, for example, in the Canada-U.S. Autopact of 1965. The "new" Third Option was to pursue a free trade agreement with the United States within the framework of rules provided by the GATT. Such an approach, while "not denying or denigrating the continued pursuit of multilateral negotiations and improved trade relations with all potential trading partners, would recognize the importance of giving the Canada-United States relationship a higher priority."[17]

In summary, the ascension of a new government in 1984, bringing with it a new political orthodoxy, would eventually ensure that public policy reflected the position that Canada's international trade interests would now be better served through the enhancement of trade relations with the United States, the Second Option in Mitchell Sharp's 1972 article. The late Hyman Solomon, a respected columnist, put it rather succinctly: "the U.S. is once more the primary focus of trade policymakers, and 'third' or other options are well down the list and looking somewhat tarnished."[18] In reaction, the *Winnipeg Free Press* more pointedly concluded:

> It has taken more than a decade for the federal government to concede that the United States is and will remain the most important single export market on which most effort should be expended.... The unstated premise of the federal government's long-delayed discussion paper ... is that the Third Option is dead. It has been dead for most of the past ten years but the department of external affairs and the prime minister's office refused to issue a death certificate until now.[19]

THE CONSERVATIVE AGENDA: BRIAN MULRONEY'S EUROPE POLICY (1984-88)

In 1984, with the largest majority in Canadian political history, Brian Mulroney ended the Liberal Party's domination of Canadian politics as the natural governing party. Mulroney's neo-conservative agenda, although Canada's Progressive Conservative party would be considered "liberal" by most American Republicans, concentrated on integrating the Canadian economy more closely with that of the United States, and also advocated a heavier reliance on foreign investment and the private sector.[20] The Liberals' FIRA, for example, was changed to Investment Canada, an investment promotion agency. The new government was initially ambivalent on the merits of free trade. The 1984 election campaign, unlike the one in 1988, was not fought on the issue of free trade. Historically, the Liberal Party had been most supportive of trade liberalization and the Conservative Party had pushed for increased protectionism. For this reason the new government initially stayed the course on a number of Liberal-era foreign policy initiatives, resulting in the government's adoption of a "constructive internationalism" that translated into support for international forums such as the Commonwealth and the creation of La Francophonie.[21] It did not specifically earmark Canada's relations with the EC for special attention, however. The Mulroney doctrine and its relationship to the CUFTA will be examined after a preliminary look at two reviews of foreign policy conducted by the Progressive Conservative government.

The first major foreign policy review since Trudeau's *Foreign Policy for Canadians* was Joe Clark's *Competitiveness and Security: Directions for Canada's International Relations* (CS:DCIR), published in 1985. The Green Paper, as the CS:DCIR was known, identified six basic objectives: unity, sovereignty and independence, peace and security, justice and democracy, economic prosperity, and the integrity of Canada's natural resources. These basics bore a close similarity to the six policy themes outlined 15 years earlier in *Foreign Policy for Canadians.* Significantly, six years later the Conservatives' last foreign policy review, the *Foreign Policy Update*, would drop the theme of "independence" from the principles underlying Canada's foreign policy.

But while both the FPC and the CS:DCIR may have been based on the same foreign policy principles, they were vastly different documents. From the Trudeau government's perspective, the world was progressing toward multipolarity as the U.S. began to be seriously challenged by Europe and Japan. In contrast, Clark's document attested to the political, economic, and military strength of the U.S., beyond which it depicted an intense contest between the U.S. and the Soviet Union. This contest between the superpowers seemed real enough, especially in the context of the second Cold War, which characterized this period. The CS:DCIR's emphasis was on Europe not as an economic threat but as the world's most important strategic site.

The importance attached to the competitiveness of the Canadian economy is what set Clark's report apart from previous analyses of Canada's international relations. A recurring theme was the changing nature of the global political economy, with an emphasis on international trade, investment, and capital flows.[22] In a clear reference to the United States, it was observed that "for Canada, protectionism poses great dangers."[23] This view was instrumental in the eventual success of the pro-free trade movement. The CS:DCIR argued that the "United States will remain the world's dominant economic power" as well as the world's foremost power generally.[24] The Trudeau government had viewed the United States' international influence as declining relative to other states and this conditioned its foreign policy orientation away from North America. Conversely, the Mulroney government saw no sign of wavering American power, even though by 1985 the U.S. had slid into the position of the world's largest debtor nation, and this was an important determinant of its foreign policy.[25]

In terms of specifics about Canada's relations with Europe, although the CS:DCIR noted that Canada was an Atlantic nation, at the same time it was "North American and not American ... a Pacific nation ... a nation of the Americas ... [and] an Arctic nation," precious little was said about Canadian interests in Europe.[26] In a one-page discussion it acknowledged the European Community as a "key player" in the international economic system since, with four of the world's ten largest economies, the EC was a major source of world investment and technology. The Canadian dimensions included a reiteration of

Canada's major postwar interests in Europe, including the fact that "fundamental Canadian political and security were engaged there"; that "thousands of Canadians have fought two world wars in Europe"; that Britain was Canada's second largest market for manufactured goods; and that Canada worked with Western European states to strengthen the mechanisms of international security and to expand East/West contacts. As a reflection of where Europe stood within the Progressive Conservatives' reassessment of foreign policy, the CS:DCIR reasserted that Canada's market access to Europe was being impeded by tariff and non-tariff barriers; that the European Community's Common Agricultural Policy had severely reduced imports of agricultural products and had turned the Community into a major international competitor for agricultural export; and, significantly, that Canada's market share in Europe had declined in the last 25 years because of structural economic change, the recession, exchange rates, and Canada's reduced competitiveness.[27]

Elsewhere in the CS:DCIR, the USSR was branded as the most ominous security threat to Canada, and Europe remained the "most critical military region in the world."[28] This position, as Rochlin points out, seemed more appropriate to 1945 than to 1985. These statements and others led observers to criticize the review for clinging to an outdated "realist" assessment of global affairs, and for failing to come to grips with the shifting international distribution of power.[29] The review was further criticized for its failure to "attach sufficient importance to the pursuit by Canada of responsible, active and idealistic external policies,"[30] and for replacing characteristics associated with a middle-power idealism with a more self-interested and egotistical appreciation of Canada's economic place in the world.

The CS:DCIR prompted analysts of Canadian foreign policy to question whether Canada was, or could be, the "principal power" of the Trudeau years, since that status was accorded to a state that was not so heavily influenced by Washington. That is, instead of Dewitt and Kirton's description of a power with a distinctive agenda, which was among the top tier of states in a multipolar world, Clark's document portrayed Canada as a loyal ally of the U.S. in a bipolar world.

With the issues raised in the CS:DCIR as its starting point, a special joint committee of the Senate and the House of Commons on Canada's international relations was formed in 1985, and it released a major report, *Interdependence and Internationalism* (I&I) in 1986. Another stark indicator of how low Western Europe and the EC in particular had slipped on the Canadian foreign policy agenda was that in the I&I, undertaken by the policy planning staff at EAITC, the amount of discussion devoted to Canada-Western European relations was grossly disproportionate to the actual resources Canada devoted to its relations with Western Europe in the political, economic, and cultural domains, and to Western Europe's position (taken as a region) as Canada's second largest trade and investment partner. In contrast, large portions of the report were devoted to Canada's relations with Asia Pacific.[31] The European Community itself was only mentioned twice in the entire review.

Let us now turn to a deeper consideration of the forces behind Canada's economic integration with the United States, which was a crucial development in the process of hemispheric integration that would occur in the 1990s and contribute to the weakening of transatlantic ties.

It is on the economic front that the new Mulroney government veered abruptly away from nearly two decades of economic nationalism as espoused by the Trudeau Liberals. Mulroney became increasingly convinced that Canada's future prosperity lay in a greater economic integration with the United States.[32] The focus of much of the national debate in 1983-85 was couched in terms of the First and Third Options of the trade policy review contrasting an industrial strategy versus free trade with the United States. The main topic was the ongoing research and consultations of the Royal Commission on the Economic Union and Development Prospects for Canada. This research project was known popularly as the Macdonald Commission after its chair, Donald Macdonald, who was a former Trudeau cabinet minister and later, as high commissioner to the U.K., a rabid proponent of the "Fortress Europe" school of thought on the impact of European economic integration.[33] With a pro-business government in power, Macdonald's recommendation was that, although Canada as a country had been created in defiance of north-south economic pressures, for the sake of national prosperity Canadians now had to be prepared to take "a leap of faith" by pursuing a more open trade relationship with the United States.[34] Canada began to negotiate a bilateral free trade agreement with the United States in 1986.

Reviews of Canada's Europe Policy

The Liberals themselves had abandoned the idea of greater trade diversification. Not the change from a Liberal to a Conservative government in Ottawa but rather an increasingly protectionist mood in the U.S. Congress and its potential to reduce Canada's access to its largest market, explain why, despite a resolve at the senior bureaucratic levels in 1983 to "move beyond" the Third Option to improve Canada's transatlantic economic links, it would actually take another four years for there to be sufficient political interest in the Prime Minister's Office for EAITC to produce a comprehensive review of Canada's relations with Europe.[35]

The Government's 1987 review of Canada's relations with Europe recommended a more integrated and proactive policy approach, and was useful in detailing the comprehensive nature of Canada's transatlantic relations, making many general recommendations, such as more ministerial trips and missions and more private sector input. Nevertheless, it was noticeably short on programs and specific means of enhancing transatlantic relations.[36] It could be criticized, in the same way that the Third Option had been, for not having a clear strategy and plan of action. In addition, any discussion of specific Canada-EC relations was overshadowed by the emphasis on Canada's security stake in Europe, a factor that may be related to the release during the same year of the Government's controversial Defence White Paper, which ironically was couched in Cold War language just as East-West tensions were subsiding.[37]

Between 1985 and 1987, concurrent with the start of the Canadian-initiated free trade negotiations with Washington, the EC took the first steps toward renewal through its White Paper in 1985 and then the Single European Act in 1987, with the latter focusing on the achievement of free trade within a single European market. Unlike a decade earlier, the priorities of Canadian and Community decision makers were now clearly diverging.

And, in terms of Brussels relations with Washington, any goodwill that the Carter administration had offered the EC was soon replaced by the old economic antagonisms and heightened foreign policy differences as the Reagan administration took office. During the early 1980s, the U.S. and the EC were on the brink of trade wars, with the biggest problem areas being steel and agriculture. The accession of Spain and Portugal to the EC in 1986, at significant cost to U.S. farm exports, exacerbated bilateral tensions and began the politicization of trade relations that were reflected in trade disputes played out in the Uruguay Round of the GATT. Differing, often opposing, positions on East-West and North-South relations affected the way the EC and the U.S. chose to trade with one another and with others. For example, the U.S opposed European sales of high-technology to the Soviet Union and its allies and also opposed EC support for the Contadora peace process, especially as this encroached on the traditional U.S. foreign policy domain.[38] The politicization of EC-U.S. relations were problematic from an institutional viewpoint since, unlike the EC's relations with Canada and Mexico, there were no bilateral organizational mechanisms to coordinate EC-U.S. policies. NATO's purview was and continues to be security and, despite the provisions for economic cooperation enshrined in Article 2 of the Charter, in practical terms excluded economic affairs. On the other hand, the EC's mandate, with the exception of the still largely dormant Western European Union (WEU), excluded military affairs. EC-U.S. disputes in the 1980s thus often fell between the two. By the end of the 1980s the growing fissures in the EC-U.S. alliance, especially as the common threat from the East bloc dissipated, highlighted the fundamental change in the relationship since the early 1970s and Kissinger's Year of Europe.

The institutional and policy making frameworks of transatlantic relations were, by 1989, in danger of becoming anachronistic and, as we shall see, attempts were made in the early 1990s to reform them. In light of the uncertain state of EC-U.S. relations, it could be expected that, as was the case in EC-Canadian relations in the early 1970s, the Commission would use its bilateral relations with Ottawa as an indirect lever in its relations with Washington. Ottawa, according to this view, would be only too eager to assert its position as the EC's "other" North American partner. At the risk of generalization, any sustained disharmony in EC-U.S. relations presents Canada with a propitious opportunity to break out of the confines of the Europeans' "two-pillar" image of transatlantic relations. However, there is no compelling evidence to show that, in the latter half of the 1980s, Ottawa actually chose to step into the breach in U.S.-EC relations. Indeed, as the following chapter will show, the Commission and the new Bush administration succeeded in patching up their differences, at least temporarily, in the year before the Treaty of Paris in November 1990, which ended the Cold War.[39] Canada, rather than being at the forefront of the rethinking of the Atlantic institutional architecture, as it had been after the Second World War, remained largely an onlooker until well into 1990.

It appears that the lack of energy devoted to relations with the EC during the 1980s should be attributed not only to the Third Option experience, but even more significantly to the Conservative government's preoccupation over free trade negotiations with the U.S. and growing interest in the Pacific Rim. Consequently, Canada's economic relations with Western Europe suffered from a case of benign neglect, albeit on the part of both partners. But such neglect is still somewhat surprising given the concern espoused by most postwar Canadian governments, with the exception of the two minority Liberal governments under Lester B. Pearson from 1963 to 1967, regarding the need to maintain Canada's independence from the United States and given also their subsequent search for counterweights. These notably took the form of closer relations with the U.K. and France and the creation of a transatlantic partnership both in political and economic terms.[40]

The 1980s were characterized by the clear bifurcation between the economic/trade and political/security tracks in Canada's policy framework for its relations with Europe. It seems somewhat ironic that running parallel with the apparent indifference to the strengthening of transatlantic economic mechanisms, was the belief that Canada's security interests were more than ever anchored in Europe and thus by extension in the transatlantic security institutions of NATO and the CSCE. Or, in the words of a Canadian journalist, the government's European policy "disclosed a curious tension between the reaffirmation of Canada's commitment to NATO and the military contribution to defence on the one hand, and, with the exception of current trade irritants, the relative indifference to developments in the EC on the other."[41]

But the EC had not become totally irrelevant to Canadian interests. The EC as an institution and as a pillar in Canada's European policy framework was, despite the fact that Canadian decision makers considered it inferior to the pillars of NATO and the CSCE, nevertheless still recognized as an important pillar in the free world to counter a resurgent Soviet threat during the increasing chill in East-West relations in the early to mid-1980s. Augmenting Canada's roles in the NATO and CSCE multilateral institutions may not have led directly to a reaffirmation of Canada-EC ties, but nevertheless ensured, as described in the 1987 Defence White Paper, that Canadian security policy in Europe was in many ways more important to Canadian interests than it had been a decade earlier during a period of détente in superpower relations. Indeed, what we see reflected in the Canadian policy discussions of this period is a regression of Canadian perceptions of the EC, mirroring Canadian and American views of the Community's importance in the transatlantic context at its founding in 1957.[42]

This chapter has covered the evolution of Canada's policy approach to Europe from the early to late 1980s. The official orthodoxy in the 1970s was that Canada had to diversify its international relations away from growing dependency on the United States; the Community was the most convenient partner in realizing this essentially political objective. This played to largely muted opposition from the Canadian business community until the late 1970s and early 1980s when a combination of a recession and unease with nationalist economic policies caused a growing realization among the private sector, increased numbers of senior federal officials, and some Liberal cabinet ministers that the U.S. market was basic to Canada's economic well being, and that success in that market would require a stable Canada-U.S. relationship. The full realization of this direction came about during the first term (1984-88) of the Mulroney-led Conservative government. In fact, the Conservative government's approach can be considered different from that of the Trudeau era in five significant ways. First, in addition to traditional ties with Britain and France there was a recognition of the increasing role that then-West Germany would play in the future of Europe. Second, there was a switch from reliance on bilateral relationships with European powers to multilateral groupings that included the United States, such as NATO and CSCE. The idea was that this would contain the United States' thrust toward unilateralism and isolationism.[43] Third, the end of détente in the early 1980s meant that security concerns, strong support for NATO in particular, rather than economic ones constituted the heart of Canada's relations with Europe, since it was believed that Canada's economic objectives could be secured in its relations with the United States. Fourth, there was a return to the quiet diplomacy of an earlier era, in the belief that by not criticizing the United States in public Canada would be consulted more often and have its views accorded more weight in Washington's deliberations.[44] And finally, the relationship with the EC as an institution and as a pillar of Canada's foreign policy approach to Western Europe was one of benign neglect. As we shall see in the next chapter, this changed by the end of the decade with momentum toward the creation of a Single Market in the Western half of Europe and the dramatic geopolitical changes in the Eastern half.

NOTES

1. Michael Hart, with Bill Dymond and Colin Robertson, "Reconcilable Differences: The Rise and Triumph of Free Trade," unpublished manuscript (1992), 14-15. All the authors had worked on the *Review of Canadian Trade Policy* in 1983.
2. Cited by Hart, *Ibid.*, 14.
3. Department of External Affairs, *A Review of Canadian Trade Policy and Canadian Trade Policy for the 1980s: A Discussion Paper* (Ottawa: Supply and Services, 1983).
4. *Ibid.*, 216.
5. *Ibid.*
6. In 1983 Trudeau in the twilight of his 16-year tenure as Canadian prime minister attempted, unsuccessfully, to mediate the growing tensions between the Reagan administration and the Soviet Union. Widely viewed at home and by the U.S. as self-aggrandizement, the peace initiative had no effect in moderating the superpower rivalries.
7. Richard G. Lipsey and Murray G. Smith, *Taking the Initiative, Canada Trade Options in a Turbulent World* (Toronto: C.D. Howe Institute, 1985).
8. In Canada, for example, arguments favouring direct negotiations with the United States to dismantle remaining barriers had been set out in considerable detail by the Senate Standing Committee on Foreign Affairs in three separate reports issued in 1975, 1978, and 1982. See particularly volume three, *Canada's Trade Relations with the United States* (Ottawa: 1982). The Senate Report was also consistent with the work of the Economic Council of Canada, which in 1975 had released a report ranking its support for Canada-U.S. free trade as the fifth among a number of possible strategies. Ahead of it were multilateral free trade; free trade among the United States, the EC, Japan, and Canada; free trade among the U.S., the EC, and Canada; and free trade among the U.S., Japan, and Canada. Its assessment was that a Canada-United States free trade agreement was probably the most attainable of all the options. See Economic Council of Canada, *Looking Outward* (Ottawa: Queen's Printer, 1975). The Economic Council's work had in turn built upon the work of economists such as John Young, *Canadian Commercial Policy* (Ottawa: Queen's Printer, 1957); Ronald and Paul Wonnacott, *Free Trade Between the United States and Canada: The Potential Economic Effects* (Cambridge, MA: Harvard University Press, 1967); Ronald Shearer *et. al.*, *Trade Liberalization and a Regional Economy: Studies on the Impact of Free Trade on British Columbia* (Toronto: University of Toronto Press, for the Private Planning Association, 1971); James R. Williams, *The Canadian-United States*

Tariff and Canadian Industry: A Multisectoral Analysis (Toronto: University of Toronto Press, 1978); and Richard G. Harris and David Cox, *Trade, Industrial Policy and Canadian Manufacturing* (Toronto: Ontario Economic Council, 1983).

9. Canada's request to negotiate a free trade agreement with the United States rekindled a debate older than Canada itself. From 1854 to 1866, Canada enjoyed the Reciprocity Treaty with the Americans. This treaty was abrogated in 1866 and Canadian Liberal and Conservative governments in 1869, 1871, and 1874 tried unsuccessfully to reawaken American interest in renewing this free trade. The U.S. rejection, according to Simpson, led in part to Sir John A. Macdonald's National Policy of 1879 which created a protected Canadian economy. In 1911, the Liberals under Sir Wilfrid Laurier, after negotiating the Reciprocity Agreement, lost the election. Their defeat would haunt Canadian governments for more than seven decades. See Jeffrey Simpson, *Faultlines: Struggling for a Canadian Vision* (Toronto: HarperCollins, 1993), 16-17.
10. Hart *et al.*, *Reconcilable Differences*, 23.
11. David Crane's views are gathered in a series of feature articles that he wrote for the *Star*. "Free trade: salvation or sell-out?" *Toronto Star*, June 8-12, 1985; and "Canada's threatened identity," *Toronto Star*, August 2-5, 1986.
12. Hart *et al.*, *Reconcilable Differences*, 6.
13. Simpson, *Faultlines*, 20.
14. *Ibid.*, 15.
15. Gotlieb and Kinsman, "Reviving the Third Option." At the time, Gotlieb was the Under-Secretary of State for External Affairs and Kinsman was the head of the policy planning unit at DFAIT.
16. Hart *et al.*, *Reconcilable Differences*, 22.
17. *Ibid.*, 23.
18. Hyman Solomon, *Financial Post*, October 22, 1983, 7.
19. *Winnipeg Free Press*, Sept. 10, 1983.
20. See D. Pollock and G. Manuge, "The Mulroney Doctrine," *International Perspectives* (Jan./Feb. 1985): 5.
21. Stated in the Throne Speech by the new Conservative government on Nov. 5, 1984, cited in John J. Kirton, *The Continuing Success of the Third Option: Canada's Relations with Europe and the United States in the Mulroney Period*, mimeo, p. 12. The speech stressed that "Canada's opportunity to influence the course of world events lies primarily in sound multilateral institutions, and therefore promised to play its full part again in the defense system of NATO" and to take part in a "renewed multilateral effort to remove ... obstructions in the international marketplace." With regard to the United States the Government pledged only "to restore a spirit of goodwill and true partnership."

22. Canada, Secretary of State Joe Clark, *Competitiveness and Security: Directions for Canada's International Relations* (Ottawa: Supply and Services, 1985), 1 [hereafter CS: DCIR].
23. *Ibid.,* 7.
24. *Ibid.,* 6a, 29.
25. Rochlin, *Discovering the Americas,* 147.
26. *CS: DCIR,* 1.
27. *Ibid.,* 36.
28. *Ibid.,* 38.
29. See, for example, A. Dorscht, T. Keating, G. Legare and J. Rioux, "Canada's International Role and Realism," *International Perspectives* (Sept./Oct. 1986): 6-8.
30. Report of the Special Joint Committee on Canada's International Relations, *Independence and Internationalism* (June 1986), 12.
31. This is illustrated in *Independence and Internationalism* and the response of the Government in its December 1986 report. While an entire chapter was devoted to the U.S. and a substantial subsection to the Pacific Rim, trade with Europe was given only passing mention.
32. The 1983 Foreign Trade Review paid lip-service to Canada's relations with Europe, but in reality was establishing the rationale for closer economic links with the United States.
33. Royal Commission on the Economic Union and Development Prospects for Canada, *Final Report* (Ottawa: Supply and Services, 1985).
34. Quoted in "Canada Must Act on Free Trade, Macdonald Says," *Globe and Mail,* Nov. 19, 1984, A1.
35. During the review of the Third Option in 1983 by senior EAITC officials, it was concluded that even if the Third Option's conceptualizaton a decade earlier had been sound, by the early 1980s it was so discredited in the public's mind that any continuation of government policy under this rubric would be counterproductive.
36. In his book on Europe Gordon Pitts noted the lamentable record of Canadian official visits to Europe between 1986-90. See, *Storming the Fortress: How Canadian Business Can Conquer Europe in 1992* (Toronto: HarperCollins, 1990).
37. Department of National Defence, *Challenge and Commitment* (Ottawa: Supply and Services Canada, 1987), Cat. No. D2-73/1987E.
38. Ginsberg, "U.S.-EC Relations," in Lodge, *The European Community,* 273.
39. Michael Smith and Stephen Woolcock, "The U.S. and the European Community in a Transformed World," 1992, draft manuscript.
40. Canada was rebuffed by its European allies in the 1950s in its attempts to strengthen its brainchild, namely, Article Two of the Charter, to give

the Atlantic Alliance more of an economic thrust rather than purely a security one. For a discussion of this, see English, *The Worldly Years,* 111, 116-18.

41. Paul Buteux, *Financial Post,* May 2, 1988, 18.
42. Smith and Woolcock, "The U.S. and the EC."
43. Kirton, *The Continuing Success,* 2. Mimeo.
44. *Ibid.,* 11.

IV

RENEWING THE TRANSATLANTIC RELATIONSHIP, 1989-91

"[T]he inclination to support the Americans, right or wrong, must contend constantly with Canada's independent assessment of the forces in the world and with its obligation to act in world diplomacy as an independent power."

— John. W. Holmes[1]

THE CONSERVATIVE GOVERNMENT of Brian Mulroney, having won the 1988 free trade election with a comfortable majority, although smaller than in 1984, and having pushed through the CUFTA, was by mid-1990 once more concerned about ending up on the spoke—rather than the hub—of a U.S.-Mexico free trade agreement. The federal government found itself in a world order characterized by the disappearance of old rules and certainties. In Canada, throughout the 1980s the left had argued that the CUFTA ensured that Canada was a dependent power; the new world order now forced a reconceptualization of Canada's role as a middle power. During this period Canadian-EC relations shifted from a condition of benign neglect to a search for new and substantive policy responses in both the economic and political spheres. While Canadian interest in transatlantic free trade ultimately would be disappointed, some progress was made on strengthening political ties with the announcement of the EC-Canada Transatlantic Declaration (TAD) in 1990.

This fertile environment for the growth of new dimensions in European relations was a result of the confluence of five defining events: (1) the collapse of Soviet domination in Central and Eastern Europe; (2) the creation of the SEM, the reconstitution of the Community through treaties on monetary and political union initialled at the Maastricht summit as well as the parallel negotiations on a European Economic Area; (3) the difficulties in completing the Uruguay Round; (4) the crisis and war in the Persian Gulf; and (5) incipient collapse of Yugoslavia. Each of these was replete with implications for Canada-EC relations. In addition, the process of restructuring post-Cold War transatlantic relations was accelerated by the dramatic haste of German unification.

This watershed in Canada's relations with the EC, however, was not just a reaction to events in Europe, but also a reaction to the evolution of Canada's relations with the United States and the latter's own renewed interest in the EC. As the discussion in the last chapter showed, the signing of the CUFTA in 1988 was the culmination of five years of intensive and divisive national debate and analysis on the future direction of Canada's trade policy and the nature of its relations with the United States. Upon implementation of the CUFTA in 1989, with Canada's trade orientation set firmly on further economic integration with its southern neighbour, the resources and energies of the Canadian Parliament and the federal bureaucracy were set free from the major national policy challenge of the 1980s.

By historical coincidence, the completion of the CUFTA negotiations happened just before the first stirrings of change in Central and Eastern Europe. As world attention turned to the economic and geopolitical developments reshaping Europe, Ottawa was not only increasingly interested in ensuring that its own European policy framework was consistent with the new realities, but also that Washington's own new-found interest in closer relations with the EC did not marginalize Canadian interests in Europe.

As is the case throughout the history of Canadian responses to the evolution of West European integration, as opposed to relations with Europe in general, reactions during 1989-90 did not consist of mass movements, advocacy groups, or Parliament. This is entirely consistent with a state-directed foreign policy process. These actors, in particular citizens' groups representing Canadians of Central and Eastern European extraction and the politically powerful lobbies representing one million Canadians of Ukrainian descent, played larger roles on

East-West issues, but they had relatively minor roles, if any, regarding Canada-EC relations.

So while Canada struggled to find a new position for itself as a middle power in the post-Cold War world, its policy directions were largely determined by domestic personalities and institutional arrangements. The choices available to Canada were contingent not only on matters of timing but also on the political leadership and personally active roles displayed by Prime Minister Brian Mulroney and his External Affairs Minister, Joe Clark, who both called for closer relations with the EC to solidify transatlantic ties and enhance multilateral responses to the changes in Eastern Europe and the Soviet Union. These choices ought to be seen in the context of the Conservative cabinet, realizing that its existing European framework was anachronistic, and of the bureaucratic politics and coalition-building at EAITC, the leading federal government department responsible for formulating Canada's Europe policy. Chronology also seems indispensable in elucidating the complicated twists and turns of Canadian, American, and European perceptions of transatlantic relations during this volatile period.

The tangled economic, political, military, and social events in Europe in 1989 forced a cautious re-evaluation of the Canadian government's overall approach to Europe. As a result of the revolutions in Central and Eastern Europe, and under pressure from the prime minister to provide his government with a menu of credible and innovative policy options, EAITC produced a second, more comprehensive review of Canada's European policy in late 1989. For the first time since the 1970s sustained political attention was being brought to bear on the totality of Canada's relations with Europe, including a specific focus on the EC.

Picking up where the 1987 report left off, this review (undertaken by EAITC's Policy Planning Staff) attached great importance to establishing a "policy framework" and, most importantly, a program of action for Canada-Europe relations in the 1990s. The program of action had an impact both in institutional and policy terms. For Canada's approach to Western Europe this translated into the "Europe 1992" component of the Government's wider, five-year (1989-94) $93.6 million "Going Global" package to develop long-term trade links. This initiative was centred on the United States and was intended to spur stronger economic and trade links with Europe, Japan, and the industrialized countries in Asia Pacific through government-supported trade development programs such as seminars, trade fairs, and outward investment support.[2] The Western European component was designed to prepare Canadian companies, through a variety of programs, for the SEM.

The review's main thesis was that Canada had a compelling interest in Europe and in European developments which it had to pursue. If not, Canadian vulnerability on the political, economic, security, and "people" fronts would increase. The Department of External Affairs recommended that Canada promote stability by: (1) influencing multilateral institutional frameworks to govern economic and political/security relations within Europe and between Europe and North America; (2) avoiding the marginalization of Canada; and (3) by securing "a seat at the table" in and with a "new Europe" based on the EC, a "refreshed" NATO, and a "reconfigured" CSCE. The views of senior EAITC officials can be summed up as concern about the risk of an inward-looking Europe and Canada's marginalization by a series of bilateral relationships such as Europe-USSR, U.S.-USSR, or U.S.-Europe. They recommended to their minister, Joe Clark, that for both domestic reasons, given the large number of Canadians of European extraction, and international reasons, as Canada was a responsible member of the world community, Canada should participate in the evolution of a "new" European architecture. The review summed up Canada's interest in Europe in one word, "stability," since it was felt that instability in Europe would lead to Canadian "vulnerability."[3]

Given the complexity and fluidity of events, it is not surprising that there was no clear consensus from the Canadian government on Canada's appropriate policy response, although EAITC consultations with other federal government departments evoked general agreement with its view that Canada had to participate actively in the transformation of Europe. Some senior federal officials who resisted an active approach, notably from the Department of National Defence and the Canadian Security Intelligence Service, expressed the view that Canada should stand back from such participation because Canada could do nothing to prevent, for example, the "rampant European tribalism" that would inevitably break out as a result of the dissolution of the U.S.-USSR condominium that had provided stability for 40 years. Other federal deputy ministers suggested that the proposed plan for a modest amount of Canadian assistance to rebuild Eastern Europe was too small; Canada would either have to spend billions or none at all, with the latter option effectively signalling its retreat from Europe. Still other senior federal officials, most notably from the Privy Council

Office and the Department of Industry, Science and Technology, were more supportive of the EAITC plan, noting that the dilemmas raised about Canada's continuing active presence in Europe invariably raised the fundamental question about Canada's place in the world. If Canada did not participate in Europe where its interests were clear, then where would it participate?[4] This comment was reminiscent of the criticism that Trudeau had faced 20 years earlier when he mused about Canada withdrawing from NATO and thereby retreating from Europe. In short, by the end of 1989, the rapid geopolitical changes in Europe, the continuing problems in the Uruguay Round of the Multilateral Trade Negotiations, and completion of the CUFTA ensured that developments in Europe gained priority on Canada's foreign policy agenda. What created further impetus for Canada to re-evaluate its European policy framework was the pace of U.S.-EC relations in this period.

THE U.S. CREATES NEW LINKS WITH THE EC

A landmark speech in Boston on May 21, 1989, in which George Bush called for a "European partnership in world leadership," was arguably the actual genesis for the separate, but parallel, Canadian and U.S. transatlantic declarations that would be signed a year later with the Community.[5] Secretary of State Baker went a step further in a speech at the Berlin Press Club on December 12, 1989, noting that as the EC moved toward its goal of a common internal market, embarked on institutional reform, and assumed increasing responsibility in certain foreign policy areas, the U.S. transatlantic relationship with the Community would have to evolve as well. He called for both the United States and the Community to achieve "a significantly strengthened set of institutional and consultative links ... whether in treaty or some other form."[6] Baker suggested a number of specific steps: (1) to explore better means of identifying and discussing potential economic conflicts before they grow into political problems; (2) to look at the possibility of more regular contacts with the EPC working groups to share views on foreign policy issues; (3) to envisage systematic U.S. cooperation with a new European environmental agency; (4) to regularly discuss a number of technical issues, such as standards, before decisions are made and can have far-ranging political effects; and (5) to discuss a more systematic, phased approach to draw Eastern economies closer to the liberalized economic system of the West.[7] As a result, there ensued a series of exploratory meetings to put some flesh on Baker's and Bush's calls for closer EC-U.S. transatlantic links

The importance of Secretary Baker's speech should not be underestimated since it reflects the evolution of the U.S.-Western Europe relationship from that of patron-client in the immediate postwar years to that of equal partners in the 1990s.[8] The EC and its member states as well as the U.S. government took up Baker's initiative in a joint declaration on December 15, 1989. Closer contacts were then agreed upon during a meeting between President Bush and the President of the EC Council of Ministers, Irish Prime Minister Haughey, in February 1990;[9] Bush and President Mitterrand also discussed the possibility of a transatlantic alliance during a meeting at Key Largo, Florida, later that spring. In addition, several EC commissioners made proposals to intensify the Community's relations with the United States in areas such as research and development, competition policy, the environment, vocational training, and high-level foreign policy coordination.[10]

It must be emphasized, however, that the Bush/Haughey announcement and the other discussions with the member states concerning the possibility of a transatlantic alliance were related to European political cooperation—an EC presidency matter—and were thus on a separate track from the U.S.-Community ministerial meetings. This is an important distinction. The Bush administration, which had distinguished itself from previous administrations by trying to broaden bilateral relations away from a fixation on trade irritants, sought consciously to develop new opportunities to insert the U.S. in the EC political process before decisions were taken. Nonetheless, it pointedly backed away from Commerce Secretary Mosbacher's ill-received remarks about the U.S. wanting a 13th seat at the EC table "at least as an observer."[11]

Mosbacher's proposal was meant as a reaction to the perceived lack of opportunity for American firms to provide meaningful input on industrial aspects of the 1992 program, such as standards development, testing, and certification. As a result of Mosbacher's complaints the EC relented and agreed on May 31, 1989 to allow U.S. technical experts to make presentations to the European Committee for Standards (CEN) and the European Committee for Electrotechnical Standardization (CENELEC), the groups assigned by the Commission to set product standards, an action that was well-received by the U.S. business community. Mosbacher declared in December 1989 that he was "very pleased" with the way the United States was able to participate in the EC decision making process. The Community, he said, "at times, allowed literally a seat" for the representatives of American interests.[12] The Europeans were not amused. But whatever negative perceptions of U.S. intentions were prompted by Mosbacher's remarks, they nevertheless pointed to the Bush administration's serious desire to enhance bilateral political links with the Community and gain enhanced access to the EC decision making process. As mentioned above, the creation, or indeed even the investigation, of a more comprehensive mechanism for managing EC-U.S. transatlantic trade ties, in addition to the GATT, was not contemplated.

Nevertheless, the stage of development reached by the EC-U.S. ministerial meetings in 1989 shows the incremental formalization of EC-U.S. relations. These meetings were chaired by the President of the Commission of the European Communities and the U.S. Secretary of State, and included a number of U.S. cabinet officers (USTR, Commerce, and Agriculture secretaries) and several European Commissioners (always External Relations, often Agriculture, Industry, Internal Market). They had been annual events for some time, and were usually tied logistically to NATO ministerial meetings in Brussels. As EC-U.S. discussions progressed on EPC during the spring of 1990, both sides reviewed proposals to make changes to upgrade the importance and increase the frequency of the ministerial meetings. This was to be achieved through a number of measures: holding the meetings twice a year; alternating the locale between Washington and Brussels; when in Washington including a meeting between the U.S. President and the President of the EC Commission; and attempting to de-link timing of the Brussels ministerial from the NATO ministerial in order to create more focused bilateral discussions.[13]

The 1990 U.S.-EC ministerials, held on April 23 and 24, were significant for three reasons: (1) they were the first ministerials to be held in Washington; (2) President Bush for the first time had a one-on-one meeting with the EC Commission president; and (3) both sides agreed that Baker's call for a transatlantic treaty was premature. Commission President Jacques Delors came out strongly in favour of transatlantic ties, pointing out that the United States and the EC could only face the new challenges to the environment, and in technological and social areas, by pooling their resources and acting as partners.[14] But it is the last reason that is the most important for the purpose of our discussion. In the *tour d'horizon* during the Delors/Bush meeting, Delors explained that the EC considered a formalized treaty to be inappropriate given the awkward stage in the Community's external relations. The EC was preoccupied with the aspirations of Central and Eastern Europe as well as the creation of a common market to include the EFTA members; and there still remained the problem of the divided competence between the Community and the member states in many areas. Delors suggested that the operationalization of a formal treaty would depend on the further progression by the EC along its path toward political union (PU).

Bush was apparently comfortable with this position and both sides agreed to concentrate instead on reinforcing dialogue under existing mechanisms.[15] Bush's comfort level at keeping the treaty proposal in abeyance was no doubt increased by the fact that the State Department had "discovered" that some form of Friendship, Commerce and Navigation (FCN) treaty already existed with 11 out of the 12 member states of the Community.[16] Following the Bush/Delors meeting and its own internal consultations, the European Council decided in June 1990 to begin talks with the U.S. government on a joint declaration.[17]

The above discussion of bilateral EC-U.S. transatlantic ties and the occasional raised European eyebrow over American presumptions is relevant to the present study on Canada-EC relations not only as background or to provide context. The discussion points to an environment in which EC-U.S. relations threatened, by burying Canadian interests in the North American pillar, to equal and then surpass Canada-EC relations in terms of institutional links

As mentioned earlier in this study, for the same reasons that Canada supported a Western Europe firmly ensconced in the Atlantic Alliance, support for European integration had been a cornerstone of American foreign policy since the start of the Cold War. European integration was believed to foster economic stability and therefore social and political stability, making it a more effective counterweight to the perceived Communist threat, and thus strengthening the Atlantic Alliance.

In addition, Western European integration was seen as a means of binding West Germany to the West. As Smith has pointed out, with the collapse of the Communist regimes in Central and Eastern Europe starting in 1989, and especially with German reunification, the European Community's integration program was once more heralded as a pillar of stability in a changing Europe. Smith calls this a "regression" of American views to the very creation of the Common Market, with the key difference being that the EC was now at least the economic rival of the United States.[18] For Canada, the Community's status as equal economic rival had dire portents since Ottawa could now foresee being squeezed between the "grindstones" of Washington and Brussels on trade policy issues.

The Community's new-found status, although not entirely comforting to U.S. and Canadian decision makers, did have the effect of raising the burden-sharing issue, especially as it related to the development of Central and Eastern Europe. Indeed, with the days of the Marshall Plan long gone, it was clear that the U.S. alone could not finance the economic restructuring that was needed; conversely, many of the EC member states had, through postwar American assistance, gained sufficient economic strength for them to play a more important financial role. As Bush expressed it, "a resurgent Western Europe is an economic magnet, drawing Eastern Europe closer toward the commonwealth of free nations."[19] That this "resurgent Western Europe" should share in a greater part of the Alliance's financial burden was made clear when Bush stated that he "was exceptionally pleased that we agreed at the Paris economic summit on a specific role for the EC in that Group of 24 effort to assist Poland and Hungary."[20] It thus seemed only logical that as European integration stimulated economic growth and, consequently, also the ability of Western Europe to shoulder an increasing share of the West's international financial burden, U.S. interests were served by support for integration. This view was mirrored among Canadian decision makers and business people alike, who were staring in the face of mounting public debt at home, a history of defaulted loans to countries such as Poland, and an overextended system of Official Development Assistance.

Canadian Reaction to U.S.-EC Dialogue

The rapprochement in EC-U.S. relations, given the history of acrimony,[21] was certainly not lost on senior Canadian cabinet ministers and EAITC officials in Ottawa and in Washington. It once more raised the spectre of Canadian marginalization[22] in Europe, which Canada had struggled to avoid over the previous two decades. It has been suggested that the reference to "transatlanticism" in the EC-U.S. bilateral discussions was bound to hit a raw nerve on the Canadian side since this concept has historically always included Canada.[23] Canadian officials were impressed by the dynamism and scope of the EC-U.S. contacts and by the commitment displayed by both sides to realizing the spirit of Secretary

Baker's Berlin speech. They noted the impressive number of cabinet-level contacts between the EC and the U.S., in addition to the breadth of the consultative agenda developing along the lines of bilateral cooperation on science and development. They saw this as reflective of an attempt to forge a broader and more cooperative bilateral dialogue in light of the "new Atlanticism."[24]

Although it may have appeared so at first glance, it was not the decision of the U.S. to reinforce and regularize its relations with the Community that most impressed Canadian officials in Washington monitoring the EC-U.S. discussions. After all, many of the changes that had been imposed and implemented were a logical extension of past activities and reflected the fact that the U.S. lacked an agreement similar to the EC-Canada Framework Agreement that ensured regular bilateral discussions at ministerial and official levels. Impressive from the Canadian perspective, rather, was the sheer interest evinced by political appointees in the State Department in pursuing a relationship with the EC that had not hitherto been evident.[25] Canadian officials noted the recognition by the U.S. of the Community's role as the single most successful integrative institution in Europe. They noted also that the U.S. would require, irrespective of the prevailing European architecture, an expanded and formalized political relationship as part of its strategy to ensure protection of its interests in Europe.

ADJUSTING TO CHANGE: OLD AND NEW CANADIAN RESPONSES TO EUROPEAN INTEGRATION

The demise of the communist regimes in Eastern Europe and the progress toward the SEM left an indelible mark; they forced Europe onto the Canadian public policy agenda. Although some Canadian academics and this author have characterized Canada's approach to the Community in the 1980s as one of "benign neglect," the geopolitical changes in Europe in 1989, coupled with the completion of the CUFTA, ensured that developments in Europe, specifically issues of security but also including the progress of European economic integration, became a priority for the Conservative government.

Growing criticism was levelled at Canada for lagging behind other industrialized countries in its policy approach to the dramatic changes in East-West relations. Prime Minister Mulroney was, for example, the last G-7 leader to travel to the Soviet Union to meet with Mikhail Gorbachev. Mulroney's November 1989 trip to Moscow thus added stimulus to the comprehensive interdepartmental policy review in Ottawa of Canada's relations with Europe.[26] The attempt to develop a fresh approach to Canada's European policy, a way of reaffirming Canada's commitment to the transatlantic relationship, was reflected in a series of important addresses by both Mulroney and Clark and in cabinet discussions in the first half of 1990. Clark, for example, referred to Canada as "a European nation," described Canadian interests in the new Europe as "real, contemporary and compelling" and said that "security in Canada has no meaning without security in Europe."[27] He believed strongly in the role that the second pillar, the CSCE, could play in projecting Canadian interests in the new Europe. On the trade side, Clark's speech at McGill University on February 5, 1990, *did* mention the increased trade opportunities for Canada in Europe in light of the Single Market, though he focused primarily, and not surprisingly, on Canadian responses to the collapse of communist governments in Eastern Europe.[28] On February 7, Clark made a special presentation to the Cabinet Committee on Foreign Policy and Defence (CCFPD) in which he stressed that if Canada did not seek to intensify its links to Europe through its three pillars—NATO, the CSCE, and the EC (in that order)—it would increasingly be marginalized in Europe.[29] Citing Baker's Berlin speech, he noted that American concerns over decoupling and marginalization in Europe were similar to Canada's and that U.S. commitment to the "new" Europe would see Canada having to commit itself as well.

The decision of the CCFPD, in light of Clark's presentation, is puzzling in certain respects. On the one hand, it was supportive of Clark's warnings and called for a continuation of Canada's involvement in Europe based on Canada's national interests and global responsibilities. This involvement would be implemented through a policy framework so that Canada's involvement in Europe would be adequate to avoid marginalization. Yet, on the other hand, the CCFPD also cautioned that whatever issue-specific policy framework was developed by EAITC in consultation with other federal government departments, it would have to give emphasis to "no cost" and "low cost" measures. Though this important constraint on the options open to Canada was understandable in light of the Government's preoccupation with the surging national debt and deficit, to maintain Canada's influential presence in Europe in the post-Cold War would certainly require more, not fewer, resources. On February 20 the Priorities and Planning Committee, comprising Mulroney's inner cabinet where the Government's major decisions were made, ratified the CCFPD's decision.

The CCFPD's decision on low-cost measures for the projection of Canadian interests in Europe also appears to fly in the face of the apparent surge in cabinet interest in relations with Europe, both West and East, reflected in the number of memoranda to cabinet during the period 1989-90. For instance in late 1989, prior to Clark's presentation, then Minister for International Trade, John Crosbie, had presented cabinet with a memorandum summarizing the state of bilateral trade irritants between Canada and the EC. As well, in March 1990, EAITC prepared a presentation to cabinet on Canada's relations with Eastern Europe and the Soviet Union.[30]

Based on this author's interviews, although by the spring of 1990 Canadian policy makers had had some forewarning of the major changes in Western Europe, that is, the momentum toward the SEM, the state of EPC, political and monetary union, they were obviously caught off-guard by the rapidity of developments in the Eastern half of the continent and in Germany. The Berlin Wall came down, the Soviet lynchpin was pulled, and there were revolutions in Czechoslovakia and Romania. The mutually reinforcing political and economic developments in Eastern Europe had, by calling for a redrawing of the face of Europe, washed away literally overnight the certainties underpinning Canada's relations with Europe. Against this backdrop, Canada faced a European Community accelerating its own integration through the European Monetary System, achieving near unanimity on the Social Charter, negotiating with the EFTA with an increased urgency, and expanding its influence into Central and Eastern Europe. With the unification of Germany, the "German Question" was once more at the heart of European politics.

In terms of architecture, the environment was equally fluid, leaving Canadian decision makers a choice of Gorbachev's "Common European Home"; EC Commission President Jacques Delors' "EC-Centric" Europe; Mitterand's "Confederation of Europe"; and Kohl's proposal for a new East-West Economic organization through the CSCE. Although none of the proposals offered detailed blueprints, they did demonstrate that the "new" Europe would in turn redefine North Atlantic and global relationships. Canadian officials perceived that the economic balance between North America and Europe was shifting at North America's expense. An open cooperative Europe based on the EC would therefore be essential.

On the security side, although it was clear to Ottawa that NATO faced an evolutionary challenge, officials and politicians were unsure as to whether it would be the instrument of change or whether a new forum was necessary. What appeared to have more consensus on the Canadian side was the CSCE as the preferred "envelope" for Canada, and the United States, to address the broad political, security, economic, science and technology, and environmental challenges facing all of Europe.

Germany Proposes a Transatlantic Declaration

Canadian thinking on Europe received further impetus when, in the aftermath of the fall of the Berlin Wall, Hans Dietrich Genscher (then German Foreign Minister and Vice-Chancellor), made a presentation to the Canadian Parliament on April 5, the day after speaking to Bush, in which he reinforced Baker's and Bush's public comments and called for a new transatlantic architecture to bind Europe more securely to Canada and the United States.[31] As he stated:

> So we are on the way to the political union of Europe, meaning the Europe of the Community, which is not the whole of Europe.... As a consequence of this process, I propose to the American government and to your government that we consider it useful at [this] time, improving relations between the European Community and the two North American democracies, to give our relationship a new quality in addition to our membership in NATO, and to have a new declaration concerning the common challenges we face in the political, economic, technological, and ecological fields. We should consider this approach in order to create a new basis of cooperation between the European Community and the two democracies in North America.[32]

It would appear that Genscher was reinforcing Secretary of State Baker's call for new thinking on the role of the transatlantic alliance and on the need to make its military focus a more political or economic one. Genscher said as much in his later presentation to Canadian parliamentarians: "It was not the German foreign minister, it was the American foreign minister [James Baker] who for the first time, when he presented his speech in Berlin, spoke of the more political character of the alliance—and I think Jim Baker is totally right in saying this."[33]

Finally, a political interpretation of Genscher's proposal led some Canadian officials to perceive the possibility that Genscher was placing the newly united Germany the same distance from both North America and the not yet defunct Soviet Union.[34]

Clark had anticipated that Genscher's visit would be an opportunity for Canada to work with its European partners "on shaping a new Europe and the institutions it shares with North America."[35] Genscher's thoughts on a transatlantic declaration complemented the Canadian position which was to impress on the Germans the desire to reinforce transatlantic links from "Vancouver to Vladivostok, via Berlin."

A senior Canadian official has pointed out that the birth of a more clearly thought out new transatlantic alliance proposal goes back to January 1990 when Genscher "first mentioned something along these lines when I called him prior to the Ottawa Open Skies Conference." The official further states that Genscher was then thinking in a CSCE context and was concerned with ensuring continued North American participation in Europe as counterbalance to a changing relationship with the Soviet Union. As it turned out, the idea of a transatlantic declaration never appeared on the agenda at the Open Skies Conference, but this did not mean that the Germans had dropped the idea. Indeed, according to this official, policy planning officials in the German Ministry of Foreign Affairs had in the meantime been trying, somewhat unsuccessfully, to transform Genscher's suggestions into a coherent text.[36]

The all-encompassing nature of the Genscher proposal, however, may have been too ambitious at that time, especially since multilateral discussions were taking place on how to broaden the CSCE and reconfigure NATO. One suggestion for this lack of immediate follow-up is that a senior official at EAITC feared that a movement on a transatlantic declaration would undermine NATO.[37] Whatever the precise reason, on the Canadian side the idea of a declaration fell into abeyance until September 1990. On the U.S. side, as we have indicated, negotiations had been underway since June 1990. But this is not to say that Canadian officials and politicians were indifferent to new mechanisms and forums to formalize transatlantic relations. After the Genscher proposal, discussions among Clark, Mulroney, and their American and European counterparts had a new urgency.

Canada Looks at Ways of Strengthening Transatlantic Trade Ties

With the CUFTA completed and with Europe demanding more and more attention, in early May 1990, Derek Burney, by then Canadian Ambassador to the United States, had his officials in Washington reflect on possible Canadian policy options in face of increasing

European economic integration, including new, more comprehensive trade arrangements between Canada and the European Community.[38] The deliberations in Washington had coincided with the arrival of a new Under-Secretary of State at EAITC, De Montigny Marchand.[39]

Two plausible explanations may account for the fact that an independent analysis of Canadian trade policy vis-à-vis the Community appeared to have been initiated by the Canadian embassy in Washington: (1) there was a perception within the senior echelons of EAITC that the Department's European Bureau was too hemmed in by operational requirements to allow for bold ideas;[40] and (2) the combination of dramatic events taking place in Eastern Europe, and the Washington embassy's own close monitoring of the increased intensity of EC-U.S. dialogue, served to make it a logical point of intellectual ferment for Canada's trade policy options. Whatever the exact reason, the conjecture that EAITC's European Bureau was not at the centre of deliberations looking at options for Canada's future relations with the Community does not strike the author as particularly unusual. In addition to his intimate involvement in the trade policy review in the early 1980s, Burney had also been Prime Minister Mulroney's closest adviser as his Chief-of-Staff and Associate Under-Secretary of State for External Affairs,[41] and could therefore offer advice unburdened by the need to develop official consensus. His well-known skepticism about putting all of Canada's eggs in the multilateral basket added to his credibility in providing this kind of advice on trade policy.[42]

The central role of Burney in Canada-EC relations at this time should certainly not be surprising to students of bureaucratic politics. According to officials at EAITC headquarters in Ottawa, Burney, as Canada's ambassador to Washington, viewed his position as one of quasi-ministerial status. This was understandable given the U.S.'s primacy in Prime Minister Mulroney's foreign policy. The net effect of Burney's high-level bureaucratic and political experiences was that Canadian foreign policy on certain issues, such as free trade and multilateral trade negotiations, was made on the PMO-Burney axis, with EAITC headquarters in Ottawa as a bystander and alerted to developments only on a "need-to-know" basis.

Burney believed that there was a causal link between the management of transatlantic trade and economic relations and the prospects for security and stability. He felt that the failure to agree on trade and economic matters could undermine prospects for security.[43] There was a concern that Canada's privileged position as the first industrialized third country to sign a commercial agreement with the EC in 1976 had long been overtaken by events, not least the Community's "1992" program, and that the GATT would also not serve as an optimal mechanism to ensure Canadian access to the new European market. According to this view, because any EC-U.S. bilateral agreement would create a privileged position for the United States while diminishing Canada's already small place in Europe, the two broad options available to Canada for enhancing Canadian access to and influence upon the EC were: (1) a Canada-EC Free Trade Agreement; or (2) an Atlantic Free Trade Association.[44] Canadian officials in Washington concluded that the latter arrangement was optimal since it permitted Canada to achieve influence that was not available through existing arrangements or, indeed, through a separate bilateral agreement. It would do so by imposing substantial obligations on the EC, as well as Canada and other participants, in areas that were within the exclusive competence of the EC and which were the principal instruments for European integration.[45]

There were a number of other indications that Canada's relations with the EC had gained priority in the Canadian cabinet. As previously indicated here, Ottawa's belated recognition of the EC as a formidable political and economic actor had been encouraged by Genscher's proposal to Joe Clark for an "EEC-North American" declaration "which would confirm shared principles and interests in openness and enhanced cooperation."[46] Underlining Canadian interest in this proposal, Mulroney, in a three-page letter to George Bush on May 8, 1990 that focused almost entirely on the need for Canadian and U.S. cooperation in emphasizing the continued vitality and complementarity of NATO and the CSCE, stated in the last paragraph that he, Mulroney, continued to be "intrigued" by Mr. Genscher's suggestion of a transatlantic declaration "designed to celebrate the values that we [EC, U.S., Canada] all share."[47] Indeed, such was the concern on the status of Canada-EC relations at the cabinet level, that when Prime Minister Mulroney met with EC Commission Vice-President Frans Andriessen on May 25, 1990 he raised the possibility of enhancing bilateral institutional arrangements to encourage more open market access on a reciprocal basis.

The "necessity" of Canada's engagement in the new Europe was again made public in a speech delivered by Joe Clark at Toronto on May 26, and repeated in his speech in the House of Commons on May 31, 1990 in which he proposed a new, more intense Canada-EC relationship.[48] Catching his officials off guard, more significantly, Clark stressed the possible virtue of examining the desirability of a formalized open trading arrangement between Canada and the EC, perhaps including the U.S. and other members of the OECD.[49] Coming at what was then thought to be the conclusion of the Uruguay Round, this declaration was important because it was the first time that Canada had attempted, in seeking to include the United States and other OECD members, to apply the multilateral security model (NATO) to its trade relations. The proposed economic and trade agreement was to be real in the sense that it would focus on issues of access, such as were found in the CUFTA, rather than just cooperation as the existing EC-Canada Framework Agreement did. In the end, because the speech was a ministerial initiative and had limited input from officials in EAITC, it was initially unclear how this transatlantic trade idea would be developed.

Transatlantic Free Trade: Antidote to U.S. Bilateralism?

Clark's "surprising policy balloon" about a transatlantic trade agreement appeared as much a reflection of Canadian concern with the U.S. tendency to bilateralism as it did Canada's desire to put its relations with Europe on a new footing.[50] The alarm signals had gone off in Ottawa as soon as Mexico and Washington began formal negotiations on a comprehensive trade agreement in June 1990. For Canadian officials, Washington's willingness to negotiate with Mexico confirmed their perception that the U.S. preferred to deal bilaterally, and thus suggested a high probability that the U.S. would turn to Brussels and also strike a bilateral deal, trade or otherwise, with the Community, leaving Canada in a vulnerable position.[51]

According to Edwards, into the summer of 1990 Canada tried "vainly" to influence the Community on trade matters, again pursuing its two-track approach "rather than combining the political and economic dimensions into a more comprehensive dialogue."[52] A new European role for Canada was clearly warranted but the question remained as to the means. In a speech at Montreal on June 20, for example, Clark averred that in light of the "new climate of cooperation between nations formerly divided by an ideological East-West confrontation" there was a need to transform the "institutions of yesterday." Clark, in keeping with the Government's desire to promote its "new" European policy and to pursue objectives in Europe that were "realistic" and "in keeping with the role expected of [Canada]," stressed the need for Canada to make "an original and tangible contribution to the development of Europe ... in order to consolidate [its] position in the Europe of tomorrow."[53] The nature of this consolidation in terms of Canadian relations with the Community was made clearer when Clark explained that he had made specific proposals to Irish Foreign Minister Gerald Collins (Ireland was holding the EC presidency at the time) about "enrich[ing]" dialogue between Canada and the member states of the European Community "particularly on major international political issues." The Canadian proposals, which were well received, included regular meetings between the Canadian Prime Minister and the President of the European Council, regular discussions between the Canadian External Affairs Minister and his European counterpart, and "much closer" contact between Canadian officials and EC experts. Indeed, these proposals foreshadowed the EC-Canada transatlantic declaration that would be signed five months later.

As a result of the Clark proposal, it was clear to middle-level officials at EAITC that a comprehensive analysis of Canada-EC trade and economic relations was needed in order to put some economic flesh on the bones of the political impetus created by Clark and Mulroney. It was equally clear that a study of this nature would require broad internal consultations in the Department.

An intradepartmental Canada-EC working group was assembled in EAITC during the summer of 1990 with the intent of submitting a final report by December. The officials responsible for developing the study were careful to point out that it would not become an economic research project, but rather a "study of the Government's political/economic priorities and judgements."[54] In other words, the project, obviously very ambitious from the start, would have had far reaching political ramifications if the Government had chosen to pursue a transatlantic trade accord. The political sensitivity of this study was further heightened because it required a detailed probing of Canada's commitment to the MTN. For example, how well would the GATT serve as a regulatory framework for EC-Canada commercial relations in the post-Uruguay Round setting? Would the system of preferential trade agreements operated by the EC significantly limit the potential for an agreement? How important was the Canadian market to the EC? And was a network of bilateral agreements the best response to the negotiating options that would face developed and developing countries after the Uruguay Round? It should also be added that this working group was also mandated to look at political issues writ large, that is, how

Canada-West European relations conformed to Canada's overall foreign policy framework.

Not wishing to create high expectations, and no doubt foreshadowing the possibility of failure if there was no sustained political will, the deliberations of the Canada-EC working group were kept strictly internal to EAITC. The question of how long the political will would last was of course crucial in understanding the outcome of this initiative. Unlike the "Going Global" trade development strategy which was generated by various geographic branches at EAITC to increase their resources,[55] the impetus for this policy came directly from Clark's office. Some officials have characterized the whole process of putting transatlantic free trade on the agenda as an exercise in "damage control." It was less the result of Canada's dissatisfaction with the existing state of bilateral relations with Brussels than it was a perception at a particular time, by Canadian politicians, that the U.S. and EC would undermine Canada's multilateral entitlements by signing a separate trade treaty.[56]

It would appear from the above review of the numerous public and private statements on Europe by Prime Minister Mulroney and Secretary of State for External Affairs Clark, and from the activity of officials at EAITC in the 12-month period ending May 1990, that during this period the Government spent more energy redrawing its European policy framework than at any other time since the development of the Third Option in the early 1970s.

European Reaction to Trade Accord Proposal

Community officials, in the midst of preparations for the Single Market in 1993 and the upcoming intergovernmental meetings, certainly had little time to study the desirability or feasibility of an EC-Canada transatlantic free trade agreement. Perhaps because the idea had not emanated from the Commission, it was given little serious attention at the External Relations Directorate (DG I) of the Community. Indeed, an official in DG I familiar with EC-Canadian relations has commented that a free trade agreement with Canada was so improbable that it was not even the subject of corridor discussions.[57] Since the broader, less defined notion of a transatlantic declaration had come originally from Genscher and there was no sustained political pressure at the Commission level at that time to develop it further, it would not be unusual for DG I to be out of the information loop.

Nevertheless, it would be an exaggeration to say that officials in the Community were completely unaware of Canadian thinking on this subject. A more likely explanation is that since the notion of a transatlantic alliance had such broad political ramifications it would in the initial stages have been dealt with directly out of the EC's Forward Studies unit which is separate from DG I. This conjecture is supported by the fact that discussions did take place between EC and Canadian policy planning officials. This author was advised that in discussion with his Canadian counterpart, Jacques Delors' main policy planning advisor was said to have been "very receptive" to ideas on an Atlantic alliance.[58] From the Commission's perspective, however, the notion of a transatlantic trade agreement never departed from the purely hypothetical.

Canada-EC Free Trade a Non-Starter

As mentioned, the intensity of European economic integration in 1990 was mirrored in the initial flurry of activity at the Canada-EC working-group level in Ottawa. A number of reports were commissioned from various bureaux at EAITC dealing with issues of trade policy in Canada-EC relations and the implications of the Single European Market for particular Canadian industries. This begs the question of how important was the role of Canadian officials in sustaining the momentum of this focus on Canada-EC trade relations.

In Canada, a cabinet faced by complexity and pressure can delegate much of the responsibility for policy making to the public service and the "public service ... stamp[s] public policy with its own values and priorities." The success or failure of political initiatives can consequently be shaped to a significant extent according to motivations and preferences of bureaucrats.[59] In the past (especially in the 1940s and 1950s) the high level of influence exerted by senior Canadian public servants was accentuated in the formulation of foreign policy, where secrecy inherent in state-to-state relations and the multifaceted, complex nature of diplomatic relations offered officials a certain autonomy in influencing policy outcomes. The influence of today's officials in EAITC may not be so great, but as the negotiations leading up to the CUFTA showed, in specific issue areas, especially trade policy, the independence of the bureaucracy remains largely intact.[60]

Bureaucratic interest waned once it became apparent that the Europeans did not share Canada's enthusiasm for exploring the modalities of a transatlantic free trade framework. At the same time, in the summer of 1990 the negotiation of a North American free trade arrangement rapidly ascended the Government's policy agenda. This had the immediate effect of reordering the bureaucracy's priorities: Derek Burney became preoccupied with ensuring that Canada was included in the U.S.-Mexico negotiations; the resources of EAITC's Policy Planning Staff were shifted on the economic front to looking at the economic and trade implications of North American free trade and, on the political front, to the implications of Iraq's invasion of Kuwait and the development of a cooperative security dialogue in the North Pacific;[61] and, the removal of the European Bureau's role as the lead bureaucratic actor further hastened the demise of EAITC's Canada-EC working-group.[62] In the end, the Canada-EC working-group died as quickly as it had been born. No final report was ever written.

Despite significant change in cabinet ministers', parliamentarians' and officials' perceptions concerning the implications for Canada of Western European integration and the revolutions in Eastern Europe, it would be wrong to view the "cognitive shift" at the political level as being in direct proportion to the radical change in the international system. In fact, it seems more plausible that the Government's sudden preoccupation with a transatlantic trade accord was no more than a policy impulse soon superseded by the more immediately pressing and obviously more significant "possession" interest of continental free trade. Transatlantic free trade was an issue that emerged at the wrong time; consequently, it became a non-issue for the Government.

It would also be incorrect to conclude that Canada was a *demandeur* (the party most anxious for movement toward more formal discussions on any given issue) during this period. There was never sufficient political will on the West European and U.S. sides to even begin negotiating a transatlantic trade accord.[63]

Canadian actions during the period covered in this chapter demonstrated that Canada only paid sustained attention to its broader relations with the Community when Western Europe forced itself on to the Canadian foreign policy agenda. It had done so in the previous year, when Brussels became the official channel, through the G-24, through which some of the Central and East European economies received Western aid. Mulroney's ranking of Canada's European pillars (NATO, the CSCE, and the EC) in his statements and speeches suggests a further conclusion. That is, since the focus of Canada's Europe interest was still firmly entrenched in the security domain, this concern militated against any *immediate* tendency away from the multilateral security dimension of Canada's Europe policy to an increased reliance on bilateral or trilateral trade and economic institutions. Nonetheless, the brief public and bureaucratic airing of the benefits of a transatlantic trade accord in the summer of 1990 indicates that the Canadian government was not indifferent to the implications of Genscher's proposal. Although a trade agreement was not feasible, a political affirmation of transatlantic ties was acceptable; Canada would become a *demandeur* in this bargaining process.[64]

NOTES

1. Holmes, *The Better Part of Valour*, 216.
2. In contrast to the European component, the Asia Pacific component program put greater emphasis on establishing closer bilateral cultural and linguistic links through, for example, separate funding for foreign-language training in Canada (Japanese, Korean, Mandarin).
3. The ethos of the review largely reflected the then Under-Secretary of State for External Affairs De Montigny Marchand's personal view about the nature of Canadian foreign policy, which he summed up to the author as the "management of vulnerabilities," given Canada's size and influence in the international system. Telephone interview with De Montigny Marchand, May 16, 1992.
4. Confidential source.
5. President George Bush, Boston University commencement address, Boston, May 21, 1989. A senior Canadian official provides an alternative view on the roots of the TAD. He avers that the idea to formulate a new treaty or declaration to bind the Atlantic allies came originally from Germany. According to this official, the story "really" begins in 1988 when Germany occupied the EC presidency, and the experiences gained in the increasingly close consultation processes of that period were carried forward. He does concede, however, that this is difficult to prove with concrete evidence since this would require an insight into what Hans Dietrich Genscher, the German Foreign Minister, was thinking at the time. Confidential interview.
6. Reprinted in *Europa-Archiv* 45, 4 (1990): D77-84.
7. As cited in Devuyst, "European Community Integration," 15.
8. For a discussion EC-U.S. relations see Michael Smith and Stephen Woolcock, "The United States and the EC: Confronting the Challenge of Political and Security Order," a discussion paper presented at the International Studies Association annual meeting, Atlanta, Georgia, 31 March-4 April 1992; and Ginsberg, "U.S.-EC Relations," in Lodge, *The European Community*, 264.

9. "Haughey and Bush Agree to Strengthen Relations," *Agence Europe* (March 1, 1990): 3-4. Canadian officials also pointed out to this author that smaller EC members such as Luxembourg were especially eager to form a transatlantic alliance. Confidential interview with Charles Court, Deputy Director West European Relations (RWR) division, EAITC, Feb. 21, 1992.
10. "Mr. Andriessen Favours Pragmatic Approach to Strengthen and Intensify Relations," *Agence Europe* (Feb. 21, 1990): 9; "Mr. Pandolfi Proposes to the Americans a Programme of Cooperation in Five Priority Areas and Welcomes the softening of the U.S. position on Telecommunications," *Agence Europe* (Mar. 7, 1990): 7; "Sir Leon Brittan Proposes a Treaty or Another Form of Agreement on Competition Policy," *Agence Europe* (Mar. 26/27, 1990): 9; and, "Mr. Van Miert for Frequent High-Level Contacts," *Agence Europe* (April 5, 1990): 8.
11. R. Mosbacher, Secretary of Commerce, Remarks at the Columbia Institute Conference on 1992, Washington, Feb. 24, 1989. On Mosbacher's views, see also Michael Calingaert, "The European Community's Emerging Political Dimension," *SAIS Review* 12, 1 (Winter/Spring 1992): 82.
12. "The European Commission and the American Administration are Reviewing Means to Strengthen Coordination in a Large Series of Fields," *Agence Europe* (Dec. 18/19, 1989): 10.
13. Telex entitled "EC/US Consultative Arrangements," YCGR 0273, sent from Canadian Delegation to the European Communities (BREEC) to Extott (the European Community [REM division]), March 21, 1990, 3.
14. "At the close of the Washington Meeting, Jacques Delors Underlines Common Responsibilities with regard to Eastern Europe Countries, for the Uruguay Round, and in the Environmental, Technological and Social Fields," *Agence Europe* (April 25, 1990): 8.
15. Confidential source.
16. Confidential source.
17. Horst J. Krenzler and Wolfram Kaiser, "The Transatlantic Declaration: A New Basis for Relations Between the EC and the USA," *Aussenpolitik* 42, 4 (1991): 366.
18. Michael Smith, "'The Devil You Know': The United States and a Changing European Community," *International Affairs* 68, 1 (1992): 115; also, Smith and Woolcock, "The United States and the EC," discussion paper, 1992.
19. President George Bush, Boston University commencement address, Boston, May 21, 1989.
20. USIS Transcript: Bush news conference, Brussels, Dec. 4, 1989, 5.
21. The history of U.S.-EC relations is peppered by periods in which there have been serious mutual recriminations. See for example, Ginsberg,

"U.S.-EC Relations," in Lodge, *The European Community*, 256-78; and also R. Talbot, *The Chicken War: An International Trade Conflict between the United States and the EEC* (Ames: Iowa State University Press, 1978); and Smith, "'The Devil you Know.'"

22. Interview with Stuart Carre, desk officer on the Policy Planning Staff, Department of External Affairs and International Trade, Feb. 13, 1992.
23. Interview with Gail Tyerman, Second Secretary at Canada's embassy in Washington, Feb. 28, 1992.
24. Confidential source.
25. Canadian officials noted that the last time there had been this concentration of U.S. attention to Europe was during Henry Kissinger's "Year of Europe" in 1973.
26. As a further measure of the interest at the political level in Canada's relations with the Community, in late 1989 a review of bilateral Canada-EC trade irritants was prepared by the Minister for International Trade for consideration by cabinet.
27. External Affairs and International Trade Canada, *Statements and Speeches*, 90/09 and 90/32.
28. Canada undertook four major initiatives in response to the dramatic changes in Eastern Europe and the Soviet Union in 1989: (1) Prime Minister Mulroney's trip to the USSR had wide-ranging political and economic significance; (2) the allocation of $10 million for the Economic Development Fund for Poland and Hungary, $12 million in food aid for Poland, and $20 million in export credits to Poland, as part of Canada's contribution to the G-24 process of aid to Eastern Europe; (3) $29.1 million to support the Polish *zloty* through the Stabilization Fund; and (4) participation in the creation of the European Bank for Reconstruction and Development (EBRD).
29. Confidential interview.
30. A senior official at EAITC informed this author of a Memorandum to Cabinet on Canada's relations with Eastern Europe and the Soviet Union.
31. Europe as a formidable political and economic actor had been encouraged by German Foreign Minister Genscher's proposal to Joe Clark for an EEC-North American Declaration which would confirm "shared principles and interests in openness and enhanced cooperation." See text of speech by Joe Clark, "Canada and the New Europe," *Statements and Speeches*, May 26, 1990, 7. Underlining Canadian interest in this proposal, correspondence between Prime Minister Mulroney and President Bush, although emphasizing the continued vitality and complementarity of NATO and the CSCE, did nevertheless make reference to Genscher's suggestion of a transatlantic declaration.

32. Minutes of Proceedings and Evidence of the Standing Committee on External Affairs and International Trade, issue no. 48, April 5, 1990, 6-7.
33. *Ibid.*, 9.
34. Confidential interview.
35. Secretary of State for External Affairs, *News Release* 063, March 30, 1990.
36. Confidential interview.
37. The Canadian Embassy in Germany did raise the matter of picking up on Genscher's proposal and putting some flesh on Canadian thinking but no follow-up was taken by Ottawa until September. Confidential interview with senior Canadian official.
38. Numerous officials at EAITC indicated to the author the centrality of Ambassador Burney to the conduct of Canadian foreign policy during this period.
39. The Under-Secretary of State for External Affairs (USS), today known as the Deputy Minister for Foreign Affairs, is the Department's top bureaucrat. Marchand started as USS in January 1990.
40. Interview with Michael Hart, Director, Economic Planning, Policy Planning Staff, Department of External Affairs and International Trade, March 1992. It was also rumoured that Clark and the top official in the Department's European Bureau did not get along, which seriously undermined the effectiveness of this Bureau in acting as a source of innovative policy advice for the minister.
41. After numerous problems in the PMO during his first term in office, Mulroney had brought in Burney from EAITC to "put his shop in order." While at EAITC Burney had risen to Associate Under-Secretary of State, making him the third-highest ranking civil servant in the Department. Burney had cut his teeth on the Liberal government's 1983 *Trade Policy Review.* As evidence of Burney's powerful role and influence in the foreign policy decision making process, it was taken as fact that on a number of foreign policy issues (particularly the free trade negotiations) the lines of communication went from Mulroney directly to Burney when he was Ambassador to the United States, circumventing altogether the normal bureaucratic reporting relationship between the Under-Secretary of State at EAITC—De Montigny Marchand at the time—and his Ambassador in Washington.
42. Interview with Michael Hart, Director, Economic Planning, Policy Planning staff at EAITC, Feb. 17, 1992.
43. Confidential source.
44. *Ibid.*, 6-7.
45. *Ibid.*, 8.
46. From text of Joe Clark's Humber College speech, "Canada and the New Europe," May 26, 1990, p. 7.

47. Confidential source.
48. Canada, House of Commons, *Debates*, May 31, 1990, 12091.
49. The assertion by the SSEA of the desirability of a more formalized, open trading arrangement between Canada and the EC was added by the Minister's staff and did not come from officials at EAITC. The Minister's staff evidently believed that what was necessary was some "general yet decisive statement" that would indicated that Canada wanted to play a serious role in the future of Europe. Confidential interview with member of Minister's staff; see text of Clark's Humber College speech, May 26, 1990.
50. Hyman Solomon was one of the few Canadian journalists who picked up the potential significance and far-reaching nature of Clark's trans-atlantic trade treaty proposal. See "Trade Deal with Europe Becoming a Major Issue," *Financial Post*, May 30, 1990.
51. Confidential interview.
52. Geoffrey Edwards, "The European Community and Canada," *Behind the Headlines* 50, 2 (Winter 1992-93): 18-23; see also, Joe Clark, notes of speech, "Canada's Stake in Europe," presented at luncheon sponsored by the Conseil des relations internationales de Montréal, June 20, 1990, p. 2.
53. *Ibid.*
54. Confidential interview.
55. It was rumoured that the Going Global exercise was a way for officials at EAITC to rationalize the need for increased funds from Treasury Board. Initially a request prepared for the Treasury Board by the Asia Pacific Branch of EAITC for increased funding to its trade development programs, it was felt by senior managers that the Department stood a better chance of getting approvals for funding beyond those stipulated in the Department's annual budget if they put a competitive spin on such requests and broadened their geographic reach. Given the Government's "competitiveness" mantra at the time (for example, it had just finished explaining to Canadians how the CUFTA would force Canadian firms to be more competitive in world markets), department officials reasoned correctly that the Government would be unlikely to turn down a more wide-ranging proposal for trade development funds. In the end, Treasury Board approved EAITC's request for a multi-year trade development program focusing on the United States, Asia Pacific, and Europe.
56. Confidential interview.
57. Telephone interview with Commission official.
58. Interview with Howard Balloch, Director General on the Policy Planning Staff at EAITC, Oct. 1991.

59. Michael Hart, "Multilateralism and Professionalism," unpublished manuscript, 525. Received by the author from Mr. Hart when he was on staff at the Policy Planning Staff in 1991-92.
60. There is, however, a countervailing force to this influence due to the organizational nature of the foreign service. With a rotational foreign ministry service, for example, the maintenance of a high level of bureaucratic support for a particular initiative can dissipate once the public servant with a vested interest in that initiative is reassigned.
61. A number of factors made EAITC's Policy Planning Staff the foreign policy bureaucracy's weathervane on the issues of greatest concern to the government in power: (1) the Director General of the Staff reported directly to the Under-Secretary of State for External Affairs, and because this position afforded the only overview of departmental operations and policy, it was a position of considerable influence; (2) due to its advisory role, the Staff provided short-term forward planning briefs (at the request of the minister or cabinet) on the impact of international economic and political developments on Canadian interests; and (3) with its cabinet liaison section in the early 1990s, the Staff formed the institutional link between the foreign policy bureaucracy and the cabinet.
62. A sure measure of the working-group's diminishing priority was the absence of senior officials, i.e., directors general, during the last two meetings of the no more than five meetings ever held.
63. Although it is true that Canada had initiated discussions for a World Trade Organization (WTO).
64. G. Bruce Doern and Brian W. Tomlin, *Faith and Fear: The Free Trade Story* (Toronto: Stoddart, 1991), 278.

V

THE REMAINS OF THE DAY: SIGNING THE TRANSATLANTIC POLITICAL DECLARATIONS

AT THE INTERNATIONAL LEVEL, the previous chapter suggests that Canada engaged its allies, in Cooper *et al.*'s words, as a "nimble dancer," by trying to define a role for itself in the new international order as the cement of the Western transatlantic alliance began to crack and Canada was no longer assured a place as a full partner in any new transatlantic institutions. The essentially normative view of Canada's middle-power status could not account for Ottawa's calculating and unsuccessful attempts to achieve a transatlantic free trade area. Nor would the vision of Canada as a "benign, responsible and selfless" middle power describe Canada's subsequent and successful role in securing a transatlantic declaration.

With the end of the Cold War it was evident that Canada's value in the eyes of its allies, based in large measure on its ability to mediate East-West tensions over the previous 45 years, had declined, if not precipitously, then certainly noticeably.[1] This came as a rude shock to many Canadian officials and politicians who had grown accustomed to being automatically consulted on any major initiatives affecting transatlantic relations. The negotiation of the transatlantic declaration would tend to support John Holmes's rejection of the thesis that Canada was a middle power because of its "moral superiority," which he viewed as a "moral arrogance [which had] crept into the concept of middle power."[2] There are, of course, shades of Canada's wounded pride as a good and deserving Atlantic partner when the Europeans and Americans appeared to be ignoring Canada's rightful place in any transatlantic negotiations. The analysis also shows that Canada's behaviour during the negotiations manifested typical middle-power roles of "stabilization" (separating, counterbalancing and mediating among other states); "negative roles" (free-riding, fence-sitting, and status-seeking); and "good multilateral citizenship."[3] These roles can be reconciled with the Holmesian view that Canadian internationalism in the postwar, and then the immediate post-Cold War period, is still "based on a very hard-boiled calculation of the Canadian national interest."[4]

THE CREATION OF A POLITICAL DECLARATION

If a free trade deal was a non-starter, what seemed to attract more sustained political attention from the United States and the West Europeans was a much more general proposal for cooperation that did not threaten existing multilateral trade institutions, but incorporated them instead. Indeed, officials on EAITC's Canada-EC working group concluded that many of the political requirements that were being served by the re-examination of EC-Canada trade relations, that is, demonstrating Canada's new approach to Europe, were already being served adequately through the Government's "Europe 1992" trade development program and its lobbying in Brussels. The prevailing view at EAITC was that if the option of a transatlantic trade treaty was not feasible, then what was needed was a declaration of goodwill and cooperation, a follow-up to Genscher's very general, ill-defined declaration proposal. The difference between Canada and the U.S. was that Canadian officials and politicians perceived a need for a transatlantic declaration to formalize high-level political ties with the Community; those formalized ties which did exist were almost entirely inter-bureaucratic mechanisms anchored by the economic and trade consultations established under the Framework Agreement. For the U.S., on the other hand, although a declaration was useful, it was *not* a necessity.

The trigger for the Canadian TAD appears to have been the result of two events. First, on September 18, 1990 discussions between the Canadian Embassy in Washington and the State Department alerted Canadian officials to the fact that the U.S. intended to issue a transatlantic declaration with the Community.[5] The EC had prepared a draft declaration to this effect. This was confirmed in discussions between Secretary of State Baker and Secretary of State for External Affairs Clark on 21 September, in which Baker explained that this declaration was to replace his more formal treaty proposal that he had made at Berlin. An EC-U.S. declaration would simply formalize bilateral U.S.-EC contacts that already de facto existed.[6] The U.S., as we have pointed out, wanted to use a declaration about common principles to reinforce the EC's commitment to consult with the U.S. before Community foreign policy decisions were set in stone. It appears, however, that the Canadian side felt it had a proprietary interest in any transatlantic declaration not least because, as officials in EAITC constantly reminded the author, Genscher had first made the proposal in Ottawa, although the record shows that he had actually made it in Washington the day before.[7] Canadian officials, Prime Minister Mulroney, and Clark all felt that Canada had a right to be full party to "any declaration on the Principles of Transatlantic Declarations," because the very term "transatlanticism" traditionally included Canada and therefore Canada's exclusion from the Declaration would have presented perceptual difficulties.[8]

THE FORMULATION OF PARALLEL DECLARATIONS

Rethinking transatlantic relations, Canada floated the idea for a short declaration that would have pulled the Community, Canada, and the United States into a new transatlantic alliance. Under this scenario, NATO would not have been replaced; rather, the new alliance would have acted as a broader overall consultative mechanism into which NATO could have been subsumed.[9] The Canadian fear was that a bilateral EC-U.S. declaration would change the nature of the existing Atlantic alliance into a bipolar European and U.S. alliance that would be detrimental to Canadian interests.

The Bush administration, however, argued that Canadian participation could lead to a dilution of the effectiveness of its declaration. That is to say, a trilateral form would: (1) not allow the administration to make as forceful a point with Congress; and (2) raise the possibility that Mexico would also seek inclusion.[10] From the Bush administration's perspective, then, the transatlantic declaration was a strictly bilateral affair. The U.S. position against a trilateral declaration was supported by the French, although they *did* believe Canada had a role to play. The Italians, who at the time had the presidency of the

European Community, wanted to move ahead quickly with an EC-U.S. declaration. Bonn, to no one's surprise, given Genscher's public pronouncements, was supportive of a trilateral approach.[11] The U.S. rejection of a trilateral declaration naturally created a certain sense of urgency on the Canadian side to be associated with and included in the exercise of a new formalization and intensification of transatlantic relations. The flow and nature of the telex traffic between officials in Canada's Washington embassy and Ottawa on this matter indicate that the Canadian government was clearly surprised at how quickly Baker's and Genscher's proposals had resurfaced, metamorphosed, and gained momentum.[12]

The second trigger was that the bilateral discussions between American and Canadian officials in Washington on the state of transatlantic relations coincided with the first state visit to Canada of German President Richard von Weizsaecker, lasting from 16 to 21 September.[13] This coincidence would merit no mention if it were not for the fact that during Dr. Weizsaecker's visit, Canadian officials apparently received a draft transatlantic declaration from their German counterparts.[14] It is unclear whether the Canadian officials had this declaration when they met with the State Department's Under-Secretary of State for European and Canadian affairs, Raymond Seitz, in Washington.[15] In any case, with Canada preferring a trilateral declaration, the U.S. refusing to have one, and the EC unwilling to issue a declaration with only one North American partner and not the other, a compromise solution was necessary. In light of the positions of Canada's interlocutors, officials at EAITC pushed for a second-best solution: they could "live with" a separate declaration signed bilaterally by the EC and Canada in addition to the EC-U.S. declaration whose drafting was already in progress.[16]

The challenge for the Canadian side was to convince the Europeans (primarily the French and Italians) and Americans that Canada had a right to insert itself into the negotiation process; that Canada's "milieu" interests had to be protected.[17] Immediately, Ottawa made several *démarches* in Europe, Ottawa, and Washington stressing Canada's integral role in any process that sought to reformalize transatlantic relations. When this did not elicit any immediate positive response, Canadian officials decided that a more proactive approach was needed. Officials in the West European Relations Division and the Policy Planning Staff at EAITC subsequently, on the basis of the German draft, drew up a draft one-page declaration outlining Canadian interests and circulated it to all the member states of the Community, to the Commission, and to Washington.[18] It is clear that the personalities of officials did play a role in influencing Canada's commitment to drafting its own text.[19] Canadian officials feared that the longer the EC-U.S. draft circulated among the member states and in the Commission and the presidency of the EC, the more difficult it would be for an EC-Canada draft to be inserted. Canadian officials sought to impress on their counterparts in the Commission and the member states that there needed to be two TADs, not just the EC-U.S. TAD.[20]

In early October, however, it became apparent that the EC-U.S. negotiations were not as advanced as the Canadian side had initially estimated. This provided the window of opportunity for Canadian officials to lobby Washington, the Community, and the member states to support a separate EC-Canada TAD that would be released along with the EC-U.S. TAD. The Italians were particularly helpful at this stage in supporting the Canadian position although there was disagreement with the Italians with regard to where and when the Canadian TAD would be issued. By mid-October a consensus was formed among all the participants that what was developing was a process of *parallel* negotiations.

Because all parties agreed that a degree of parity was desirable between the U.S. and Canadian TADs, the U.S., the Commission, Italy, and other member states all had to be satisfied with the initial Canadian effort. The Americans and the Commission, in particular, were not. They wanted a more "substantive" declaration. Over the course of six weeks, various longer drafts of the Canadian TAD were produced and distributed, in addition to German, American, and Italian draft transatlantic declarations already in circulation. Not surprisingly, given the U.S. rejection of a trilateral declaration, during this period there was little cross-fertilization of ideas on the substance of the declarations between U.S. and Canadian officials as they drafted their respective TADs. Indeed, the Canadian side received a working copy of the EC-U.S. TAD in confidence from sympathetic officials of a member state, which was rumoured to be the United Kingdom.[21] If Canadian officials did receive it from this source it would not be surprising since Clark had a good working relationship with Douglas Hurd, the British Foreign Secretary, who supported Canada's position that it had a right to be fully involved in any transatlantic negotiations. But lest the impression be given that Canada could rely on support from only the key member states, it must be stated that Canada also received support from Spain and Portugal, widely regarded as the most pro-Community of all the member states.

Due to the parallel negotiations, the Canadian government wanted the TADs to be issued simultaneously. Timing, however, became a problem: the Italians wanted to sign the EC-U.S. TAD during Prime Minister Andreotti's visit to Washington in mid-November; and the Canadian side wanted to issue the EC-Canada TAD on 22 November in Rome, since this would coincide with Prime Minister Mulroney's trip to Europe to attend the Paris CSCE meeting. The Canadians were particularly concerned about a prior release of the EC-U.S. TAD. Any time gap between the public announcement of the EC-U.S. TAD and the EC-Canada TAD would have proved "awkward" for Canada: the notion of a Canadian prime minister going to Washington to sign a tripartite or bilateral declaration during an official visit by another head of state, in this case Italy's Andreotti, would, according to Canadian officials, have been a political embarrassment at home.[22]

Within the Canadian bureaucracy there was also a problem of defining the focus of the declaration. There was a flurry of activity in EAITC to determine whether the Declaration was to be purely political or more trade and economic oriented. In the end, the PMO, the PCO, and Clark's ministerial office took into consideration the concerns of the trade officials, particularly the trade-oriented staff at Canada's mission to the EC in Brussels, but nevertheless decided that the TAD's focus should remain political.[23] There was also considerable concern among Canadian officials that the EC-U.S. and EC-Canada texts be similar with regard to shared transatlantic principles, values, and consultative mechanisms, so that Canada would not be viewed as a "second-class" transatlantic citizen.[24] But perhaps the most important reason for the PMO's strong interest in bilateral relations with the Community and therefore in a transatlantic declaration was the impact domestically of the dizzying pace of developments in Europe. As a result, officials in EAITC consulted with and provided the PMO with ongoing reports on the status of negotiations.[25]

In the end, after much consultation and drafting, it would be tendentious to try to assert which country had the most input in the final product. An idea that had initially started out as an American treaty proposal, that was recast as a transatlantic declaration by the Germans, and had, in the final phase, considerable Canadian participation, was transformed into the EC-U.S. and the EC-Canada TADs. In the fall of 1990, following discussions between Ottawa and Washington and the

Community's own internal consultations on establishing enhanced political relations with Canada and the U.S., the Declaration on European Community-Canada Relations was unveiled in Rome by Prime Minister Mulroney and Italian Prime Minister Andreotti on November 22, 1990.[26] The Transatlantic Declaration with the U.S. was issued a day later in Brussels.[27]

THE SIGNIFICANCE OF THE TRANSATLANTIC DECLARATION

It should be noted, in the first instance, that the TAD was "issued" rather than signed, indicating that Canada and the EC were not legally bound to adhere to the Declaration's terms, giving it a more symbolic rather than substantive quality.[28] Second, as Edwards observes, when compared to the signing of the Charter of Paris, the day before, on November 21, by the 34 participating states of the CSCE, which formally declared the end of the Cold War, the institutionalization of bilateral political and economic relations through the TAD was a fairly modest achievement.[29]

That said, the process of negotiations leading up to the TAD and the document itself raised a number of questions about the nature of Canada's place in the new Atlantic order. How important were high-level political ties? What about the impact of institutional changes in the EC? How many *new* bilateral links were actually created and how important were they? Did the TAD fill the "legitimation vacuum" in transatlantic relations? However, before attempting to answer these questions, it would be useful first to compare the Canadian and American TADs. Despite their similarities, there are important differences between them that illuminate the differing natures and foundations of American and Canadian relations with the Community.

Comparing the U.S. and Canadian TADs

In making this comparison it is difficult not to ascribe a certain "me-tooism" to Ottawa. Given the parallel sets of negotiations it is not surprising that the texts of the declarations are strikingly similar. Most generally, both the Canadian and American declarations emphasized the need for multilateral institutions such as the UN to be responsible for worldwide conflict mediation; they called for strengthening the multilateral trading system through the implementation of GATT and OECD principles to reduce the number of non-tariff barriers in industrial and agricultural trade, services, competition policy, transportation policy, standards, telecommunications, and other areas. Assistance to Central and Eastern Europe was also encouraged.

More practically, as a result of the TAD, meetings would take place "regularly" in Canada and in Europe between the Canadian Prime Minister and the President of the European Council and the President of the Commission (see Figure 5.1 at end of this chapter). Second, biannual meetings were scheduled on each side of the Atlantic, between the Canadian Secretary of State for External Affairs and the President of the Council of the European Communities and the Commissioners for External Relations and Trade Policy. At the time the TAD was issued these two portfolios were held by the same Commissioner. Significantly, under the U.S. TAD the U.S. president would meet "biannually" with his European counterparts and not just "regularly" as was the case for Canada's prime minister. Furthermore, rather than being new, as in the Canadian case, the "biannual" meetings between the U.S. president and the president of the EC member state holding the six-month presidency of the Community had already been occurring for several years prior to the Declaration, a fact that serves to highlight the lack of a similar Canadian political will in relations with the Community at this time.[30]

It has been conjectured that the use of the word "regular" in Canada's TAD was a tactical move on the part of Canadian officials who believed that the imposition of "annual" meetings on the prime minister would have created a "failure trap" since they were not convinced that a Canadian prime minister (given Mulroney's and Clark's track record on European issues prior to 1989) would have been able to live up to this type of commitment.[31] Having "regular" meetings meant that Canada could be spared the "embarrassment" of missing some future high-level meetings; Canadian prime ministers would instead be able to "work their way up" to annual meetings.

At the level of officials, the U.S. TAD stipulated an annual meeting between U.S. officials and the political directors of the EC presidency's Troika, which was essentially a continuation of existing practice. Canadian negotiators felt that regular access via the Troika was not necessary since they would be briefed at the ministerial level following EPC meetings.[32] There was also an "evolution" clause in the U.S. Declaration which provided for an adjustment of the existing structures of cooperation to the progress made in European integration, whereas there was none in the Canadian Declaration, presumably because Canada already had the Framework Agreement. Significantly, the EC and the U.S. retained the option to specify contractually the arrangements upon a greater cohesion in EC foreign policy and to make them legally binding.

Finally, the Canadian and American TADs also called for cooperation, or "cooperative security," on such transnational issues as terrorism, drug trafficking, control of population migration, and the environment. The reference to encouraging bilateral investment in the Canadian TAD, something not found in the U.S. Declaration, lent it more of an economic flavour than its American analog, although the intents of both declarations were clearly political. More pointedly, given this study's assertion that Canada's approach to its relations with the EC continued to be state-led, there was no mention in either declaration of the need to bring the transatlantic business communities closer together; indeed, there were no consultations with the private sectors on this initiative.

The Importance of High-Level Political Ties

Returning to the set of questions posed above, the key element of the Canadian TAD was the establishment of a new transatlantic institutional framework. The Declaration reaffirmed the need for the full use of the mechanisms established under the Framework Agreement and of the already existing political contacts, such as the annual meetings between the Canadian Secretary of State for External Affairs and the EC Commissioner for External Relations and Trade Policy under the Joint Cooperation Committee.

Since the Declaration did go some distance to meet Canadian officials' persistent requests for a more elaborate range of political consultative mechanisms, it succeeded in making bilateral relations less unidimensional and focused on trade irritants; it provided a broader bilateral context within which these irritants could be discussed. Second, the Declaration established political relations between Canada and the EC on a level comparable, as we have discussed, to that of the U.S. Certainly, at the time, Canada had "exclusive" access to the Community in comparison to other middle powers such as Australia and New Zealand.[33] The Japanese, in fact, used the Canadian TAD as a model in their own negotiations with the EC in 1991.

A senior official in Canada's mission to the EC in Brussels viewed the TAD as a "powerful top-down tool" that allowed both sides to keep abreast of the relationship and make appropriate adjustments because it "suffuse[d] an entire range of formal and informal bilateral contacts on international issues of mutual interest with a renewed spirit of dialogue and cooperation," and it "broaden[ed] the interaction at the personal and institutional level and considerably enhance[d] Canada's ability to promote its interests and pursue its bilateral and multilateral political and economic agenda."[34] An example of the broadened interaction at the personal level was the Canadian SSEA's twice-yearly consultations with the member state foreign minister who is President of the Council of the European Communities. This was highly symbolic (the President "invited" the Commissioner of External Relations and Trade Policy to these meetings) because it stressed contact between Canadian and European politicians rather than between officials, the latter having previously been the norm. Although the formalization of bilateral political links was clearly an advance, given the evolution of bilateral relations by the end of 1993 (see Chapters 9, 10, and 11), it was premature for senior Canadian officials to have stated unequivocally in 1990 that the TAD was a "powerful" tool.

TAD and the Reinstitutionalization of Canada-EC Relations

In looking at Figure 5.1 it can be quickly established that the two *new* links established by the TAD were: (1) the Canadian Prime Minister meeting with the President of the European Council and the President of the Commission; and (2) the SSEA meeting with the President of the Council of the European Communities. The other stated links, the Canadian SSEA's meeting with the Commissioner for External Relations and Trade Policy and the contacts between Canadian missions and EPC, already existed. The Canadian SSEA and the EC Commissioner for External Relations and Trade Policy were theoretically supposed to have met annually to discuss bilateral relations through the Joint Cooperation Committee established under the Framework Agreement (see Figure 5.2).[35]

Another example of increased political cooperation was the debriefings on EPC decisions for non-member states. Canada did not have the same level of access to the EPC decision making process as the U.S. As noted, Canada's links to EPC were formalized in the early 1980s when it began to receive a general briefing on the Community's final decisions along with other "like-minded" (mostly OECD) non-member states. Starting in 1988, it received more exclusive access through the biannual separate bilateral "political directors" meetings. This being said, in the domain of EPC, it was unclear how much more Canadian access had been brought about through the TAD, although there were now presumably more ad hoc links between the Canadian Mission to the EC in Brussels and the EPC expert groups as well as between the Mission and the EPC Secretariat and the EC Council's Secretariat for EPC.

Also, with the additional links created as a result of the TAD there was initially some doubt whether the practice of having high-level ministerials, which predated the 1976 Framework Agreement by four years, would need to be continued.[36] In establishing the net number of bilateral institutional links, it becomes apparent that there was a fair amount of redundancy in the bilateral institutional structure. Of course, this was to be expected in the short-term before some of the old links were either abolished outright, indefinitely suspended, or subsumed under new institutional links. At the time of writing, the high-level ministerials had not yet been subsumed under the new links established by TAD. It was unclear what significant benefit their continuation would bring to bilateral relations.

Decisions not to eliminate certain structures thus fed the perennial criticism in the academic and corporate communities that the conduct of bilateral relations was over-bureaucratized. The creation of new institutional links represented an accretion of organizational mass; there was an inherent belief in the bureaucracy that more was always better. Although officials in Ottawa contended that Canada's relationship with the EC was considerably greater than the government-to-government dialogue that they had fostered through the TAD, even a cursory examination of the history of bilateral relations and a review of the institutionalized nature of the relationship (Figures 5.1 and 5.2), would leave the analyst with the impression that the process appeared to have become an end in itself. Indeed, such observations do not differ greatly from those of Boardman *et al.*, who, writing about the Framework Agreement in the early 1980s, stated that:

> The largely exploratory and technical work undertaken within the Working Groups of the continuing machinery of the JCC constitutes, in a sense, its own justification. The product is the process ... and not what might actually emerge from it in the form of contracts and deals in trade and investment areas.[37]

While the TAD's "product" was clearly political, the problem remains the same. This assessment, however, must be qualified since the process-driven nature of bilateral relations can be traced to the inherent difficulties for Canadian policy makers when dealing with an international organization that displays both supranational and intergovernmental characteristics.

Finally, another problem, highlighted by Boardman *et al.*, was Canada's reluctance to pursue a strategy whereby issues would be linked. Therefore, even with the reinvigoration of bilateral relations as a result of the TAD, the structure was still vulnerable to the charge that the combination of general reviews of the relationship, through regular and private meetings at the political level, with "intense, narrow and isolated exercises in trade negotiation and cooperation," would cause opportunities to be missed for constructive linking of issues in which both sides could gain something.[38]

Filling the "Legitimation Vacuum"

A more intangible, short-term outcome of the TAD was that at a time of great institutional uncertainty in transatlantic relations between 1989 and 1991, it filled the legitimation vacuum on both sides of the Atlantic created by the end of the Cold War. It marked a new epoch in Canada-West European relations in so far as it represented an attempt by Canada to maintain its status as an equal partner with the Community. In many ways, though, as the post-TAD Community pushed for greater economic, monetary, political, and even defence integration, Canada was destined to become a distinctly *unequal* partner. There was now the likelihood that the economic asymmetry in the relationship (see Chapter 7), traditionally balanced by the security guarantee offered by Canada's membership in NATO as evident in the negotiations leading to the 1976 Framework Agreement, would become increasingly politicized and put Canada in an increasingly disadvantageous position.

More tangible evidence of the attempt to fill the legitimation vacuum was found in the TAD's reference to increasing transatlantic cooperation on such "soft" security issues as migration, illegal drugs, and terrorism. This was a partial way of filling the void created by the decreasing need to cooperate on transatlantic "hard" security issues since Canada was no longer needed to "symbolically" defend Western Europe from Soviet attack. This void was widened two years later when, as part of the 1992 federal budget, the Mulroney cabinet decided that in the absence of the Cold War Canada would no longer maintain troops in Europe; it was decided that all permanently stationed Canadian troops would be withdrawn by the end of 1994.

More generally, what hope did the Declaration have of stimulating the type of Atlanticist impulses in the Canadian government that were discussed in Chapter 2? From a pro-Atlanticist view, such as that proffered by Halstead,[39] Canada should have been able to negotiate directly with the EC on a bilateral declaration to assert its role as a member of the transatlantic alliance and to create a "counterweight" to U.S. influence.[40] This, of course, presupposed a convergence and balancing of interests that existed, for example, in the 1970s, but that clearly no longer existed by 1990. There is also implicit in the above assumption a suggestion that Canada-EC negotiations on potentially precedent-setting bilateral initiatives could exist independently of, or even contradict, what Washington would consider its vital national interests. But this assumption of Ottawa's independent ability to negotiate bilaterally with the Community requires closer examination and may exaggerate Canada's relative power in transatlantic relations. Why? Put quite simply, given the history of West European sensitivity to U.S. perceptions,[41] it was always difficult for Canada to negotiate independently with the Community. For instance, the Commission would never have negotiated the Framework Agreement in 1976 without prior assurances from Washington. Indeed, this returns the discussion to the schema outlined in Chapter 1 on the four determinants of Canada's relations with the Community: it reaffirms the U.S.'s important role in setting the parameters of Canada-EC relations.

Apart from the political rhetoric on both sides of the Atlantic, it was doubtful that in the immediate aftermath of the TAD that Europeans saw Canada as a nation with a "right" to a seat at the European table. While this author would argue that Canada had and continues to have real and pressing interests in Europe, there were those who questioned the ultimate utility and seriousness of the TAD as a mechanism to reinforce Canada's Atlanticist ties. In other words, not only did the non-Atlanticists probe the significance of TAD as a framework within which to strengthen Canadian-EC relations, but they challenged the entire premise that TAD provided a Canadian seat at the European table.

They also did not see Canada's political, commercial, and military retreat to its continental shell as solely a reaction to European integration. In their view, a number of factors were at play. As a result of budget cuts, Canada's diplomatic posts were severely cut by the early 1990s,[42] development and aid programs scaled down, and the national focus redirected south to the United States. No more symbolic manifestation of this Canadian drift from Europe was the decision in the spring of 1993 by Ottawa, as part of the federal government's deficit reduction program, to eliminate fully one-third of the 318 jobs at the Canadian High Commission in London. Given the U.K.'s dual position as a pillar of transatlanticism and Canada's eyes and ears on the Community this was both an administrative and symbolic cut.

In the non-Atlanticist view, then, although the existence of the TAD may have strengthened the emphasis on relations with Europe in official Canadian rhetoric in the early 1990s, this declaratory foreign policy was in fact belied by economic and strategic reality which ensured the decline of the Atlantic idea. Long-time analysts of Canadian foreign policy such as Kim Nossal pointed out that as wartime bonds faded, with exchange rates shifting Canadian exports to the United States, with the CUFTA and NAFTA creating a continental economy, with the Pacific Rim creating a new pole of attraction for Canadian policies, with changing demographic patterns as, by the early 1980s, most immigrants to Canada came from Asia, and with the rapid decline of the former Soviet threat, there was a full-blown challenge to the Atlanticist orthodoxy in the Government's rhetoric. Nossal asserted that "Canadians came to believe that they had less concrete need for an Atlantic connection; they no longer were as inclined to buy the arguments of the Atlanticists that being in Europe gave Canada a seat at the table; or allowed Canada to add a moderate tone to the North American voice in the alliance; or provided a counterweight to the United States."[43] Others went so far as to point out that seeing Canada as an Atlantic nation, or a Pacific nation, or an Arctic nation was a futile attempt by some Canadians to transcend their reality, to make Canadians "anything but what [they were]—a nation of the Americas," an attempt to deny the "incontrovertible fact of geography that makes Canada an American nation."[44] From the non-Atlanticist perspective, the whole legitimation argument in favour of the TAD was moot.

This chapter has shown that the significance of the TAD should not be overstated. On the one hand, it provided a framework within which existing bilateral mechanisms could be used and new ones developed. It was a recognition by Canadian policy makers that the strategic management of Canada's relations with the Community in the years to come would have to be broadened from the prevailing focus on trade irritants. The TAD was important because it started a process, but the question remained whether it could develop into a vehicle of real cooperation in the 1990s. While it obviously cannot be compared to the roles played by NATO and the CSCE as pillars in Canada's European framework, it did act as the foundation of a renewed effort to strengthen Canada's approach to the European Community.

What the Declaration did not do was to introduce any fundamental changes to existing institutional mechanisms, particularly not to the unfulfilled 1976 Framework Agreement; there were no *binding* contractual commitments to make the TAD really effective. Because the TAD has such a broad, all-encompassing mandate, there was a concern that mechanisms set up under it to facilitate political ties would become ritualistic, as some observers contended existing bilateral mechanisms already were.

Were false expectations along the lines of the Third Option once more being created? There are parallels recalling a former Liberal external affairs minister who, in reflecting on the disappointment of the Third Option, said he could not help being reminded of "sound and fury signifying nothing," and then changed the metaphor to the "mountain labouring and bringing forth a mouse." Because the TAD was a strengthening of Canada's European policy by another name, great care must be taken that the public, politicians, and bureaucrats judge the declaration on its own merits, rather than on larger issues that Canada and the EC have failed to agree on.[45] This may prevent the feelings of cynicism that have always dogged the Framework Agreement.

Even more skeptically, and less generously, since November 1990 it has been hard to see the immediate substantive results of the Declaration apart from institutionalizing high-level political contact.[46] After all, the bilateral Canada-EC memoranda of understanding (MOUs) and mutual recognition agreements (MRAs) on a number of issues, such as competition policy, fisheries, standards, and science and technology, would have been negotiated irrespective of the TAD's existence. Moreover, with regard to the big, highly politicized bilateral issues such as the offshore fisheries dispute, it is difficult to conclude with any certainty that Portuguese and Spanish fleets began to respect the NAFO quotas for fish caught off Canada's East Coast as a result of Prime Minister Mulroney's entreaties during his private meetings held in April 1993, under the auspices of the TAD, with the Portuguese president of the European Council and President Delors of the Commission.

Furthermore, this study's description of the process leading to the issuance of the TAD reinforces the perception that the conduct of U.S. foreign policy limits the options available in the conduct of Canadian foreign policy. This has both positive and negative consequences for Canada. On the one hand, without the cooperation of the U.S., Canada would not have achieved the institutionalization of high-level political links in such a short timeframe. On the other hand, the process of achieving the TAD had also, in European eyes, no doubt reinforced the traditional two-pillar theory of bilateral relations in which Canada either had to be excluded entirely or included in the American pillar. Despite having provided text for the TAD, it was not clear that Canada was viewed by the EC as anything other than an adjunct of the U.S.; once more there were suspicions on the Canadian side that the EC had difficulty in making clear distinctions between Canadian and U.S. interests.

Perhaps the best way of putting the development of the TAD into perspective is to note that there was no one *predominant* causal factor: not the momentum of EC-U.S. discussions, although they undoubtedly had an important trigger effect; nor the effect of the dramatic geopolitical developments in Eastern Europe on the thinking of the Canadian cabinet (would it have been as desirous an Agreement if the U.S. had not been engaged in negotiations?); nor the role played by Canadian officials, primarily at EAITC in interpreting and reacting to the developments in Eastern and Western Europe by undertaking two major reviews of Canada's policy framework toward the regions. Rather, these were all mutually reinforcing variables.

What does the TAD say about the manoeuverability of a middle power such as Canada in the post-Cold War era? While the musings of Clark on the desirability of a transatlantic trade agreement, spawning his department's short-lived Canada-EC working group, did not bring about any direct results and has only a tenuous link to the political document that is the TAD, nevertheless this action along with the Government's other internal reviews in 1989 and 1990 of its European policy framework highlights the Canadian desire to strengthen ties to Europe.[47] The process of negotiating the TAD itself shows Canada as *demandeur* in the negotiations, and as highly dependent on its relations with member states, specifically the U.K. and Germany, to ensure policy outcomes in its favour. Canada's courting of the EC can also be linked to Prime Minister Mulroney's ambition to be seen as an international statesmen, as had been his aim in gaining the support of the Commonwealth to impose sanctions on South Africa in the mid-1980s. The personal challenge for him between 1989 and 1991 was how to insert Canada as a major player in refashioning the post-Cold War order.[48]

All in all, the processes leading up to and including the TAD demonstrate three aspects of Canada as a middle power in the post-Cold War era. The first is Canada's ability to modulate U.S. tendencies toward bilateralism. The Canadian TAD was Ottawa's attempt in light of the tremendous changes in Europe to create a lever; it was and is Ottawa's most visible attempt not to be left out of the Washington-Brussels axis. Second, it demonstrated Canada's capacity to lever its limited clout by acting quickly and persuasively to influence its larger international interlocutors. Finally, we are left with the irony that if the TAD is considered a limited "counterweight" to the Washington-Ottawa axis, its achievement was inextricably tied to the momentum of EC-U.S. relations.

FIGURE 5.1:
PRE-TAD CANADA-EC INSTITUTIONAL LINKS

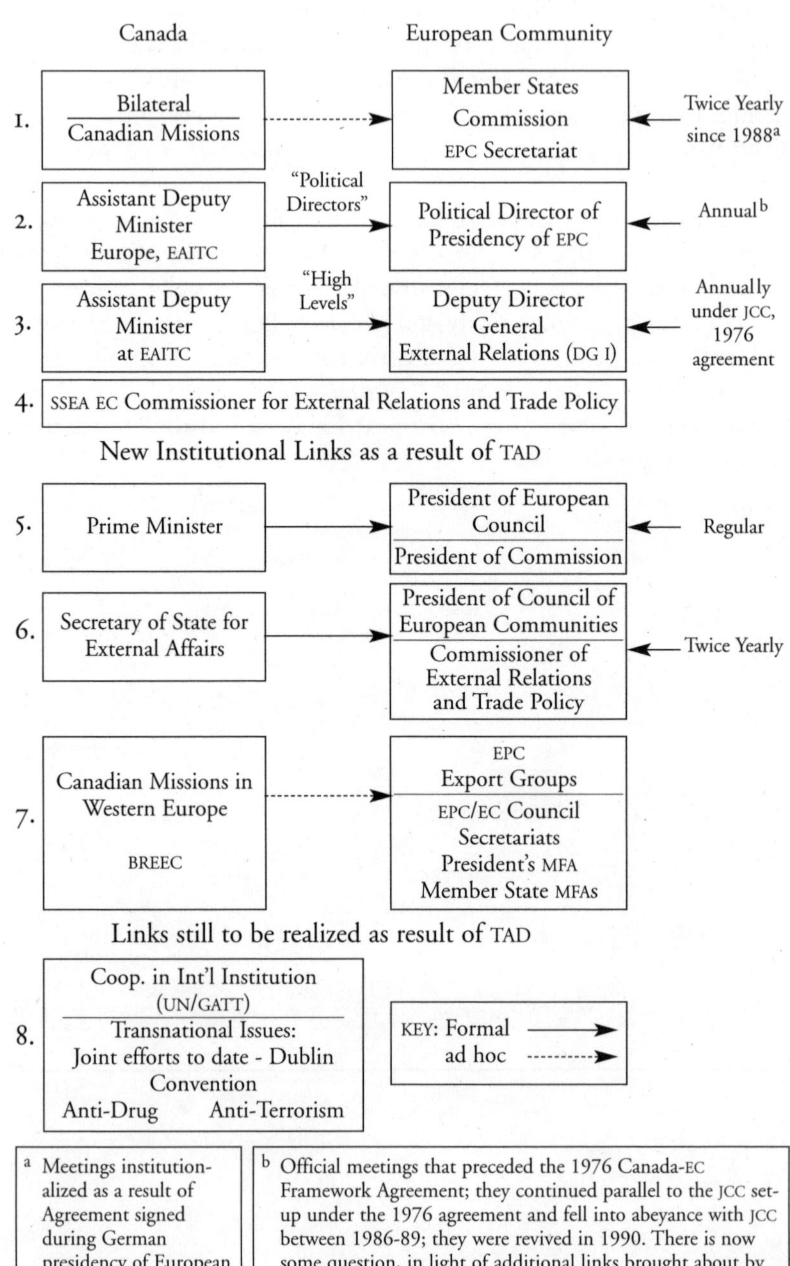

FIGURE 5.2:
1976 FRAMEWORK AGREEMENT

- annual forum for ministerial-level meetings
- facilities industrial and S&T collaboration between Canada and the EC

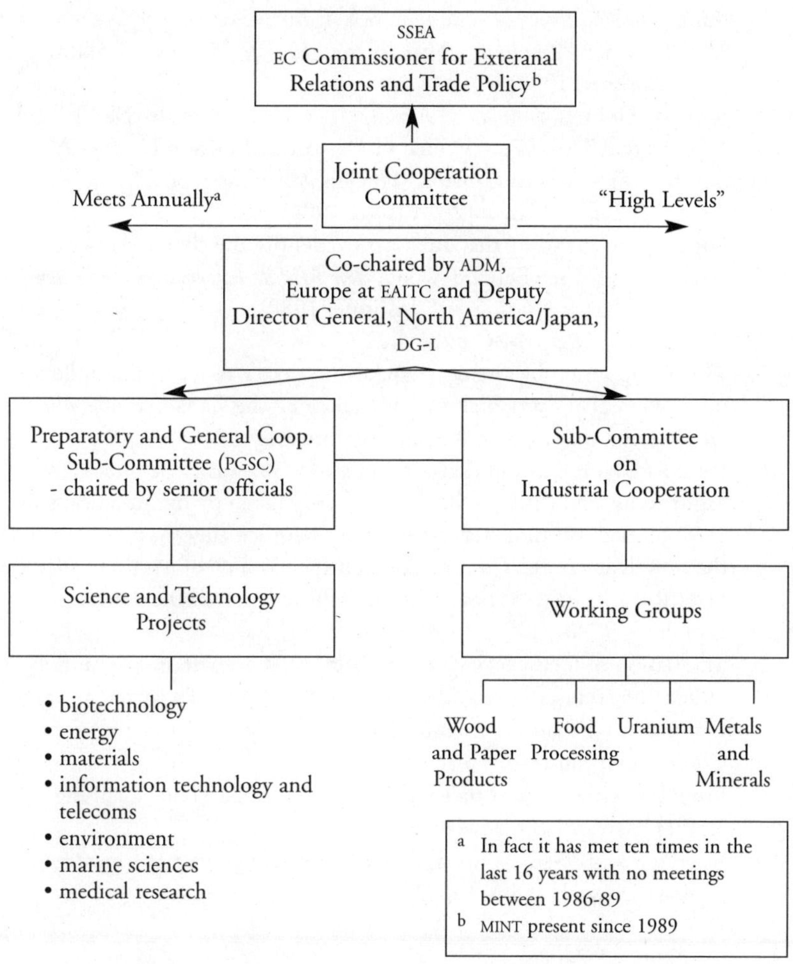

NOTES

1. Arthur Andrew, a former senior Canadian diplomat, traces the decline of Canada's international influence from the end of the Golden Age of Pearsonian diplomacy in the late 1950s to the loss of independence during the Mulroney government. See Arthur Andrew, *The Decline of a Middle Power: Canadian Diplomacy from King to Mulroney* (Halifax: James Lorimer, 1993).
2. John W. Holmes, *Canada: A Middle-Aged Power* (Toronto: McClelland & Stewart, 1976), 37, as quoted in David R. Black and Heather A. Smith, "Directions in Canadian Foreign Policy Literature," *Canadian Journal of Political Science* 26, 4 (Dec. 1993): 761.
3. For an excellent study that attempts to identify the characteristics of middle powers, see Bernard Wood, *The Middle Powers and the General Interest* (Ottawa: North-South Institute, 1988).
4. Holmes, *A Middle-Aged Power*, 6.
5. This is supported by a senior Canadian official's assertion that follow-up on Genscher's proposal was only taken by the Canadian side when "it appeared that the U.S. was moving forward."
6. Peter Riddell points out that the American TAD was to be phrased in vague terms and confirm the action already taken by the Americans in 1990 to establish more regular meetings between the U.S. president and the presidency of the Commission and the Council of Ministers. See Peter Riddell, "U.S.-EC ties to be strengthened," *Financial Times* (London), 9 Nov. 1990.
7. Translation of Genscher's speech in front of White House on April 4, 1990, from transcript provided to the author by the Department of External Affairs and International Trade.
8. Confidential source.
9. Interview with Howard Balloch, Director General, Policy Planning Staff at EAITC, March 24, 1992.
10. Interview with Gail Tyerman, Second Secretary, posted to Canadian embassy in Washington, Feb. 28, 1992.
11. *Ibid.*
12. Confidential source.
13. The visit to Canada provided an opportunity for discussions on German reunification, the state of bilateral relations, and the "historic changes under way in Europe." See Press Release, Office of the Prime Minister, August 9, 1990.
14. Interview with Gilles Landry, Director, West European Relations division (RWR) at EAITC, March 26, 1992.
15. Again, it may be entirely coincidental that both the Assistant Deputy Minister, Europe, and the Assistant Deputy Minister, Political and

International Security Affairs, were in Washington on September 18 and also met with Seitz.

16. Confidential source.
17. See Wolfers, *Discord and Collaboration*, 67-80. Wolfers discusses national goals under the categories of milieu goals, general possession goals, and specific possession goals. The former seeks to influence the nature of the international environment beyond the country's borders (e.g., the UN, the multilateral trade system), while the last two goals seek to protect and promote the things that are possessed by the country.
18. As a measure of the amount of responsibility that is devolved to select officials in making Canadian foreign policy, it should be noted that the first-draft Canadian declaration was the product of four officials in two bureaus at EAITC. It does not appear that the document was a product of consultation with other bureaus within EAITC or other federal government departments. Nor does it appear that SSEA Clark's own staff had any direct involvement, much less the Prime Minister's Office or the Privy Council Office, with a document that was going be hailed as a new mechanism to reinforce Canada's transatlantic ties.
19. Howard Balloch, who was then the Director General of the Policy Planning Staff at EAITC, was one of the drafters of the Canadian text. In terms of reporting relationships within EAITC during the period when the TAD was being drafted, Balloch and his counterpart in the Europe Bureau, Assistant Deputy Minister, David Wright, had direct access to the Under-Secretary of State (USS), De Montigny Marchand, through a once-a-week operations committee meeting and a policy committee meeting. All other contacts between the USS and his senior officials would have been ad hoc or through the USS's executive assistant.
20. Confidential source.
21. Interview with Commission official at DG I responsible for Canadian affairs.
22. Confidential source.
23. Confidential interview.
24. Confidential source.
25. *Ibid.*
26. Government of Canada, "Canada-European Community Agree on Transatlantic Declaration," *News Release*, Nov. 22, 1990.
27. "Declaration on EC-US Relations," in *European Political Cooperation Press Release*, 23, Nov. 1990.
28. Signing would have required ratification by legislatures on both sides of the Atlantic.
29. Edwards, "The European Community and Canada," 18.
30. Although it should be noted that President Bush was not initially in favour of having biannual meetings.

31. Confidential interview.
32. *Ibid.*.
33. Confidential source.
34. Confidential source.
35. Since 1989, the Minister for International Trade (MINT) has accompanied the SSEA to the JCC meeting.
36. Since 1976 the practice has been to have the "high-levels" on the same day that the JCC meets.
37. Boardman, *et al.*, *Canada-European Communities*, 57.
38. *Ibid.*, 26. There has been explicit linkage of issues in the history of bilateral relations, such as the purchase of Leopard tanks by Canada, a decision which assured Bonn of Canada's commitment to NATO and of the political acceptability of the Framework Agreement.
39. John Halstead, "Atlantic Community or Continental Drift?," 162-63.
40. For a good historical discussion of Atlanticism, see Robert Wolfe, "Atlanticism without the Wall: Transatlantic Cooperation and the Transformation of Europe," *International Journal* 46, 2 (Winter 1990-91): 137-63.
41. As noted in Michael Smith, *Western Europe and the United States: The Uncertain Alliance* (London: George Allen & Unwin, 1984); also, see Ginsberg, *Foreign Policy Actions*; Ginsberg, "U.S.-EC Relations," in Lodge, *The European Commuity*, 256-78; and, Michael Smith and Stephen Woolcock, *The United States and the European Community in a Transformed World* (London: Royal Institute of International Affairs, 1993).
42. In 1983, Canada had 124 diplomatic posts in 85 countries; in July 1993, it had 106 posts in 77 countries. Some EAITC officials have concluded that Canada's international priorities consist basically of the G-7 plus Mexico. Madelaine Drohan, "Home Alone," *Globe and Mail*, July 10, 1993, D1, D5.
43. Kim Richard Nossal, "A European Nation? The Life and Times of Atlanticism in Canada," a paper presented at the Conference on Canadian Foreign Policy, Toronto, December 10-11, 1991, 31.
44. Hart, "Canada Discovers its Vocation," 83; see also, Donald S. MacDonald, "Should we break our bond with Europe?" *Globe and Mail*, April 10, 1992, A17. In the same article, from an Atlanticist perspective, Gijs M. De Vries, a Dutch member of the European Parliament, argues that Canada's withdrawal of its troop commitment to Europe is a mistake considering that it could become an important economic partner for the Community.
45. For instance, in negotiating the 1976 Framework Agreement, records show that the European interest was mainly resource-oriented whereas on the Canadian side the most important element of the agreement

was industrial cooperation. Thus it should come as no surprise that once the Europeans were no longer faced with a situation in which their resource supplies were threatened their interest in the Framework Agreement waned.

46. As a postscript, officials in EAITC would counter this less positive appraisal by pointing out that the TAD had already had a positive impact. This was evidenced by the visit to Canada by the Portuguese Prime Minister and Commission President Delors on April 24, 1992, to meet with Prime Minister Mulroney as part of the process of formal political consultations. The Canadian officials further point out that in the practice of Canadian foreign policy although a foreign policy issue may not rank high on the SSEA's agenda, it is a fact of life that once it lands on the prime minister's agenda it pulls with it the attention of the entire cabinet.
47. These reviews resulted in more resources devoted to Canada's trade development programs for Eastern and Western Europe.
48. The final example of Prime Minister Mulroney's desire to be seen as an elder statesman manifested itself three years later, after he had announced his intention to resign, when he engaged in personal diplomacy with G-7 members to support Russian President Boris Yeltsin's request for increased Western assistance.

VI

CANADA AND THE CHALLENGE OF THE SINGLE EUROPEAN MARKET

THE IMPLEMENTATION OF THE SINGLE MARKET program had far more important and numerous consequences than were first expected, due to the exigencies of increased integration. Therefore, it is a serious underestimation to limit the assessment of the external impact of the 1992 program to the changes in the functioning of the EC market and to modifications in EC external trade policy. The SEM required the Community to intervene in new policy territories and to reinforce some other common policies. Thus we must acknowledge that Canadian industry was not only affected by, for example, changes in the "horizontal" elements of the 1992 program, such as public procurement legislation and changes in standards and certification procedures, but also by how these changes affected "flanking" issues; that is, phytosanitary, plant and animal health, environmental, and science and technology policies. These issues were more indirectly affected by the SEM, demonstrating the breadth and depth of the integration process.

The purpose of this chapter is fourfold: (1) to describe the anticipated benefits of the SEM and the concerns it generated among Canadian decision makers; (2) to outline Ottawa's program response as it encouraged Canadian investment, particularly by SMEs, in the EU in advance of the Single Market's creation; (3) to examine the actual experiences of Canadian industries, particularly in the telecommunications

TABLE 6.1: SECTORS MOST AFFECTED BY THE SEM

IMPACT	SECTOR	MNE INVOLVEMENT	GAINERS
1. Reduction in protection and increased competition	a. Financial services	High	Europe, Japan, and Canada
	b. Telecommunication services	High	Europe and U.S.
	c. Pharmaceuticals	Medium	Europe
2. Shift from fragmented local to integrated EC market	a. Distribution	Low	Europe
	b. Food Processing	Medium	
	c. Transport	Low	Europe
3. Gain of technical economies of scale through sale of standardized goods	a. Electronics	High	Japan
	b. Packaging	Medium	Europe, U.S., and Canada
	c. Consumer goods and services	Medium	Europe and Japan
4. Dependence on public procurement	a. Computer equipment and services	High	Europe, Japan, and Canada
	b. Defence contractors	Low	Europe and U.S.
	c. Telecommunications equipment	Medium	Europe, U.S., and Canada
5. Industries where the single market leads to import subsitution (EC goods instead of imports)	a. Chemicals	Medium	Europe and U.S.
	b. Electrical components	High	Japan
	c. Office equipment	High	Japan

Sources: John Dunning, "MNE Activity: Comparing the NAFTA and the EC," in Lorraine Eden, ed., *Multinationals in North America* (Calgary, AB: University of Calgary Press and Industry Canada, 1994), 289, Table 3. The conclusions on Canadian gains are drawn from: Royal Bank of Canada, "Is Canada Ready for Europe 1992?," *Econoscope*, 16, 1 (Feb. 1992): 13-16; *Europe 1992: Implications of a Single Market, Part 1* (Ottawa: EAITC, April 1989); *Europe 1992: Your Business Opportunity* (Ottawa: EAITC, 1989); and a survey of Canadian firms with major interests in Europe.

and financial services sectors, in light of the EU's move to reduce internal barriers to market access; and (4) to highlight the SEM's spillover effects by looking at "flanking" issues in two select areas—Canada-EC Science and Technology (S&T) cooperation and the forestry industry, the main source of Canadian exports to the EU. Obviously, not all Canadian industries can be covered in this chapter. This would require a book-length analysis along the lines of the sector-by-sector treatment in Hufbauer's *Europe 1992: An American Perspective.*[1] By examining the differentiated response of Canadian SMEs and MNEs to the creation of a West European free trade area, and by evaluating the state and private-sector motivations and strategies, we will demonstrate the validity of describing Canada's approach to its economic relations with the EU as being state-led.

But before looking at the sectors most affected by the SEM, we will first set the stage by outlining the forecasts of the trade diversion and trade creation effects of the SEM and how Canada, along with other third countries such as the United States, Australia, and New Zealand, initially responded the prospect of a West European trade "bloc."

THE BENEFITS OF THE SEM

As mentioned, the SEM while continuing the process of trade liberalization among the EC members, also raised some fears among third countries. The projections of the expected growth generated by the SEM, not surprisingly, have varied among the Commission, scholars, and other analysts. As a rigorous analysis of all these projections is already set out elsewhere,[2] it is sufficient for us to note the various estimates of trade creation and trade diversion and then to look at the estimated impact of the SEM on Canada's trade patterns with the EC. It is impossible, as Redmond cautions, to isolate with any precision the impact of the SEM on the EC external trade partners. This is because governments, companies, and consumers inside and outside the Community are continuing to adjust.[3] What can be done is to identify the principal trade effects; that is, the internal trade creation, trade diversion, external trade creation, trade suppression, and so on.[4] To this author's knowledge, no public studies have attempted a rigorous quantification of the effect of the SEM on Canada's overall trade patterns with the EC, although there were many such studies on the impact of the CUFTA on Canada's trade with the U.S.

What was the evidence available to Canadian decision makers that the SEM was leading to an increasingly protectionist EC trade bloc? While this is a complex issue, one indicator of protectionism was the degree of trade diversion that took place between 1986 and 1993, for which one rough measure was the increase in the "regional bias ratio," or the ratio of intra-regional trade to the share of world trade. Prior to 1986 intra-Community trade had largely benefitted from the creation of a customs union and the integration process more generally. Demers and Demers state that the regional bias in the EC rose from 1.28 in 1980 to 1.77 in 1989, a more important increase in regional bias than in any other regions such as North America or East Asia.[5] Under another measurement, from 1958 to 1986, intra-EC trade grew by a factor of 36 in nominal terms, while EC trade with the outside world grew by a factor of 16. Compounding this increased intra-EC trade was the impact of the EEA and the evolving economic links with Central and Eastern Europe. The magnetic pull of the SEM on these countries also, in general, increased regional European trade flows at the expense of European exports to non-European countries.

Yet this did not necessarily mean that there was greater trade diversion than trade creation. In the case of the impact of EC integration on EC-U.S. trade, for example, estimates made by Yannopoulos suggest that the formation of the original common market of six led to trade creation in excess of trade diversion to the extent of US$18.5 billion (in 1988 prices); the further enlargement to nine members generated a positive balance of approximately US$800 million; and the subsequent enlargement to 12 had the effect of reducing U.S. exports.[6]

As for Canada, it is likely that the creation and enlargement of the EC has historically been more detrimental to trade. This was noticeable when the United Kingdom joined the EC in 1973, causing the disappearance of preferential tariffs for Canadian products in the British market. Canada's exports of grain to the U.K., for example, went from $400 million to $30 million.[7] In addition, free trade agreements between the EC and some of Canada's main competitors for forest products, notably the Nordic countries, also hampered Canadian exports to the EC. For example, the Community imported Finnish rather than Canadian newsprint. But trade diversion did not necessarily mean that overall bilateral Canada-EC economic relations had been eroded as Canadian firms chose to use European subsidiaries to serve their European markets.

So what were the SEM's possible effects on Canada's export position? Assuming that the income elasticity of Canadian exports to Europe was not lower than 1.5[8] and taking the Cecchini report's fairly conservative estimate of 4.5 percent GDP growth, Potter and Bence have estimated the trade-creating effects of the SEM would raise the level of Canadian exports by a further $776 million or about 6 percent (based on 1993 total export value).[9] Another Commission study estimated that the merchandise trade diversion effect of the Single Market program could represent up to 2.6 percent of overall EC imports, which in the case of Canada would amount to $300 million.[10]

Whether the economic gains accruing to Canada as a result of the SEM would be $300 million or $776 million, Canadian observers calculated that if the SEM produced the expected growth, then trade creation would, all things being equal, exceed trade diversion. However, if the growth stimulus of the Single Market did not occur, the trade diversion effect would be more threatening. For instance, it was recognized that lack of growth coupled by increasing competition from not only the EFTA countries but also the EC's southern tier (e.g., Greece) would create additional pressure on traditional Canadian exports such as textiles where Canada faced tariff barriers.[11] Exacerbating this scenario was the calculation that since the successive GATT rounds had reduced tariff barriers what was even more worrisome was the prospect of the multitude of possible non-tariff barriers.[12] Canadian observers of European integration were thus very concerned about the impact of measures such as anti-dumping duties, rules of local content and origin, technical standards and requirements for certification, and environmental regulation.

Other regional integration movements such as the creation of the North American free trade area reinforced any trade-diverting or trade-creating effects of the SEM on Canada-EC economic relations. It could be expected, for example, that since the Canada-U.S. economic relationship was the world's largest bilateral economic relationship, that further bilateral economic integration through the CUFTA and the NAFTA would affect the bilateral trade and investment flows between Canada and the Community.

A number of factors, such as exchange rates, diminishing levels of demand in Canada and abroad, the composition of exports to the EC and the U.S., or downturns and upturns in the global economy, obviously make it difficult to isolate with any precision the trade-creating and trade-diverting effects of CUFTA. If the objective of Canada-U.S. free trade was to increase Canadian access to the American market then statistics show that there was significant trade creation. Canadian exports to the U.S. market increased by an annual average of 0.56 percent between 1986-93 or approximately $900 million per year. Or, put another way, trade in goods with the U.S. became eight times greater than trade with the EC, although the ratio in trade in services remained constant. Schwanen, for one, surmises that in those sectors liberalized under free trade, two-way trade between Canada and the U.S. rose sharply, relative to trade between Canada and the rest of the world between 1989 and 1992.[13]

Can it be concluded, therefore, that North American economic integration created an incentive for Canadian trade diversion away from Europe or that the SEM created an incentive for intra-North American trade and investments? In the absence of a sector-by-sector comparison of Canadian exports to the United States and the EC we can only posit a correlation between the CUFTA and this greater intra-North American trade, where the estimated $900 million increase would have certainly compensated the Canadian economy for any trade diversion resulting from the SEM.

INITIAL THIRD-COUNTRY REACTIONS TO THE EC's SINGLE MARKET

By 1988 the EC was at pains to reassure the world community, through communiqués[14] and speeches by its Commissioners,[15] and through the document "Europe 1992: Europe World Partner,"[16] that a "Fortress Europe" was not in the offing. But the Community's industrialized third-country trading partners such as Canada, the United States, Japan, Australia, and New Zealand could have been excused for being wary of the SEM's initial intentions for them. The Cockfield White Paper contained only a single sentence on relations with third countries, and a menacing one at that: "Moreover the commercial identity of the Community must be consolidated so that our trading partners will not be given the benefit of a wider market without themselves making similar concessions."[17]

In general, the increasingly assertive use of rules of origin and "local content" regulation by the Community in the late 1980s created the initial impression among industrialized third countries that the SEM had a protectionist agenda. The debacle surrounding semiconductors, for example, raised suspicions about "forced investment" and indirect protection of EC manufacturers. The SEM also raised the issues of Voluntary Export Restraints (VERs) and quotas in sensitive areas: whereas prior to 1992 these were at the national level, after the completion of the Single Market they were to be established at the Community level.

Canadian policy makers, although obviously concerned at the possibility of a Fortress Europe, appeared more willing than either the Americans, Australians, or the New Zealanders to accept Brussels' post-1988 vows to make the Community a world partner. Based on the trade-diversion and trade-creation calculations noted above, the Canadian reaction was largely positive because of the belief that the SEM would facilitate access for Canadian exporters and direct investors.[18] Ottawa saw a number of advantages:

- the opening of public procurement in the previously excluded sectors;
- the prospect of a European Monetary Union (EMU) that, by eliminating all exchange-rate uncertainty among EC countries and the transactions costs involved in operating in more than one currency, offered considerable savings;[19]
- the single EC financial markets offered Canadian banks and their investment dealer affiliates interesting opportunities, especially since Canadian banks had expertise in mergers and acquisitions, one of the most important areas of activity in the completion of the Single Market; and
- it was felt that direct investment by Canadian firms would complement Canadian exports, as previous empirical work had demonstrated for U.S. multinationals.

By 1989, the EC's granting of "Single Licences" in the financial services area and the fact that third countries such as Canada were permitted to have input into the European standard-setting process had gone some way to mollify Ottawa. Because the composition of Canadian exports to the Community over the decades had become less concentrated in agriculture and raw materials, Canada's response to the 1992 program was not overshadowed by its concern with the efforts to liberalize agricultural trade within the GATT.[20] Indeed, what differentiated Canadian responses in the late 1980s and early 1990s from those at the time of the EC's creation was that, although the CAP was a continuing concern, it no longer dominated Canada's perception of the impact of Europe's integration on its economic interests. In essence, there was no longer the knee-jerk antagonism toward the process of European integration that had typified earlier Canadian responses.

There were three other major reasons for Ottawa's more balanced reaction and the Canadian business community's general indifference to transatlantic policy convergence. Ever since the findings of the 1985 Royal Commission on Canada's Economic Union, the perception in Canada was that Western Europe had been supplanted by the United States and Asia Pacific as the major sources of economic threat. With the CUFTA in hand and with the negotiations started on the NAFTA, the federal government and the business community had achieved their goal of a "level playing field" with Canada's largest trading partner. The foundation was thus laid for a future anchored outside the Atlantic Community. The United States, in contrast, saw a "new" economic superpower on the horizon just as it had defeated the Soviet military superpower.

Second, the major bilateral irritants outlined in the next chapter (oil seeds, wine appellations, the fishing practices of EC member states) all predated the 1992 process and were not directly affected by it.

Third, Canada's response to the SEM should be seen, as Woolcock perceived the case to be with the United States, as one which did not treat the 1992 process in isolation but which subsumed the process within the larger question of market access in both the EC and Canada and the evolution of the multilateral trade negotiations in the Uruguay Round. Ottawa's key concern, having observed EC-U.S. frictions over steel and agriculture, was that the coexistence of the SEM with the Uruguay Round and the fact that EC-U.S. relations were central to the GATT would lead to Ottawa being "side-swiped" by U.S.-EC trade disharmony. This would be especially so if an agreement in the GATT became intertwined with important aspects of the SEM, and if problems encountered in the Uruguay Round fed back into attitudes toward the SEM itself. By the spring of 1991, after the failure of the Round to make progress on agriculture in particular, Ottawa's worst fears appeared to have been confirmed.

Problems in the interlinkage between the SEM, Canadian foreign economic interests, and the GATT were not just confined to agriculture, but rather manifested themselves in the actions of the Community in a range of trade disputes. On certain issues, the EC, for example, had a tendency to stonewall when facing arbitration under the GATT's dispute-settlement mechanism. Thus a number of international trade disputes over non-tariff barriers (e.g., rules of origin, quantitative restrictions) that were the basis of negotiation during the Uruguay Round became inseparable from the challenge of the SEM strictly defined. For example, as far as Japanese car exports from the United States or Canada were concerned, it seemed the EC would recognize them as Canadian or American. Canadian officials emphasized to both the EC and Japan that products from Honda, Toyota, and CAMI assembly facilities were Canadian products and should have been considered for export to the EC and not included in any quantitative restrictions between the EC and Japan. There was nevertheless a concern in Ottawa that the EC and Japan would quietly negotiate a voluntary restraint system that would limit exports from Canadian plants.[21] Although

Ottawa monitored the rules of origin and quantitative restrictions issues closely, in retrospect they were much more central to EC-U.S. and EC-Japan trade relations, and the effects of these disputes on Canada's market access to the Community, apart from in the telecommunications sector, were negligible. Nevertheless, they demonstrated how the overlap between the SEM and the Uruguay Round agendas had the potential to squeeze Canadian foreign economic policy between the often conflictual relations of the triad members.

To conclude, on one level Ottawa's approach to its bilateral relations with Brussels focused on the external implications of the 1992 program and whether this represented a move toward a Fortress Europe. On a second level, however, the debate concerned bilateral relations in terms of market access issues in the EC and Canada and how this interrelated with the multilateral system, a discussion that covered the old festering disputes going back to the early days of the Common Market and the CAP, and to the early- to mid-1980s dispute over fisheries. In these cases, the impact of the SEM was indirect but nonetheless important.[22]

OTTAWA'S PROGRAM RESPONSE TO THE SEM

Two major factors shaped Ottawa's program response to the SEM. First, Ottawa was prepared to agree with the Commission that tariffs were generally low on its exports to the Community and that, in any case, the 1992 program was about eliminating non-tariff barriers. A second, related point is that for Canadian firms to be more internationally competitive and thus by definition for them to be more adept at penetrating the larger, more efficient Community market, Canadian federal officials concluded that: (1) Canadian firms would have to be encouraged by government to invest abroad, which would entail a fundamental change in Canada's international business development strategy; and (2) that government would have to simultaneously push at the level of the EC member states and multilaterally to put in place investment regimes that both encouraged and protected Canadian Foreign Direct Investment (CFDI).

Ottawa's approach reflected a growing realization that due to structural changes in the global economy, it was no longer heretical for government to promote FDI, since research showed that there was not a clear trade-off between outward direct investment and jobs lost in the domestic economy.[23] With the Canadian labour movement battered by the setback of the CUFTA, a consensus was achieved between the business community and the Mulroney government on the benefits of strengthening the forward and backward links between international business with the domestic economy,[24] which meant that it was difficult for Ottawa to discourage Canadian companies from exporting jobs to the EC.[25] The Mulroney Government's position was that an expanding Community would require Canadian companies to position themselves increasingly within the EC through outward investment, strategic alliances, and joint-ventures.[26] In 1991, approximately 70 percent of Canadian business alliances were made with other Canadian firms, but it was recognized that a growing number were also being organized with foreign companies.[27] A number of federal programs were thus developed to promote technology-transfer and investment as complementary techniques to exporting. The overarching framework for this international competitiveness strategy was the federal government's 1989 "Going Global" international business strategy.

"Going Global": A New International Business Strategy

With Going Global, Ottawa for the first time not only privileged investment, but also sought to integrate investment strategies with technology innovation, production, and marketing. The reasons were not difficult to discern. Investment in distribution channels and service facilities that provided customer services in local markets promoted exports to the home company. Alternatively, when a Canadian parent could sell components to its affiliate in Europe, exports would follow Canadian foreign investment in the EC, whereas without the Canadian presence in Europe the EC market could be lost to competitors. Chapter 3's findings and this chapter's investigation into the types of Canadian investment in the EC demonstrate that patterns in Canada-EC economic relations reflected a more general phenomenon in the global economy: increasingly exports followed investment rather than the historic pattern of investment following exports. Going Global's significance was that it demonstrated that Ottawa was beginning to wean itself off its reliance on the traditional export-oriented trade development strategies based on trade fairs and ministerial-led trade missions and recognize the complementarity of trade and investment. The Government recognized that the promotional aspect of Canada's international business strategy would have to be de-emphasized in favour of a greater concern about how Canada's Trade Commissioner

Service, rather than just Canada's trade negotiators, could increasingly monitor and react to emerging market access issues, such as investment, labour, social and environmental policies.[28]

The SEM, which promised to change the contours of the European economy, therefore had the effect of highlighting the anachronistic nature of Canada's traditional international business-development programs and was an incentive for the above-mentioned changes in Ottawa's strategy. First, the new EC regulations and market access concerns that resulted from the 1992 program, particularly at the Commission and in major capitals such as Bonn and London for environmental standards and regulations, and Brussels on Canadian forestry practices, were precisely the types of market access issues that the Canadian government and business would be facing in other parts of the world. And second, as will be noted in the next chapter, although the proportion of Canadian exports to the EC composed of end products had steadily increased since the creation of the Common Market, raw materials and low manufactures still represented more than 50 percent of Canada's exports. Canadian officials recognized that these goods, if they continued to be only exported, would become increasingly vulnerable to environmental restrictions as a result of the emerging pan-European market that stemmed from the spillover effects of the SEM.

The Europe 1992 Component of Going Global

The West European, or "Europe 1992" component of the Mulroney government's Going Global strategy was two-pronged, consisting of: (1) the European Trade and Investment Development Strategy, with its investment development component, known as Strategic Ventures, receiving an unprecedented $505 million worth of funding;[29] and (2) targetted programs to strengthen Canadian capabilities in priority high-technology sectors. Under the new Europe 1992 program, traditional market development programs (such as EAITC's Program for Export Market Development [PEMD]) were de-emphasized in favour of the Strategic Ventures program whose objective was to foster links between Canadian SMEs and small, rapidly growing high-tech firms in Europe. This, Ottawa felt, would help Canada's commercial relations with Europe to become more investment- and technology-driven, to improve Canadian competitiveness more directly, and to increase the value-added of Canadian exports to EC markets.[30] It is significant to note that unlike the more universal trade-development programs of years past, Going Global targetted Canadian SMEs to help them become more outward-oriented; Canada's MNEs were considered to have adequate resources and, so it was rationalized by Ottawa, did not require what amounted to indirect subsidies.

As well, with Canada as partner to the CUFTA, Ottawa wanted to sell Canada to European companies as a North American base. It was noted by Canadian federal officials that Canada's reputation as a less competitive market than the United States ironically served it well as the initial springboard. In addition, with the high level of EC investment in Canada, Canadian subsidiaries of EC companies could benefit from the Canada-U.S. Free Trade Agreement's provision for enhanced access to each other's public procurement markets.

It was not surprising that the Mulroney government focused on investment in the trade response to the SEM, in contrast, for example, to the lower emphasis placed on the investment in the Asia Pacific dimension of Going Global. Given the high dependence of Canada's forestry sector on the EC forestry products markets, Canadian officials predicted that a failure for this sector to engage in joint ventures or mergers would endanger its future export prospects. Indeed, using the calculation of 15,000 Canadian jobs resulting from $1 billion in exports, officials calculated that significant losses in this sector's market share in Western Europe would have serious economic repercussions for Quebec and New Brunswick.

In other cases, the choice between exporting to or investing in the EC was affected by protectionist measures adopted by the EC. For instance, Canadian firms in the telecommunications sector faced the choice between expanding plant, equipment, and Research and Development (R&D) in the EC or in Canada, and many decided to locate in the EC simply because of the origin and local-content rules, even if cost considerations would have otherwise favoured a Canadian location. And, although the issue of "screwdriver" plants was a volatile one in Japan-EC relations, what attracted more attention in Canada, as exemplified by the DeHavilland case, was how the EC's competition policy would exert an important influence on bilateral investment patterns through the treatment of proposed mergers and acquisitions.[31] For these reasons, Canadian policy makers saw how protectionist tendencies in the EC could lead to distortions in direct investment patterns as well as a reduction in the benefits of the integration process for Canadian and non-EC firms. Thus it was in the interest of Ottawa to push for both a bilateral competition policy agreement with the Commission as well as an international investment regime.

In sum, then, Ottawa believed that Canadian industry needed to have a better understanding of whether its products and services could be sold on an EC-wide basis or whether national markets would remain paramount, and, if exports were uncompetitive, whether investment was warranted. For this reason, under the EC 1992 component of Going Global started in 1989, EAITC embarked on a two-year informational program in Canada to apprise Canadian industry of the implications of the SEM. Although this exercise, which entailed 21 sector studies, six general guides for investors and exporters,[32] and numerous seminars and conferences, was organized by industry associations such as the Canadian Exporters' Association and the Canadian Pulp and Paper Association, it was financed almost entirely by the federal and provincial governments.

This largely passive Canadian business response to the SEM contrasted sharply with the keen interest displayed by the Canadian private sector in any trade policy initiatives undertaken by Ottawa with the United States. Here, Canada's business community needed no prodding and was willing to both participate and fund independent analysis of the CUFTA's and the NAFTA's impact. The state-led nature of Canada's response to the SEM will be detailed in the following sections on specific sectors.

THE CANADIAN PRIVATE SECTOR RESPONSE TO THE SEM

As Table 6.2 (see Appendix 2) shows, based on a survey[33] of the most active Canadian firms in the EC and calculations by the Royal Bank of Canada (see Table 6.1), the Single Market was of least benefit to the Canadian food processing, food products, metals and minerals sectors, while its greatest benefit was in highly specialized niche markets for Canadian firms such as in telecommunications and computers and in traditional sectors such as financial services. It was estimated that the Canadian machinery and equipment sectors would be more adversely affected, as firms in these sectors met increased competition from European producers. In fact, it was conjectured that the development of Canadian exports to the EC was hampered even more by the 1992 phase of European economic integration than it had been by the U.K.'s accession and, before that, the creation of the Common Market. This was due to the rapid increase of intra-EC trade and EFTA preferences.

Thus, while the 1992 program may not have been as protectionist as initially anticipated, neither was it going to present Canada's private sector with boundless opportunities. Furthermore, at the peak of the preparation for the SEM, most Canadian businesses were still adapting to the new environment created by the CUFTA. The following section analyses the specific impacts on Canada of the "1992" program.

Standards and the Elimination of Technical Barriers

According to the Cecchini report,[34] technical barriers, such as technical standards or regulation and certification procedures, constituted the most important obstacle to intra-Community trade. Before 1985, and in the absence of a new approach to standards and technical regulations, the European Community had tried to reduce technical barriers to trade through harmonization measures (including directives aimed at adopting similar technical rules for all member states).[35] In nearly all sectors, this approach proved to be inefficient.

In a resolution dated May 7, 1985, the Council adopted a new approach in favour of more flexible rules. Harmonization was still accomplished through directives in a limited number of cases, but these directives only laid down essential requirements in critical areas related to public health, safety, and environment. With the exception of these essential requirements, national standards became subject to mutual recognition, a principle derived from the 1979 decision of the European Court of Justice in the "Cassis of Dijon" case. This principle of mutual recognition appeared to make it harder in theory for an EC member state to discriminate against an EC-based subsidiary of a non-EC firm.

Parallel to this process, European standardization bodies (CEN, CENELEC, ETSI)[36] began to develop non-compulsory, European-wide standards to the maximum extent. For instance, Woolcock *et al.* note that by 1990 1,250 ENs (European standards) had been worked out, although national standards in the member states still exceeded those at the European level by a factor of nine to one.[37] The Commission therefore demonstrated a willingness to move as quickly as possible, although it was recognized that the complete harmonization of standards at the European level would take a great deal of time because of the complexity of the problems involved.

But there remained some uncertainties and concerns about the European standard-making process, starting with the need to produce to EC technical regulations or to promote acceptance of third-country products not made to voluntary European standards. Related to this, despite improvements in the transparency of the process, was the fact that third countries, except those of EFTA, had historically had little if any direct input into the policy process. Second, the EC's strict essential requirements related to health and safety affected third-country producers, although here the effect was more pronounced on developing as opposed to developed countries. Third, there was the fear that the EC would introduce technical standards for high-tech products in order to exclude, at least temporarily, foreign competitors and to allow time for its own industries to become competitive.

That said, it was true that most EC standards were actually inspired by international standards produced by such organizations as the International Standards Organization (ISO). Third countries such as Canada *had* input (one vote) here, although not as much as the Europeans who could pool their votes (*viz*., the EC, Germany, the U.K., and the other member states each had one vote). Thus it was no accident that Canada was highly active in the various steering committees, not only of the ISO but also the other international standard-setting bodies.

Because Canada recognized that the new harmonized EC standards would be closer to the existing international standards, Ottawa was very keen to transmit its views on specific standards to the European standardization bodies through its crown corporation, the Standards Council of Canada (SCC). While it was recognized that the purpose and structure of the European Standardization System were both significantly different and considerably more complex than the National Standards System in Canada, many of the responsibilities assigned to elements of the proposed new European Standardization Council were markedly similar to those in corresponding elements of the SCC.[38] The Canadian side used this similarity in order to stimulate increased cooperation and transparency and convince the Europeans of the benefits of an arrangement between the SCC and CEN and CENELEC in the form of an information exchange.[39] In 1992, Canada and the Commission began to negotiate an MRA on standards; in the same year the Canadian Standards Association opened an office in Brussels. Because Canada's highly centralized standards-setting system made its system more compatible with the European approaches (indeed the Europeans looked to the Canadian system as a model for their proposed Council) than the highly decentralized American system, Canada was able to exert more influence on European standards decisions.[40]

Another concern for third countries such as Canada was the EC policy on testing and certification. Until 1991, while EC-wide procedures on mutual recognition of national testing and certification procedures were implemented internally, there was no system to manage relations between the EC and third countries. Canada was concerned that its private sector would be forced to undergo much more costly and time-consuming approval procedures than its EC competitors. The Commission eventually allowed third countries, including Canada, to establish trial procedures for mutual recognition so that foreign laboratories were able to certify the "Euro-worthiness" of their exports.

It is difficult to make a general statement about the impact on Canada of changes in the EC's standards and certification regimes, since these regimes affected different sectors in different ways. In comparison to, say, the United States with a higher value-added percentage of exports to the EC, standards were less of a concern for Ottawa's policy makers than they were for Washington's. Obviously, the principle of mutual recognition was good for Canada in that Canadian manufacturers could expect to see a considerable cut in the time required for approval for the export of their goods to a given member state. But, in the high-end sectors of communications and electronics, the standards issue was still very much on the minds of Canadian industry, especially in high-technology industries (see discussion on telecommunications). Institutionally, given similar structures, standards is one issue-area of the 1992 program where there appeared to be substantial convergence between Canadian and European policy approaches.

Public Procurement

Liberalization of public procurement markets in the EC was one of the major goals of the Single Market program. Public purchasing among the 12 member states varied between 10 and 20 percent of GDP, and was significantly higher than the average of 8 to 12 percent of GDP estimated for all industrialized countries.[41] The economic stakes were thus considerable, with state and local governments accounting for about 70 percent of all government purchasing in the EC. The other purchasing was done by central government departments and by bodies which benefitted from exclusive rights granted by public authorities. The main components of this latter category were the four traditionally excluded sectors of energy, telecommunications, water, and transport.

The European Commission saw important economic consequences emerging from the opening up of procurement markets in the formerly excluded sectors, since it affected areas where public demand was capable of providing Community firms with a sufficiently large market to enable them to strengthen their competitiveness in world markets. Since detail on the main legislative changes to liberalize EC public procurement is available elsewhere,[42] we will focus on how these changes affected Canada's market access.

With respect to third countries, the Commission envisaged two kinds of measures when it appeared that European firms did not get from a third country the equivalent access that third country's firms enjoyed in Europe, or when European companies did not enjoy national or MFN treatment. In particular, the Commission would first conduct negotiations with the third country to try to solve the differences. If the issue was not resolved, the Commission could implement some measures to limit third-country access to the EC market.

Changes in EC regulations were intended to open public contracts more effectively to all Community-established firms. Consequently, European subsidiaries of Canadian firms were to receive the same access throughout the Community to government purchases and contracts as European companies. Suppliers from outside the EC continued to be governed by the GATT code on Government Procurement. Signatories to the code had agreed to provide mutual, non-discriminatory access to public procurement markets in specified sectors. However, the multilateral procurement code was insufficient, and thus the liberalization of public procurement in the EC created incentives for Canadian investment.

The concern in Canada was that some provisions of the EC's utilities directive would hamper Canadian industry's ability to take advantage of more open public procurement. To begin, under this directive external bids did not *have* to be considered. If they were, of particular concern were: a 50-percent value-added rule which enabled public authorities to reject a bid if more than 50 percent of the value of the goods was generated outside the EC; a mandatory 3 percent price preference granted to EC bids over equivalent offers of non-EC-origin; and a provision that described the circumstances under which entities could have obtained waivers from adhering to existing European standards in favour of national standards. In addition, there was an EC requirement for reference to European standards in public procurement contracts, and the public authorities did not even have to consider a non-EC tender if it did not meet the content requirements.

But perhaps the biggest problem for Canada was that procurement practices in the excluded sectors were characterized by close relationships between the procurement agencies and national suppliers. Between 70 and 95 percent of the procurement in these sectors was sourced from national suppliers, with the result that intra-Community trade was very small. Compounding this natural difficulty in displacing host nation suppliers, Canadian suppliers did not have assured access to procurement bodies in the EC in the excluded sectors because these sectors were excluded from the disciplines of the GATT Government Procurement Code.

The protectionist implications of this situation must be qualified, however. First, Canadian officials repeatedly expressed their frustration to this author that even though Canadian business had been provided with ample opportunity to bid on Community public procurement contracts, there was little interest.[43] Second, Canadian firms benefitted from the piecemeal liberalization of procurement that took place in the excluded sectors. Much of this was linked to privatization efforts in the U.K. (where the bulk of CFDI in the Community was located), the greater role of the private sector in infrastructure development, and the Commission's agenda to end the Post, Telephone, and Telegraph (PTT) monopolies in the provision of services and equipment other than basic voice telephony.

In sum, it was felt that the creation of SEM would result in significantly improved access of EC-based suppliers to the previously excluded sectors in all the member states, and that this would open up new opportunities for Canadian firms. At the same time, it was also recognized that the new entrants would face formidable challenges. Those challenges included strong competition from existing suppliers, high start-up and distribution costs, the 50 percent local content provision and, during the transitional period, ongoing technical and certification barriers to trade. In short, it appeared that although Canada produced a range of internationally competitive products that were compatible with the needs of the EC procurement entities, the effect of strong EC competition combined with the high institutional, commercial, and non-tariff barriers would limit future direct export opportunities to a handful of products, primarily in the telecommunications sector, which will be discussed in the following section.

Telecommunications

Perhaps nowhere was the impact of the liberalization of public procurement practices felt more than in the telecommunications market. This was a particular target for the Commission, given its significance for Europe's economic future. Woolcock *et al.*, for example, point out that the EC market for telecommunications services was one of its largest and most dynamic sectors, worth about 80 billion ecus (1988 figures) and projected to grow at a rate of 11.5 percent to 154 billion ecus by 1995.[44]

In Canada, as well, telecommunications equipment and services was a major sector of the Canadian economy. In fact, by 1991, as a percentage of Canada's exports it had outstripped lumber. Widely considered a world leader in the telecommunications field, the carriage and manufacturing industries in Canada in 1991 together generated more than $23 billion in revenues and employed some 125,000 people, representing 3.5 percent of Canada's exports.[45] It was also one of the fastest growing sectors, with the telecommunications share of GDP having a real growth rate of 5.8 percent in 1991 compared to a decline of 1.1. percent for the national economy.[46]

How, then, did the procurement changes prompted by the Single Market program affect export opportunities for Canadian firms in the telecommunications market? To start, EC tariffs on telecommunications equipment were low—between 5.1 percent and 7.5 percent—although as mentioned in the last section this was the least of Canadian suppliers' concerns. In the period leading up to 1992, the EC was the second largest export market for Canadian telecommunications equipment after the United States. The major markets for Canadian telecommunications parts and equipment in the EC were the U.K. and Ireland, which together accounted for 80 percent of total Canadian exports to the EC. As would be expected, given the changing investment and export patterns, a significant portion of these sales consisted of exports of Canadian parts, components, and sub-assemblies to manufacturing operations owned by Canadian firms in these two countries. In the U.K. it was Northern Telecom's STC PLC subsidiary, Newbridge, Mitel, and Gandalf; in France, Northern Telecom, and in the Netherlands, Gandalf. It has been estimated that, in 1990, sales to the EC by the four largest Canadian telecommunications companies, Northern Telecom, Mitel, Gandalf, and Newbridge Networks totalled $490 million. In August 1992, the Commission approved the partial acquisition of Matra Communications, a French company, by Northern Telecom.[47] This joint venture (see Table 6.3 in Appendix 2) with public networks in France provided the Canadian multinational with new markets in the European Community. This acquisition was consistent with the trend among Canadian multinationals (see Table 6.2 in Appendix 2) to invest in the EC by entering into joint ventures, not only with firms in the U.K. but also with firms from the other member states.

A few observations about Northern Telecom's international activities would perhaps also highlight some of the broader trends in Canada-EC economic relations. Indeed, the experiences of Northern Telecom make for an interesting case study. For our purposes, suffice it to note here that the evolution of Northern Telecom from an essentially North American company in 1988,[48] to one of the top three "outward-oriented" Canadian communications firms by 1993, with foreign assets of 61 percent of its total, demonstrates the impact of globalization and the pull of regional integration (CUFTA, SEM) on the strategy of one of Canada's largest multinationals.[49]

In fact, so great was the pull of the European market that just over half of all Northern's outward investment between 1986 and 1993 (see Table 6.3 in Appendix 2) was made in the EC. In the wake of the US$2.8 billion acquisition of STC PLC, a large British telecommunications company, 26 percent of Northern Telecom's sales were generated outside North America and it became the eighth largest telecommunications equipment supplier in the EC.[50] By the end of 1993, Northern Telecom's identifiable assets in Europe exceeded those in either Canada or the U.S.

With the notable exception of Northern Telecom, and even with low tariff barriers, Canadian industry found the telecommunications equipment market largely closed to competition from suppliers from other member states, much less third countries. This would explain the high degree of intra-firm trade between Canadian manufacturers and subsidiaries in the EC. As mentioned, the main barrier to entry was the monopoly purchasing power of the telecommunications authority and its close working relationship with certain national suppliers. Between 70 and 90 percent of contracts awarded by telecommunications administrations were found to have gone to national producers. The ratio was highest in those member states that had a strong national industry, such as Germany and France.[51]

There were other problems for Canadian suppliers, too. For example, there were market access restrictions for terminal equipment through standards and standard-setting procedures; testing, certification, and attachment policies; and, in some cases, foreign investment policies. Large companies such as Northern Telecom as well as smaller third-country suppliers faced high costs in meeting different national standards in the EC. Company executives complained that it cost millions of dollars every time a new product was taken through the redevelopment and approvals process needed to enter the new European market. The markets for terminal equipment were maintained in separate national markets because the state-administered authorities monopolized domestic sourcing, importation, and supply of terminals. In some countries, notably France, Italy, and the U.K., companies were required to fulfill certain nationality or residency requirements before they could even enter the approvals process; having an agent to circumvent this requirement also proved costly. In some member states, Canadian firms found that procurement decisions by PTTs were overtly political. Northern Telecom, for example, apparently encountered interference when trying to bid for a switching system for the Italian telephone company.[52] To mitigate these problems, some large Canadian telecommunications firms invested heavily in the EC market. This would explain, for example, Northern Telecom's acquisition of STC PLC, which enabled it to be classified as a domestic supplier.

In terms of value-added service providers, many of the member states imposed restrictive terms and conditions. With the significant exception of the U.K., the price of leased lines was kept artificially high by PTTs, particularly in Germany, Spain, and Italy, to deter the development of private networks. Over the years, some member states used regulations to close their domestic telecommunications markets to foreign companies by prohibiting foreign ownership of basic facilities and denying foreign providers the right to establish enhanced services.

The relationship between purchasers and suppliers in the telecommunications industry in most member states had become one of near-monopoly in procurement, counterbalanced by an oligopolistic supply industry. Even with liberalization, it was clear to both Canadian officials and to the Canadian business community that it would be difficult for new entrants to displace existing national suppliers such as Alcatel, Siemens, and Ericsson, as well as the second-rank suppliers such as Bosch, Philips, and Italtel/ATT.

The telecommunications sector, the only one in which Canadian companies were world class, was also the one in which an open, unified Europe promised greater export opportunities as well as increased returns on direct foreign investment. It was forecast that the increased export opportunities would likely be in the terminal equipment market, since this was to be liberalized unconditionally. In contrast, increases in direct exports were less likely in the network equipment market due to its high entry barriers together with the 50 percent value-added rule. Thus, for this market segment investment, licencing arrangements or joint ventures would be necessary for Canadian firms. Finally, it seems obvious that as European firms benefitted from economies of scale they would also pose increased competition for Canadian firms in their domestic markets.[53]

What can we conclude about the Canadian telecommunications sector's response to the SEM? First, it is significant that exports of half a billion dollars in telecommunications equipment by four Canadian companies (not to mention Northern Telecom's investment) was only about $100 million less than the total value of softwood lumber exported by Canada to the Community in 1992. Thus, the effect of the expansion of the Canadian telecommunications sector was not only that it further diversified Canada's export mix to the EC, but, instead of investment replacing exports, the magnetic pull of the SEM created increases in Canadian investment flows and exports.

It appears then that although Canadian firms had been successful in competing against EC firms in third markets (based on the principal criteria of competitive prices, product quality, technical and financial reliability, and product compatibility with existing systems), in the previously excluded sectors the presence of strong, well-connected national suppliers in most member states meant that Canadian firms would have had a very hard time competing unless they did so with a strong local partner.

For the above reasons, the Canadian federal government encouraged joint venturing and other forms of partnership as an integral part of Canada's response to the SEM. Another impulse was not only to use strategic alliances for their marketing and distribution benefits but also to permit Canadian firms to tap into foreign research. For example, in an innovative industry such as telecommunications, it was recognized that for Canadian firms to remain competitive they would have to have access to world-class technology, much of which resided in the EC. This was Northern Telecom's strategy when it gained another R&D facility in the U.K. through its purchase of STC PLC, complementing its existing R&D facility at Maidenhead.

Reciprocity for EC Firms in Canada

The EC adopted a comprehensive procurement offer which operated at all levels of government. This had the effect of putting pressure on countries such as Canada and the U.S., who were signatories to the GATT Public Procurement Code, to in turn pressure their sub-federal units. At the time of writing, the GATT Public Procurement Code covered purchases by central governments only, but excluded purchases in a number of major sectors such as power generation, telecommunications, transportation, construction, and services contracts. In fact, the Code covered less than 5 percent of the total non-defence purchases of its members.

Therefore, the other side of the liberalization of the EC's lucrative procurement market was that the Commission had made it clear that it expected EC-based firms to be given preference in procurement decisions in the excluded sectors in the absence of multilateral or bilateral agreements ensuring "comparable and effective" access for EC firms in third countries. How then did the Commission view its "comparable and effective access" to the Canadian market? In the telecommunications industry, for instance, EC officials charged that Canada had refused to open its lucrative yet much smaller market by not allowing the Europeans to break into vertical supplier arrangements. The Europeans had an interest in seeing a deregulated domestic telecommunications market, preferably with Northern Telecom no longer enjoying a privileged-supplier relationship with Bell Canada. EC officials note rather wryly that Northern Telecom was "sitting rather pretty," since Canada did not intend to introduce competition from Alcatel and Siemens.[54] In addition, the Europeans complained that the regulations for common carriers and pricing set by the Canadian Radio-Television and Telecommunications Commission (CRTC) also worked to exclude EC companies from providing services and selling their products. The issue of "reciprocity" brought out by the 1992 program that had so exercized American decision makers in the late 1980s, raised in Ottawa's mind the issue of whether to protect Canadian commercial interests in Europe by negotiating a bilateral procurement agreement with the EC, or encouraging the EC to negotiate improvements under the GATT Public Procurement Agreement.

Another risk high in the minds of Canadian decision makers was the disruptive effects on Canada of a U.S.-EC bilateral deal on procurement, especially if such disharmony was over the telecommunications sector and caused Canada to be side-swiped. In the first scenario, Canadian officials realized that this would almost certainly cause Canadian telecommunications equipment suppliers to source their products to the EC from their U.S. operations.

Ottawa was also served notice by the Commission that it would be looking at the major provincial utilities such as Quebec Hydro, Ontario Hydro, and British Columbia Hydro. In this regard, the Community was very interested in the attempts in Canada to remove existing inter-provincial barriers to trade in public procurement. One success was the Intergovernmental Agreement on Government Procurement, covering goods only, which was signed in November 1991 and came into effect in April 1992. Although Quebec did not sign this agreement, it did state at the time that it would comply with its stipulations. Western Canada and the Maritimes had regional agreements in effect that extended beyond the national agreement in terms of lower thresholds for covered goods contracts and some services.

Despite the movement in both Canada and the Community to increase access to public procurement, Canadian officials had to be realistic about how much progress could be made given the relative power of Canada to negotiate bilaterally with the EC on this issue. In 1992, the total Canadian public procurement market was worth about $84 billion compared to the $1.7 trillion value of the total public procurement market of the members of the GATT Public Procurement Code. In reality, then, despite the excessively optimistic projections of Canadian government trade officials, what the liberalization of EC government procurement meant was enhanced Canadian export opportunities in all the formerly excluded sectors, but with the greatest returns coming from investment in the transportation and telecommunications sectors.[55]

Financial Services

In the financial services sector, the SEM sought the elimination of many internal Community barriers. Again, this process raised the question of the EC's leverage to press for "effective market access" vis-à-vis its trading partners. The Commission raised the issue of the Canadian financial market having the same financial sector concessions as provided to the United States under the CUFTA.

The Banking Directive was considered the bellwether for how the Community would deal with third countries in financial services. Early drafts of the directive gave grounds for fears of narrow reciprocity. The final draft called for "national treatment offering the same competitive opportunities [to EC credit institutions] as are available to domestic credit institutions" and "effective market access comparable to that granted by the Community to credit institutions from [third countries]." This wording was less overt in demanding sectoral reciprocity than earlier formulations, but its precise significance depended on the criteria used to determine "effective market access comparable to that granted by the Community." Similar "effective market access" requirements existed in the insurance directives.

In practice, however, the EC's commitment to grandfather existing authorized operations of foreign financial institutions in the EC alleviated many Canadian concerns. In particular, the EC grandfathered Canadian institutions both with respect to their ability to continue current operations and to branch out. The ability of a Canadian bank to make acquisitions in the EC could, however, still be undercut by reciprocity requirements.

The EC, especially the U.K., complained about Canada applying the federal 10/25 rules to all countries except the United States. Under existing Canadian policy, the transfer of shares in banks (Schedule A), federally chartered life insurance companies and trust companies cannot result in any single non-U.S. non-resident owning more than 10 percent of a company incorporated in Canada; nor can it result in non-U.S. nonresidents owning collectively more than 25 percent of the company's shares.

In addition, the commercial logic and effect of the directives was expected to increase intra-EC collaboration between member states' financial firms. This would result in a stronger European financial sector which would promote the expansion internationally of European firms in the financial services industry. At the same time, Canadian banks did not appear interested in using the benefits of the Single Market to expand their European operations. This was because of their retreat from the more competitive EC markets, which preceded and succeeded the implementation of the Single Market program. Indeed, the Royal Bank, Canada's largest chartered bank, announced in 1992—after having released a study that was quite positive on Canadian opportunities in the single market—that it was retreating from its retail operation in continental Europe.[56] Finally, the effect of the SEM on the Canadian securities and insurance sector was estimated to be small. In the securities sector, London was the focus for Canadian interests and essentially no barriers existed for traders; the Canadian non-life insurance sector was foreign dominated.

Some Canadian officials considered an early bilateral initiative with the Community in the financial sector in response to the EC's request for further liberalization of foreign access to Canada's markets, particularly in the banking sector. The benefits to Canada of the approach were not clear in Ottawa. Canadian officials considered negotiating with the EC the same treatment provided to the United States under the CUFTA. It was felt in Ottawa that timing was of the essence if Canada were to obtain any benefits. In particular, the Canadian side wanted to carefully assess: (1) the extent to which the EC would put pressure on Canada to provide "effective market access" as the implementation of the various 1992 directives got under way; and (2) the results of the services negotiations in the Uruguay Round, before developing firm views regarding an initiative in the financial sector. Because financial services had been negotiated within the Uruguay Round negotiations on services (General Agreement on Services), there had been no formal requests to the Community by Canada for a bilateral Canada-EC agreement on financial services as there had been on science and technology, competition policy, and on standards and certification. Again, this demonstrates the intersection of the SEM and the GATT in Canada's foreign economic policy. The following two sections of this chapter examine the indirect impact of the SEM on Canada-EC relations in S&T and in the forestry products sector.

THE SEM's SPILLOVER EFFECTS

Canada-EC Cooperation on Science and Technology

By 1989, two years after the Single European Act had come into effect, Canada became very keen to exploit the advantages of the SEM in the area of S&T. With the Single Market program having accelerated the Community's research programs, Willy de Clerq, then External Relations Commissioner, gave Ottawa what it took to be the green light to pursue a bilateral S&T agreement with Brussels by stressing the possibilities of international cooperation in science and technology, space, transport, and communications.[57] The needs and benefits of closer S&T links with the Community, in Ottawa's view, stemmed from Canada's relatively modest role in the field of international S&T: it contributed only 4 percent of the world's scientific literature and 2 percent of the world's global technology pool. This performance was reflected downstream in R&D activities, as illustrated by the growing deficit in Canada's trade in technology-intensive products despite the impressive growth in the communications sector. As we will see in our discussion of Canada's competitive position later in this chapter, this lack of S&T was a contributing factor to the continued reliance on the exports of low-manufactures and raw materials. At the same time, Canada faced increasing competition from the opening of Eastern Europe and the former Soviet Union[58] and the increased technical sophistication of the Pacific Rim countries.

In a global economy that placed a premium on value-added goods and services, all of which required a strong technical foundation to remain competitive, it was easy to see why Canadian policy makers were very eager to raise the profile of Canada/EC S&T collaboration. The existing arrangements, for example, of bilateral S&T ties with Germany, France, and the United Kingdom and some provincial arrangements were seen as insufficient by the late 1980s. In institutional terms, Ottawa increased its S&T resources so that by 1989 EAITC had five S&T officers, three of whom were in Europe, plus one "space" officer in Paris; by 1992 the number of S&T officers had risen to seven and were supported by an S&T division at EAITC, with eleven technology development officers. As well, EAITC earmarked $175,350 for Contributions for Technology Development with Europe in the fiscal year 1992-93, an amount that was, however, dwarfed by the Department's $1.8 million contribution to the Japan Science & Technology Fund.[59]

To provide some perspective on the state of EC-Canada S&T relations in the period leading up to the SEM, although the Framework Agreement was intended to intensify scientific and technological cooperation, in actual fact Canada's formal cooperation with the EC in this sphere had never gone much beyond the exchange of information and scientists, and the occasional joint research project between laboratories. Until the end of 1992, access to the major Research and Technology Development Framework Programs of the Communities was restricted to European partners only. As research was tied directly to the goals of the Single Market, both to improve trans-S&T capacity and international competitiveness, Ottawa considered Canada excluded from the EC's economic/trade objectives. The fear in Canada was that to the extent that the Single Market program incorporated a greater degree of pan-Europeanization, this in turn would lead to pressures on each constituent member state and also on other European countries (most notably the EFTA members) to look to others in Europe for more S&T collaborations. This would be at the expense of potential collaboration with non-EC nations such as Canada.

But Canada was not completely frozen out of the Community's S&T programs. Canada's most focused experience in collaboration with Western Europe took place in conjunction with the EUREKA program.[60] To support Canadian companies interested in EUREKA, Ottawa had established a $20 million program called Technology Opportunities in Europe (TOEP). However, because the program was not widely used by Canadian firms, it was terminated in 1989.

Given its spotty record on S&T collaboration with the EC, the Canadian government, starting in 1989, began to approach the EC with a view to negotiating a bilateral S&T agreement.[61] However, after the disappointment of TOEP, the renewed impetus from the Canadian side was based on the belief that such a framework agreement would build on and tie together activities that already took place bilaterally and through multilateral forums such as IIASA, IASC, the OECD/CSTP, NATO Science Program, and ESA. A 1990 study produced under the auspices of the Going Global strategy called for a more focused approach to bilateral relations with the EC on S&T. The idea was that an Agreement on Cooperation in Science and Technology would help to match consortia and R&D networks, the assessment of standards, and cataloguing international interests and priorities of Canadian universities and corporations, with a view to permitting Canadian organizations to get access to the Community's S&T programs.[62]

With the Commission receiving the mandate in mid-1992 to negotiate an S&T agreement with Australia, Canada saw a strategic opportunity to push again for its own S&T agreement. In June 1992, the Canadian government presented a "strengths" paper to the Commission, highlighting the scope for S&T partnerships given that many of Canada's strategic sectoral priorities mirrored the Community's.[63] The Canadian paper noted that with the particular technologies featured in the Community's Third Framework Program there were Canada-EC "complementarities" in light of Canadian strengths in communications technologies, information technologies, the development of telematics of general interest, environmental research and technology development, agriculture, forestry, non-nuclear energy, nuclear research and development, and biotechnology.

The Europeans appeared interested in taking increasing advantage of the link between S&T activities, trade, and investment highlighted in the Canadian study for a number of reasons. First, particularly in the high technology sectors, conventional marketing was being replaced by strategic alliances based on licensing, joint ventures, coproduction, subcontracting, and marketing arrangements. Second, as the CUFTA and the NAFTA were phased in, the Community recognized that Canada would become increasingly attractive as the entry point into the North American market and, significantly, Canada had a well-established community of SMEs which would be attractive to EC SMEs. Undoubtedly, this was one of the reasons why the Commission saw the benefits of having Canada join its BC-Net system. In early 1993, the Commission received the mandate to negotiate an S&T agreement with Canada, although at that time it was estimated that it would take a year or more for the agreement to get through the Council.

In summary, the above discussion demonstrates: (1) the spillover effects of the SEM; (2) the asymmetrical nature of Canada-EC relations, with Canada as the *demandeur*; (3) that the 1976 Framework Agreement had failed to expand S&T relations; and (4) the general lack of enthusiasm within the Canadian private sector for government assistance to participate in EC research programs.

The Impact of the Environment on Canada's Forestry Exports

Between 1991 and 1993, concerns with the environment were at an all-time high internationally. The destruction of tropical rain forests focused attention on the Earth's biomass. With 10 percent of the world's forest products of Canadian origin and half of Canada's land mass consisting of forests, it was perhaps not surprising that the management of Canada's forestry resources were coming under increasing domestic and international scrutiny. To the extent that the Single Market process had raised the profile of environmental issues in Europe, this raised the question of whether Canada's forestry practices affected Canada-EC economic relations in the late 1980s and early 1990s. As it turned out, Canadian forestry practices created a major bilateral Canada-EC economic and political irritant; so much so that, as in the case of the fisheries, this conflict succeeded in overshadowing and undermining the multiplicity of other bilateral contacts.

Before describing the conflicts, it is important to understand that the largest component of exports from Canada's forestry sector comes in the "commodity" sectors of lumber, wood pulp and newsprint, as opposed to further value-added sectors.[64] As well, forest industry development within Europe must be recognized. There has been a growth in newsprint capacity and changes in the EC's preferential arrangements (particularly with regard to the Nordic countries).

To begin, the EC was the world's largest importer of, and Canada's second largest customer, after the United States, for forest products. Canadian forest-product exports to the EC comprised more than a quarter of all Canadian exports. The reason that access to the European market was vital to Canadian interests was that with net exports exceeding $19 billion annually, making up 14 percent of Canada's total world exports, the forest-products sector was the largest contributor to Canada's balance of trade and the second largest export sector after automobiles.[65] For this reason, both Ottawa and the provincial governments were very concerned that the Canadian share of the EC market would be deleteriously affected by: the European environmental movement, which had received support from some members of the European Parliament; the EC's technical standards on forestry products; EC phytosanitary and plant health policies; and the prospect that Canada's market share would be eroded by competing European producers at both ends of the value-added spectrum. At stake directly were 45,000 domestic jobs.

Criticism in Western Europe of Canadian forest products and practices was concentrated in the U.K., where the criticism focused on the issues of recycling, sustainable yield, and destruction of virgin forests, and in Germany, where the criticism focused on acid rain, forest management, and mill effluents.[66] The media coverage, both in Canada and the spillover into the European press, pushed by what the Canadian government and industry referred to as "fringe groups,"[67] could not be ignored. Canadian government and industry were forced to act. As both the European Commission and the European Parliament increasingly expressed concern over the state of the tropical forests of the world, as well as of Europe's own forests, environmental standards started to figure prominently on the EC agenda, particularly on processing using chemicals and preservatives. This occurred despite the fact that, historically, management of forestry resources had rested solidly with the member states. As a result of contact between certain Euro parliamentarians, primarily the Greens and Socialists, and Aboriginal groups in Canada, the European Parliament was exposed to Canadian forestry practices and the issue gained a high visibility. That discussions in the European Parliament[68] would link national and domestic issues such as Aboriginal land claims with disputes over the efficacy of managed clear-cutting in British Columbia and Canada's export quota of newsprint, stung Ottawa particularly hard.

There was also a strong economic anchor, smacking of protectionism to Canadian observers, to the protests of some Euro MEPs who demanded that the Commission initiate anti-dumping actions on both Canada and Scandinavia on the grounds that, because their industries were not engaging in ecologically sound forest management practices, they were able to dump pulp on the Community market and thus caused serious damage to the EC's forestry industry.[69]

In addition to these environmental concerns, there were a number of specific barriers to Canada's exports of forestry products. The EC Construction Products Directive (CPD), put in effect in June 1991 and dealing mainly with codes and standards affecting engineering and design, concerned Canadian industry because it appeared set to precipitate a large number of testing and certification procedures. The process was driven by the Commission, with technical committees appointed by the EC.[70] There was some debate on the effect of Eurocode 5, the attempt to set a common EC building code for wooden structures, on Canadian interests. There was also concern in Canada that the new standards, such as those that applied to fire testing, might be inconsistent with Canadian standards and that Canadian suppliers could therefore face adjustment problems.[71] The feeling among EAITC officials was that because the code would be product-neutral (containing no product information) it would not pose a large barrier.[72] What was of greater concern to them was the development of product standards, since, once completed, these Euro-standards would replace member-state standards and would thereby directly affect Canadian interests. Ottawa's approach, therefore, was to get as many Canadian products included in the product standard lists.

In order to ensure that Canada had direct input into the product standards decision making process, so that Canada would have a say on drafts produced by the European technical committees responsible for drafting product standards (including those pertaining to timber), Ottawa made sure that the Confederation of Forest Industries of British Columbia (COFI),[73] which had an office in London, had representation on the Eurocode technical committees. COFI tracked CEN work on standards through the U.K. members of CEN such as BSI. Apparently, the impetus to get COFI more intimately involved in standards monitoring came from EAITC, which provided COFI with a stream of grants; by 1993, COFI was one of the few Canadian industry associations still receiving direct subsidies from EAITC.[74] According to a senior Canadian official who was interviewed, COFI's eight-person London office (reduced to three at the end of 1993) had always been structured to act as a marketing and trade promoting arm of the Canadian forest industry rather than a shop monitoring trade policy issues.[75] The implication was that Canadian industry was not equipped financially to deal with EC market access issues by itself as the debacle over the Pinewood Nematode (PWN) worm in 1991 would demonstrate.

The Pinewood Nematode and Canada's Lumber Exports

The PWN was one of the most contentious of bilateral EC-Canada issues in the period leading up to the SEM. By 1991, Canada had for many years been exporting lumber to the EC, which in that year had a total value of $1 billion of which $700 million was so-called "green" or untreated lumber. Lumber was Canada's single biggest export item to the EC.

The pinewood nematode is endemic in North America forests and is primarily found in the pine tree species. The PWN is transmitted from one tree to another by a vector (a beetle) that enters host trees which are weakened or decaying. However, the PWN apparently does not result in significant losses to North American forests due to climatic conditions; the PWN needs a temperature of minus 20 degrees Celsius to develop. In contrast, the PWN has caused serious damage to Japanese pine forests, where it is widely accepted that the PWN was transmitted many years ago from North America by the export of full tree logs with bark on.

Until January 1, 1991, there were no common EC rules on import conditions for lumber from North America to safeguard against the introduction of the PWN. Some countries required a drying treatment to bring the moisture content down to below 20 percent—so-called kiln drying. This process was supposed to kill off any PWN, but was considered a time-consuming and costly process increasing with the size of the lumber. Other countries, such as the U.K., which was a prime importer, had for 10 years been practicing a less rigorous requirement demanding that the lumber be debarked and inspected for grubholes to verify the possible presence of the PWN. This verification was undertaken by the sawmills in exporting countries, producing the so-called "mill certificate" accreditation.

In the early 1980s Finland detected the presence of PWN in a consignment of Canadian wood (chips), and as a consequence prohibited the entry of coniferous wood from Canada and the U.S. This led to the request for common EC import rules and the phytosanitary-related requirement to kiln-dry all Canadian softwood lumber, which took effect on January 1, 1992. Thereafter, all imported coniferous wood from North America had to be treated by kiln drying to less than 20 percent moisture content. However, at that time Canada and the U.S. had insufficient kiln-dry capacity to fulfill this requirement. Consequently, the EC granted them a temporary derogation applicable for one year and for ten member states, allowing them to export lumber under the mill certificate system under the auspices of Agriculture Canada and USDA.

In the meantime, a joint Canada/Community research program, initiated in 1991, was verifying the effectiveness of the kiln-drying requirement and alternative methods including the mill certificate. This research concluded that an effective method to kill PWN and the vector was to pasteurize (heat treat) the wood to obtain a minimum wood-core temperature of 56 degrees Celsius for 30 minutes.[76] These requirements were approved by the Standing Committee on Plant Health (SPC) in July 1992 and were implemented into Community legislation by Commission decision in December 1992. Upon presentation of the results of the scientific study, both Canada and the U.S. in September 1992 requested the measures only be applied to high-risk species, primarily pines, and that less stringent requirements apply to medium- and low-risk species.

Canada's attempt to have less stringent requirements brought the arguments to a head since the scientific evidence produced by Canada was considered inconclusive by the SPC. The SPC proposed having heat treatment for all high-risk species (pine and mixtures) starting in June 1993; making non-pine and non-thula lumber imported into the Community that was under the mill certification program at that time also submit to the heat treatment, but only after a phase-in period of 8-12 months; and allowing large dimension wood to be exempted from the heat treatment until such time that technical developments would allow heat treatment. Canada's reaction was that it wanted to differentiate among species of wood. The member states, however, showed no readiness to accept this, with the exception of the large dimension non-pine wood, provided that this type of wood still had a mill certificate. The reason was that the danger of transmission of the PWN from non-pine to pine was considered real.

On the Canadian side, there was much consternation at the Commission proposals and the member state reactions. Officials responsible for Canada-EC relations at EAITC found themselves spending, in the words of one official at the height of bilateral discussions in the summer of 1992, "80 percent of his time" on just the PWN issue.[77] Indeed, it was projected that because Canadian industry's capacity for heat treatment was still inadequate, there would be significant disruption in the exports of lumber from Quebec, the Maritimes and coastal British Columbia. Further, the requirement to have all lumber heat treated without allowing Canada and the U.S. to justify their case would result in significant increases in the costs of exports to the EC.

Based on the above description of the PWN as a bilateral trade irritant, lumber exports was one area where there was a clear causal link between an EC non-tariff barrier and changes in Canada's export patterns to the EC. In 1993, U.K. inspectors found a PWN larvae which led to a ban on Canadian lumber imports. In Canada's exports to the U.K. (the largest importer of Canadian lumber), the addition of the higher production costs associated with heat treatment on top of the U.K. importers' existing requests that Canadian lumber be cut to special sizes, combined to lead to a significant loss in green lumber exports. For the aggregate EC market the loss was an estimated $200 million (based on exchange rates) in green lumber exports between 1990 and 1992, plus an estimated $100 million in additional loses due to the uncertainty created by the PWN. The hardest hit region of Canada as a result of the PWN was the lumber industry in Nova Scotia; the least affected region was the British Columbia industry since it still had the Pacific market.

As in other bilateral disputes, this Canada-EC trade irritant was taken to Geneva under a draft agreement in the GATT discussions on Sanitary and Phytosanitary Measures (SPS-Agreement). The finding was that the European importer had the right to take protective SPS-measures, determined by the level of protection against risks. The importers' measures had to be the least trade restrictive in achieving this objective, not be maintained against available scientific evidence, and be proportional to the risk. It was up to the exporter, however, to demonstrate that his measures were equivalent to the importer's requirements in order to avoid any risk.

Another observation that arose out of the PWN case study is the role of a key member state such as the U.K. with which Canada has a special relationship. As told to this author by a Canadian official,

Canadian interests were stymied by one U.K. official in particular who was responsible for coordinating the EC's forestry research program. It appeared from the example of the U.K.'s position on the PWN, that although Canada could count on the U.K. to represent its interests on many issues, it could not do so for one that posed so significant a threat to Canadian commercial interests. This should not strike one as surprising especially as the machinery of government in the U.K. adjusts to increasing integration with the Community machinery and the shift in Britain's foreign policy from the Atlantic and Commonwealth to Europe becomes in Wallace's words "incremental and pragmatic."[78]

If the EC's phytosanitary restrictions caused Ottawa headaches over Canada's lumber exports, then the situation over Canadian newsprint exports was largely self-inflicted. Together, both highlighted the fact that Ottawa had been on the receiving end of a "double whammy" from the EC with regard to its forest exports. Pulp and newsprint were generally traded duty free; tariffs on planed lumber, the bulk of Canada's exports, were 4 percent, and 10 percent on panel products beyond a duty-free quota. There was a quota of 600,000 tons for tariff-free newsprint, beyond which a levy of 4.9 percent was charged (9 percent if not waterlined). The story on the Canadian quota, as told to the author by Canadian officials, is that in 1986 Canada's Minister for Trade, James Kelleher, miscalculated when, rather than waiting to see what the Commission would offer in terms of a duty-free quota for Canadian newsprint, he went into negotiations with the Europeans and "low balled" with an offer of 600,000 tons, which the Commission officials to their delight apparently promptly accepted.[79] Canadian officials believed that the EC would have accepted a higher Canadian quota and therefore pointed to this as a major bungle that ended up costing Canadian exporters for years after.

What can we conclude from looking at developments in the forest-products sector in the period leading up to the SEM? While non-tariff barriers, such as environmental concerns, standards and certification procedures, plant-health issues such as the PWN, and poorly negotiated quotas certainly all had an impact on Canada's most important export sector with the EC, it should be remembered that these were not the only and, perhaps, not the most important factors.

In weighing the relative impact of the SEM on Canada's forestry sector, it should be kept in mind that it was the combination of a larger, more efficient market being created, plus the EC's preferential agreements with other European states that reduced Canadian competitiveness.

The outlook for Canadian exports to the EC, although reasonably favourable in volume terms in the early 1990s, would clearly have been better if there had been an agreement on free trade in forestry products, thus eliminating the duty advantage enjoyed by the EFTA members, notably Sweden, Finland, and Austria. Canada's traditional export products to the EC—paper, paperboard, market pulp, newsprint, and unseasoned construction-grade lumber—were under increasing competition from new low-cost producers, with only slight growth forecast in the coming two decades.[80] Meanwhile, market growth for solid products, such construction-grade lumber, was expected to face increased competition from low-cost sources such as the Baltics, and the Commonwealth of Independent States, and the Nordic countries;[81] and the EC and Nordic countries were moving quickly toward self-sufficiency in higher value-added products. Even when Canada attempted to focus on the growth in demand for printing and writing papers, it was clear that Scandinavian producers already dominated the EC market; Canadian suppliers were not easily going displace their innovative Nordic competitors. In short, Canada was in the uncomfortable position of witnessing market-share erosion at both spectrums of the forestry sector, its most important export sector to the EC.

That said, other factors may still have had a greater impact on the ability of Canadian suppliers to compete in the EC market than tariffs and quotas. There were problems in exchange rates, investment climate in Canada, product innovation (R&D), increased capacity in the southern United States and Latin America, and environmental constraints. In terms of the impact of EC tariff barriers, the price effect of EC tariffs on Canadian forest products was offset in the late 1980s and early 1990s by the shift in exchange rates.

All in all, the emergence of a Single Market had less impact on Canada's forestry sector than it had on, for example, the Canadian telecommunications sector. Nevertheless, issues related to the SEM, such as the environment, and the expansion of preferences to the EFTA states and the countries of Central and Eastern Europe, *did* significantly hinder the access of Canadian forestry products to the EC market. And furthermore, the Canadian forestry industry, accustomed to promoting its goods rather than tracking market-access issues, appeared particularly ill-prepared and dependent on the federal government to protect its interests in environmental campaigns launched from Europe and on specific non-tariff barriers such as the PWN.

EVALUATING THE BUSINESS AND GOVERNMENT RESPONSE TO THE SEM

Given the SEM's breadth, any evaluation of the Canadian response risks being weakened by its lack of precision. Yet, a number of observations can be made and are supported by the statistical evidence in this chapter, the data on the investment decisions of individual Canadian firms, and this chapter's more qualitative discussion of the challenges and opportunities for third countries resulting from the Community's attempt to legislate an end to inefficient non-tariff barriers.

In general, it is striking to discover that, despite Ottawa's efforts to respond aggressively to the SEM on both the trade policy front, calling for global free trade, negotiating reduced tariff rates on those products heavily represented in Canada's export mix to the EC, promoting new regimes on investment and other emerging trade policy issues, and proposing and negotiating bilateral sectoral accords with the Commission and also on the international business front, through Going Global, the combined results were decidedly mixed. Nevertheless, it is probably too soon after the implementation of the SEM to label the Canadian response as a disappointment as was the case with the Third Option. On the one hand, Ottawa's effort probably did reduce the amount of trade diversion at Canada's expense that arose from the economic repositioning leading up to the SEM; on the other, it is unlikely that the Mulroney government's response would, in the medium to long terms, succeed in fundamentally reversing the trend of weakening transatlantic economic links. The reasons are fivefold:

1) Although the SEM first affected large European companies it also had very real ramifications for large non-EC companies in non-EC markets. However, the breakdown of the Canadian corporate sector indicates the paucity of large, global, and majority-owned Canadian companies. Those that did exist were restricted to those certain sectors (mining, forestry products, engineering) that were less affected by the SEM but more vulnerable to the EC's preferential agreements.

2) Those large Canadian companies capable of responding aggressively to the SEM were in many cases subsidiaries of U.S. firms, and the strategies for the Single Market had already been elaborated by the parent firms.

3) Some of the strong Canadian sectors (mines and resources, forestry, and fishery products) were only indirectly affected by the SEM, although the case of the PWN showed that even an indirect effect could have deleterious

domestic economic consequences for Canada. As well, although these sectors may have been less affected by the SEM they were more vulnerable to the EC's growing network of preferential trade accords.

4) Canadian supply was weaker in sectors such as agri-food and public procurement, in which the impact of the Single Market was significant.

5) For many Canadian companies, especially SMEs, the U.S. and Mexico were more obvious markets. This was because the elimination of non-tariff barriers, which was the hallmark of the 1992 program benefitted those Canadian suppliers, usually not SMEs, who could afford to invest in the EC.

For an evaluation of the Canadian response to have any value a distinction must first be made between how Canadian MNEs and SMEs responded both to the SEM and to Ottawa's planned approach to European economic integration. Historically, Canada's largest, mostly resource and financial services firms had been responsible for the vast majority of Canadian investment and exports to Europe.

The concentration of Canadian trade and investment with Europe in a few MNEs was quite extraordinary and can be discerned from Table 6.2 in Appendix 2. For instance, it is significant that of the 30 Canadian firms with the largest interests in Europe, 16 were among the 30 most outwardly-oriented Canadian-based firms,[82] and 11 of Canada's 20 largest firms also happened individually to have made the largest investments in Europe.[83] Furthermore, based on the survey data compiled on Canadian firms with the largest interests in Europe and aggregate Canadian Foreign Direct Investment (CFDI) data,[84] the 11 Canadian firms with the largest interests in Europe were responsible for approximately 80 percent of the total investment in the EC between 1988-92.[85] And to reinforce the point even more, it is instructive to recall that if 60 percent of Canada's exports were from 20 of Canada's largest firms, we may surmise that the same large Canadian multinationals (listed in Table 6.2) responsible for the preponderance of CFDI in the EC were also responsible for the majority of Canadian exports to the region.

Thus, what the emergence of the SEM did was to further increase the concentration of Canadian MNE activity in Canada's investment and trade patterns with the EC, something that may not have been anticipated or planned by Ottawa in its focus on SMEs and its desire to diversify transatlantic links across all firm sizes.

But, as Table 6.2 shows, there were some positive benefits to Canada's state-led response to the SEM. Indeed, of Canada's inter-

TABLE 6.4: INTERNATIONAL TECHNICAL ALLIANCES OF CANADIAN FIRMS, 1990-91

Sector	U.S.	EC	Japan	Other*	Total	% Distr.
Advanced Materials	10	10	2	2	24	15
Biotechnology	16	27	3	2	48	30
Electronics	16	30	10	10	66	41
Transportation	9	8	4	1	22	14
Total	51	75	19	15	160	14
Total (%)	**32**	**47**	**12**	**9**	**100**	—

* Mostly Korean firms; there were no Mexican firms among the "other."
Source: J. Niosi, "Foreign Direct Investment in Canada," in Eden, ed. *Multinationals in North America*, 382.

national alliances, Europeans were by far the most popular partners. During the 1980s, the number of strategic alliances formed by European firms increased dramatically, partly in response to research and development programs and regional initiatives. From 1990 through 1991, Niosi indicates that Canadian firms concluded more foreign technical alliances with the EC than with American partners. Table 6.4 shows that alliances with EC partners constituted almost half the total foreign alliances of Canadian firms. American alliances were less numerous than EC alliances across the board, except in transportation equipment. In short, after 1989, there was a significant shift of Canadian MNEs abroad but, despite the CUFTA, Canadian investors considered the EC to be at least as good a destination as the United States.

The findings on strategic alliances, for example, those between BCE/Northern Telecom group in Europe, with Matra in France and Mercury in Britain, and Bombardier, with the Transmanche consortium and Aérospatiale in France, as well as the lure of small Canadian biotechnology firms that attracted large European pharmaceutical firms, like Allelix and Biochem Pharma, can be explained by the complementarity of European and Canadian industries. It can also be explained by the more widespread use of strategic alliances in the EC than in the United States through the many inter-European programs launched since 1984, including the previously discussed EUREKA S&T program and the SME-oriented BC-Net (to be discussed below).

Although strategic alliances were up, what Ottawa apparently could not do was to induce Canadian SMEs to form alliances with EC firms. As noted in Table 6.2, the Canadian partners of international alliances were most often large corporations with significant FDI. Of course, it is true that certain SMEs, particularly in the technological sectors such as computers or telecommunications or biotechnology, adopted measures to reinforce their presence in the EC through alliances, but this appears to have been the exception rather than the rule.

But the rather discouraging response of Canadian SMEs to Ottawa's inducements to penetrate Community markets and to participate through strategic alliances in Community S&T programs, rather than causing federal officials to move resources out of Western Europe to other regions, instead appeared to strengthen the resolve of the Government. It so happened that in the late 1980s while the Canadian Chamber of Commerce was exploring the modalities of mechanisms to help its membership exchange trade leads and strategic alliance information through electronic means, the EC was at the same time exploring ways of linking the SMEs of the member states. At that time, the Commission's SME matching system, known as BC-Net, was not yet open to third countries such as Canada. It was this focus on the promotion of strategic alliances for SMEs that in July 1993 led to the accession of Canada to the European Commission's BC-Net, for the first time allowing Canadian SMEs to be linked to the EC's SMEs.[86] The rationale on the Canadian side was that the BC-Net was consistent with both government and business strategies to help Canadian SMEs, which flowed from the belief by Canadian decision makers that Canada would only be brought out of its recession in the late 1980s and early 1990s through an export- and investment-led economic recovery, spearheaded by SMEs.

The state-led nature of the BC-Net initiative was readily apparent. Ottawa hoped that this program would help to diversify Canada-EC relations away from their state-to-state character by creating a separate channel for Canada-EC business links. Although the Canadian dimension of BC-Net was promoted as a "private sector-led" initiative with the Canadian Chamber of Commerce acting as the private-sector link in Canada, and was "supported" by the federal government departments of Industry, Science, and Technology Canada (ISTC), EAITC, as well as the provinces of Ontario, Quebec, British Columbia, and Nova Scotia, it should be noted that neither the Chamber nor any other Canadian private-sector actor evinced any interest in setting up this transatlantic business network independent of government funds. In fact, the Chamber only agreed to act as the Canadian business partner once it was assured by the Industry department that it would not be responsible for the start-up costs. This was in stark contrast to the Chamber's willingness to pursue setting up private-sector trade offices in the United States, something it presumably could ask its 170,000 members to support.[87]

Interestingly, the focus on joint ventures between Canadian and EC firms, through the mechanism of business cooperation centres, had been called for nearly 20 years before at a forum on Canada-EC relations.[88] As noted by Hodges at the time, while governments propose, nongovernmental actors "dispose, negate or bring to fruition links set up at the governmental level."[89] Thus, the success of the BC-Net in fortifying non-governmental Canada-EC ties would rest largely on the interest of Canadian SMEs in pursuing commercial opportunities. Canada's historical track record in this regard was not good.

Another point that emerges from the creation of BC-Net is that not only was it not private-sector led, but the lead government department was ISTC, since it was responsible for the government's SME strategy,[90] and not EAITC, further reinforcing the thesis that the management of Canada's foreign and trade policy was increasingly becoming fragmented. That being said, the almost corporatist character of BC-Net fit nicely into the calls by both the federal government and the private sector for a new form of public-private sector partnership in the promotion of Canada's commercial interests abroad.

In sum, the Mulroney government's response to the SEM between 1986 and 1993 did not appear to have made any significant changes in the way Canada's business community reacted to the SEM. This is because the state's programs targetted SMEs, yet the vast majority of the investment, exports, and strategic alliances was undertaken by Canada's few large MNEs. Indeed, it would be expected that with the major Canadian MNEs (Bombardier, Northern Telecom, Seagram, and McCain) having already made most of their investments in the EC before 1990 (see Table 6.2 and cross-reference with aggregate investment flows in Table 7.4 in Chapter 7), the fear of Canadian officials would come true, namely, that Canada would become an increasingly residual supplier to the EC market.

In the past, it was suggested that the Third Option had failed because it was state-led, yet the case of the Canadian response to the SEM suggests that there was not so much of a failure on the part of government as there was relative disinterest on the part of private actors.

A number of conclusions may be drawn from this chapter. First, while the creation of the SEM may have removed many of the statutory barriers, it also revealed in starker terms many of the structural impediments that existed in Europe.

Second, as difficult as it was to measure empirically the impact of the SEM on specific Canadian industries because the evidence was often fragmentary and anecdotal, the case study of the PWN in this chapter showed that there was an unambiguous link between this non-tariff barrier and the precipitant drop in Canadian lumber exports to the Community between 1990 and 1992.

Third, it appeared that Canada's responses to the SEM were both similar to, and different from, those of its larger neighbour, the United States, and those of other middle powers to which it is frequently compared, notably, Australia and New Zealand. It is not hard to see why. Although each country was in the proverbial "third" concentric circle in terms of the EC's external relations and therefore had similar general concerns about the third-country impact of the 1992 program's horizontal measures, there were clear differences in these countries' sector-by-sector level of response to the SEM since each country had qualitatively and quantitatively different export and investment profiles in its relations with the Community. For instance, Canada was less concerned about the SEM in terms of automotive parts exports in comparison to the United States and Japan, although it shared these same countries' concerns about access to European telecommunications markets; Canada was less concerned about agricultural exports (although they were of course still important) in comparison to, say, Australia and New Zealand; but it was certainly much more concerned about phytosanitary requirements than were the United States, Japan, Australia, and New Zealand.

Fourth, spillover from the 1992 process raised contentious issues in specific sectors such as European concerns about plant health in terms of Canadian lumber shipments, which often occurred against a background of existing trade frictions such as European and Canadian environmental campaigns to force changes in Canadian forestry practices.

Fifth, the response of the Canadian business community was most highly visible through the reactions of a handful of Canadian multinationals. These multinationals were active in their response to the SEM and required little prompting from Ottawa. They did, however, provide substantial evidence that Canada continued to face discrimination as a third-country supplier in important areas such as public procurement. The response from SMEs targeted by the Canadian government was generally one of indifference given the pull of the U.S. market in the aftermath of the CUFTA.

And finally, as vexing as bilateral trade problems were for both Ottawa and Brussels, the major bilateral issue between 1987 and 1993, was *not* directly related to trade or the SEM: the incendiary fisheries dispute, that would escalate to the point of armed confrontation with a Spanish vessel, puts into perspective the overall impact of the SEM on Canadian economic interests in Europe.

NOTES

1. See, Gary C. Hufbauer, "An Overview," in G.C. Hufbauer, ed., *Europe 1992: An American Perspective* (Washington, DC: Institute for International Economics, 1990).
2. Ali M. El-Agraa, "Japan's Reaction to the Single Internal Market," in John Redmond, ed., *The External Relations of the European Community: International Responses to 1992* (London: Macmillan, 1993), 13-17. El-Agraa provides a good review of the various projections for trade creation and trade diversion that have been attributed to the SEM.
3. Redmond, *Ibid.*, "Introduction," 5.
4. Trade diversion arises when a European firm replaces a lower-cost third-country supplier with a European supplier due to the removal of non-tariff trade barriers in intra-Community trade. Trade creation occurs when the EC increases its imports from third countries because of the economic growth generated by the Single Market program.
5. Michel Demers and Fanny Demers, "Europe 1992: Implications for North America," in Fen Osler Humpson and Christopher J. Maule, eds., *Canada Among Nations, 1992-93: A New World Order?* (Ottawa: Carleton University Press, 1992), 196.
6. G.N. Yannopoulos, *Customs Unions and Trade Conflicts* (London: Routledge, 1988).
7. Bob Merner, Counsellor Commercial, Canadian High Commission. Interview, July 31, 1994.
8. William Cline, *United States External Adjustments and the World Economy* (Washington, DC: Institute for International Economics, 1989), 172-74, Tables 4A.2, 4A.3. Cline estimates that U.S. exports' income elasticity to Europe is 1.9.
9. Calculated as follows: (1992 Canadian exports to the EC, $11.5 billion) times (assumed income elasticity of European demand for Canadian exports, 1.5) times (Commission medium-term macroeconomic gains, 4.5 percent) equals $776 million.
10. Michael Emerson *et al.*, "The Economics of 1992," *European Economy*, no. 35 (Luxembourg: European Communities Directorate-General for Economic and Financial Affairs, March 1988), Table A.5.
11. Canadian officials told this author that they had, by 1993, already begun to see this type of additional competition on clothing exports where dresses made in Canada were slapped with a 14 percent tariff rate and were uncompetitive against the same type of product being

exported within the Community from Greece and Italy. Interview with Cécille Latour, Counsellor (Commercial), Canadian High Commission, July 31, 1994.

12. Stephen Woolcock identifies three broad categories of "barriers to market access": tariff barriers, two types of non-tariff barriers ("industrial policy-related" and "regulatory policy-related"), and structural impediments. As was shown in the previous chapter, tariff barriers have been significantly reduced through the GATT trade negotiations over the past 30 years. What Woolcock calls "industrial policy-related non-tariff barriers" are all those governmental measures that are specifically aimed at promoting international competitiveness of an industry or company, or providing protection from import competition. The "regulatory policy-related non-tariff barriers" are those that result from national regulatory policy. See Stephen Woolcock, *Market Access Issues in EC-U.S. Relations: Trading Partners or Trading Blows?* (London: Chatham House Papers, Royal Institute of International Affairs, 1991), ch. 1.
13. Daniel Schwanen, "Were the Optimists Wrong on Free Trade? A Canadian Perspective," *Commentary* 37 (Toronto: C.D. Howe Institute, October 1992), 2.
14. Hanover Summit Communiqué, June 1988; and the Rhodes Summit Communiqué, December 1988.
15. Speech by Willy de Clerq, "The European Community in a Changing World," Fundacion Jorge Esteban Roulet, Buenos Aires, August 2, 1988.
16. Commission of the European Communities, *Europe 1992: Europe World Partner* (Information Memo P-117, October 19, 1988).
17. As quoted in John Redmond, *External Relations*, "Introduction," in *Ibid.*, 4.
18. Demers, "Europe 1992," 193.
19. *Ibid.*, 195.
20. Juliet Lodge, "New Zealand, Australia and 1992," in Redmond, *External Relations*, 165.
21. Confidential interview with trade official from the Department of External Affairs and International Trade.
22. The use of a broad definition of market access issues is borrowed from Woolcock, *Market Access Issues*, ch. 1. Woolcock points out that a narrow definition of "market access" was used in the Uruguay Round of trade negotiations in the GATT, in which a number of negotiating groups—including tariffs, non-tariff barriers, agriculture, and textiles and clothing—are referred to as the "market access issues." A broader definition of market access as used in this chapter includes all those questions being addressed in the other negotiating groups, such as services, investment, government procurement, and standards.

23. See Robert Stranks, "Outward Direct Investment: Implications for Domestic Employment," *Commentary* (Ottawa: Policy Staff, EAITC, March 1994).
24. This recognition prompted a flurry of private and public-sector financed studies between 1991 and 1992 that examined ways of improving Canada's international competitiveness. See, for example, *Prosperity Final Report* (Ottawa: Industry Canada, 1992); Rugman and D'Cruz, *Fast Forward*; and Michael E. Porter and the Monitor Company, *Canada at the Crossroads: The Reality of a New Competitive Environment* (Ottawa: Business Council on National Issues, 1991).
25. For a bureaucrat's perspective on the changing international business environment and investment's role therein, see Section III of Andrew Griffith, "From a Trading Nation to a Nation of Traders: A Second Century of Canadian Trade Development," Policy Planning Staff Paper (Ottawa: EAITC, 1992).
26. *Ibid.*, 89.
27. Lynn K. Mytelka, "Strategic Alliances," in Fen Osler Hampson and Christopher J. Maule, eds., *Canada Among Nations, 1993-94: Global Jeopardy* (Ottawa: Carleton University Press, 1993), 129.
28. On the shift away from trade promotion to monitoring and reacting to market access barriers, see Evan H. Potter and Murray G. Smith, "Trade Policy and Trade Development: Making the Market Access Connection," a discussion paper prepared for the International Business Studies Division at EAITC on the occasion of the 100th anniversary of the Trade Commissioner Service, July 1994.
29. It is noteworthy that under the Going Global program only $135 million was allocated for the promotion of CFDI to Asia Pacific. See Andrew Griffith, "Straight Talk on Why Canada Needs to Reform its Trade Development System," *Canadian Foreign Policy* 1, 1 (Winter 1992-93): 61-68.
30. Pentland, "Europe 1992," in *Canada Among Nations 1990-91*, 139-40.
31. Ottawa did not have to wait too long after the EC Merger Regulation came into force in September 1990 to feel its effects. In its first two years, the Commission's Merger Task Force reviewed 136 notifications and of that total, only one, the proposed acquisition of DeHavilland aircraft company of Canada by France's Aerospatiale and Italy's Alenia, was blocked. For an excellent summary of the major issues at play in this case, see Industry Canada, Micro-Economic Policy Analysis Staff, "Formal and Informal Investment Barriers in the G-7 Countries: The Country Chapters," *Occasional Paper* 1, 1 (May 1994): 286-89.
32. See, for example, *Moving Into Europe* (Ottawa: EAITC, 1991); *Link '92: The Experience of Successful Canadian Companies in Europe: United Kingdom, France, Germany, the Netherlands* (Ottawa: EAITC, 1991);

The European Community: A Canadian Perspective (Ottawa: EAITC, September 1989); *1992: Implications of a Single Market, Part 1* (Ottawa: EAITC, April 1989); *Europe 1992: Your Business Opportunity* (Ottawa: EAITC, 1989); *The European Economic Community: A Guide for Canadian Exporters* (Ottawa: EAITC, 1989).

33. The survey of Canadian firms with major interests in Europe had been conducted in the summer of 1992. To indicate whether there was an increase in investment activity starting in the late 1980s, both pre-1986 and post-1986 acquisitions are indicated. The top 30 Canadian firms with interests in Europe are reflected in Table 6.2 in Appendix 2.
34. Paolo Cecchini, with Michel Catinat and Alexis Jacquemin, *The European Challenge 1992: The Benefits of a Single Market* (Aldershot, U.K.: Wildwood House, 1988).
35. Between 1968 and 1985 the EC adopted a total of 270 standards directives. See Stephen Woolcock, Michael Hodges, and Kristin Schreiber, *Britain, Germany, and 1992: The Limits of Decentralization* (London: Royal Institute of International Affairs, 1991), ch. 4.
36. CEN: European Committee for Standardization; CENELEC: European Committee for Electrotechnical Standardization; ESTI: European Telecommunications Standards Institute.
37. Woolcock, Hodges, Schreiber, *Britain, Germany*, 47.
38. Correspondence from George Archer, President of Standards Council of Canada to John Mogg, Deputy Director General, Directorate General for Internal Market and Industrial Affairs, Commission of the European Communities, February 6, 1991, 1.
39. Beginning in 1991, Canadian firms through the Standards Council of Canada were given the opportunity to comment on various standards proposals before they were passed at the various technical committees at CEN and CENELEC.
40. On EC-U.S. approaches to standards and certification, see Woolcock, *Trading Partners or Trading Blows?*, ch. 6.
41. *Ibid.*, 71.
42. *Ibid.*, ch. 5 on public purchasing.
43. Confidential interviews with EAITC trade commissioners in Europe.
44. Woolcock, Hodges, Schreiber, *Britain, Germany*, ch. 5 on ("Telecommunications"), 59.
45. For a good summary of Canada's telecommunications industry see Steven Globerman, Hudson N. Janisch, Richard J. Schultz, and W.T. Stanbury, "Canada and the Movement Towards Liberalization of the International Telecommunications Regime," in Claire Cutler and Mark W. Zacher, eds. *Canadian Foreign Policy and International Economic Regimes* (Vancouver, BC: University of British Columbia Press, 1992), 237-85.

46. “Overview of Telecommunications Policy Developments: Canada and the European Community” (Ottawa: Delegation of the European Communities, April 1993), 1.
47. The joint venture fell within the scope of the EEC Merger Regulation since the four main sectors affected by the transaction, namely, public switching, private switching, telephone sets, and mobile telephony, were felt to be in largely different geographic areas. Delegation of the European Communities, *European Community News*, Ottawa, August 12, 1992.
48. Its non-North American sales accounted for less than 5 percent of total sales. See Fernand Amesse, Louise Séguin-Dulude, and Guy Stanley, “Northern Telecom: A Case Study in the Management of Technology,” in Steven Globerman, ed., *Canadian-Based Multinationals* (Calgary, AB: University of Calgary Press and Industry Canada, 1994), 439.
49. K. Knubley, M. Legault, and S. Rao, “Canadian Foreign Direct Investment in North America,” in Lorraine Eden, ed., *Multinationals in North America* (Calgary, AB: University of Calgary Press and Industry Canada, 1994), 86, Table 4.
50. The attraction of the EC for Northern Telecom apparently was that it expected Europe’s telecommunications market to grow at a rate of three times that of the U.S. domestic market from 1991 to 1995. Amesse *et al.*, “Northern Telecom,” 439-40.
51. A 1986 U.S. Department of Commerce report states that in Germany local suppliers benefit from elaborate technical requirements although there is no “buy Germany” bias per se; it has been very difficult for foreign suppliers and their French subsidiaries to get approval from the French Directorate General of Telecommunications. At the time of this report, there had been no opportunities for North American firms to bid on central office switch contracts in France.
52. Confidential report.
53. The major value-added telecommunications services provided in Canada were mostly provided by U.S. or EC-controlled firms such as Motorola, Novatel, and Ericsson-GE Mobile Communications.
54. Shannon Day, “Canada Risks Sideswipe in U.S., EC Telecom Spat,” *Globe and Mail*, June 30, 1993.
55. This was the conclusion of the Royal Bank of Canada in its February 1992 report, “Is Canada Ready for Europe 1992?” *Econoscope* 16, 1 (Feb. 1992).
56. *Ibid.*
57. *Agence Europe*, No. 4775, 8.
58. The countries of Eastern Europe occupied the second tier, after the EFTA nations, in terms of access to EC S&T programs, a fact not lost on Canadian officials responsible for developing Canada’s S&T policy approach in Europe.

59. Department of External Affairs and International Trade, *1994-1995 Estimates, Part III, Expenditure Plan* (Ottawa: Ministry of Supply and Services, 1994), A-115.
60. On Canadian access to Community high-technology projects, see J. William Galbraith, "EUREKA: What implications for Canada-EC Technology Relations?" *Journal of European Integration* 11, 2-3 (Winter/Summer): 141-61.
61. Canada as a third country could only negotiate at the project level, and not the program level, of the European Framework Program. What this meant was that a Canadian firm could bid on an EC project as long as there were at least two other EC partners. The author thanks John Klassen, Director, European Community division (RWM) at EAITC for this point.
62. See, Department of External Affairs and International Trade, *Canadian Science and Technology: Moving Forward to Cooperate with the Research and Technological Development Framework Programs of the European Community* (Ottawa: Government of Canada, June 30, 1992).
63. *Ibid.*
64. The other forestry products sectors consist of other papers, and paperboard; the value-added paper products category includes: (1) the likes of corrugated containers, folding cartons, packaging products; (2) sanitary tissue and other consumer disposables; (3) specialty commercial paper; (4) specialty institutional paper; and (5) wallpapers.
65. Michael Hart, *Trade—Why Bother?* (Ottawa: Centre for Trade Policy and Law, Carleton University, 1992), 14, 17.
66. Report on the Meeting of Canadian Forest Products Commercial Offices in Western Europe, Brussels, May 21-22, 1991, 7-8.
67. *Ibid.*, 8.
68. On the question of newsprint, in 1993, Palu Lannoye, co-president of the European Parliament's Green Group and also a member of the EP's "delegation for relations with Canada," called for the suspension of the preferential import rate of Canadian newsprint into the Community. In addition to the Canadian government, Canadian multinationals in the forestry industry (especially McMillan Bloedel, International Forest Products, and British Columbia Forest Products) were blamed for the negative consequences of the destruction of primary forests on Aboriginal populations. *Europe*, No. 6091, October 22, 1993. See also European Parliament, Delegation for Relations with Canada, Political Affairs Committee, "Broken Promises: Canada and its Aboriginal Peoples," January 8, 1992, a paper by Gijs de Vries, Chairman of the EP delegation for relations with Canada; European Parliament, Session Documents, "On the Massive Deforestation Caused by Timber Felling in Canada," July 10, 1992, B3-0898; and also questions by Euro MPs

on Canadian forestry management in *Official Journal*, No. C 195/6-7, 19.7. 1993; *Official Journal*, No. C 65/28, 8.3. 1993; and *Official Journal*, No. C 51/19, 22.2. 1993.

69. *Europe*, No. 6052, August 28, 1993.
70. Government of Canada, *Report on the Meeting of Canadian Forest Products Commercial Officers in Western Europe* (Brussels: Government of Canada, May 21-22, 1991), 32.
71. Demers, "Europe 1992," in *Canada Among Nations 1992-93*, 200.
72. *Report on the Meeting of Canadian Forest Products*, 32.
73. COFI is the major vertical industry association of the lumber producing industry. As such its focus is different from the powerful Canadian Pulp and Paper Association whose members comprise the value-added components of the forestry products sector.
74. For example, in the fiscal year 1992-93 COFI received $395,891 in grants from EAITC. *1994-95 Estimates, Part III*, 116-III.
75. Confidential interview.
76. Thuja wood was excluded from this requirement not being susceptible to infestation with PWN and could therefore continue to be exported under the mill certificate.
77. Interview, John Klassen, Director, European Community relations, at EAITC, June 14, 1994.
78. See William Wallace, *Britain's Bilateral Links within Western Europe* (London: Royal Institute of International Affairs, 1983), esp. ch. 3.
79. *Ibid.*
80. According to a study by Woodbridge Reed & Associates, December 1988.
81. As an example of the latter trend, in 1993, 45 percent of Scandinavian forestry exports to the EC were in solid wood; Canada's share of solid wood exports had dropped to 15 percent of its total forestry exports to the EC.
82. Appendix 2, "List of Top Outwardly-Oriented Canadian-Based Firms," in "Canadian-Based Multinationals: An Analysis of Activities and Performance," *Working Paper Series*, no. 2 (Ottawa: Industry Canada, July 1994). The top 30 include the Canadian subsidiary of Ford Motor Co.
83. This figure is achieved by cross-referencing the list of 20 largest Canadian-based firms and the list of 20 Canadian firms with largest interests in Europe (see Appendix 2). For the list of largest Canadian-based firms, see Knubley, Legault, and Rao, "Multinationals and FDI in North America," in Eden, ed., *Multinationals*, 166.
84. This figure was derived from a list of 253 firms with major interests in Europe that was compiled by the European Community Division of EAITC in July 1991, and passed to the author.

85. The survey provides the companies' history in the EC market, describes the type of investments that these companies had made before 1986 and after 1986 (including the names of the European partners or acquisitions), and details what the SEM meant for their industry sector.
86. BC-Net was eventually linked to over 23 non-EC countries in the world. Since 1988 it helped over 38,000 businesses find new markets, undertake joint research and development, co-manufacturing and co-marketing, as well as helping SMEs to identify investors and arrange transfers of technology. "Canada Links up with International Business Network," *Press Release*, Toronto, January 26, 1994, 1.
87. On this point it should be noted that the agreement between the Chamber and the government and provincial partners calls for the Canadian BC-Net to be self-financing by 1995.
88. Michael Hodges, "Canada and the European Communities: Problems in the Management of the North Atlantic Interdependence," in *Les Relations extérieures de la communauté Européene: Le cas particulier du Canada* (Montréal: Université de Montréal, July 1975), 54-55.
89. *Ibid.*, 56.
90. Confidential interview.

VII

THE STATE OF CANADA-EUROPEAN UNION ECONOMIC RELATIONS

FROM AN HISTORICAL PERSPECTIVE, the reason for the high degree of transatlantic economic interdependence was that Western Europe and Canada had, over the course of more than three decades, adopted converging economic policies. They both pursued international trade liberalization, promoted stable exchange rates, and created regulatory institutions to ensure greater transparency. As would be expected, in the 1980s and early 1990s domestic policy choices on both sides of the Atlantic, in reaction to domestic interests and the changing dynamics of the international system, in part, determined the level of transatlantic economic interdependence. However, what differentiated interdependence in this decade from earlier decades was that it was no longer possible to draw a distinct separation between what was domestic and what was international.

This chapter analyzes the state of Canada-EU economic relations to the end of 1996 by examining bilateral trade and investment patterns as well as the series of persistent bilateral trade irritants that transcended the creation of the SEM. In order to give the reader a flavour of the constraints and opportunities facing Canadian leaders as they looked across the Atlantic, it begins with a general discussion of the domestic and international economic environments facing Canada in the post-TAD early 1990s and closes with observations on Canada's inherent economic vulnerability vis-à-vis the EU.

THE DOMESTIC ECONOMIC ENVIRONMENT

Following from the discussion in Chapter 3, starting in the early 1980s, a consensus had formed among both private and public sector elites that Canada was slipping further and further behind its major Asian and European competitors because of its long-protected industries and the low value-added of its exported goods. It was recognized that although Canada's trade-dependent economy was undergoing a painful transition to a more knowledge-intensive, and internationally oriented economic base, its export mix was still heavily dependent on raw materials and low manufactures. To facilitate the transition from a protected economy to a more liberal and competitive one, the Mulroney government, rejecting the protectionist legacies of previous Conservative governments, adopted an outward-looking trade policy centred on the United States as one of its most important policy levers. The Government committed itself to improving Canadian access to foreign markets through CUFTA, NAFTA, and the successful completion of the Uruguay Round. Ironically, just as the Government was making progress at the international level, it faced the more intransigent domestic interprovincial trade barriers that were costing the Canadian economy an estimated $5 billion annually.[1]

The right mix of domestic policies was also seen to be critical to Canada's competitiveness. Adopting sound fiscal and monetary policies, creating a more skilled labour force, removing internal market barriers, establishing tax and regulatory policies that encouraged investment, and human resource development were all essential ingredients in any framework to promote increased Canadian competitiveness. With an average rate of unemployment of 10 percent between 1988 and 1993 and a domestic economy that was likely to remain subdued for several years, Ottawa had a keen interest in assuring that all of its economic policy levers were aligned with the objectives of improved international competitiveness. More specifically, increasing the exports of Canadian SMEs, the fastest growing segment of the private sector, was seen as critical to this enhanced national competitiveness because, as government economists had calculated, every billion dollars in exports created 12,000 jobs in Canada.[2]

Globalization created not only a more competitive environment for Canada but a qualitatively different one as well. For example, commercial services, those that could be traded,[3] accounted for perhaps 20 percent or approximately $1 trillion, of world exports by the end of

1992.[4] Given Canada's dependence on trade, it was not surprising that services accounted for more than 60 percent of national economic output and fully 72 percent of all jobs, and proportions were likely to rise in the future.[5] Although the manufacturing and resource sectors both remained critical to generating economic value-added and export earnings, firms in these sectors also formed a core customer base for service providers since services typically represent a significant portion of the value of traded manufactured goods. Policies that promoted competitive service industries were therefore also seen to have a great potential to bolster Canada's manufacturing competitiveness. With one of the largest service sectors relative to GDP in the world, Canada had strengths in a number of commercial service industries, including telecommunications, insurance and other financial services, transportation, engineering, construction management, and various technical and professional services, which were precisely the industries most affected by the SEM.

But perhaps the single most important factor affecting Canada's economic viability was its fiscal performance. In the space of little more than a decade between 1981 and 1993 Canada's accumulated federal and provincial debt more than doubled from $300 billion, or around 42 percent of GDP,[6] to close to $700 billion,[7] which represented over 95 percent of GDP (in contrast, the U.S. ratio was only 51 percent). This made Canada one of the most debt-burdened countries in the industrial world; its debt was greater than all the OECD countries except Belgium, Italy, and Ireland. Even more troubling, however, was that by 1993 Canada owed $300 billion more to foreign creditors than was owed to it. The high ratio of foreign indebtedness to overall economic resources was also revealed by the fact that Canada's external debt was more than 165 percent of annual exports. This ratio is the generally accepted measure of a country's ability to finance itself. In contrast, the U.S.'s external debt was 120 percent of its exports; Japan's was minus 75 percent.[8]

This bleak and deteriorating fiscal picture ensured that for both the federal and provincial governments fighting the debt and deficit through austerity programs and government downsizing, and enhancing national competitiveness through, for example, increased R&D expenditure and government-funded trade promotion programs targetting SMEs, became twin and linked key national policy objectives by the late 1980s and early 1990s. Finally, Canada's economic recession that began in 1989 was exacerbated by the political instability arising from the failure of the Meech Lake constitutional accord in 1987 and by the subsequent rejection of the Charlottetown accord in 1992, both of which had been designed to, among other things, achieve a national consensus on Quebec's future role in Confederation.

THE IMPACT OF GLOBALIZATION

If one were to try to separate out the international dimensions of Canada's policy environment from the above discussion, the major global factors shaping Canada's international economic policy between 1983 and 1993 were: (1) globalization, characterized by increased import penetration along with, as mentioned, the emphasis on knowledge-intensive production and trade in services; (2) a more complex trade policy agenda including, for example, investment, intellectual property, research and technology, regulations of service industries, and competition policy; and (3) regionalism, assuming that trade would continue to grow more within regions, North America, Europe, Asia Pacific, than between them.

First, starting in the 1960s but particularly during the course of the 1980s, there were dramatic changes in industrial organization and international trade, with the latter led by knowledge-based industries and services.[9] Previous declines in the relative value of natural resource and agricultural trade were thus accelerated.

Second, trade had become investment driven, conducted on an intra-firm and intra-industry basis, particularly in OECD markets.[10] For instance, there was a fourfold increase in stock of world outward foreign direct investment from $519 billion in 1980 to $2 trillion in 1992.[11] As companies competed more and more on a global basis, investment flows also grew almost four times as fast as trade flows.

Third, the emerging regionalism of Europe, Asia, and North America at the same time forced companies to develop a distinct presence and approach for each region. As a result, companies themselves became more sophisticated; trade, technology, and investment were now viewed as complementary tools to international business development.[12] Despite the impressive growth of trade in goods, cross-border flows of services, portfolio finance, foreign direct investment, and technology became the main forces driving international economic integration.

As a result of the above trends, Canada's economy became much more open and exposed to international commerce, especially vis-à-vis its most important markets in the U.S., Europe, and Japan. As Canada's total world exports increased, reflecting in part industry's adjustment to the CUFTA, NAFTA, and the post-Uruguay Round, import penetration in the domestic market also increased. In 1991, the share of the Canadian market for manufactured goods held by imports reached a record 45 percent, up from just 27 percent in 1980.[13]

Another reaction to globalization was the changing composition of Canadian trade with the Triad between 1970 and 1990, with end products forming an increasing percentage of Canada's merchandise exports. In 1980, 23 percent of Canadian manufacturing shipments were exported. By 1993, the figure had approached 50 percent.[14] However, as we shall see below, this dramatic shift to manufactured goods was not reflected in the composition of Canada's exports to the EC, where there continued to be a substantial, if declining, dependence on raw materials.

Lower tariff and non-tariff barriers and the reduced requirement for suppliers to be located close to manufacturers of course raised the question of how prepared were Canadian SMEs, touted by Ottawa as the vanguard of economic recovery in the early 1990s, to compete on a global basis. Despite the pace of globalization, it appears that many firms lacked the necessary motivation to compete. Judging by the statistics, Canadian companies in general still felt they could survive and prosper by concentrating on domestic markets or by looking no further than the United States. The statistics are telling: by 1993, 60.4 percent of all Canadian exports were made by just 100 mostly resource companies. More startling still, given Canada's dependence on trade, was the fact that only 7.6 percent of all Canadian firms exported, and only 15.4 percent of those firms were listed as manufacturers. But most disturbing of all was the fact that SMEs, the only segment of the economy that had seen increases in employment in the late 1980s, represented only 9 percent of Canadian manufacturers' exports.[15] Finally, when the Canada-U.S. trade figures and intra-firm transactions were calculated out of these numbers, the number of SMEs involved in business transactions outside Canada's borders was even smaller.

In the face of this discouraging export performance, the Mulroney government made substantial commitments to trade promotion and investment development programs to encourage Canadian firms to diversify their markets overseas. Veering away from the more universal export programs of the past, Ottawa now employed a more targetted approach, anchored by SMEs, to secure global niches in those knowledge-intensive industries such as telecommunications and biotechnology and services where Canada had and could have a competitive advantage.[16] But resources alone could not change attitudes. Canada's dependence on resource-based production, close proximity to the U.S., limited size, and its high dependence on foreign investment had all historically combined to undermine the incentives to develop a more outward-oriented economy.

On the matter of investment, the CUFTA marked a significant change in attitude toward foreign direct investment (FDI) in the Canadian economy. It put an end to a 100-year strategy of encouraging investment in Canada to serve the Canadian market. In fact, until as late as 1984, Canadian officials were still not permitted to promote outward direct investment.[17] Time had eroded the relevance of such a strategy, however. By the mid-1980s, Canada, through Investment Canada,[18] began to compete actively for investment to serve the North American market and global markets, a trend which was to accelerate with the creation of a free trade area in North America. With regard to Europe, as opposed to previous decades when the Canadian government's emphasis was on promoting Canadian exports, it now included the aggressive promotion of outward and inward investment in response to the creation of the SEM.[19]

BILATERAL CANADA-EU TRADE AND INVESTMENT FLOWS

Although the EC as a bloc was, after the United States, Canada's second-largest trading partner, by the time of the signing of the Maastricht Treaty at the end of 1993, trade with the EC accounted for a much smaller percentage of Canada's total world merchandise trade. Figures 7.1 and 7.2, along with the detailed breakdown of yearly export and import statistics in Tables 7.1 and 7.2 (in Appendix 3), show Canada's trading relationship with the EC between 1958 and 1993.

Significantly, during the decade of the 1980s, the benign neglect of Canada-EC relations and the renewed attention to the U.S. market were reflected in a steady erosion of the Canada-EC trading relationship. In 1982, for instance, Canada's exports to the EC accounted for 9 percent of total exports and imports accounted for 8.4 percent; in 1993, Canadian exports to the EC amounted to just 5.7 percent of total exports and imports accounted for 8.7 percent of total imports. Three years into the SEM program (and with the inclusion of three new member states), Canadian exports to the EC had barely risen to 5.8 percent of total exports. In marked contrast, Canada became more dependent on the U.S. market over the same time period: in 1982, the U.S. was the destination of 68.2 percent of Canada's merchandise exports and the

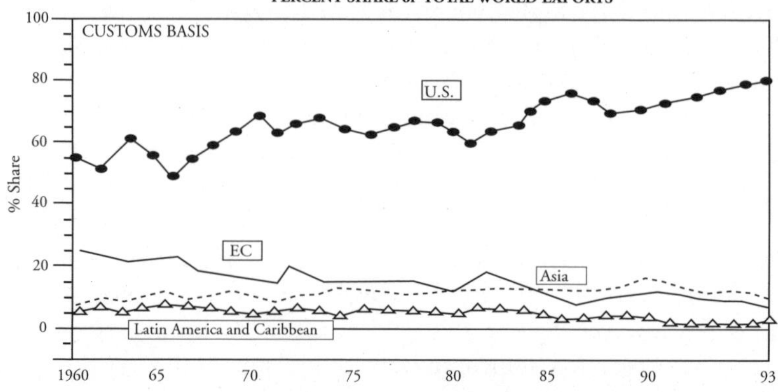

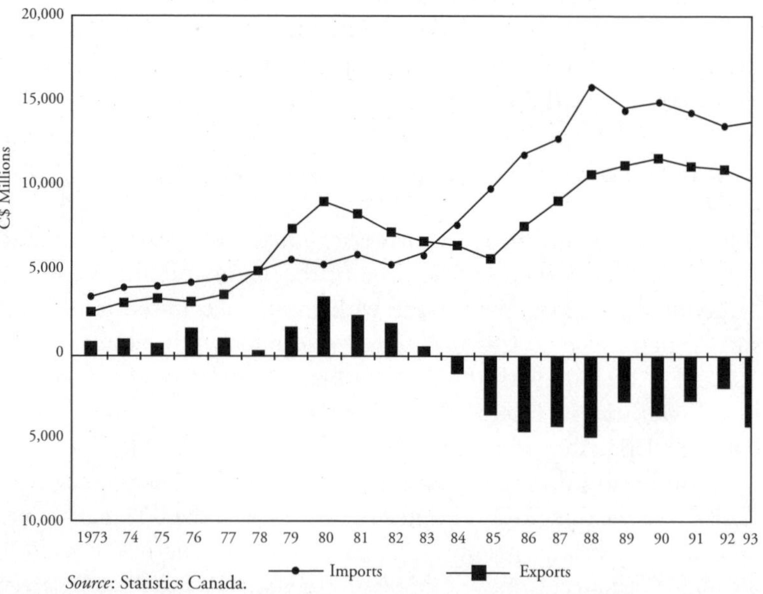

Source: Statistics Canada.

source of 70.5 percent of Canada's imports; by 1993 Canada's exports to the United States for the first time broke the important "psychological barrier" of 80 percent, while its imports from the United States remained steady at 67 percent. This increasing percentage of exports to the U.S. was destined to continue unabated throughout the decade. In the period since the CUFTA went into effect in 1989, Canada's trade with the U.S. as a percentage of its world trade increased by almost 2 percent annually. In the same time period, Canadian exports to Asian markets remained level in percentage terms, hovering just below 10 percent. And as shown in Figure 7.1, and Table 7.1 (in Appendix 3), in 1984 Canadian exports to Asia for the first time surpassed Canadian exports to the EC. For the EC, meanwhile, trade with Canada represented less than one percent of its total world trade.

From the creation of the EC in 1957 until 1984, Canada had usually posted an overall trade surplus with the EC, except in 1975. However, the relative stability in exports to the EC, due to a favourable Canadian exchange rate, coupled with the increase in imports from the EC, combined to produce for the first time a deficit of slightly more than $1 billion in 1984. In 1993, the deficit for bilateral trade with the EC amounted to $4.1 billion. If one includes the EFTA members to create the European Economic Area, this trade deficit increased to $5.3 billion by 1993, $6.7 billion by 1995, and $7.9 billion by 1996.[20]

If we look at Canada's trading relations in terms of blocs, trade figures show that Canada's total trade with the U.S. rose throughout the course of the 1980s and early 1990s. It rose with Latin America in the early 1990s,[21] in general was flat with Europe (EC, EFTA, and some of the larger Central and East European countries), and declined with the Pacific Rim, from $17.1 billion in 1988 to 15.7 billion in 1992. In fact, in the same way that Canadian observers had anticipated the trade-diverting effects of the Community's creation in 1957 and again when Britain joined, the creation of the SEM once more raised the question of whether renewed European economic integration, this time through increases in intra-EC trade and EFTA preferences,[22] would be protectionist or trade-liberating for Canada.

The process of European integration could also be seen as an incentive for North American integration. There was concern among some analysts in Canada that the CUFTA was contributing to more trade creation in North America and less trade diversification away from North America.[23] The Mulroney government had, after all, predicted that CUFTA, by making Canadian firms more competitive, would lead to greater not lesser trade diversification. To take an example, between 1992 and 1993 Canadian exports to the U.S. increased by more than the increase in its exports to all other OECD members combined, thus further reinforcing the world's largest bilateral trading relationship, valued in excess of $350 billion annually or almost 10 times that of Canada-EC trade.

In addition to the erosion of the transatlantic trading relationship, another characteristic of Canada's trade with the EC was its weakness in manufactured exports. This confirmed the maxim about Canada's role in global commerce, that it was "a hewer of wood and drawer of water." Trade opportunities for Canada in Europe fell into two basic categories: the price-sensitive and the less price-sensitive. The former included most forestry products, metals and minerals, construction materials, fish, and other unprocessed products.

Despite improvement, notably the rise of office machinery and equipment which comprised Canada's third-largest export to the EC in 1993, Canadian exports continued to be concentrated in fabricated and crude materials. In fact, the two main exports during the period examined in this study were, and continue to be, wood pulp and similar pulp, softwood lumber, and newsprint. These commodities were worth $3.1 billion in 1992 or fully 27 percent of the value of Canada's total exports to the EC, with other metals and ores coming in fifth place. Neither Japan nor the United States were the recipients of such a highly resource-dependent export mix from Canada. By contrast, imports from the EC, with the exception of crude oil, consisted mostly of end products and fabricated materials such as airplanes, automobiles, and auto parts, with organic chemicals strongly represented.

On the services side, nearly 60 percent of Canada's business services receipts were attributed to the United States, half from related companies. Corroborating the earlier observation about the increased trade in services worldwide, Table 7.3 (Appendix 4) indicates that there was an extraordinary 80 percent increase in Canada's exports of business services to the EC between 1986 and 1992, due in large measure to the creation of the SEM, with the EC making up 17 percent of total EC worldwide receipts with over 30 percent from affiliates. The most important business services sectors for Canada were transportation, insurance, financial, and communications services.[24] Not surprisingly, the patterns of Canada's service trade with the EC mirrored the pattern of its goods exports, with the U.K. by far the largest market. But as large an increase as there was in service exports to the EC, service sales to the EC nevertheless made up a declining percentage of Canada's world service exports.

Investment

Canada was a significant exporter of capital during the 1980s.[25] As Table 7.4 shows, between 1982 and 1993, the stock of Canadian Foreign Direct Investment (CFDI) abroad more than tripled, from $35.6 billion to $170 billion, increasing at a faster pace than the global stock of direct investment and as a greater percentage of Canadian GDP (from

8.7 percent to 14.4 percent).[26] What factors accounted for the dramatic increase Canadian FDI observed in Tables 7.4 and 7.5? How did the geographic distribution of CFDI change between 1951 and 1993? Was there a marked shift in its industrial composition away from primary and resource-based manufacturing industries toward services and technology-intensive manufacturing industries? And how well do the general observations about changing Canadian investment trends account for Canada-EC investment patterns?

To answer the above questions, it would be helpful first to examine three broad trends in CFDI: (1) a much faster growth rate in CFDI abroad than in inward foreign direct investment to Canada; (2) a decline in the U.S. share of CFDI in the second half of the 1980s, largely in favour of Europe; and (3) the increasing importance of the financial services and chemicals and chemical products industries.[27] In 1993, research by Industry Canada, building on earlier work by Dunning, Cantwell, Rugman, and Globerman, examined some of the major push and pull factors that explain the rapid expansion of CFDI relative to incoming foreign direct investment into Canada. Those factors included a recession in the late 1980s that pushed investment away from Canada, the changing structure of international commerce, the changing profitability of foreign locations, increased non-tariff barriers, exchange rates, and greater aggregate demand in Canada.[28] The conclusion drawn from this research was that the increased outward orientation of Canadian firms was due less to exchange rate and labour force costs,[29] and more to the emergence of mature and strong Canadian firms, the increased importance of scale economies, the threat of non-tariff trade protection in the U.S. and post-1992 Europe, the need for market diversification, and the emergence of niche markets.[30]

Tables 7.4 and 7.6 show that Canadian FDI to the EC increased by almost 400 percent between 1982 and 1993, although it had stagnated during the early 1980s. By the end of 1996, as indicated in Table 7.5, 20.4 percent of all Canadian foreign direct investment abroad was in the EC, with by far the greatest percentage of investment flow and stock in the U.K.[31]

A number of other significant trends also come to light. Why, for instance, was CFDI in the EC in 1989 and 1990 for the first time higher than CFDI in the rest of the world (denoted as "Other" in Table 7.4 and excluding the U.S. and Japan)? And what would account for the fact that between 1988 and 1991 the annual percentage increases in CFDI flowing into the EC *exceeded* that flowing into the United States? At

TABLE 7.4: TOTAL CFDI ABROAD, 1980-96
(C$ millions)

Year	United States	EC/EU	Japan	Other	Total
1980	16,781	4,440	109	5,637	26,967
1981	22,356	4,827	99	6,565	33,847
1982	23,781	4,612	110	7,055	35,558
1983	26,576	4,076	200	9,007	39,859
1984	32,151	5,573	231	9,467	47,422
1985	37,074	6,803	232	10,014	54,123
1986	39,424	7,849	225	10,994	58,492
1987	43,365	10,395	242	12,792	66,794
1988	46,497	11,880	354	13,415	72,146
1989	50,341	15,200	395	14,843	80,779
1990	52,800	18,046	770	16,270	87,886
1991	54,639	19,988	1,721	18,087	94,435
1992	61,527	20,611	2,641	21,755	106,534
1993	65,072	22,763	2,973	24,567	115,375
1996	95,006	37,073	2,676	46,602	181,357
Increase, 1983-88 (%)	80	134	77	81	
Annual average ($)	3,984	1,361	51	6,457	
Increase, 1988-92 (%)	30	73	646	48	
Annual average ($)	3,757	2,183	577	8,597	

Source: J. Niosi, "Foreign Direct Investment in Canada," in Eden, *Multinationals in North America*, 380; and author's calculations.

TABLE 7.5: RELATIVE DISTRIBUTION OF CFDI ABROAD, 1951-96, IN %

Year	United States	EC/EU	Other	Total
1951	78.2	6.9	14.9	100
1961	66.4	13.2	20.4	100
1971	52.0	14.3	33.7	100
1981	66.1	14.3	19.6	100
1984	71.7	8.9	19.4	100
1988	64.4	16.5	19.1	100
1991	57.9	21.1	21.9	100
1993	56.4	19.7	23.9	100
1996	52.4	20.4	27.2	100

Source: Statistics Canada, *Canada's International Investment Position: Historical Statistics, 1926-1991* (Ottawa, 1993), cat. 67-202.

first glance, this would appear to have been a very unusual trend given the U.S.'s proximity and historic source of foreign investment. Indeed, the share of Canadian FDI going to the U.S. dropped from 71.7 percent in the mid-1980s to 52.4 percent by the end of 1996, with the relative decline being picked up by Europe.

TABLE 7.6: CANADIAN FOREIGN DIRECT INVESTMENT (CFDI) IN THE EC/EU, 1971-96
(C$ millions)

Country	1971	1979	1982	1984	1986
France	87	278	229	121	402
Germany	87	327	269	415	649
The Netherlands	33	211	277	434	572
Belgium/Luxembourg	35	68	63	101	146
Italy	46	112	122	141	225
U.K.*	—	2,188	2,779	3,415	4,558
Spain*	—	—	—	—	186
Portugal*	—	—	—	—	19
Greece*	—	—	189	285	285
Denmark*	—	125	74	39	22
Ireland*	—	148	394	622	785
Total CFDI in EC	**288**	**3,457**	**4,396**	**5,573**	**7,849**
Total CFDI	6,538	20,496	35,558	47,422	58,492
CFDI in EC as % of total	4.4	16.8	12.4	11.8	13.4
CFDI in U.S.	3,399	12,165	23,781	32,151	39,424
CFDI in U.S.as % of total	52.0	59.4	66.9	67.8	67.4
CFDI in Japan	58	82	110	231	225
CFDI in Japan as % of total	0.9	0.4	0.3	0.5	0.4

Country	1988	1990	1992	1993	1996
France	1,450	1,671	1,970	1,801	3,604
Germany	666	837	1,066	1,774	1,180
The Netherlands	836	1,528	1,557	1,901	1,919
Belgium/Luxembourg	410	625	1,349	1,955	2,577
Italy	178	368	839	785	768
U.K.	7,050	11,292	11,360	12,907	17,809
Spain	271	541	401	342	161
Portugal	106	110	176	235	100
Greece	76	89	91	102	108
Denmark	76	46	36	27	38
Ireland	814	939	1,766	2,542	6,872
Austria	—	—	—	—	202
Sweden	—	—	—	—	222
Finland	—	—	—	—	—
Total CFDI in EC	**11,933**	**18,046**	**20,611**	**24,371**	**35,560**
Total CFDI	72,146	87,866	106,534	115,375	181,357
CFDI in EC as % of total	16.5	20.5	19.3	19.7	20.4
CFDI in U.S.	46,497	52,800	61,527	65,072	95,006
CFDI in U.S.as % of total	64.4	60.1	57.8	56.4	52.4
CFDI in Japan	354	770	2,641	2,973	2,676
CFDI in Japan as % of total	0.5	0.9	2.5	2.6	1.5

* Figures are not provided for years prior to a country's membership in the EC.
Source: Statistics Canada, *Canada's International Investment Position*, cats. 67-202 and 65-007.
Note: Figures for the final two years may not be strictly comparable.

One explanation for this development is that real aggregate demand in the U.S. between 1980 and 1985 increased by 3.4 percent, compared to only about 0.9 percent in the EC. However, the growth of real aggregate demand in the U.S. declined to 1.7 percent between 1985 and 1992; meanwhile, the real aggregate demand of the EC increased by 3.1 percent in the same time period, with the significant improvement in the relative profit position of the U.K. reflected in its position as the major host of Canadian FDI in Europe.[32] Another explanation is the aggressiveness of Canadian firms. The total growth of Canadian FDI in the EC from 1984 to 1990 was about 10 times less than that of American investment over the same time period ($12 billion compared to US$100 billion). This meant that, proportionate to the size of their economies (the U.S. economy is about 10 times bigger than Canada's), the increase of Canadian investment in the EC was about the same as that of American investment. In fact, it would appear that Canadian firms were just as aggressive as their U.S. counterparts. This is because U.S. investment stock was mature. Therefore, much of the annual capital flows into the EC were reinvested earnings.[33] Canadian capital flows had also been in reinvested earnings but there had been a greater degree than in the U.S. of greenfield investment or acquisitions.

But, as the previous chapter showed, any analysis of the Canadian private sector's strategy to the SEM must differentiate between large firms and SMEs. The characterization of Canadian investment toward Europe as "aggressive" can only be ascribed legitimately to the few, very large Canadian multinationals which made significant investments in niche markets in Western Europe. Canadian SMEs, as pointed out, were not outward-oriented, unlike for example those of Germany, a country with a similarly high trade/GDP ratio. If they exported and invested at all, smaller Canadian firms preferred to invest and/or transfer technology to the United States rather than to the EC, probably because of more limited resources and knowledge of the European markets.[34] In sum, the explanation for the sharp increase in CFDI in the EC between 1986 and 1991 appears to rest on: (1) the magnetic pull of Western Europe with the formation of the SEM and the associated fear of a Fortress Europe; and (2) the increased aggressiveness and global orientation of large Canadian firms.

The first conclusion in the above explanation is supported by the fact that with the completion of the SEM, the pull of Western Europe as a host of CFDI waned. After 1991 there was a decline in the annual percentage increases in CFDI in the EC, a decline in CFDI in the EC as a percentage of total CFDI, and a noticeable diversion of Canadian investment away from both the Community and the United States to Asia and Latin America.

With regard to the composition of CFDI in the EC, as Table 7.7 shows, the growing share of services and technology-intensive industries is consistent with the structural changes in the global economy mentioned earlier, such as the decline in prices of resources and resource-based manufacturing and the liberalization of financial services. But despite a discernible shift in the composition of Canada's worldwide CFDI, it is noteworthy that the shift was less pronounced in CFDI in the EC, where resources and resource-based manufacturing continued to account for a large share of Canada's total stock of CFDI in the EC. For example, in 1991 investment in non-ferrous metals constituted 31 percent and wood/paper products 25 percent of total CFDI, with both sectors showing significant increases between 1985 and 1988.[35] In addition to beverages (26 percent), financial services (a traditional sector, including corporate/personal banking, investment dealers, and insurance), accounted for a still-significant but declining share of CFDI, amounting to 7 percent of the total in 1991. Significantly, more than 10 percent of Canadian investments was in computer technology. What is striking about the composition of Canada's investment stock is that in the years preceding the SEM, with the exception of the emerging presence of Canadian computer and electronics firms, the new investments reflected Canada's traditional strengths. There was little diversification.

Canada as a Host of EC Investment

Since this chapter is measuring the level of Canada-EC economic interdependence, it cannot ignore the Community's stake in its economic relations with Canada. While European companies were preparing themselves for a more open internal market, many EC firms turned to North America in the late 1980s, partly in response to the CUFTA. As EC MNEs advanced their relative global positions, by 1990 their overseas investment in North America was larger by far than North American (Canada and the U.S.) FDI in the EC. The Community's FDI into Canada during the period 1983 to the end of 1992 rose from $13.4 billion (17.3 percent of total inward investment stock) to $31 billion (23 percent of total inward investment stock), with the

TABLE 7.7: COMPOSITION OF CANADIAN DIRECT INVESTMENT IN THE EC, 1985-91
(C$ millions)

Industry	1985	1988	1991	Increase, 1985-88 (%)	Increase, 1985-91 (%)
Beverages	1,424	2,431	2,789	71	15
Non-ferrous metals	1,784	2,109	3,292	18	56
Wood and paper products	721	1,716	2,608	138	52
Iron and iron products	187	553	801	196	133
Chemical and allied products	254	257	495	1	93
Other manufacturing	130	318	548	145	72
Manufacturing subtotal	**4,499**	**7,384**	**10,531**	**64**	**43**
Merchandising	201	387	451	93	17
Mining and smelting	130	73	151	-44	107
Petroleum and natural gas	655	856	1,055	31	23
Utilities	166	30	164	-82	447
Financial	1,054	2,617	1,474	148	-44
Other enterprises	98	534	1,230	445	130
Total	**6,803**	**11,880**	**19,988**	**75**	**68**

Source: J. Niosi, "Foreign Direct Invstment in Canada", in Eden, *Multinationals in North America*, 382; based on, Statistics Canada, *Canada's International Investment Position*, cat. 67-202.

U.K. accounting for more than half the investment. While the previous discussion showed how important the U.K. was as a destination for Canadian FDI, Canada was also important for the U.K., ranking fourth as a destination of U.K. investment; over 650 British firms had subsidiaries in Canada.[36] From Table 7.8, the annual average increase between 1983 and 1988 was $2.3 billion and slowed to $1.9 billion annually, on average, between 1988 and 1991; between 1987 and 1988 EC FDI in Canada increased by a startling 20 percent. In 1989-90, the EC, as the second largest source of total FDI stock in Canada, had the distinction of, in aggregate, replacing for the first time the United States as the leading foreign investor, in terms of annual inflows, in Canada. Canada had become as attractive a destination for European investment as the United States.

We can attribute the large jump in annual Canada-EC investment flows between 1986 and 1990 to the magnetic pulls of both North American and European economic integration and the significant degree of globalization underway. In terms of North America, it should be noted that the substantial growth of FDI flows had also greatly increased the economic links between the EC and the United States. In 1991, for example, EC investors owned more than half the FDI stocks

TABLE 7.8: TOTAL FDI IN CANADA, 1950-96
(C$ millions)

Year	United States	EC/EU	Japan	Other	Total
1950	3,549	468*	n.a.	81	4,098
1965	14,408	3,075	10	371	17,864
1983	58,446	13,454	1,611	3,902	77,413
1984	63,355	14,118	1,790	4,122	83,385
1985	66,013	14,860	1,925	4,428	87,226
1986	67,025	18,164	2,291	4,921	92,401
1987	71,806	20,485	2,479	7,073	101,483
1988	73,710	24,963	3,149	8,723	110,545
1989	78,217	27,488	4,104	9,149	118,958
1990	80,931	31,094	4,138	10,425	126,588
1991	83,775	30,786	5,345	11,724	131,360
1993	90,600	31,604	6,249	13,040	141,493
1996	120,370	38,042	7,828	13,275	179,515
Increase 1983-88 (%)	25	88	106	131	43
Annual Average ($)	2,943	2,380	340	1,019	6,681
Increase 1988-91 (%)	14	23	70	34	19
Annual average ($)	3,355	1,941	732	1,000	7,028

* Figure for the U.K. only.
Source: J. Niosi, "Foreign Direct Investment," in Eden, *Multinationals in North America*, 370; and Statistics Canada.

in the U.S., while two-fifths of American-owned FDI stocks were located in the EC. At historical prices, these investments together were worth more than US$420 billion,[37] substantially dwarfing the $50 billion in Canada-EC investment stock.

The growth evident in bilateral North America-EC investment flows thus supports the thesis that, globally, growth in foreign investment was outstripping growth in world merchandise trade. For this reason, it was clear that investment would be of increasing importance in Canada's relations with the EC. For example, as the trade statistics show, the precipitous decline in average annual percentage increases in the value of Canadian exports to the EC between 1986 and 1990 (from 18 percent average annual increases between 1986 and 1988 to 4 percent between 1988 and 1990), which turned into annual percentage *declines* from 1990 to 1993, were partially offset by the annual percentage increases in Canadian FDI flows during the same time period. This shift in the value and nature of Canada's economic links to the Community can be explained not only by the trade-diverting aspects of, say, the CUFTA and NAFTA, but also by Canadian companies having decided to replace their exports by investment in the Community.

Policy Implications of Investment Regimes

What, then, were the policy implications for Ottawa of: (1) the high level of CFDI; and (2) the high level of CFDI in the Community? With the rapid increase in Canadian investment abroad, there was more pressure on Ottawa, not surprisingly, to create effective international investment regimes. For this reason, Canadian policy makers pressed for a number of initiatives, including the inclusion of investment provisions in both the CUFTA and the NAFTA, the review of the OECD Code of Liberalization in Capital Movements, the OECD Code of National Treatment Instrument (NTI), the trade-related investment measures (TRIMs) in the MTN, and the bilateral foreign investment protection agreements. The concern from the Canadian standpoint was that without a single European standard of entry for investment, Article 58 of the Treaty of Rome, it remained under the jurisdiction of the individual member states, allowing for a wide variety of discrimination on foreign direct investment across the Community.

As discussed earlier, from the EC's point of view, since Canada accorded national treatment on investment to the U.S. under the CUFTA and with the improved North American investment regime under NAFTA, similar treatment was of interest to the EC and the member states, particularly without an OECD-wide obligation for Canada to extend the CUFTA threshold levels for foreign direct investment. In 1993, threshold levels were still higher for U.S. investors than they were for investors of other countries. This issue was an irritant for EC countries and arose in the context of the OECD Code of Liberalization of Capital Movements, since the preferential treatment accorded to the U.S. was inconsistent with the non-discrimination obligation of the Code. What this meant was that the NAFTA, through its substantial liberalization of investment and services, would benefit those EC interests that already had a substantial business presence in one of the NAFTA countries. The exceptions were automobiles and textiles, where more stringent rules of origin applied.[38]

The Canadian side was slow to move on EC concerns, because even if it had extended thresholds to OECD member countries this would not have resulted in any reciprocal treatment for Canadian firms. This is because, as mentioned, the EC had no formal policy on foreign direct investment. Brussels had not gained competence in this area from either the Treaty of Rome or subsequent Community law. Thus, it was the member states, not the European Commission acting for the

Community, that had had to individually adhere to FDI-related international obligations in multilateral forums, such as the OECD, or in bilateral arrangements, such as bilateral investment treaties.[39] In short, Canadian policy makers realized that they would receive nothing in return from the OECD member states. This was a major concern given that a number of larger member states, notably France and Germany, presented significant markets for Canada and had considerable and effective formal and informal barriers to inward foreign investment.[40]

THE CONTEXT OF CANADA-EU ECONOMIC RELATIONS

Having examined the trade and investment trends, it is important to understand the context of Canada's economic relationship with the EU. This includes Canada's relative place in the EU's external relations, the level of tariff barriers facing Canadian goods, and the key bilateral trade irritants. Additionally, it is important to examine the implications of EU enlargement for Canada.

For both historic and economic reasons, the EC maintained a multi-layer system of trade preferences vis-à-vis third countries on both a reciprocal and unilateral basis.[41] About 60 percent of EC imports originated from preferential sources, with the full Common Customs Tariff (CCT) applied only to Canada, the U.S., Japan, Australia, New Zealand, and South Africa. Preferences were granted in the context of free trade agreements, through a wide range of association and cooperation agreements[42] and the Community's Generalized System of Preferences (GSP) scheme.

The EU's external trade was conducted through a hierarchy of preferential trading agreements built around a network of about 50 bilateral agreements, introducing strong elements of discrimination into the multilateral trading system. Its most important preferential ties were with other states in Europe, usually described as the first and second concentric circles of influence.

The EFTA represented the first concentric circle of third countries and was the EU's largest single trading partner, accounting for more than one-fifth of trade outside the Community. The EEA, ratified by all the EFTA countries in 1993, promised to significantly expand the size and importance of the SEM. Canadian policy makers anticipated that the EEA would be but a short step before some EFTA states received full EU membership, which happened on January 1, 1995 with the accession of Austria, Finland, and Sweden. The second concentric ring represented the former COMECON states, most of which, after 1989, had signed individual association agreements with Brussels.

The impact of the emergence of a pan-European economic zone on Canada and other industrialized non-European middle-sized states (Australia, New Zealand) meant they were relegated further to the third, or outer, ring of the EU's external relations. Policy makers in Ottawa watched with some apprehension as the spillover from the SEM program to the first and second concentric circles promised to lead to a further increase in intra-European trade and thus to fewer opportunities for Canadian products to be price competitive.

In general, EU tariffs on Canadian exports were relatively low. For instance, from the mid-1980s onward, the simple average tariffs were 6.4 percent for industrial products and 12.4 percent for agricultural products, although it was less the tariffs that were a concern to third countries than the variable levies and quotas imposed on agricultural exports.[43] And with a range of raw materials, including wood pulp, hides and skin, unwrought copper, nickel matte, and tin, that were subject to very low or zero tariffs, Canada, with a large proportion of its export mix (wood pulp) in raw materials, was affected less by EC tariffs than, say, the United States or Japan.

However, this was not to say that tariff rates were not a concern for Ottawa. Since the Commission imposed low or zero tariffs on primary, unprocessed products and increased its tariffs as the degree of processing of a particular product increased, Canada faced particular barriers to upgrading its natural resource exports. For instance, a variety of other wood products, such as wood panels, faced a series of escalating tariffs the more these products were processed; semi-fabricated copper goods faced duties of 5 to 6 percent; aluminium, lead, and zinc in metal form faced tariffs of 3 to 6 percent; and steel faced both import quotas and tariffs.

The above description leads to two observations. First, the increasing depth and breadth of the EU's preferential trading arrangements with its European neighbours, including arrangements for freer trade in precisely those sectors (most prominently wood products) that mattered the most to Canada's transatlantic trade, ensured that even a one or two percent tariff rate on Canadian products would make them uncompetitive in relation to the same tariff-free products entering the Community from Nordic or East European suppliers. And second, in the absence of a Canada-EU free trade agreement, it is easy to see why Canadian trade officials were especially motivated to use the MTN to push for zero tariffs across a range of products, including steel, pharmaceuticals, and medical equipment, but particularly for forestry products, including paper and wood.[44]

When combining the bilateral trade and investment flows, there was no question that the Community remained Canada's second most important economic partner after the United States. Given the overall volume of economic ties, it is not surprising that a number of major trade conflicts arose over the years. For the most part, however, the EU and Canada were able to resolve their differences bilaterally through compromise. For a few seemingly intractable problems, both sides resorted to trade dispute settlement mechanisms within the GATT framework.

What were the major bilateral trade irritants? From the European perspective they included Canadian countervailing duties on certain EC beef exports, discriminating provincial liquor board practices, and the appropriation by Canadian winemakers of certain European geographical names. On the Canadian side, the major ones in rough chronological order were: the allegedly reduced access to the EU market for Canadian grains due to the EU's Common Agricultural Policy; the size of the Community's tariff-free quota for Canadian newsprint; the impact of plant-health issues on the export of untreated Canadian lumber; allegations of European overfishing just outside Canada's 200-mile economic zone on its east coast, and Ottawa's ban, starting in 1986, of EC vessels from Canadian ports;[45] and the Commission's threat to ban furs from animals caught in leg-hold traps.

To be sure, bilateral Canada-EU trade conflicts were overshadowed by the larger economic stakes in Canada-U.S. trade relations. Nevertheless, the nature of the former disputes should not be downplayed since they had very real domestic political and regional economic ramifications in Canada and tended to, as mentioned earlier, make bilateral relations appear irritant-driven to publics on both sides of the Atlantic.

The Canada-EU fisheries dispute, which came to a head in March and April 1995 and is described in greater detail in Chapter 10, perhaps best illustrates how the relationship was perceived by both sides. Although the fishing dispute had its origins in the early 1980s, it took another decade before the prospects of the eradication of certain fish stocks forced Ottawa to declare a moratorium on their harvesting and thus pushed Canada headlong into a conflict with the Europeans, who insisted that Canada was unreasonable and inflexible in its conservations policy and that several years of restructuring were needed before the Spanish and Portuguese fishing industries could adjust to lower quotas. The continued perception in Canada of the deleterious effects of European overfishing in violation of NAFO quotas, particularly by Spain and Portugal, ensured that there was considerable domestic political and economic pressure on Canadian politicians to confront Brussels. The dual economic and political pressure is easy to understand, since with the largest source of employment in Newfoundland and Nova Scotia now gone and 30,000 workers unemployed, Ottawa was forced to increase its transfer payments and to offer compensation to the Maritime provinces—the traditional "have-nots" of Canadian Confederation. Although it would have been possible to sustain such expenditures in previous decades, by the early 1990s with recessions and burgeoning provincial and federal debt, the European actions came to be seen as an attack on the very economic survival of Canada's Maritime provinces. The Europeans, on the other hand, considered themselves scapegoats for Canada's own mismanagement of its fish stocks.

Another important dispute was linked to a 1985 Canadian countervailing duty on European beef imports. Although the EC won a GATT ruling on a technical point, Canada rejected the ruling and the countervailing duty remained in place. The EC's phytosanitary requirements, such as the concern over the pinewood nematode (PWN), also posed a serious restriction (depending on exchange rates) on exports of forestry products, a $30 billion dollar export industry and Canada's second largest export earner after automobiles and auto parts.

What can be concluded from the range of bilateral irritants? First, the impact of the disputes was larger in certain regions than in others: in the case of forestry products, for example, Eastern Canada, in particular Quebec and New Brunswick, suffered more than British Columbia, which had alternative markets in the Pacific Rim.

Second, with regard to the resolution of disputes, there appeared no interest by either side to use the bilateral mechanism, the Framework Agreement, that ostensibly had been set up for this very purpose. Article II of the Agreement, for example, discourages restrictive trade practices by firms in either Canada or the EU and creates an obligation to resolve trade disputes by "cooperat[ing] at the international level and bilaterally in the solution of commercial problems of common interest, and us[ing] [the parties'] best endeavours to grant each other the widest facilities for commercial transactions in which one or the other has an interest." Furthermore, Article IV provides the rudiments of a dispute settlement mechanism. This article envisaged that the Joint Cooperation Committee (JCC) would meet at least once a year. The article stipulates that special meetings "shall be held at the request of either Party. Subcommittees shall be constituted where appropriate in order to assist the Committee in the performance of tasks." In fact, the history of the JCC showed that it met infrequently—not once between 1986 and 1989—and had become a "rubber-stamp for industrial cooperation and other bilateral activities in the area of environment and science and technology."[46] After analyzing the Agreement, Roseman criticized both Canada and the EC for the Framework Agreement's underutilization and went so far as to say that it was a "misused" resource.[47] He advocated the selection of a few low-level trade irritants for resolution within the JCC to increase its credibility in the eyes of Canadian and European officials as well as the respective business communities. The suggestion was not adopted and trade disputes continued to be dealt with through GATT mechanisms or through the separate semi-annual high-level consultations.

Third, as we examined in greater detail in the previous chapter, the "reregulation" of Europe fostered by the SEM in tandem with an increase in absolute terms of the volume of bilateral trade promised to cause more contested bilateral trade issues, not necessarily fewer. This would prove to be the necessary incentive to re-examine the conflict resolution methods available to both parties and the utility of other bilateral trade agreements. Finally, to put the impact of Canada-EU irritants on the bilateral trading relationship into perspective, it should be noted that while bilateral irritants affected approximately 10 percent of two-way trade, or $2.5 billion, in Canada's much larger trading relationship with the United States, they affected a smaller percentage—about 5 percent—but a larger value at $15 billion.[48]

CANADA'S ECONOMIC VULNERABILITY

What concluding observations can be distilled from this chapter's analysis of bilateral trade and investment flows? From Ottawa's perspective, and borrowing from David Baldwin's analysis of "sensitivity" and "vulnerability" interdependence, the transatlantic economic relationship displayed "asymmetrical vulnerability interdependence." It was "asymmetrical" because the cost of altering the relationship was much higher for Ottawa than it was for Brussels, since trade with Canada represented less than one percent of the EU's world trade and was the location of about 5 percent of the total foreign investment stock of the EU member states. Furthermore, the review of historical statistics showed that although there was an erosion in Canada's trading relationship with the Community from the mid-1980s on, there was also a significant increase in bilateral investment between 1986 and 1991 as private sectors on both sides of the Atlantic responded to regional economic integration. This surge in investment was, however, followed by a decline in subsequent annual bilateral FDI flows.

The erosion of bilateral trade ties, the post-1991 decrease in bilateral investment flows, the relegation of Canada to the third concentric circle, and the higher growth rates in Asia Pacific did not, however, displace the EU from its position as the second most important economic (comprising trade, investment, and portfolio investment) partner for Canada. Indeed, by 1996 the over $70 billion in bilateral investment stock ensured sufficient economic interdependence that neither side of the Atlantic could ignore the other over the short- to medium-terms, something that was evident in mutual concerns over prevailing investment regimes. In fact, there was a clear paradox in Canada's trade relations with the EU: the erosion in bilateral trade was offset by surges in bilateral investment, particularly in the EU's FDI to Canada. In 1988, for the first time, the value of Canada's investment stock in the EC ($11.8 billion) exceeded the value of total exports ($11.2 billion). European and Canadian business were now favouring investment rather than trade ties in transatlantic relations, whereas historically exports had preceded investment.

It would be conjecture to attribute this growth in bilateral investment solely to the emergence of regional trading blocs in North America and Europe, yet the fact remains that the emergence of these blocs in conjunction with, or as a response to, the structural transformation of the world economy contributed to *greater* not *lesser* economic ties between Canada and the Community. However, judging from the response of Canadian policy makers to the bilateral relationship until 1989 (during the decade of "benign neglect"), the consensus was that as a foreign economic policy interest, the EU was less of a priority than Asia Pacific or even Latin America. This (mis)perception, no doubt fed by memories of the Third Option, was also due to the fact that observers tended to focus on trade imbalances rather than on the overall context of the economic relationship. There was less of an appreciation of how much bilateral economic convergence there was due to increasing bilateral investment flows.

Another factor that was frequently overlooked was that even with only a minute share of the EU's world trade, Canada still received a disproportionate amount of the Community's attention, a fact that can be attributed to Ottawa's penchant for multilateralism and its ongoing contacts with Western Europe at a cross section of international forums.[49] One senior EAITC official termed this the "hidden leverage" that most observers of transatlantic relations, on both sides, grossly underestimated.[50] Of course, changes in regulations in either Europe or North America, whether on investment regulations, tariff-rates, or non-tariff barriers, often led to trade conflicts and always placed Canada in a more vulnerable negotiating position since it had more at stake in bilateral economic relations.

Nowhere was this vulnerability more apparent than in the catch-22 situation that Canada found itself in with diversifying its export base. Here Canada faced a double whammy. First, in response to the decreasing importance of raw materials in the postindustrial age, Canada sought to increase the value-added proportion of its export mix, but as it did so these goods were destined to be slapped with higher EU duties. Nonetheless, Canada appeared to have no choice but to upgrade its exports due to increasing competition, particularly in resource exports, from non-EU European countries. Canadian officials concluded that, based on current trends, there was a looming danger that Canada would eventually become only a residual supplier to the West European market. Second, as was discussed in the previous chapter, while Ottawa recognized that the Community's Single Market program would provide increased opportunities for precisely those types of non-resource-based industries (high-technology, services) that it felt would fuel Canada's future economic growth, at the same time it saw the potential for value-added Canadian products to face protectionism by another name since EC 1992 also represented a "reregulation" of the West European economy.

NOTES

1. See Canadian Manufacturers' Association, *The Aggressive Economy* (Toronto: Canadian Manufacturers' Association, 1992).
2. Morley Martin, "Exports and Job Creation," *Policy Planning Staff Paper*, No. 93/06 (Ottawa: External Affairs and International Trade, June 1993), 15.
3. International services are defined as transborder transactions with non-residents of Canada which cover travel, freight and shipping, business services, government transactions, and other services.

4. Jock Finlayson, "Directions for Canadian Trade Policy: A Private Sector View," *Canadian Foreign Policy* 1, 3 (Fall 1993): 114.
5. *Ibid.*, 115.
6. Alan S. Alexandroff, "The Global Economy and Canada: Meeting and Managing Change," 43. Draft Report (1994) prepared for the *Canada 21 Report*, made available to the author.
7. Finlayson, "Directions," 116.
8. *Ibid.*
9. For a review of the literature on this phenomenon see Lorraine Eden, "Bringing the Firm Back In: Multinationals in International Political Economy," in Lorraine Eden and Evan H. Potter, eds., *Multinationals in the Global Political Economy* (London: Macmillan, 1993), 46-48.
10. See discussion of the impact of investment on the global economy in Lorraine Eden, "Foreign Direct Investment in Canada: Charting a New Policy Direction," *Canadian Foreign Policy* 2, 3 (Winter 1994): 43-60.
11. Industry Canada, "Canadian-Based Multinationals," i.
12. See chapters by Raymond Vernon, Raphael Kaplinsky, and Sanjaya Lall, in Eden and Potter, *Multinationals.*
13. The observations on the impact of globalization on Canada is adapted from Finlayson, "Directions," 113-17. See also Canadian Manufacturers' Association, *Aggressive Economy*, 45-47.
14. Finlayson, "Directions," 115.
15. Presentation by Industry Canada to the Canadian Council for International Business, January 13, 1994, "Canada's Competitiveness Challenge," quoted in Alan S. Alexandroff, "Global Economic Change: Fashioning Our Own Way," in Maureen A. Molot and Harald von Riekhoff, eds., *Canada Among Nations, 1994: A Part of the Peace* (Ottawa: Carleton University Press, 1994), 39.
16. For a list of these government programs, see Andrew Griffith, "Straight Talk on Why Canada Needs to Reform its Trade Development System," *Canadian Foreign Policy* 1, 1 (Winter 1992/93): Appendix.
17. Interview, Jim Hyndman, former senior DFAIT official, June 6, 1994.
18. Under the Trudeau government's Foreign Investment Review Act (FIRA) the emphasis was on screening and restricting inward FDI. This caused considerable consternation among Canada's principal economic partners, especially the United States, who viewed this policy as highly discriminatory. In 1985, the Mulroney government replaced FIRA with Investment Canada. Mandatory reviews of all new investments were eliminated and Investment Canada emerged with a new mandate: to promote foreign direct investment. Between 1985 and 1993, Investment Canada had a double mandate: to screen FDI and to promote FDI, that is, to have an open-door policy for most inward

investments with a narrow screening window for sensitive areas such as biotechnology (Connaught Laboratories) and cultural industries (book publishing).

19. *Foreign Policy Framework, 1991: Managing Interdependence* (Ottawa: Policy Planning Staff, Department of External Affairs and International Trade, October 1991), 22.
20. In the end, while bilateral imbalances of themselves are not the sole indicator of the economic health of a relationship, they do point to underlying problems and important issues. Moreover, in the political world persistent imbalances translate into the perception of lost jobs for the domestic economy, although if a bilateral imbalance is offset by a surplus elsewhere there is no reason one imbalance should be considered good or bad.
21. See Rochlin, *Discovering the Americas*, 187 and Tables A.1 and A.2.
22. A good example of the preferences was the fact that, starting in 1986, Scandinavian wood products and newsprint began entering the EC at zero rates of duty, while Canada remained outside these preferences.
23. See Keith Christie, "The Day After: An Agenda for Diversifying Free Trade," *Policy Staff Paper*, no. 94/04 (Ottawa: Department of Foreign Affairs and International Trade, January 1994).
24. Statistics Canada, *Canada's International Trade in Services, 1991-92*, cat. no. 67-203 (Ottawa, 1992), 39.
25. Much of the detail on investment in this chapter is from a briefing note on Canada's investment in the European Community prepared by the European Community Division at External Affairs and International Trade Canada.
26. Industry Canada, "Canadian-Based Multinationals," i.
27. *Ibid.*, 8.
28. J. Cantwell, *Technological Innovation and Multinational Corporation* (Oxford: Basil Blackwell, 1989); J.H. Dunning, *Multinational Enterprise and Economic Analysis* (Cambridge: Cambridge University Press, 1982); and S. Globerman, "CDIA: The Private and Public Interest" (Vancouver: Simon Fraser University, 1993), monograph.
29. Industry Canada, "Canadian-Based Multinationals," 13.
30. *Ibid.*
31. This significant jump in investment since 1988 (from $11.9 billion) was, among other things, influenced by the Reichmann's Canary Wharf project in London. Within the EC, the U.K. was by far the largest recipient of CFDI. Between 1982 and 1992, the last year for which a breakdown is available, CFDI in the U.K. more than quadrupled, growing in size to $11.3 billion, with the most significant increase between 1988 and 1990, although there was significant divestiture between 1991 and 1992, with its share of total CFDI in the

Community decreasing from 59 percent in 1988 to 55 percent four years later.

32. Industry Canada, "Canadian-Based Multinationals," 13-15.
33. Interview with Jeoffrey Lowe, Bureau of Economic Analysis, U.S. Department of Commerce, January 28, 1992.
34. Jorge Niosi, "Foreign Direct Investment in Canada," in Eden, *Multinationals in North America*, 381.
35. Not only were the foreign activities of Canadian firms highly concentrated, with the top 20 firms in 1991 contributing about 80 percent of the total foreign assets and sales of all Canadian MNEs, but these same firms' activities were concentrated in the resources sectors. Industry Canada, "Canadian-Based Multinationals," 16-17.
36. From a Briefing Note provided to the author by an EAITC official at the Canadian High Commission in the U.K., July 1994.
37. European Commission, *1993 Report on U.S. Barriers to Trade and Investment* (Brussels: Commission of the European Communities, April 1993), 7.
38. Richard G. Lipsey, Daniel Schwanen, and Ronald J. Wonnacott, "Inside or Outside the NAFTA? The Consequences of Canada's Choice," *Commentary*, 48 (Toronto: C.D. Howe Institute, June 1993), 2.
39. Industry Canada, "Formal and Informal Investment Barriers," 279. This report notes, however, that the situation on the EC's lack of jurisdiction on investment is changing. For example, at international forums such as the OECD and the European Energy Charter negotiations, the Commission of the European Communities now speaks on behalf of member states, following consultations among the 12 members on a Community position.
40. For instance, unlike the relatively streamlined procedures for foreign investment in Canada, of all the EC member states, France (and to a lesser extent Italy) has the most obstacles running the gamut from nationality requirements for personnel, multiple authorization requirements for different federal authorities, to reciprocity requirements. Germany's investment regime is characterized by financial-commercial links that effectively block foreign takeovers. For the impediments to investment in the large member states, see *Ibid.*, iv, v, Chs. 1 (France), 2 (Germany), 3 (Italy), and 4 (United Kingdom).
41. For an excellent review of the Community's preferential trading areas, see Anna Michalska and Hellen Wallace, *The European Community: The Challenge of Enlargement* (London: Royal Institute of International Affairs, 1992). The major preferential agreements were with the Lomé countries and the ACP states.
42. While cooperation agreements only seek to establish a thorough economic cooperation, association agreements go much further in terms

of cooperation and financial assistance. Association agreements can be a preliminary step before integration (as in the case of Greece in 1962) or just aim to create a customs union. The EC had association agreements with most Central and East European states by 1993.

43. An example of variable levies restricting access was in the area of processed food products containing sugar, milk, or flour.
44. In tandem with their American colleagues, this was the strategy adopted by Canadian officials at the 1993 Quadrilateral meeting held in Tokyo.
45. The Canadian government argued that the Europeans, particularly the Spanish and Portugese, by not respecting NAFO quotas, overfished and dangerously depleted North Atlantic fish stocks at a time when Canada was reducing its own domestic quotas for preservation purposes. For a discussion of Canada-EC fishing relations, see, Gordon R. Munro, "Evolution of Canadian Fisheries Management Policy under the New Law of the Sea: International Dimensions," in Claire Cutler and Mark W. Zacher, eds., *Canadian Foreign Policy and International Economic Regimes* (Vancouver: British Columbia University Press, 1992), 306-08.
46. Roseman, "Canada-European Community Relations," 9.
47. *Ibid.*, 10.
48. The 5 percent figure quoted is from an interview with Canada's ambassador to the United States, Raymond Chrétien. "No Scapegoat," *Ottawa Sun*, July 31, 1994.
49. As a measure of Canada's importance and the EC's limited resources, the officer responsible for Canada in DG 1 is also responsible for Community relations with the United States and Australia. The fact that the Eurocrat responsible for Canadian affairs is also the point person for U.S. relations may partially explain why it may be easier, in light of time and resource constraints, to lump Canada in with the United States on a cross section of transatlantic issues.
50. Interview with Michel Duval, Director of the West European Relations (RWR) division, Department of External Affairs and International Trade, July 11, 1993.

VIII

FREE TRADE OR NOT?

FOLLOWING THE EUPHORIA at the end of the Cold War there was some puzzle as to what would replace the values-driven transatlantic agenda. By 1992-93, with the move to create a SEM in full swing, the economic track of transatlanticism became much more important than the security track. This effectively increased the importance and profile of the EU as a European institution in transatlantic affairs. At the same time, there was a growth of regional free trade agreements (Hemispheric free trade by 2005; Asia Pacific free trade by 2020). The notion of "open regionalism" as a step to increased multilateralism was gaining more and more adherents.

In the context of transatlantic relations, the problem, with the exception of a few industries, was no longer "at border" issues such as tariffs and quotas, but as described in previous chapters, a host of "new trade issues" such as competition, technical standards, labour market, and environmental policy as well as various regulatory regimes in investment and finance.[1] The multilateral system had not yet succeeded in resolving barriers to market access in these areas.

It was not surprising, then, that following the signing of the NAFTA in 1993, there was more energy from the North American side to devote to re-imagining the transatlantic economic relationship. But, following the TAD, this was to proceed in fits and starts throughout the 1991-97 period. The idea of a TAFTA was not raised formally by the Canadian government until late 1994, only to be rejected, and replaced over the next two years by U.S.-EU and Canada-EU Action Plans.

However, before examining the transformation of the TAFTA idea into two action plans it is important to place Canada's transatlanticism within the context of economic relations in the Triad. The first section of this chapter outlines the evolution of the EU's global influence. Since this study has already demonstrated Canada's vulnerability to problems in U.S.-EU relations, the second section, therefore, extends this vulnerability thesis to the growth of Japan's economic might and how Canada has been affected by problems in U.S.-Japan and EU-Japan relations. Canada's vulnerability is a function of three deep-seated structural features of transatlantic economic relations in the 1990s: the relative increase in the economic muscle of the EU and Japan at the expense of the United States; the inexorable loss of Canada's Atlanticist influence (discussed at greater length in Chapter 9); and continued growth in economic interdependence without commensurate progress in policy convergence between Canada and the Community. This raises questions about the respective roles of Canada and the EU in the world economy and how they have coped with the link between domestic structure and demands of ever more integrated economies. The third section examines the options Canadian decision makers contemplated as they sought to reconfigure the economic framework for Canada-EU relations. The final part of the chapter describes the debate over the TAFTA and the negotiations leading up to the action plans.

CHANGING HEGEMONS: THE EU IN A MULTIPOLAR WORLD

The EU's trade and investment relations with the outside world are characterized by two contradictory trends. On the one hand, there is an ever-closer economic interdependence which creates a high level of policy interdependence.[2] On the other, there appears to be a tendency toward increasingly fractious political relations associated with claims and counter-claims about the construction of regional trading blocs. The global trading system is radically different if we consider Europe as a single unit rather than the sum of its constituent parts. As it devotes more and more of its attention to a pan-European preferential trading area, there is a greater tendency for the EU to shape the international system rather than for it to be a passive taker.

The EU's claim to global power-player status was hotly debated in the 1970s, when the EC was considered a "civilian superpower."[3] It appeared legitimate finally with the 1992 program and the move toward monetary and political union. This status was now less controversial and a more empirically supportable assertion. Indeed, a fundamental change in the world economy was the growing weight of the EU. The EU's 1995 population of 375 million was more than 12 times larger than Canada's, almost 115 million larger than that of the United States, and more than 200 million larger than Japan's. Until the ratification of the NAFTA, the EU represented the largest trading area in the world, with a total GDP that exceeded US$8.5 trillion in 1996. Community competence, as pointed out in this study, had also been extended to more and more policies of relevance to international commerce, creating a magnet effect on neighbours.[4] If the GDPs of all the EFTA member states were added to the EU's GDP to create the European Economic Area, the GDP of this pan-European market easily exceeded that of the North American bloc.

Another indicator of the EU's economic stature was that, by 1996, exports originating in the EU accounted for 39 percent of total world exports (down by 2 percent from 1990), including exports to other EC member states, and almost 25 percent of Community GDP.[5] In contrast, Canada's exports made up less than 4 percent, while U.S. exports accounted for about 15 percent of total world exports. In terms of investment, by 1990, for the first time since the end of the 1970s, the EU had larger direct investment flows than the United States,[6] for example, accounting for 41 percent of U.S. FDI in that year.

But perhaps the most illuminating trend was not that the EU's world trade was surpassing that of the North American bloc or that it was taking significant amounts of North American investment, but rather the degree to which it was internalizing multilateralism, reflected in the fact that although its share of world exports increased by 5 percent from 36 percent in 1980 to 41 percent in 1990, much of this was due to intra-EC trade.[7] In fact, excluding intra-EC trade, the Community's 16 percent share of world exports had actually decreased slightly between 1985 and 1990, a trend attributed to the growing importance of the newly industrializing Pacific Rim economies.[8] Indeed, as this study has noted, the high level of intra-Community trade, almost 60 percent, likely explains the increasingly weak correspondence between Canada's trade links with Europe.[9]

The EU was becoming a powerful political organization as well. It includes two of the world's five nuclear powers and four G-7 members, in addition to have an observer role itself. Moreover, if the G-7 Summit is considered the premier post-Cold War international forum for the industrialized world, then it is significant to note the steady economic decline of the United States relative to the EC and Japan: for example, at the inception of the Summit in 1975 the United States by itself commanded 45.5 percent of the Group's economic power (as expressed in Gross National Product [GNP] in 1995 U.S. dollars); in 1993 it commanded 39.5 percent.[10]

The U.S.'s declining economic power relative to the EU has led observers of U.S.-EU relations such as Michael Smith to note the regression of North American images of the EC in the 1990s.[11] According to Smith, the key difference between North American reactions in the 1950s and reactions in the 1990s to transatlanticism was that in the 1990s the EU not only acted at least as the equal of the United States on the economic front, but began striving to act as its political equal as well.[12] The EU's role in aiding the political and economic revival of Eastern Europe after 1989 is proof of this. Furthermore, despite the Community's internal economic difficulties in the early 1990s (characterized by low annual growth rates and high unemployment), the steady way in which the Community progressed to enacting the 282 directives to create a fully integrated market as part of the 1992 program demonstrated that it had become more disciplined compared to the period in the 1970s when it had lost its momentum. In addition, the EU's move toward monetary union was very significant and sure to change the perceptions of its international partners, since the EU had never had a single voice in monetary and exchange-rate policy.

This decline in U.S. power also had implications for the manoeuverability of smaller states such as Canada. The changing status and role of the U.S. influenced Canada's perceptions of the Community. Thus, while the Community was largely irrelevant to Canadian policy makers in the early to mid-1980s, there was a cautious change in perception in the 1990s at the official level. It was certainly not a full return to the great expectations of Canada-EC relations in the 1970s, in large measure because Canada's economic relations were now oriented firmly to the United States and Asia Pacific.

CANADA AND THE TRIAD

Canada's major political and economic relations are formed within the Triad. The relations between its partners in the Triad have powerful ramifications for Canada in its policy approach to the EU. The focus in the following discussion will be on EU-Japan relations, since the EU-U.S. dimension is addressed throughout the present study.

It has been the mantra of Canadian government officials, based largely on the existence of the Framework Agreement, that Canada's relations with the Community have historically been more "special" and "privileged" than those of Japan or the United States. This view was not necessarily shared by the Commission, however. Willy de Clercq, the EU's former Commissioner for External Relations, once remarked that he was surprised that Canada-EC ministerial-level contacts were considerably less frequent than those between the EU and the U.S., and the EU and Japan. Nevertheless, most commentators on EU-U.S. and Japan-U.S. relations would agree that generally they have been conducted on an ad hoc basis, according to multilateral ground rules. Ottawa is actually not as privileged as it would like to believe, since most bilateral trade conflicts in its relations with the Community have been taken likewise to the GATT and now the WTO.

As described, EU-U.S. relations have historically been characterized by periods of intense bickering over specific trade irritants and misunderstanding as Washington preferred to deal bilaterally with the member states or exercise its power in Europe through its leadership in NATO. El-Agra observes that relations with Japan also tended to be cool if not outright hostile.[13] Starting around 1989, however, there was a general rapprochement in both EU-U.S. and EU-Japan relations as both Washington and Tokyo adopted a more positive outlook on the Community's post-Cold War role both in Europe and globally.

Conceptually, Canada can be seen as an appendage in an EU-U.S.-Japan trade triangle although, as Nanto points out, this triangle really does not exist. Instead, there is a dynamic of three separate bilateral relationships, "each varying in intensity and balance," with the EC-U.S. link historically the strongest and deepest, followed by the Japan-U.S. link, and the Japan-EC nexus the weakest.[14] Canada, therefore, had the option of using its leverage through its special relationship with Washington to improve its access to the European market and European decision makers. However, given the much weaker Japan-EU axis, prior to 1990 Ottawa saw little benefit in indirectly pressing its interests to the Community via Tokyo. The Tokyo-Brussels route gained more legitimacy in Canadian eyes in the 1980s once Japan was pushed away from increasing exports to the United States and pulled to larger markets in Europe. At the same time, Europe was looking to the higher growth rates of Asia Pacific.

By the early 1990s, with the duels over Japanese "screwdriver" plants no longer aggravating Japan-EU relations and with Brussels for the most part viewing Tokyo as a more responsible actor in the international trade system,[15] Ottawa found itself increasingly using its diplomatic goodwill with Tokyo[16] to move the Community on specific bilateral issues. At the same time, Ottawa also sought to benefit from the EC's efforts to reduce market access barriers in Japan that were, in Brussels' eyes, the cause for its substantial trade deficit. Of course, there was also the danger that this liberalization would be skewed to the EC's advantage and therefore to Canada's disadvantage. For this reason, Ottawa saw particular benefit to teaming up with the EC in pressing for a multilateral trade negotiations track in Asia-Pacific, thereby liberalizing Japan's market.

It is somewhat ironic that Canada, which had begun in the 1980s to disavow its "Europeanness" in favour of its "North Americanness," was in the early 1990s using its European connections to secure its interests in Asia Pacific. This is not surprising, however, since Canadian policy makers by the late 1980s viewed Asia-Pacific, especially China,[17] as vital, both economically and politically, to Canada's international standing into the next century.[18] The Asia Pacific region, with a population of almost two billion, an aggregate gross national income twice that of the European Community and growing rapidly, and containing four of Canada's ten largest export markets (Japan, China, South Korea, Hong Kong) representing just under 7 percent of Canada's world exports compared to the EC's 6 percent share, had by the end of 1993 become a region hard for Canadians to ignore.

How much of a "free rider" was Canada in these evolving bilateral relations within the Triad? On the one hand, the apparent rapprochement in bilateral EU-U.S. and EU-Japan relations boded well for Canada. It allowed Ottawa to reinforce its bilateral negotiations with Brussels by selectively using its influence in Washington and Tokyo, where Ottawa/Washington and Ottawa/Tokyo concerns overlapped vis-à-vis the Community. At the same time, Canada could use a selective alliance with the Community to further its separate interests in Washington and Tokyo. On the other hand, Canada could no longer claim with any legitimacy that it was the only industrialized third country with a privileged relationship with the Community, thus creating the potential that its interests would be marginalized as the EU's relations became more institutionalized with Japan and the United States.

Thus, the extent to which bilateral relations within the Triad became less or more conflictual had very real implications for a small open economy caught between the larger members of the Triad. It seemed likely that with their growing economic power, largely at the expense of the United States, the EU and Japan would increasingly lock horns with the U.S. as the other shaper in the international system, leaving Canada in the vulnerable position of being sideswiped as the three giants grappled.

NEW FRAMEWORKS FOR CANADA-EU ECONOMIC RELATIONS[19]

Canada's limited room to manoeuver in this three-way configuration of economic power made any meaningful initiative to improve Canada-EU relations both more difficult and more necessary. The next challenge for Canadian policy makers tasked with rethinking Canada's European policy framework in 1993 was a revisitation of the transatlantic options articulated by Derek Burney and his officials at the Washington embassy. The options were seen in the following way:

- an improved EU-Canada Framework Agreement
- a traditional EU-EFTA-style link/an EEA-type link
- Canada-EU Free Trade Agreement
- a Transatlantic Free Trade Agreement
- bilateral sectoral and issue agreements.

There was a consensus that the first choice, namely, the status quo, was no longer appropriate for managing transatlantic relations. The Framework Agreement had had a very limited impact on trade and investment flows and it was thought unlikely that restructuring it would make any significant difference to bilateral economic relations.[20] And given the asymmetry in economic relations, it was felt that the Europeans would have no interest in a bilateral free trade agreement with Canada.

For Canada and the United States, the GATT was the primary mechanism that governed the terms of access to the EU and Canadian and American markets, provided dispute settlement procedures, and served as a forum for Canada and the United States in the multilateral trade negotiations. The GATT, however, applied to trade in industrial products only. It had also not prevented the erection of preferential barriers to North American goods by virtue of the EU's network of bilateral trade agreements with non-member European countries, former colonies, and other dialogue partners.

Virtually every nation that had entered into a cooperation agreement with the Community had found it insufficient for the overall management of its relationship with the EU. Many of these countries had seen their cooperation agreements as temporary second-best solutions, or steps to achieving full member status. This was the point of the EU's bilateral agreements with the EFTA member states and the thinking behind the European Economic Area, a free trade agreement between the EC and the EFTA that was completed in 1994.

It was recognized that if Canada and the United States had tried to emulate a traditional EFTA-style link this would have been restricted to free trade in industrial goods, through the abolition of tariffs and quotas. It would not have included trade policy issues including procurement, subsidies, and trade in services—precisely those issue areas that would greatly affect Canada's value-added exports. Additionally, in the financial services area, the lack of mutual recognition on rules governing trade in bank supervision and trade in securities had been a major obstacle to bilateral trade in the EFTA-EU case.

However, a major question arose as to whether the expanded harmonization of trade policies envisaged by the EEA could be extended to North America, since this would undermine the preferential nature of the EU's agreements with EFTA not to mention the preferential rights of the NAFTA signatories.

The inadequacies of the other arrangements led to renewed speculation on the usefulness of a free trade agreement with the Community. Indeed, it was anticipated that a new Third Option for Canada's relations with Europe of the 1990s could be an Atlantic free trade association that would embrace Canada, the United States, Mexico, the EU, and potentially the EFTA countries.[21] In its most broad conception, it was thought that it could also be extended to an OECD member such as Japan. Its objective would be, under the overall umbrella of the TAD, to act as the new economic architecture for North American interests in Europe, and to protect European interests against the risk of a protectionist bloc in North America.

It was argued that a North American-EU free trade scenario could be modeled on the CUFTA or it could go beyond an EEA-style agreement. It would include the elimination of tariff and non-tariff barriers to trade and services, including those arising from product standards, restrictive rules of origin, and government procurement restrictions. In addition, agriculture was a consideration, but this was a very sensitive area for all parties. This scenario would expand conditions for investment and services liberalization through national treatment, building either on the Uruguay Round's General Agreement on Trade in Services, the CUFTA, and the OECD's NTI. It would also facilitate conditions for fair competition within the free trade area and establish effective procedures for the joint administration of the agreement and the resolution of disputes modeled on the CUFTA and NAFTA, including binding dispute settlement in trade remedy cases. Finally, it would lay the foundations for further bilateral and multilateral cooperation to expand and enhance the benefits of the agreement.[22] A permanent secretariat would be charged with institutional management and servicing the dispute settlement mechanism.

Such an agreement would give Ottawa a level of influence not available to it through current arrangements or indeed a separate bilateral agreement. It would finally give North America a seat at the European table. Of course, in weaving itself and the United States into the European preferential trading system, it was recognized that Canada would still be faced with the perennial dilemma that the EU and the United States would dominate such an arrangement and Canadian interests in EU eyes would not be seen as distinct from U.S. interests.

During a fact-finding trip to Europe in the summer of 1992, a Canadian parliamentary subcommittee had raised just this possibility with their European contacts. The interest was not just confined to Canada. Certain quarters of the U.S. academic and think-tank community were voicing similar opinions. Allowing that a confrontational approach to the EU was not in U.S. interests, a detailed call for joint action was issued by the Carnegie Study Group on U.S.-EU Relations in July 1993. That report, *Atlantic Frontiers*, called for building a single market, based on broader and improved contacts over a range of new areas, including better coordinated microeconomic, environmental, and monetary policies. The aim of the report was to expand and deepen the constituencies that support Atlantic ties.[23] The European response was "yes, but please not now."[24] At the time, the EU was preoccupied with a host of internal matters such as the implementation of the Single Market, ratification of Maastricht, the question of enlargement, and the Uruguay Round negotiations.

There were other significant reasons why there was little possibility of a GATT-consistent, free trade agreement with the EU. Countries with much closer ties with the EU member states had had to settle for partial coverage, with preferential access but not barrier free. The EFTA countries came the closest under the EEA, but the EU had been careful to reserve substantial discretionary powers in managing these relationships. Moreover, as mentioned, in Brussels' eyes, countries such as Canada, the United States, and Mexico, were likely always to rank in an outer, or "third concentric ring," behind the EFTA nations and the Central European nations. On specific trade policy issues such as government procurement, resources, and liquor boards, where subnational governments are involved, it would be particularly difficult to guarantee the EU reciprocity without also admitting the Canadian provinces and the U.S. and Mexican states to the negotiating table. This was in addition to administering two free trade agreements with differing provisions on rules of origin, dispute settlement, procedures, and contingency measures.

In comparison to the SEM, the CUFTA, it was pointed out, was a modest initiative: it had abolished tariffs between Canada and the United States over a 10-year period, something the EU had abolished 20 years previously. There was thus the question of the lessons of European economic integration for North American integration: the EU's single banking licence versus the fact that all financial institutions in the United States and Canada had to comply with host country regulations; the principle of mutual recognition on standards and norms between member states and pan-European standards in matters of health, safety, and the environment versus the fact that mutual recognition of standards is not a formal part of CUFTA; competition in the realm of public procurement and the transparency of tendering procedures versus the fact that the CUFTA did not cover provincial, state, and local governments and thus opened up only a small segment of the U.S. and Canadian procurement markets; and finally, a successful monetary union, slated for the end of the decade, meant a single European currency and central European bank. Nothing of this nature was being contemplated at the time by Canada, the United States, and Mexico.[25]

It was this lack of parity in respective levels of integration that did not bode well for European interest in a comprehensive transatlantic agreement, not to mention that European integration had gone beyond the economic arena to encompass social policies, including joint legislation on such fundamental issues as environmental laws and human rights. The side agreements on environment and labour between Mexico and the United States under the NAFTA were a step closer to broadening the integration process and thus the competitiveness of North America, as were steps to removing Canada's deleterious interprovincial trade barriers. But the progress of North American integration was still far behind that of Europe.

After a review of the options, officials in Ottawa came to the conclusion that the vital question was: How much were the smaller Canadian and Mexican markets worth to the EU? It was an uncontestable fact that with the trend of increasing intra-EU trade, the Canadian market was steadily losing its significance. Niche markets, where Canada had a comparative advantage, and where the EU would still look to Canada, were primarily in the telecommunications and power-transmission sectors.

There was also the problem of how Canada could ensure equal terms of access for its still resource-heavy export mix to the Community. The non-tariff barriers of phytosanitary controls and environmental limitations were and would continue to be significant hurdles for Canadian suppliers.[26] As the case of the pinewood nematode showed, the EU had given little ground on Canada's access concerns in these areas.

In the absence of a viable free trade option it was the considered opinion of trade policy specialists that, in addition to the GATT, a network of bilateral sectoral and issue agreements would likely be the foundation of Canada-EU economic relations in the future. This is precisely what happened.

- In 1993, the European Council gave the Commission the mandate to start negotiating a Science and Technology agreement with Canada. The Standards Council of Canada and the European Organization for Testing and Certification (EOTC) began working on a Mutual Recognition Agreement (MRA) for products in non-regulated sectors; for regulated products, the Commission gave Canada notice that it was ready to negotiate.[27] An MRA on national testing and certification procedures would enable Canadian laboratories to certify the Euro-worthiness of Canadian exports across a number of specific categories of products and would level the playing field for Canadian business in these categories. The EOTC would also be able to test and certify conformity to Canadian standards.
- A 1992 Canada-EU fisheries agreement was awaiting ratification.
- And in March 1993, Canada signed on as a partner of BC-Net, to which Mexico had previously been given access. This was the Community's partnering network that allowed small- and medium-sized Community firms to source strategic partnerships.

- National treatment of investment was of particular interest for the Canadian side as a way for smaller Canadian firms to form alliances in Europe.

With the advent of sectoral agreements, the idea of a TAFTA appeared finally to be dead, or was it?

THE RE-EMERGENCE OF THE TAFTA IDEA

International Trade Minister Roy MacLaren, in a September 1994 address to the Canada-U.K. Colloquium and in a subsequent speech to the European Community Chambers of Commerce in Canada, asked rhetorically: if we can contemplate free trade with Latin America and with Asia Pacific, why not negotiate a free trade agreement with our traditional trading partners in Europe? Liberal Prime Minister Jean Chrétien floated the idea of a NAFTA-EU partnership in a November 1994 speech to the French Senate.[28] In other speeches MacLaren further developed the idea of a transatlantic free trade area, calling for "removal of industrial tariffs by a specified date," and for agreements in competition and investment.[29] MacLaren was subsequently credited with launching a transatlantic dialogue between North America and Europe.

Thus after having lain dormant for two years, the idea of a Transatlantic Free Trade Agreement, successor in fact to Lester Pearson's idea of an Atlantic Community, was once more on the transatlantic agenda. The idea was favourably received by two of Canada's staunchest European partners, the United Kingdom and Germany, as well as by Italy, Sweden, and the Netherlands. Roy MacLaren had the full support of Klaus Kinkel, the German Foreign Minister, and Malcolm Rifkind the then British Foreign Minister, to develop the concept of a free trade agreement between Canada, the United States, and the European Union. However, there was not much appetite for this idea in the United States and France.

It is worth noting that a new transatlantic dialogue had not been anticipated by the new Liberal government that came to power in October 1993. Nowhere in the *Liberal Foreign Policy Handbook*,[30] the Liberal Party Red Book,[31] or even the November 1994 parliamentary review of Canada's foreign policy, *Canadian Foreign Policy: Principles and Priorities for the Future* (hereafter, FPR),[32] is there mention of transatlantic free trade. The review was distinctly inconclusive on the future of the EU. On the one hand, it noted that the EU was the "dynamic core" of Europe and with expansion to Eastern and Central Europe it has the "potential" to play a major world role. On the other, it also stated that the "idea" of Europe had not yet achieved practical expression as its members were still preoccupied with building their own institutions and with the task of broadening and deepening the Union. For this reason, concluded the FPR, the EU was not yet able to shape the international trading system that its size, wealth, culture, and traditions would indicate.[33] Trade Minister MacLaren's references to the EU in his speeches from November 1993 to September 1994 largely echoed the FPR's ambivalence, and provided no hint of his subsequent conversion.[34]

What were the new centripetal forces putting TAFTA on the political agenda? As mentioned, there was a belief that regional agreements could be used to build up to multilateralism. As well, Canada's values and its approach to trade policy issues were closer to those of Europe than to the United States, creating a greater affinity in the Ottawa-Brussels axis and making it easier for Ottawa to rebroach the idea of a free trade zone with the Europeans.

These centripetal forces were more than offset by countervailing forces, however. The United States, for its part, has a historical legacy of being leery of multilateral entanglements. Only a few years before the Americans had rejected the German call for a transatlantic treaty. A transatlantic declaration was settled for instead. The Clinton administration, although much more willing to negotiate with the Commission than the Bush administration, was faced with a Republican-dominated Congress for whom such a treaty was a non-starter. Federal regulatory agencies such as the FDA, OSHA, EPA, and others were said to have balked at the prospect of giving up their independence as a result of closer transatlantic regulatory cooperation. So unpopular was the idea in American government circles that soon the term "free trade" was no longer being used in connections with the transatlantic dialogue. Instead, the EU and the United States agreed to carry out a study on the "New Transatlantic Marketplace."

The Europeans were of two minds on TAFTA. Given the other regional free trade agreements that were being signed, the lack of a transatlantic agreement was conspicuous by its absence. European leaders realized that their countries had much greater cultural, political, and economic affinities with North America than they had with Asia or Latin America. Certainly, the prospect of being shut out of an Asia Pacific free trade zone forced some to rethink their ambivalence to transatlantic free trade. That being said, the European Commission, focused as it was on stabilizing its Eastern neighbours and preparing for monetary union, had little energy to embark on a new set of comprehensive negotiations.

Although the French had been keen on extending the EU internationally to balance American influence, it would have been politically difficult to advance the idea of a TAFTA with Paris at bay on culture and threatened by the liberalization of agriculture, over which the GATT had nearly broken down. The question of agricultural reform—the CAP—was a major sticking point and would have had to be dealt with internally (before 1999) in advance of any serious discussion of creating a free trade zone.

In Canada, the push for TAFTA came almost exclusively from Minister MacLaren's office. No great enthusiasm was evinced by the business community, for many of the same reasons that the SEM did not elicit great interest, or, for that matter, the senior echelons of Ottawa's trade bureaucracy. This was because it was recognized that the North American side of TAFTA would be dominated by U.S. interests. As trends in world economic relations showed, Canada could not have the same political will as the United States to strengthen economic relations with the EU because the EU as an economic partner was going to be much more important to the United States than it was to Canada in the coming years.

The supporters of TAFTA went to great lengths to position it as a step closer to greater multilateral liberalization and not a new protectionist zone. But it was hard to justify opening a third front of trade negotiations when greater transatlantic cooperation in specifically targetted areas could be achieved within the existing multilateral machinery (e.g., World Trade Organization [WTO]).

The Europeans have always looked to Washington first before settling on any major transatlantic institutional arrangements. With Washington still showing no willingness to pursue a free trade track, the idea of TAFTA was politely shelved. But, as in the case of the TAD, something had to be found to replace the idea of a treaty. Since the TAD had been largely symbolic, a new transatlantic protocol, or action plan, was developed to project a sense of movement and progress in transatlantic relations. Canada's ultimately unsuccessful attempt to trilateralize this action plan with the Americans and Europeans and the emergence of two action plans exhibits striking similarities to the negotiations leading up to the parallel TADs.

U.S.-EU Action Plan

In the spring of 1995, following an approach by Spain, the United States agreed to negotiate a new U.S.-EU partnership. What would explain the U.S.'s desire to negotiate bilaterally on transatlantic issues? Unlike Canada, the United States still had a major share of its trade in Europe; more than half of foreign direct investment in the U.S. was European. This enormous mutual interdependence explains the preference for bilateral negotiations. By adopting a building-block or sector-by-sector approach to their transatlantic relations the EU and the United States were setting the stage for both freer trade and greater cooperation in the multilateral arena. Indeed, the conclusion to the multilateral negotiations on telecommunications and information technology demonstrated that when the EU and United States pulled together they constituted a powerful agenda-setting bloc. The Clinton administration was also aware of the EU's penchant for negotiating separate sectoral deals with countries in Asia and Latin America, an ability that forced the United States to take the EU more seriously as a negotiator.

When the discussions began between the U.S. and EU on the possibility of a joint action plan, the Canadian government pressed for a trilateralization of the negotiations to obviate the danger of two parallel trade agreements. Canadian officials had warned that with its greater economic and political weight, the United States would negotiate better access to the EU than Canada and would also become a more attractive location for European investment. Ottawa knew it could count on the U.K.'s and Germany's support in its attempts at trilateralize transatlantic negotiations. Nevertheless, Ottawa did not get a seat at the table with its two larger Atlantic partners for many of the same reasons that it failed to trilateralize the TAD. The Clinton administration feared that concessions would have to be made to Mexicans. Additionally, as U.S.-EU relations had become more institutionally dense, there was a strong impulse in Washington and Brussels to draw up a very comprehensive set of measures to add a new dimension to a relationship that was dominated by security and bilateral trade irritants. The Clinton administration was willing to go even further than the Bush administration in engaging the Commission bilaterally on these matters. Finally, from a practical sense, the existence of additional parties to a negotiation, with potentially different core interests, meant that negotiations would inevitably be slowed down—something that did not appeal to Washington and meant that it did not want to share the action plan.

Canada's seizure in March 1995 of the Spanish fishing vessel, *Estai*, in international waters ensured that no exception would be made to this non-trilateralization rule. The effect of Spain assuming the presidency of the Council of the European Union on July 1, 1995, and thus acquiring control of the EU agenda for the next six months, was that Canada-EU relations soured for more than a year.

On December 3, 1995, the Joint U.S.-EU Action Plan was unveiled with four shared goals: promoting peace and stability, democracy and development around the world; responding to global challenges; contributing to the expansion of world trade and closer economic relations; and building bridges across the Atlantic (the transatlantic business dialogue and cooperation in science and technology).

Canada-EU Action Plan

In the absence of trilateralizaton, the Canadian government began to proceed along a track parallel to the U.S.-EU negotiations. In October 1995, Germany proposed a Canada-Germany Working Group on Canada-EU relations whose final report was presented by Canada to the European Commission and the Italian presidency in January 1996. The document was part of a larger strategy to inject Canada directly into the debate on the renewal and revitalization of relations between the EU and North America from which it had been excluded. This formed the basis of the Canadian government's negotiations with the EU on an action plan, and covered three main areas: economic and trade policy; foreign and security policy; and justice and home affairs or "new global challenges" (migration, combatting sex tourism, coordination of developing the information highway). It was thought that by solidifying its relations with Germany on this initiative at an early date, Canada would make progress toward the long-term objective of a TAFTA.

The action plan negotiations were an attempt to achieve a bilateral agreement to fill the gaps in the multilateral framework. There was no significant difference between the German-Canadian document and the final EU-Canadian Action Plan except for the addition in the latter document of cooperation on the sustainable development of the Arctic. The focus of the Canadian document, more so than the American one, was again economic: the conclusion of the aforementioned series of bilateral sectoral agreements that were under negotiation; an early-warning system to prevent trade and investment disputes; the reduction of non-tariff barriers by harmonization and a completion of WTO negotiations on procurement; the completion of negotiations on telecommunications and cooperation in other service sectors; and a more active Transatlantic Business Dialogue.[35] However, it was on the business dialogue track of the U.S.-EU Action Plan that the United States was far ahead of Canada. Indeed, this Business Dialogue, spear-headed by U.S. and European firms, would be responsible for finally achieving an agreement on standards and certification in June 1997.

Canadian negotiators saw an opportunity in their action plan to target non-tariff barriers such as product standards, testing and certification procedures, which had been a persistent concern for Canadian exporters. For example, with North American certification and testing for telecommunications equipment at the time of the negotiations not acceptable in Europe, Canadian-made telecommunications equipment had to be retested and recertified for use in Europe, meaning that firms such as Newbridge Networks would have incurred an additional cost of $30 million to certify all its products in Europe.[36]

Although Canadian policy makers were interested in focusing on the new trade policy agenda in transatlantic relations, this did not mean that the old trade policy agenda was absent. The EU still levied significant duties on products such as aluminum, copper and nonferous metals, chemicals, telecommunications equipment, fish and consumer packaged fish products, agricultural products, and wood products. Duties on these goods ranged from 3 to 20 percent, but up to 25 percent for certain fish products.[37] As noted, although many of Canada's leading exports already entered the EU duty free or were subject to quite low tariffs (3.6 percent on a trade-weighted basis post-Uruguay Round), some EU tariffs remained sufficiently high in certain sectors to restrict important Canadian exports. To cite just two examples, although the EU is one of the world's most promising aluminum markets, the EU tariff of 6 percent on aluminum ingot was an effective barrier to Canadian aluminum exports. Canadian leading technology companies such as Newbridge Networks found that the EU tariff facing the company's telecommunications equipment exports had been *revised upward* from 4.5 to 7.5 percent. These types of cases increased the incentive for Canadian negotiators to use the action plan to prompt greater tariff reductions in the context of multilateral negotiations.[38]

However, any commitment to undertake another round of tariff reductions under the WTO was absent from both the Canadian action plan proposal and the Commission document. In contrast, the U.S.-EU Action Plan commits the United States and the EU to explore the possibility of negotiating a package of tariff cuts on industrial products and to consider accelerating tariff reductions already agreed to under the Uruguay Round.

Negotiations Reach an Impasse

On March 18, 1996, Sir Leon Brittan met in Ottawa with Prime Minister Jean Chrétien and his ministers of Foreign Affairs and of International Trade to launch the negotiations on the action plan between Canada and the European Union. The Commission proposals were approved by the Council of the European Union on March 25, 1996. However, negotiations between Canada and the EU could not be concluded in time for an approved ceremony in Rome on June 26, 1996 between Chrétien, European Commission President Jacques Santer, and Italian Romano Prodi.

Just days before Prime Minister Chrétien left for Rome, the negotiations on the Canada-EU Action Plan were suspended. The Spanish had managed to derail the negotiations by raising objections to Canada's fisheries policies. The disagreement arose over language in the proposed action plan calling for cooperation to combat the extraterritorial application of national laws. This section of the plan was intended to promote Canada-EU cooperation in the fight against the U.S. Helms-Burton (HB) legislation, which both Brussels and Ottawa strongly condemned for its extra-territorial provisions (see discussion in Chapter 10).

The Europeans argued that it was inconsistent for Canada to oppose the principle of extraterritoriality in HB legislation while at the same time applying Canadian fisheries law in the North Atlantic outside the internationally recognized 200-mile limit of national jurisdiction. As noted in a 1996 Canadian Senate report, two possible options would have satisfied EU objections to Canada's fisheries law. Canada could have rescinded Bill C-29, which amended the Coastal Fisheries Protection Act to enable the Canadian government to enforce the protection of straddling fish stocks outside the 200-mile limit or it could have offered to modify Bill C-29 to exempt EU fishing vessels from the application of the law.

The negotiations over the Action Plan came to an impasse as Canada was not prepared to accept either option. Therefore, the successful completion of the Action Plan then hinged on whether Canada and the EU could resolve the outstanding bilateral fisheries issues.

Needless to say, what turned out to be Canada's parallel Action Plan was stalled by the Spanish. The majority of member states felt it was necessary to have language in the plan to deal with extraterritorial law. The Canadian side at first balked at this. But in May 1996 Ottawa included cooperation on extraterritorial matters under the heading of legal cooperation. There was some confusion when it turned out that the Canadians were referring to HB and the EU was referring to the fisheries, at which point Ottawa wanted to withdraw reference to legal cooperation. Spain, for its part, insisted that this section of the text be read as referring to the fisheries. By September and October 1996 this deadlock was confirmed. In December at the OECD meeting in Lisbon, Foreign Minister Lloyd Axworthy talked to his Spanish counterpart. Ottawa-Madrid then hastily convened talks during the Dublin Summit. On December 17 the Joint Action Plan was unveiled.

For Canada, the Joint Action Plan was one more institutional layer beyond the Framework Agreement and the Transatlantic Declaration. The Canada-EU Action Plan represents the latest hierarchical level in Canada's institutional links with the EU and differs from its U.S. counterpart because it emphasizes the higher education and science and technology agreements. In 1995, Canada was the first non-European country to sign an S&T agreement with the EU; by the end of 1997 the education project between Canada and EU had approved 13 projects, and a technical standards MRA had finally been signed. But the question remains, was this really an action plan, or, like the TAD before it, was it another Canadian "me-too" document that conveniently papered over the failure of Ottawa to get its Atlantic allies to seriously consider a new transatlantic treaty? It could be argued that it created the necessary political will to force the conclusion of a number of outstanding bilateral sectoral negotiations. But it did not set Canada-EU relations on a new footing nor would the mere use of the word "action" in the title necessarily translate into more energy on the policy front being directed to Canada from Brussels. For Ottawa it was an important agenda-setting document that officials in the foreign ministry hoped to transform into concrete programs, especially by linking the Plan's "global challenges" section, including references to increased cooperation in information technology, justice and home affairs, and combatting sex tourism, into the third pillar of the Maastricht Treaty (see discussion in next chapter).

Thus far in this study we have examined and appraised the Canada-EU relationship from a Canadian perspective in a number of fashions: historically, by outlining Canada's approach to West European integration from the immediate aftermath of the Second World War to the formation of the Common Market; by charting the vicissitudes of the Trudeau and Mulroney governments' differing approaches to the EU, from the STAFEUR Report, through the 1976 Framework Agreement and to the negotiations leading to the TAD; and by looking at the state of bilateral economic relations as well as the impact of the SEM during the first term of the Chrétien government.

This chapter, by looking at the likelihood for new economic arrangements in Canada-EU relations, has emphasized how the politics of structural change, and the recognition of fundamental shifts by policy makers, are clearly at the root of many transatlantic policy difficulties. Although the policy agendas of both Canada and the EU had begun to diverge significantly after 1985, the radical transformation only began after 1989. The collapse of the Soviet Union, the move toward economic, political, and monetary union in the Community and its implications for the rest of Europe, the completion of the CUFTA and the NAFTA in North America combined with the completion of Uruguay Round and the start of the WTO, all meant that policy makers on both sides of the Atlantic were confronted with a radically transformed set of choices and issues.

In the end, what are we to conclude from the above cost-benefit analysis of transatlantic economic arrangements and the choices facing Canadian decision makers and their European counterparts? With both sides of the Atlantic experiencing budgetary deficits, it made sense to increase cooperation on a host of areas, whether in the economic, development, or security domains (see next chapter). Indeed, the underlying theme of the new transatlanticism of the next century will be coordination and cooperation. Part of this process is the movement toward freer trade, although, as we have seen, not to the creation of a comprehensive free trade zone. For a host of reasons, including the desire not to damage multilateralist approaches to solving the problems of the new trade policy agenda, TAFTA was set aside. Instead, with a view to targetting the remaining market access barriers, a sectoral approach was adopted to transatlantic trade negotiations, in medical devices, pharmaceuticals, and telecommunications. It was envisaged that these negotiations would become the building blocks for a new transatlantic market place.[39]

The two major lessons to be drawn from this chapter's discussion is the importance of political will and the power of even one member state to affect Canada's ability to negotiate with the EU. The key prerequisite for any new transatlantic Canada-EU or Atlantic Community mechanism is a strong political commitment of time and resources to fostering this relationship. A first step in this direction was the TAD which was then supplanted by the Action Plan. That being said, given the asymmetrical economic relations between Canada and the EU, and the fact that the EU was preoccupied with its own internal interests, the most important variable was how interested the Europeans were in such an initiative, and whether it would come in the short, medium, or long term. At the time, however, there was no political will in Europe and Canada had to content itself with the small victories of gaining bilateral sectoral or issue-specific agreements.

The suspension of the negotiations for the Action Plan illustrates vividly the problems for Canada in dealing with the European Union. That is, its relations with the EU can easily be held hostage to a dispute over a single issue involving primarily the interests of one member state. In such cases, a problem with one member country automatically translates into a problem with the entire Union.

NOTES

1. "Perspective on Transatlantic Relations," a background report initiated by the Forward Studies Unit of the European Commission (November 1995), 19.
2. Woolcock, *Market Access Issues*, 7.
3. See discussion by P. Tsoukalanis, "The Defence of the European Community," in Juliet Lodge, ed., *Politics of European Integration* (London: Pinter, 1989), 320-360.
4. Smith and Woolcock, *The U.S. and the EC*, 36.
5. Royal Bank of Canada, "Is Canada Ready?," 8; and for the figure on total world exports see, Smith and Woolcock, *The U.S. and the EC*, 35.
6. *Ibid.*, 9.
7. *Ibid.*, 36. Or, put in another way, intra-EC exports have risen from 54 percent of total EC exports in 1982 to more than 60 percent in 1990; while on the import side the increase is from 50 percent to 58 percent during the same period.
8. Royal Bank, "Is Canada Ready?," 9.

9. Knubley, Legault, Rao, "Multinationals and FDI," in Eden, *Multinationals in North America*, 151.
10. Figures from John J. Kirton, "The Diplomacy of Concert," paper prepared for conference entitled, "Canada and the 1995 G7 Halifax Summit: Developing Canada's Positions," sponsored by the Centre for Trade Policy and Law, Carleton University, April 3, 1995. This revised paper appears in *Canadian Foreign Policy* 3, 1 (Spring 1995): 63-83.
11. Michael Smith, "'The Devil you Know'," 87.
12. On the increasing relative political and economic weight of the Community, see Mark S. Mahaney, "The European Community as a Global Power: Implications for the United States," *SAIS Review: A Journal of International Affairs* 14 (Winter/Spring 1993): 79; Smith and Woolcock, discuss the relative weight of the EC and the United States in the world economy (*The U.S. and the EC*, 34-40); Mark Nelson, "Transatlantic Travails," *Foreign Policy* 92 (Fall 1993): 80-84, talks about the EC replacing the United States as an international power.
13. Ali El-Agraa, "Japan's Reaction," in Burton, *External Relations*, 16-17.
14. Dick K. Nanto, "The U.S.-EC-Japan Trade Triangle," *CRS Report*, 92-500 E (Washington, DC: June 4, 1993), Summary, 3, 11-16; and Nanto, "European Community-Japan Trade Relations," *CRS Report*, 86-166 (Washington, DC: 1986), 36.
15. The impetus for improvement in this bilateral relationship came from both sides. For Japan, the motivation came from a concern over continued and/or possible future protectionism. Second, Japan desired greater involvement in the new institutions which would shape Europe, such as the EBRD. The Community's strategy, on the other hand, came to be greatly influenced by the record of U.S.-Japan economic relations. For example, the EC expressed concern that it might be discriminated against as a result of the Structural Impediments Initiative between Japan and the United States.
16. This good will is a function of Canada's particular expertise and capabilities in its diplomacy in the Asia Pacific region (peacekeeping, verification, surveillance, and confidence-building) in Brian L. Job and Frank Langdon, "Canada and the Pacific," in Hampson and Maule, *Canada Among Nations, 1993-94*, 288-89. The authors point out that although the Japanese are not very supportive of Canadian efforts to create multilateral security regimes for Asia Pacific, they are very keen on learning, for example, from Canadian expertise on peacekeeping.
17. Stephen Lavergne, "China 2000: The Nature of Growth and Canada's Economic Interests," *Policy Staff Paper*, No. 94/10 (Ottawa: Department of Foreign Affairs and International Trade, May 1994).
18. See Keith Christie, "Different Strokes: Regionalism and Canada's Economic Diplomacy" *Policy Planning Staff Paper* (Ottawa: External

Affairs and International Trade, 1993); also see, Christie, "The Day After."

19. This section draws from Evan H. Potter, "The Impact of European Economic Integration on North America: Adjustment Versus Radical Change," in Donald Barry *et al.*, eds., *Toward a North American Community? Canada, the United States, and Mexico* (Boulder, CO: Westview Press, 1995), 241-67.
20. The EU and Canada have always had different expectations for the Framework Agreement. Measured against these differing expectations it is not surprising that a 1992 Canadian parliamentary report goes so far as to call the Agreement a failure. It has neither prevented, nor helped to resolve many of the bilateral irritants over the last 10 years. See, House of Commons Standing Committee on External Affairs and International Trade (sub-committee on International Trade), *Canada's Relations with the New Europe* (Ottawa: Queen's Printer, June 1992), 8.
21. Telephone interview with senior EAITC official at Washington Embassy, April 1992.
22. See Gary Hufbauer's outline of such an approach in "Beyond GATT," *Foreign Policy* 77 (1989-90): 64-76.
23. Nelson, "Transatlantic Travails," 89.
24. Commons Standing Committee on External Affairs and International Trade, *Canada's Relations*, 9.
25. Royal Bank, "Is Canada Ready?," 6.
26. For example, the flanking issue of the environment was very important in terms of Canadian exports, where the EC took 17 percent of all Canadian pulp and paper exports in 1993. The major environmental issues in the early 1990s were: PNW, forest management (U.K.), chlorine bleaching (Germany), and recycling.
27. See "Canada and EC Mutual Recognition Agreements," in *Europe 1992 Trade Winds* (Ottawa: Standards Council of Canada, January 1992). The regulated products are under EC technical harmonization directives and corresponding to CEN/CENELEC/ETSI standards. The EC Commission is presently awaiting its mandate from the EC Council of Ministers to open discussions with third countries.
28. The original proposal was a Canada-EU free trade agreement, but the minister was convinced by his officials that this would not be well received and the wording in the text was changed to NAFTA-EU free trade.
29. Roy MacLaren, "Canada's Trade Policy for the 21st Century: The Walls of Jericho Fall Down," notes for an address by Roy MacLaren, Minister for International Trade, to the Centre for International Studies and the Centre for International Business, University of Toronto, Toronto, January 18, 1995, cited in the Senate of Canada, *European Integration: The Implications for Canada, Report of the Standing Senate Committee on Foreign Affairs*, July 1996, 129.

30. Lloyd Axworthy and Christine Stewart, *Liberal Foreign Policy Handbook* (Ottawa: Liberal Party of Canada, May 1993).
31. Liberal Party of Canada, *Governing for the 1990s* (Ottawa: September 1993), ch. 8. This blueprint (known as the "Red Book") for Liberal government policy was released during the 1993 federal elections. Chapter 8 on Canada's international relations, largely a rewriting of the *Handbook* published earlier in the year, focused on a Liberal foreign policy. Noteworthy is that it focused on the commercial potential of Asia Pacific and Latin America.
32. On November 15, 1994 a joint parliamentary committee presented its final report to Parliament. Report of the Special Joint Committee of the Senate and the House of Commons, *Canada's Foreign Policy: Principles and Priorities for the Future* (Ottawa: Publications Service, Parliamentary Publications Directorate, November 1994).
33. *Ibid.*, 27.
34. See especially, Roy MacLaren, "The Road from Marrakech: The Quest for Economic Internationalism in an Age of Ambivalence," *Canadian Foreign Policy* 2, 1 (Spring 1994): 1-8.
35. Senate Report, *European Integration*, 123.
36. *Ibid.*, 130.
37. *Ibid.*, 132.
38. *Ibid.*, 129.
39. At the time of writing, December 1997 was the anticipated due date of the 1997 EU-U.S. joint study.

IX

REACTING TO MAASTRICHT: FOREIGN POLICY AND SECURITY ISSUES

THERE IS AN INSTITUTIONAL DENSITY and untidiness that has complicated Canada's approach to European security. At the same time that Canada was repositioning itself within the Triad and reacting to the SEM, it felt the loss of its Atlanticist influence in Europe as a result of the policy struggles that were part of NATO reform. In 1990, the North Atlantic Cooperation Council (NACC) was set up,[1] along with the Partnership for Peace (PfP). Other factors were the evolution of the CSCE/OSCE and the development of a European security and defence identity (ESDI) in the form of the EU's own Common Foreign and Security Policy (CFSP) for which the WEU,[2] for a short time, appeared to be its chosen instrument.

From the Canadian perspective, then, there was some confusion about the appropriate European institutions with which to pursue the hard and soft tracks of transatlantic security relations. The question was whether Ottawa saw the EU becoming as important a security player as NATO and the OSCE. And, if so, how did the intersection of West European (WEU, Eurocorps) and Atlantic (NATO, OSCE) security institutions and the expansion of Community competencies to justice and home affairs affect Canada's security interests? In short, how does Canada fit into Maastricht's second (CFSP) and third (home affairs) pillars?

This chapter is concerned with the transatlantic security debate only in so far as it has affected Canada-EU relations. The rationale for the following discussion is that just as there was an unambiguous link between Canada's security commitment to Western Europe in the 1970s and its ability to gain closer institutionalized relations with the Community, there was a similar attempt made between 1990 and 1996 to link Canada's emphasis on cooperative security, the thesis that national security is enhanced through consultation on the whole range of political, economic, environmental, and social, interstate relations,[3] with its ability to forge a new basis of mutual interests with the Community. Certainly, the economic dynamic of the relationship still far outweighed the political and security dimensions, although the TAD and the Action Plan show that there was now interest on both sides to broaden contacts. Indeed, the second and third pillars of the Maastricht Treaty promised to precipitate more, not less, interaction between Canada and the EC on European and international security issues.

For the first time in their respective bilateral histories, each party faced the other across a broader range of bilateral security issues, running the gamut from the hard security issues of non-proliferation, arms control, and crisis management to the ascendant soft or cooperative security issues, which included battling international crime, promoting good governance and human rights, and managing of refugee flows and asylum seekers. The problems since the end of the Cold War in reconfiguring the transatlantic security architecture have been twofold: the difficulties associated with the "communitization" of sensitive domestic matters, such as in the areas of justice and policing; and the difficulty in reconciling the Europeans' search for greater independence in security and defence policy with a continued, active North American involvement in the traditional Atlantic institutions of NATO and the OSCE.

But before looking at the EU-Canada dimension of transatlantic security, it is important to outline briefly the major transatlantic security debates and Canadian responses. There are a number of issues here, but the most important from this study's perspective was the problem of coordination between NATO and the WEU and the uncertainty over the U.S. role in Europe.

EUROPEAN SECURITY DEBATES OF THE EARLY 1990s

From the early 1980s onward the strongest advocates of an independent West European defence structure were France and Germany, countries at the forefront of setting up European security and defence structures in the form of security competence for the new European Political Union, and of upgrading the WEU and establishing a Franco-German army corps.[4] While France was more vocal, Germany stood by its side at every important juncture. Official documents always refer to basic compatibility between NATO functions and ESDI, even though most participants involved agreed that the process was very competitive and had impaired the Atlanticist spirit that united NATO during the Cold War. After the collapse of the Soviet Union, these fissures in the transatlantic security framework widened. Simply put, the authority and relevance of NATO, and thus the North American role in Europe, were being diminished. Where did Canada fit into this evolving debate? Moens cautions that although not much should be read into Canada's weakened position in European councils, there were nevertheless tell-tale signs as we shall discuss below.[5]

It is not necessary here for a detailed review of Ottawa's policy zigzags on European security during these years.[6] Canada's "three-pillars" approach to Europe announced in Joe Clark's Humber College speech in the spring of 1990 seemed quite optimal at the time. Since NATO, the CSCE, and the EC were in flux, it behooved Canada to try and engage all. Historically, the ability of Canada to gain privileged economic access to the European Community had been based, to a significant extent, on Canada's participation in the postwar transatlantic security framework. Canada was rewarded for playing a support function in the military security provided by the United States. Suffice it to say that Canadian planners had a difficult time making Canada's voice heard, given the competition among the various institutions, compounded by the civil war in the former Yugoslavia and the unforeseen UN role on the continent. It is even difficult to place Ottawa's position firmly in any one school of thought since the Mulroney government was itself divided, with EAITC scrambling not to lose any ground in any European institutions and to avoid any initiatives that might offend Canada's European allies.

Beginning in the summer of 1991, Canada made a major contribution by deploying troops to the EC monitoring mission in Yugoslavia, and later two battle groups to the UN Protection Force in Yugoslavia (UNPROFOR). The Canadian commitment, for a time, became the second largest contingent of peacekeepers in Yugoslavia, after the French.

However, the apparent Canadian commitment to European security must be balanced by the domestic constraints in Canada and the ongoing rivalry between the departments of External Affairs and

National Defence (DND) on the appropriate Canadian role in Europe. By 1992, with the combination of a recession at home, a rising national debt and deficit, and the search for a peace dividend after the Cold War, the Department of National Defence's budget—the largest of any federal department—came under increasing scrutiny. That it would be cut again there was no question, the only question was how and where. The political calculus of the Mulroney government was that it would be impossible to close domestic military bases (historically part of Ottawa's regional industrial development) for budgetary reasons, and leave Canada's European bases open. In this environment, National Defence, burdened with aging equipment, the victim of ongoing budget cuts, and prohibited from closing unneeded domestic bases, supported the withdrawal of Canadian troops from Europe.[7] This position was not shared by officials at External Affairs who argued that Canadian troops in Europe were an important signal of Canada's commitment to European security and were crucial to keeping NATO North American. This view was overridden by the Conservative cabinet, however.

Prime Minister Mulroney, after stating in the fall of 1991 that Canadian troops would stay as long as they were "needed and wanted," decided by the spring budget of 1992 that they were no longer needed. Despite protests by Canada's European allies that echoed the displeasure 20 years earlier over Trudeau's downsizing of Canada's military presence in Europe,[8] Mulroney decided to withdraw all permanently stationed Canadian troops from Europe by 1994.[9]

This state of affairs had put Canadian policy makers in a tricky position and reignited the Atlantic "burden-sharing" critique that the Europeans and Americans had directed at Canada since the early 1970s. If NATO became *the* inclusive collective security organization in Europe[10] rather than one that developed its security role in close cooperation with the partners of the NACC and further strengthened the CSCE to become a regional security organization under Article 52 of the UN Charter,[11] then for Canada not to dissipate whatever influence it still had with its European and American allies, it would have had to begin thinking about reversing its decision on troop withdrawals. But apart from the peacekeeping commitment to Yugoslavia, the Mulroney government had no political will to flip-flop on its European security policy and commit new troops. Compounding this perceptual problem were the debates within the Canadian government on whether to support a NATO-first or CSCE/OSCE-first policy on European security.

Changes in Europe further obscured Canada's future security role within the Alliance. On the margins of the Maastricht Summit in December 1991, it was decided that an expanded WEU should embody the ESDI and should also serve as the European pillar of NATO. At the Petersberg Ministerial Meeting in June 1992, it was agreed to make the WEU more operational, through the creation of a military planning cell to refine three main tasks for WEU forces: humanitarian and rescue, crisis management, and peacekeeping.[12] Some of these activities, especially crisis management, were already being pursued by European organizations such as the CSCE. From a Canadian perspective, further complicating the issue of institutional overlap, was the creation of the Franco-German army corps which it was agreed would be placed under NATO command in crises ranging from war to international peacekeeping. Canada was seeing its internationally recognized role of peacekeeper usurped.

These developments raised serious questions about the relationship between the WEU and NATO and, by extension, the role for Canada, as a North American partner, in crises on European soil. As Canada's former ambassador to NATO, John Halstead, has noted, the question was whether the focus of defence planning and consultations among the European members of NATO should take place in NATO or in the WEU, and should the WEU eventually have an independent military role? If the former, how could the EC develop an ESDI? But if the latter, how could the United States and Canada continue to be involved in European security?[13] The view in Washington at the time was that the ESDI should develop in whatever way the EC wished, as long as it did not affect NATO's role as the forum where all the allies made common security policies and took decisions to execute them.[14] The United States supported the idea of a common European security policy, provided it was brought to NATO for debate and adjustment to the alliance position. There remained concern in Washington, however, that some European allies would want to establish policy making in the European Defence Community (EDC) as an alternative to NATO. If this were to happen, it would put in question the essential underpinning of the transatlantic link.

The formulas that were eventually reached to reconcile the mandates of the NATO and the WEU[15] could not alter the fact that between 1990 and 1993 there was an inherent tension between the transatlantic and the European view of the alliance, which served to complicate the construction of a new European security architecture and thus undermined transatlantic solidarity, including the prospects for free trade.

So, where did Canada fit into this complicated landscape of crosscutting interests and how did this affect its relations with the EU? Clearly, without a permanent troop commitment in Europe, it became increasingly difficult for Canada to have much influence on any major Alliance decision. That being said, there was a major structural transformation, namely, the growing interpenetration of economic and security issues. A case in point was Canada's formulation of a "cooperative security" approach to its international security relations and its pursuit of European relations based on the logic of this concept, as exemplified by the entrenchment of cooperative security elements in the TAD and the Action Plan, as well as its attempt to organize the OSCE around these principles. Thus, perhaps it can be said that the distinguishing feature of the early 1990s was that the objective change predicted in the academic literature on interdependence in the 1970s was now matched by a "cognitive shift" on the part of policy elites.[16]

The cognitive shift, though fundamental and substantial, was not complete by the early 1990s; it had not been thoroughly incorporated into policy processes and political dialogue on both sides of the Atlantic. In many ways it contributed to the institutional overlap and confusion outlined above that characterized the transatlantic relationship. This overlap began to sort itself out starting in 1995, but is worth examining in greater detail.

THE EU's COMMON FOREIGN AND SECURITY POLICY

Part of the process of the Europeanization of European security was the formulation of the EU's CFSP. The common foreign and security policy and justice and home affairs elements of the Maastricht Treaty (titles V and VI of the Treaty) correspond to the second and third pillars, respectively, of the European Union. Unlike the first pillar (the economic treaties), the decisions under these pillars remained intergovernmental since authority in these areas was not devolved to the supranational institutions of the Commission, Parliament, or Court of Justice. It had been hoped that the CFSP, unlike its forebear EPC, would finally allow the EU to project its political weight on the world stage commensurate with it economic power. This was not to be.

The first indication that the introduction of CFSP did not foreshadow an aggrandizement of the EU's international political stature was its inability to prevent the crisis in Yugoslavia from deteriorating into a brutal civil war. To be sure, it was hamstrung by problems such as the lack of proper interconnectedness between Maastricht's three pillars and questions about whose budget (the Community's or member states') would be responsible for expenditures under CFSP.[17] An additional confusion was the connection between the EU and the WEU, which was supposed to assume the EU's defence identity but in practice demonstrated little ability to do so. This was not surprising given the four classes of WEU membership, the overlapping membership between the EU, the WEU, and NATO, and the fact that it was impossible to consider merging the WEU and EU when a number of the neutral member states (e.g., Ireland) had no intention of seeking membership in either NATO or the WEU.

The challenge of operationalizing the CFSP's security component was achieved at the January 1994 NATO Summit, which gave European NATO members permission to use Alliance resources and facilities for their operations under the Combined Joint Task Force (CJTF) concept. This had the effect of allowing the EU to embark on out-of-theatre missions using NATO assets, but without involving the United States or Canada. It also went some way in solving a nettlesome policy conundrum for European decision makers, namely, how to develop a way for the EU to have an instrument of military means without threatening its neutral members. What emerged was a WEU-EU link on security matters, while on matters of defence there was a WEU-NATO link. The WEU thus became the European pillar of NATO. But as the breakdown of order in Albania in 1997 revealed, these neat conceptual reconfigurations did little in practice to elevate the WEU's standing as an operational body.

The Europeanization of European Security

Despite the push for a ESDI in the first half of the 1990s, which presupposed that Europe could increasingly take care of its security needs and was manifested through the growth of the Franco-German corps and a reinvigorated WEU, it was soon recognized that European security had to be built within NATO rather than constructed in a single self-contained European pillar. There were sound reasons for this. First, the debacle of European indecision in the former Yugoslavia served to confirm Europe's lack of willingness to take control of security on its continent. Second, European leaders realized that their taxpayers could not be asked to bear the burdens of trying to duplicate all NATO's assets, particularly NATO's intelligence and transport infrastructure. And France's return to NATO's military committee after 30 years made it easier to contemplate a European defence identity inside NATO, not to mention that this change put the WEU's role as the EU defence identity in serious doubt.[18] A final element to the Europeanization of security has been the parallel processes of NATO and EU enlargement, with some Eastern countries looking to the EU as a bridge to NATO membership. Officials from NATO and the EU have strenuously emphasized that there is no linkage between the two processes.

In summary, what happened in the period 1990 to 1993 was a shift away from NATO to other security institutions, such as the WEU and OSCE, and back to NATO. But between 1994 and 1997, the WEU, rather than acting as a vanguard for an independent European security arm, had become the European arm of NATO. In an effort to give the EU's CFSP a boost, the 1997 Inter-Governmental Conference allowed that once principles of a particular foreign policy issue had been agreed to by the EU's leaders, decisions on how to implement action would be subject to qualified majority voting rather than unanimity. As well, the Commission established a new Directorate-General for External Political Relations, which demonstrated the continuing desire of the EU to move in the direction of a common security policy. It could not, however, achieve a common defence policy. As long as the EU was not able to take aboard the commitment of the WEU Treaty, then it needed the WEU to have access to NATO assets.

In the end, for all the shifts in institutional focus, which may improve the EU's foreign policy making mechanism, "it is unlikely to produce stronger common policies or to result in more decisive joint actions unless the collective will exists on the part of the member states."[19] The WEU has lost its role as the basis of European defence to other organizations such as the UN and the OSCE, which will have larger roles, while NATO will continue to provide the "bedrock of European security."

Implications for Canada of Changes in European Security

Once there was a consensus that the means for handling a crisis in Europe was firmly bound with NATO rather than a non-Atlantic institution, this implied that Canada would continue to retain a voice, albeit diminished, on European security matters. The challenge was how Ottawa would make the best of this opportunity.

According to a 1996 Canadian Senate Foreign Affairs Committee report, Canada needed to maintain its security links to Europe "(b)ecause

Canada has limited defence resources of its own; membership in NATO acts as a 'force multiplier' which helps to guarantee Canadian national security."[20] The report goes on to note that Canada's membership in a European alliance actually supports the Chrétien government's objective of helping to preserve global security by having Canada participate in NATO peacemaking activities such as the Implementation Force (IFOR) in Bosnia and by participating in NATO outreach programs such as the NACC and the PfP which keep Russia and the countries of Eastern Europe engaged with NATO.

Another objective of Ottawa's security policy through institutions such as NATO is that it needs to keep U.S. multilateralism alive. The U.S.'s role in Europe is just one example of this involvement. However, to exert any influence in this regard, Canada must have credibility in the eyes of Washington. The withdrawal of all permanently stationed Canadian troops in Europe in 1994 has meant that this leverage is no longer there.

Canada has been trying to re-establish a foothold in European security matters by picking and choosing low-cost areas. This is in keeping with Foreign Minister Lloyd Axworthy's avowal that Canada will be projecting more "soft power," in the future; that is, intellectual leadership or what one observer has referred to as "software."

The Europeans view this as trying to buy a seat at the European table on the cheap. Intellectual leadership in crisis management and Canada's expertise in peacekeeping is being proffered in lieu of a commitment of assets. This will not be accepted in the absence of tangible evidence of permanent hardware. It is true that Canada has much to teach the Europeans about peacekeeping, but even this may no longer be a growth industry. Finally, there was some puzzlement when Canada refused the chairmanship of the OSCE.

The sign of Canada's declining profile in European eyes is evident across a number of fronts. It has been alleged, for example, that this lack of profile in the "new Europe" accounted for Canada being given only observer status at the Contact Group in 1994. It was further suggested that such a dissipation of profile will lead eventually to the exclusion of Canadians from certain command positions within NATO. The Europeans were also not impressed by the appointment of Admiral John Andersen (1994-97), a professional soldier rather than a political appointee, as Canada's Ambassador to NATO, not because of any failure of competence on the part of Mr. Anderson, but because it did not send the right political message.

There is a sense that Canada can be a niche player in European security, but its role as a player to be consulted on major decisions has been irretrievably lost. It is destined to be a peripheral player on military security matters. Arguably, the Europeans have undervalued Canada's presence. After all, the Dutch and French have also withdrawn their troops from Germany.

THE THIRD PILLAR

Under the "third pillar" or Title VI of the Maastricht Treaty, nine areas of justice and home affairs are subject to judicial cooperation: asylum policy, following from the Schengen Agreement's rules governing people crossing the external borders of the member states; immigration policy and the residence rights of third-country nationals; combating unauthorized immigration and establishing rules governing residence and work by third-country nationals; combating drug trafficking; combating international fraud; developing judicial cooperation on civil and criminal matters; customs cooperation; police cooperation to combat terrorism, drug trafficking, and other serious crimes through the creation of a European-wide policy intelligence office, known as Europol.

The role of the EU's supranational institutions is limited under this pillar. The Commission has a right to initiate policy, but it shares this right with the member states in six of the nine areas covered by the third pillar. The European Parliament, for its part, has the right to be kept informed, the right to be consulted on the principal areas of judicial cooperation, and its view are supposed to be taken into consideration. It has shared right of initiative in six areas. In practice, the European Parliament is rarely consulted by the Council Presidency, and this despite the outcome of the 1997 Inter-Governmental Conference which gave it and the Commission more powers over member states' immigration, asylum, and visa policies. In reality, the Council has the strongest role in pillar-three items. The problem with pillar three is that the structure at the EU level does not overlap national and bilateral cooperation.[21] As in the case of CFSP, difficulties also stem from the lack of a clear demarcation between the EU pillars; in this case, the Community pillar and the justice and home affairs pillars.

Canadian Interests

It is noteworthy that justice and home affairs issues have been included in the Canada-EU Action Plan. Specifically, the inclusion of these issues offers an opportunity to beef up the cooperative security track of transatlantic security relations as Canada's role within other European security institutions, such as NATO and the OSCE, becomes smaller. Canada wanted to deal with EU on the basis of single unified policies affecting immigration, asylum, organized crime, drug trafficking, and other third-pillar issues because it would be less costly and more effective for Canada to negotiate an agreement with one actor, rather than with 15 national governments, but it would also help prevent criminals, terrorists, and illegal immigrants from exploiting differences in bilateral treaties between Canada and the EU member states.[22]

Ottawa views pillar three as a means to reposition Canada within transatlanticism and to, in the words of a Canadian diplomat, "instrumentalize" the relationship. But there is a great skepticism attached to this in Europe. The legislation within the EU is not advanced enough to allow EU competency in the areas that Canada is targetting. It was felt that the EU has first to resolve its own problems concerning competencies before engaging with third countries. And, when it was ready to negotiate with third countries in this area it would be with the countries of Eastern Europe where it has already established programs. Moreover, there was resistance within the EU to negotiate with outside countries. For example, in June 1995, the EU Justice Council announced new rules which restricted the EU's ability to negotiate in this area with third countries. These new rules were put into effect because of French concerns about third-country involvement in internal EU affairs.[23]

As Gretchen MacMillan has observed, the member states were reluctant to surrender sovereignty in many of these areas, especially in sensitive areas such as immigration. However, in other areas such as terrorism and drug interdiction, the Commission would eventually be allowed to take a higher profile role.[24] For Ottawa this meant that many pillar three items would be the subject of intergovernmental negotiations in the near term and thereby require bilateral diplomacy with the member states. It is worth noting that not all the EU's interlocutors have preferred dealing with only the Community on these issue areas. The Clinton administration, for example, was content with the split of competencies between the EU and its member states. This simplified life: if a message from one member state is contrary to an American position, the United States can still negotiate with other member states which are more receptive. The "open skies" treaty, for example, was gained by negotiating individually.

The Commission has been playing a larger role in pillars one and three and has an overall perspective in the latter area. There was also a move from unanimity to qualified majority in certain areas such as asylum/justice policy. What remains to be seen is to what extent certain elements of the third pillar can be "communitized." The Commission has been targetting Central and Eastern Europe on pillar three cooperation, for example, with police forces. There is not much interest left over for Canada, although there may be scope for greater EU-Canadian cooperation on combatting illegal traffic in human begins.

How should Canada target itself at pillar three? Canada is a *demandeur* on third pillar. The European Parliament is supposed to be consulted by the Council presidency, but in fact Parliament has a weak role on pillar-three items. It is rarely consulted. It has shared right of initiative in six areas. In reality, the Council has the strongest role in pillar-three items. The problem with pillar three is that the structure at the EU level does not overlap national and bilateral cooperation.

If the SEM produced the first cognitive shift for Canadian policy makers on Canada's future relationship with the EU, then Maastricht's focus on the second and third pillars produced the second cognitive shift. Because Canadian policy makers expected that Canada's future participation in transatlantic security would likely be in cooperative security-type issues, Ottawa strove to enshrine such security issues in the TAD. As the EU was developing its own apparati to perform these functions, it was, however, increasingly difficult to see how Canada might benefit from performing a European role that would actually no longer be seen by the EU as a support function in a prioritized policy agenda. Herein then lay the dilemma for Canadian foreign policy makers. It was entirely unrealistic to expect Canada to have the same amount of influence in Europe in such a reformulized policy agenda. It was patently obvious that cooperation on transnational security issues such as terrorism, refugee management, drug trafficking, and nuclear non-proliferation as outlined in the TAD and then the Action Plan, was not likely to produce the same type of close-knit, value-driven transatlantic relationship that had bound Canada to Western Europe during the Cold War.

Regardless of the level of adjustments to existing architecture, Ottawa had to ask itself on what policy congruence and with what rewards it was going to build stronger political ties with Brussels if it was destined to have less and less influence in an expanded NATO, the primary European security institution. Finally, if Canada did indeed want to build cooperative security relations with the EU, one had to question how serious Ottawa was. The evidence suggests that between 1990 and 1993 Ottawa was intent on making the CSCE, not NATO, the linchpin of its European security architecture. In the next three years, once the debate over WEU/NATO had sorted itself out, Ottawa came down on the side of NATO.

What also comes through the analysis is an interesting change in the complexion of Canada's relations with Western Europe. On the one hand, on one range of broad, overarching issues such as aid to Eastern Europe and the former Soviet Union, the desirability to complete the Uruguay Round, and assistance to the developing world, there is a basic consensus between Canadian and Community elites on both the goals and the means, with the exception perhaps on the means of resolving agricultural disputes within the Uruguay Round. This may not be surprising. What *is* notable is the other range of broad issues discussed; that is, the future of Europe's security architecture and transatlantic economic relations. The policy conclusions or actions to these developments on the part of the EC and Canadian elites are notable for their lack of general agreement.

Compounding the problem of making transatlantic interests more convergent was the fact that both Canada and the Community appeared to view the solutions to their respective Atlantic frameworks in fundamentally different ways. This book's analysis of the various options open to Canadian policy makers in the early and mid-1990s points to Ottawa's need to redefine the balance between prosperity and security; basically spending less on European security and gaining more from an expanded European market by investing more in West European trade and investment development efforts. However, it is not clear that there was a convergence of Canadian and European interests in this regard.

Not only this, but domestically there appeared to be no consensus on the appropriate Canadian response to European integration. If we recall the discussion in Chapter 6, with the exception of the few Canadian multinationals, the Canadian business community was relatively indifferent to the Community market in spite of the federal government's exhortations, incentives, and programs. Canadian business leaders talked about the "maturity" of the West European markets and lobbied government to spend *less* not more on trade development schemes for this region. And, at the same time that an aggressive, unified Canadian response to the SEM—that is, a "Team Canada" approach in which business and government would "sing from the same song sheet"—was missing in Canada, on the EC's side, the process of revising its role in Europe was almost entirely in the opposite direction from Canada's. So, in the two years after the TAD, while policy makers in

Ottawa were framing their approach to the Community around the prospects for new bilateral trade arrangements, in Western Europe the debate had turned upon the ways in which a concern for security could be grafted on to the traditional civilian power base established through Community activities and institutions. This apparent divergence of Canadian and European strategies and outlooks was a major hammer-blow to transatlantic interdependence; Canada, as a result, became much more of a *demandeur* in transatlantic relations. The extent to which Canada could intensify its relations with the Community now depended more than at any other time in its history on what the Community's interests were. The next chapter returns to how Canada's interests played out across a number of high-profile transatlantic disputes and how enlargement will affect Canada's future negotiating positions.

NOTES

1. A forum to which the NATO members and the former Warsaw Pact members and the successor states of the Soviet Union belonged.
2. The WEU emerged from the transformation of the 1948 Brussels Treaty through the accession of West Germany and Italy, and the addition of new political and military functions. From the time of its creation in 1954 as an organization for regional defence and arms control to the early 1980s it lay virtually dormant.
3. For a definition of "cooperative security" see Christopher Anstis, "CSCE Mark II: Back to Helsinki from Paris via Berlin and Prague," *NATO Review* 2 (April 1992): 18-23.
4. See Charles Pentland, "European Security after the Cold War," in D. Dewitt, D. Haglund, and J. Kirton, eds., *Building a New Global Order: Emerging Trends in International Security* (Toronto: Oxford University Press, 1993), 76; and see also, David Haglund, *Alliance Within the Alliance? Franco-German Military Cooperation and the European Pillar of Defense* (Boulder, CO: Westview Press, 1991), esp. chs. 1 and 7.
5. Alexander Moens, "A New Security Strategy for Europe," in Molot and Riekhoff, *Canada Among Nations, 1994*, 165, and ch. 7, endn. 23.
6. Moens provides a good summary in *ibid.*, 162-65.
7. *Ibid.*, 163.
8. Moens states that Canada unilaterally withdrew its troops even though several allies (he does not name which ones) had "quietly" offered Ottawa "very substantial help" in covering costs or base and equipment costs. *Ibid.*, 163.

9. This withdrawal did not mean, as Canadian diplomats were careful to emphasize to their European counterparts, that Canada was eliminating its operational commitment to NATO. Canada's navy, for instance, continued to provide a minimum of one destoyer/frigate to the Standing Naval Force Atlantic as it had done for the previous 25 years on a continuous basis. In addition, Canada's military would continue to provide numerous operational and staff positions within the NATO command structure.
10. Canada 21 Council, *Canada and Common Security in the Twenty-First Century* (Toronto: Centre for International Studies, 1994).
11. John Halstead, "International Security Institutions: NATO and the CSCE," *Canadian Foreign Policy* 2, 1 (Spring 1994): 45-62.
12. Diarmid Williams, *The Atlantic Council Letter* (June 1993).
13. Halstead, "International Security," 55.
14. Former U.S. Ambassador Williams H. Taft IV, *The Atlantic Council Letter* (July 1993).
15. Under the various options proposed, NATO and the WEU would be mutually complementary, with neither being subordinate to the other, and would work together in a spirit of full cooperation and sharing of information. NATO would remain the centre for defence planning and coordination for all its members, while the WEU, as the "European pillar" of the alliance, would play the role of a bridge between NATO and an increasingly integrated European Union.
16. I am indebted to my colleague, Prof. Alexander Moens, for this point.
17. Senate Report, *European Integration* (July 1996), 94.
18. *Ibid.*, 97.
19. *Ibid.*, 102.
20. *Ibid.*, 102.
21. *Ibid.*, 109.
22. *Ibid.*, 111.
23. *Ibid.*
24. The Germans were somewhat mystified that terrorism should be an interstate security concern that would involve extensive consultations between foreign ministries and would find itself on the transatlantic security agenda. For them, terrorism was solely a police issue.

X

THE NEW TRANSATLANTICISM

BY THE MID- TO LATE-1990s, relations between Canada and the EU began to take on a qualitatively different nature. Ottawa was no longer responding to largely unidimensional disputes, such as the appellation of wines or high tariffs on computer equipment, but rather faced "clusters of entangled problems" encompassing trade rules, animal rights and, in some cases, the rights of indigenous peoples.[1] This chapter will look at two high-profile disputes in recent years in Canada's relations with the Union: the war of words over fisheries that culminated in the boarding of the Spanish trawler, *Estai*; and the ban on leg-hold traps that threatened Canada's fur exports to the EU. These disputes reinforced the perception of a relationship that was based in the public's eye on trade irritants. For a number of years they created a dark cloud over Canada's relations with the EU and some of its member states and caused the emergence of pro- and anti-Canada camps within the EU.

If the nature of the disputes between Ottawa and Brussels began to change, then, it would not be surprising to discover that the nature of bilateral cooperation changed as well. Another very visible case study of the new dynamics of bilateral cooperation is found in Canada's and the EU's approaches to the United States' Helms-Burton Act. Whereas it first appeared that Ottawa and the Commission were presenting a unified front against Washington's discriminatory extra-territorial legislation, upon closer examination it turns out that Brussels preferred to exclude Canada and negotiate separately with the United States.

Obviously, to have a full understanding of these disputes and the nature of transatlantic relations, the focus cannot be on only the EU's institutions. It goes without saying that the views and positions of member states on Canada-EU relations are also critical in determining future bilateral relations. For this reason, the chapter examines the changing nature of Canada's relations with the United Kingdom and Germany.

Finally, conjectures about the future problems and directions in Canada-EU relations cannot ignore the prospects of a significantly enlarged Union within the next decade. The last section of the chapter points out that with Canada already on the outside concentric circle in terms of its place in the EU's external relations, such an enlargement promises to make Ottawa's leverage within European decision making bodies even more tenuous and will further diminish its European profile. In fact, Canada is still seeking compensation from previous enlargements.

THE DISPUTES

The Fisheries

The EU and Canada have had difficulties in their fisheries diplomacy going back to the arrest of a German vessel in the mid-1980s, when mutual recriminations began over areas regulated by the North Atlantic Fisheries Organization (NAFO). The differences between Canada and the EU were substantial and were directly related to several issues. These included the internal politics within NAFO, the domestic politics in Canada and in member states such as Spain and Portugal, the decision making process within the EU, and differing interpretations of international law. The main issue for Canada was enforcement; for the EU it was quota division. It also rested on clashing philosophies. For example, for the longest time, while Canada petitioned the EU for a bilateral fisheries agreement, the European response was that it did not negotiate bilaterally on issues that were multilateral (i.e., dealt with by NAFO).

The matter of Totally Allowable Catch Size (TACS) was a particular lightning rod. After Spain and Portugal were sanctioned by NAFO for exceeding their quotas, the EU protested by setting very high autonomous quotas, an act which, with some Canadian stoking, isolated it within that organization. It also put Ottawa and the Commission on a collision course. The Canadian government had been monitoring the steady decline of the cod stocks since 1989 and viewed the culprit as foreign, mainly Spanish, overfishing. The moratorium on fishing that was finally called by Canada in April 1992 and the EU in July to save the stock led directly to the collapse of the East Coast fisheries industry. It so happened that this industry was the mainstay of Canada's poorest province, Newfoundland, and thus a hot political issue for ambitious Canadian politicians who sought to deflect any Canadian culpability for overfishing the Grand Banks to foreign shores.

The Europeans were particularly concerned with Ottawa's creeping jurisdiction on the high seas. Not only were the Europeans barred from fishing inside Canadian territorial waters unlike the Russians and Cubans, but their boats were being boarded by armed Canadian Department of Fisheries and Oceans' officers on the high seas beyond Canada's 200-mile economic zone as well. For the Europeans this was a flagrant violation of international law.

On enforcement, the Europeans and Canadians differed significantly. Ottawa's priority was to ensure that all vessels from NAFO member states fishing so-called straddling stock off the 200-mile limit had neutral observers aboard. In addition, the Canadian side pushed for and received inspection platforms on the high seas. Starting in 1991, the EU provided an inspection vessel and soon had inspection vessels in operation 10 months of the year. But such was the mutual suspicion that even with greater enforcement, Canada still felt it necessary, much to the Europeans' dismay, to send fisheries officers to Europe to do port-side inspections and to "observe the observers."

Binding arbitration became a particular sore point. Brussels pointed out that Canada defended objection procedures in all international organizations except at NAFO. The Canadian government, in European eyes, wanted binding arbitration so that it could turn NAFO into a supranational body; the EU, on the other hand, preferred an objections procedure that preserved NAFO's intergovernmental character. Each side did so to protect its own interest. Canada pushed binding arbitration to force the EU to force its member states to respect the lower TACS, while the EU defended the objection procedure because it provided it with breathing space in internal negotiations with its member states, who were themselves feeling domestic pressure.

Between 1990-92, fruitful negotiations between Canada and the EU led to a greater convergence of interests. The EU, for example, ceased to provoke fellow NAFO members with autonomous quotas. Canada pressed the EU for a fisheries agreement which culminated in an agreement that was initialled by both sides in December 1992. The agreement was to be a permanent solution on the area known as 23KL and provided for, among other things, access to Canadian ports by EU vessels and access to surplus stocks. In December 1993, the European Council agreed to ratify the agreement. At the time of writing Canada still had not ratified the agreement. At the same time, Canada made some NAFO members uneasy by not accepting the NAFO Scientific Council's findings on declining stocks.

The Canada-EU brinksmanship on fisheries then rapidly escalated when it became clear at the October 1994 NAFO annual meeting that no agreement would be possible on quotas for Greenland halibut stock (also known as turbot). The TACS for halibut was set at 27,000 tons, of which Ottawa insisted on receiving 75-80 percent, with only 11 percent going to the EU. Once the EU indicated that it was asking for 75 percent, based on the previous year's catch, the two sides were headed for confrontation. Certainly, no compromise was possible when the EU's final position was an autonomous quota of 77 percent. What weighed heavily on the minds of the EU negotiators was that the halibut was seen as replacing the loss of the cod fisheries for the Spanish. For Canada this was a non-negotiable issue since it felt that the halibut also required protection. In fact, the Community received a diplomatic démarche for overfishing. Ottawa had now deliberately targetted Spain through its position. Canada proceeded to insist on a vote on a proposal to fix a quota on the allocation of stock. When the EU lost the vote (6 to 5 in favour of Canada's position) under the NAFO's majority voting system, it was awarded 5,000 tons. The EU's reaction was to use the objection procedures and then to fix unilateral autonomous quotas.

By January 1995, the brinksmanship was becoming grave. Officials responsible for fisheries in the Commission's DGXIV began warning their External Relations colleagues in DGI that Canada's position would become more and more aggressive and that Ottawa appeared to want confrontation. In their view, it was not beyond the realm of probability that Canada would begin to arrest vessels at this stage, although this advice was apparently dismissed by the DGI officials who believed that Ottawa was posturing, albeit very aggressively, but ultimately would not dare to up the ante any more.

The climax came in February when, before arresting the Spanish trawler, *Estai*, in international waters, the pursuing Canadian ship sent a shot across her bow. For Canada, not known for its gunboat diplomacy, it was a shot heard—and meant to be heard—around the world.

For other countries fishing in the areas under dispute it was a barely disguised signal. The immediate impact, besides the huge public relations campaigns on both sides to justify their actions, one in which the Canadian side kept the upper hand, was the freezing of all Canada-EU contacts. The "turbot war," as it became known, soon overshadowed all of Ottawa's other trade disputes with the EU. However, despite the war of words, and to the relief of Canada's Department of Foreign Affairs and International Trade, which had advised against any precipitant military actions but had been overruled by the prime minister, the Canadian and EU sides were not prepared to let the EU-Canadian relationship flounder on the Grand Banks. Following around-the-clock negotiations for three weeks in March and April, a bilateral protocol was signed on April 16. It provided for strict control and enforcement measures, emphasized a multilateralization of measures, and came to an understanding on the distribution of the turbot stock in the coming years. The momentum from the agreement also led to the opening of Canadian ports to EU vessels in 1996.

While there is no doubt that the 1995 protocol averted any major lasting damage to EU-Canadian relations, in the ensuing years it was far from forgotten in Europe. In Canada, the "war" briefly captured the collective imagination as an unusual display of raw machismo—a far cry from the stereotype of Canadians as conciliators. For the Commission, and especially Spain, Portugal, and France, the protocol was tinged by suspicion since it still left the 1992 agreement unratified. The Canada-EU rapprochement in 1995-96 did not bring the two sides any closer on access to surplus stocks and the introduction of dispute settlement mechanisms within NAFO. As well, Canada remained keen to push through Bill C-62, which gives Canada extraterritorial enforcement rights on the high seas. The Commission responded with several *notes verballes* in protest.

The Canada-EU fisheries episode is certainly a complicated one and cannot be adequately illustrated in a more general work. Nevertheless, it prompts the following observations. The boarding of the *Estai* cast a long shadow across bilateral relations; fish odour hung like a cloud over Canada's relations with the EU for at least a year after the seizure of the *Estai*. The timing is important because it was during this period that Canada was also attempting to negotiate and trilateralize a new transatlantic agreement with the Americans and the Commission. The episode demonstrates Canada's aggressive unilateralism when provoked and provides yet another case study that will help to lay to rest the myth that Canada only acts multilaterally.[2] It also points to the creation of clear pro- and anti-Canadian camps within the EU. The U.K., for example, which felt similarly aggrieved by Spanish and Portuguese overfishing, took a keen interest in pushing the Canadian message in the EU's decision making centres.

Leg-hold Traps

Like fish, the controversy over the exports of fur demonstrates the new policy complexity of transatlantic relations. In 1990, a European directive banned leg-hold traps and halted the import of furs from nations that used such traps. The European Commission, however, never enforced the trade ban for fear of opening a trade war with the main fur exporters of Canada, the United States, and Russia. In fact, four deadlines for the imposition of the ban were skipped.

The Commission chose instead to regulate the issue with the three countries through an agreement on humane trapping standards, which would apply both to the exporters and European countries. In this way, the Commission believed it could avoid going to a WTO dispute settlement panel. This was because the WTO was looking to bring trade liberalization and the environment closer in line by using the leg-hold trap issue as a test case. For their parts, the three countries would be exempted from any further regulations. A deal to do just this was finally passed by qualified majority on June 19, 1997.

For Canada, this issue was a public relations nightmare on the scale of European protests over Canadian seal-hunting methods in the 1970s and 1980s. It was also a much greater emotional issue for the Canadian side than it was for the American or Russian sides. Indeed, Ottawa did most of the lobbying against what it perceived to be extraterritorial and aggressively unilateral EU legislation. No such lobbying effort was forthcoming from the United States and Russia. The United States, in fact, dropped out of the negotiations over trapping standards because it felt that it could not provide a guarantee to implement these standards since trapping regulations are set by individual states rather than the federal government.

The level of attention devoted by the Department of Foreign Affairs and International Trade to this problem was very high. In fact, some European Commission officials with experience in dealing with Canada went so far to describe Ottawa's attention to the matter as "unprecedented." Commission officials were surprised at the responsiveness of their Canadian counterparts on this issue in comparison to the much greater resistance on questions of fisheries. It is conjectured that the reason for this reaction was not only because 100,000 Canadian jobs were directly or indirectly linked to the export of furs to Europe, but also because the interests of Aboriginal Canadians were at stake. In the aftermath of being severely criticized domestically and internationally for its treatment of its native peoples, Ottawa was extremely sensitive to the charge that it was shirking its responsibilities with regard to their welfare.

From Ottawa's perspective, the original European directive was aggressively extraterritorial and unilateral. That being said, given the Commission's desire to look for alternatives to the WTO route for resolving the matter, it is clear that Brussels had also been sensitized by lobbying from Canada and not just by the well-funded European (mostly U.K.-based) animal rights groups.

The European Commission was itself very divided over the issue, with Sir Leon Brittan, the trade commissioner, who did not favour linking leg-hold traps as a trade issue with the environment, at odds with the environment commissioner, Ritt Bjerregaard, who did. Sweden, Denmark, Austria, and the U.K.—the latter often an ally of Canada's—all viewed the leg-hold trap issue more through the prism of the environment.

The case of leg-hold traps is an example of the type of clustered bilateral policy issue, encompassing the rights of indigenous peoples, animal rights, and trade rules, that will be increasingly common in the coming years. It is not clear how interconnected the components of the cluster are, with each component having a separate set of interests. This makes dealing with the EU all the more difficult for Canadian policy makers.

The Helms-Burton Act

Besides the fisheries and leg-hold trap disputes, no bilateral issue in recent years more clearly illustrates the dynamics of Canada-EU and transatlantic relations than the European and Canadian responses to the United States' Helms-Burton Act. The Act is a piece of extraterritorial legislation that discriminates and punishes European and Canadian firms wishing to do business in Cuba. At first glance, the response to the Act appears to be a tailor-made case study proving how the EU-Canada axis of the Canada-U.S.-EU triangle can be used to moderate U.S. unilateralism. Upon closer inspection, however, Helms-Burton highlights Ottawa's fundamentally inequitable position in the North Atlantic triangle, and demonstrates the dominance of the United States in Ottawa's foreign-policy calculus. It also indicates the lingering mistrust in Canada-EU relations at a time of supposed greater cooperation.

The Helms-Burton Act violates the spirit and letter of NAFTA (specifically chapters 11 and 16) and international trade rules. Canada and the member states of the EU are facing a growing number of secondary boycotts as a result of the plethora of American federal, state, and municipal sanctions. For this reason, the Europeans moved to set up a WTO panel to challenge the American legislation, which was eventually to proceed as far as choosing and naming the panel members. Steps were also taken to prepare a NAFTA challenge, but action actually stopped short of demanding a panel. A variety of reasons were cited for this reluctance, the most important of which was that Canada did not wish to forsake the overall tone of its bilateral relations with the United States for the sake of one piece of extraterritorial legislation.[3] The Europeans wanted Canada to be a full member of the WTO challenge rather than only an observer; the Canadian side, meanwhile, insisted on the sidelines and held the NAFTA challenge in reserve.

By the spring of 1997, Ottawa was growing progressively more suspicious of European motives. The Commission, on the one hand, was pushing Ottawa to launch a NAFTA challenge, while on the other it remained engaged in bilateral negotiations with the Americans while excluding the Canadian side. Unsaid, but hanging over Canada's position in the eyes of the European negotiators was the fact that Canada was no stranger to unilateral actions that contravened international law.[4] The "turbot war" between Canada and Spain in 1995 and Bill C-62 had surprised the EU and significantly undercut Canada's credibility as a champion of international law. And the Europeans were especially unhappy with Canada's reluctance to call for the NAFTA panel. Furthermore, they felt that Canada was trying to ride their coattails by acting as only an observer at the WTO panel. Ottawa's strategy, despite pressure from the Europeans, was to maintain the threat rather than carry it out. Such a position did not preclude Ottawa from eventually pursuing the WTO and NAFTA settlement options. However, had Ottawa acted as a full member of the WTO panel, it would have eliminated its ability to make a NAFTA challenge.

After engaging in a game of brinksmanship over Helms-Burton in February 1997 and going so far as to select the members for the WTO panel, the EU and U.S. signed an agreement on April 11 that suspended the panel until that October. The Europeans, having supported Canada's hard-line stance, putting antidote legislation in place, not attaching conditionality to a bilateral Canada-Cuba 14-point plan on greater cooperation against Helms-Burton in 1996, then refused to trilateralize their agreement with the Americans to include Canada because of their continuing annoyance at Canada's reluctance to proceed with the NAFTA panel. An obvious other consideration was that it would be easier to find a settlement without having to factor in the interests of a third party. Ironically, Canada received its information on the state of EU-U.S. negotiations from the American side. This is a reversal of the typical transatlantic pattern of negotiations among Canada, the U.S., and the EU: the Europeans were usually the ones pushing for Canada to be included, while the Americans rejected Canada's inclusion.

The explanations for the weak transatlantic coalition against Helms-Burton are varied. Part of Canada's ambivalence toward a strong coalition with Europe was that Canada's sights had drifted to Asia Pacific and Latin America and away from Europe. This ambivalence toward a coalition was matched on the European side since Canada had not been above tabling its own extraterritorial legislation. The Action Plan did little to reverse these centripetal forces.

RELATIONS WITH MEMBER STATES

Canada-EU and transatlantic relations past, present, and future can only be understood in the wider context of Canada's bilateral relations with the member states. As Roy Rempel notes, "since Germany is the most important power in Europe, the nature of Canada's relationship with it is ... a crucial indicator of the strength of Ottawa's commitment to the very idea of the Atlantic link."[5] Canada's Atlantic vocation has been linked inextricably to both the stationing of troops on the continent and its bilateral relationship with Germany. As argued in the previous chapter, Canada certainly marginalized its position within both NATO and, adopting Rempel's thesis, its bilateral relationship with Germany by its decision to withdraw forces from Europe. But while there was disappointment in Bonn with the Mulroney government's decision, this has not prevented German foreign ministry officials from talking about their relationship with Canada in glowing terms, namely, that it is one of the few industrialized countries with which Germany has few problems. The problem with a problem-free relationship, of course, is that it does not translate into a higher profile.

The relationship with London is of a higher profile, but beset by a more pessimistic outlook. The historical relationship between Canada and the U.K. has been a potent glue, making Britain the closest of all Canada's bilateral partners within the EU. London and Ottawa work closely together in international organizations such as the WTO, NATO, UN, and the Commonwealth and hold very similar approaches to most global issues such as ODA, defence cooperation, sustainable development, etc. The U.K. is the largest investor in Canada behind the United States, with 600 British companies in the country. As noted in Chapter 7, Canada's investment earnings in the U.K. are about equal to the rest of the EU combined. The U.K. is the third-largest trade market for Canada in manufactured products and is the gateway for European trade.

But despite the natural affinities, the "special relationship" is atrophying around the edges. For instance, while the U.K. is a natural ally on many issues, this should not imply that there are no differences between Ottawa and London (e.g., leg-hold traps). The official message from Whitehall is stark. Canada is taking the richness of bilateral relations, including the U.K.'s good offices within the EU, for granted. London feels that the U.K. is expending increasingly valuable political capital within the institutions of the EU—for example, during the fisheries crisis—while Canada is not doing enough to project its interests in Europe. There is a perception that Ottawa is content to sit on the sidelines and watch while London and Bonn, as its key partners, press its various cases (fish, TAFTA, fur). In short, say British officials, a greater commitment is needed at the "sharp" end from Ottawa. Lacking even the symbolic commitment of a small number of permanently stationed troops following the closure of bases in Germany, and, notwithstanding the commitment of Canadian peacekeepers in Bosnia, it is understandable that Canada's European partners view it as an even more marginal player in European security. As one British official noted dryly in response to the assertion that Canada made a commitment to European security in Bosnia, there were in fact more Malaysian troops than Canadian troops. In the long term, say British officials, they disconnect Ottawa's official rhetoric on Canada's active commitment to Europe from the facts.[6]

In contrast to Bonn's relative satisfaction with Ottawa's European policy approach, London feels that Canada needs to put some visible commitment behind its European rhetoric. This is to be expected. Given the colonial history and special relationship that continues to exist, British expectations are naturally higher than those of Germany. It is then somewhat ironic that, despite the mutual history, there are, in fact, very few structural relations between the U.K. and Canada. It is a distinctly unmodern connection. There is, for example, not even a Canada-U.K. parliamentary association. Using the spur of the Canada-EU Action Plan commitments, in early 1997 Canadian officials began the process of bilateralizing the Action Plan in order to modernize Canada-U.K. relations. Such efforts are, however, aggravated by the gradual disappearance of the "old-boys" system that historically had provided the glue between Canadian and British academic, political, and commercial networks. The German government, in comparison, is making a concerted effort to establish a German face in Canada through the sponsorship of, for example, academic chairs at select Canadian universities.

No one country will act as Canada's cornerstone in transatlantic relations, although Germany's role in an expanded EU should continue to grow since: (a) the enlargement will be eastward into its natural sphere of influence; and (b) there should be a reform of the weighting of votes in the Council of Ministers where Germany and other large EU member states are currently underrepresented. Therefore, Canada's bilateral relationship with Bonn will grow in importance. The question is whether an increased German role will diminish the U.K.'s role. The fear in London is that the U.K., relegated to finding "floating issues," will find itself in a minority all the time. Such a position would lessen the value to Ottawa of Britain's good offices in the Council of Ministers since, with the existing voting system, London will start to face permanent alliances and will be relegated to becoming a constant minority.[7]

IMPLICATIONS FOR CANADA OF EUROPEAN UNION ENLARGEMENT

Within the next decade it is anticipated that the EU will expand from its current 15 member states to as many as 28. This will have several implications for Canada. First, EU enlargement will raise tariffs against some Canadian exports, decreasing Canadian business opportunities, particularly in Eastern and Central Europe, in the process.[8] It will also affect exchange rates and therefore Canadian exports, particularly once

Central and Eastern European countries have devalued their exchange rates. Second, but related, is that as the EU increases in size it will become a more powerful trade negotiator, given the harmonization of trade rules and the integration of additional emerging markets. Third, enlargement will increase the political and economic leverage of the EU relative to Canada, through an increase in the membership of European countries to several international organizations such as the OECD and the WTO to which Canada also belongs. Fourth, disputes between Canada and the EU are likely to increase as the EU will be forced to defend a wider range of national interests.[9]

Although the EU's trading partners are entitled, under GATT Article XXIV, to negotiate compensation for the loss of markets that inevitably occurs with enlargement, satisfactory results are not usually garnered by outside countries such as Canada. The EU often provides compensation through increased outside access in a different commodity, or even in an entirely different sector from the one in which enlargement caused the trade diversion to occur. Third countries such as Canada find that there is little they can do to alter this unsatisfactory situation. It is difficult, for example, for Canada to raise import tariffs against the goods of one EU member state without sideswiping imports from another country in the process.[10]

It may be useful at this point to highlight the detrimental effects past EEC and EU rounds of enlargement have had on Canadian exports. Canadian agricultural exports, particularly wheat, were hard hit after the U.K.'s accession to the EEC in 1973. There were several reasons for this: British tariffs on Canadian goods were raised to EEC levels; EEC competitors gained duty-free access to the British market, as did outside countries that had trade agreements with the EEC; and CAP subsidies artificially stimulated British domestic agricultural production. At the time of writing, Canada's request for compensation remains unsatisfied.[11]

Most Canadian exports were not affected by the accesssions to the EU of Greece (1981), Spain (1986), and Portugal (1986) due to the high tariffs that existed previously in these countries. Salt cod, newsprint, and barley, however, were exceptions. Compensation to Canada for the loss of market access for Canadian barley exports was not resolved until December 1995, while compensation for the loss of market access for Canadian newsprint and salt cod remains unresolved, although the newsprint problem should be resolved with the elimination of the duty on newsprint imports by the EU in 2002.[12]

With the accession of Austria, Finland, and Sweden to the EU in January 1995, tariffs were increased on Canadian exports of fish and seafood, aluminum, and snowmobiles. Due to a lack of compensation provided by the EU for these tariff increases, Canada threatened to raise tariffs on imports of EU-produced perfume, vodka, shoes, and glassware. This threat was delayed, however, when the EU reduced tariffs on newsprint.[13]

The loss of market access caused by the four rounds of EU enlargements just alluded to forced Canada and the EU to the bargaining table on December 5, 1995 to discuss compensation to Canada. Agreements were reached on a number of issues. The EU agreed to eliminate tariffs altogether on items such as certain paper products and durum wheat and will reduce tariffs on items such as fish, frozen lobster, lead, zinc, and snowmobiles. The EU also agreed to improve market access for Canadian pork. Certainly, it can be expected that Canada, along with other so-called third countries, will face further negotiations over the loss of market access that the next round or rounds of EU enlargement will cause to those countries outside the EU.[14]

At the risk of repetition, another implication of EU enlargement for Canada is the increasing economic and political leverage Europe will be able to exercise through international organizations.[15] For example, Europe now accounts for 20 of the 26 members of the OECD.

Finally, Canada is also likely to find that it is involved in more disputes with the EU after enlargement since Brussels will be put in the position of defending the individual interests of more and more countries. As the fisheries dispute illustrates, Canadian disagreements with a single member state have the potential to disrupt Canada's relations with the entire EU. Canada, as a middle power, already finds itself at a huge disadvantage when dealing with a comparatively much more powerful large bloc of countries such as the EU. This disadvantage is only going to increase as the EU becomes economically and politically more powerful with each round of enlargement.[16]

This chapter's discussion of high-profile Canada-EU and transatlantic trade disputes, Canada's relations with key member states, and the ramifications of enlargement points to a major challenge for Ottawa. Where will it have to concentrate its diplomatic resources if it can foresee more trade disputes due to enlargement, a more complex type of dispute, and scepticism among policy makers in even the most pro-Canada member states who will be asked to provide a sympathetic ear to Canada's positions? This once more raises the question of whether to concentrate on bilateral or multilateral negotiations with Europe. In 1996 the Canadian Senate Foreign Affairs Committee, for example, urged the government in a report to multilateralize (in the OECD or WTO) transatlantic conflicts so as to counterbalance the growing EU's power. In light of Spain's role in holding up the Canada-EU Action Plan, the Committee reasoned that multilateralizing trade conflicts would prevent future member states from sabotaging transatlantic sectoral agreements that are favoured by Ottawa. It would indeed be ironic that if instead of using transatlantic dialogue to provide leadership to resolve global economic, political, security, and development problems, what occurs instead is that Ottawa attempts to internationalize its particular disputes with the EU so as to be on a more level playing field. The many international institutions in which Canada, the member states, and the Commission meet, would then be turned into Canada-EU battlegrounds.

As regards relations with member states, the special relationship with London is rooted in history; the one with Bonn is about the future leadership of the Atlantic community. The combination of a presidency that will come around fewer times due to enlargement and a continuing intergovernmentalism in the second and third pillars (albeit a waning one in the latter), will require a blend of bilateral and multilateral diplomacy from Ottawa. A major shift of Canada's diplomatic resources away from key member states such as Germany, France, and the U.K. to Community institutions in the belief that the progressive "communitization" of public policy issues in Europe will render bilateral diplomacy essentially anachronistic, would be premature in the near term. The bilateral diplomacy that will occur with an expanding number of member states on pan-European problems will as often be on an issue-by-issue basis: for example, Canada could target London as an ally on fisheries issues but not on leg-hold traps. Finally, the case of Helms-Burton dispelled any illusions in Ottawa that the EU was necessarily a natural ally. It re-established the principle of national interest in transatlantic relations.

NOTES

1. For a useful discussion on the increasing complexity of defining public policy issues, see Leslie A. Pal, *Beyond Policy Analysis: Public Issue Management in Turbulent Times* (Toronto: Nelson, 1997), 3-4.
2. Canada's multilateralist impulse is held up to scrutiny in Cutler and Zacher, *Canadian Foreign Policy.*
3. Evan H. Potter, "Canada and Helms-Burton: The Perils of Coalition-Building," paper presented at CPSA, Memorial University, June 10, 1997, 18.
4. *Ibid.*, 23.
5. Roy Rempel, *Counterweights: The Failure of Canada's German and European Policy, 1955-1995* (Montreal & Kingston: McGill-Queen's University Press, 1997), 194.
6. Author interview with senior British official responsible for North American affairs, Foreign and Commonwealth Office, April 1997.
7. *Ibid.*
8. Senate Report, *European Integration* (July 1996), 72.
9. *Ibid.*
10. *Ibid.*, 80.
11. *Ibid.*, 81.
12. *Ibid.*
13. *Ibid.*, 81-82.
14. *Ibid.*, 82.
15. *Ibid.*, 84.
16. *Ibid.*

XI
FUTURE DIRECTIONS

WHAT WILL BE CANADA's major role in Europe in the next century? On the security side, will the emphasis be on transnational security issues, regional security organizations, or maintaining the stability of the East? Will the tools be greater investment in regional institutions or new types of bilateral relations? On the trade front, what will engage Canada—more sectoral agreements or a renewed push for comprehensive free trade? Is the overarching goal to participate in European security and economic institutions so that they can act as catalysts for increased global security and multilateral economic liberalization? In short, how will Canada define itself to Europeans? As crisis manager, peacebuilder, humanitarian intervenor, or partner in the creation of new rules to respond to the new trade policy agenda?

By the time the Canada-EU Action Plan was completed at the end of 1996, vestiges of the seminal 1969 STAFEUR Report final recommendations were still evident in Canada's policy toward Europe. In Ottawa's declaratory policy and in its foreign policy actions (such as sending Canadian peacekeepers to Yugoslavia), it was clear that Canadian decision makers still considered Canada's security to be intimately, although, given Canada's exclusion from the Contact Group, perhaps no longer inextricably, linked with that of Europe. In keeping with the STAFEUR report's predictions, although Western Europe and the EU had become increasingly self-reliant, European leaders nevertheless recognized that they still had to maintain a basic interdependent relationship with North America. After a period of introspection on the possibility of an independent European security structure, there was a reaffirmation by the Europeans of NATO as the primary organization of European security. There was, however, also the recognition that with second and third pillars of Maastricht, the nature of this interdependence was now becoming different. At the same time, more progress was made on securing mutual commitments to decrease barriers to transatlantic economic ties. And with the creation of a pan-European economic area dominated by the EU, the security and economic tracks of transatlantic relations had a tendency to criss-cross more often, heightening transatlantic frictions.

This study has shown that, with the end of the Cold War, it is no longer possible to rely on shared perceptions of interest shaped by the awareness of dominant conflicts and powers, as was arguably the case in the 1950s, 1960s, 1970s, and well into the 1980s. Put crudely, there is more than ever a need for the *definition of shared interests* and the *identification of clashing priorities* in the Canada-EU relationship. At the same time, however, conditions make this infinitely more difficult than in the past. How can Canada rebuild the leverage with Europe that it has lost in the aftermath of the Cold War? In the thorny area of value differences, how can the decreasing "psychic" link be reversed or at least measures taken to demonstrate the importance of common understandings and values which bind Canada and Europe?

In order to maintain a linkage between the greater concern with cooperative security issues and the Canada-EU economic relationship, it is time for Canada to consider launching an overarching dialogue with Europe, beyond the TAD and the Action Plan, on the future of the transatlantic relationship. This discussion must include trade, investment, monetary and fiscal policy, defence, and cooperation in helping to resolve global problems. This process would involve a number of levers in addition to Canada's membership in NATO and the OSCE: fulfilling the Action Plan objectives; strengthening relations with the Commission and the European Parliament; regular contact with the new Commission secretariat responsible for CFSP; relations with the key member states, with specific focus on Germany as the EU's economic engine; and relations with the countries of Central and Eastern Europe. These avenues would allow a number of practical steps to be taken, many of them bilateral initiatives that would not sit well with Canada's multilateralist traditions.

While Canada has not made up its mind about what role it wants to play in Europe, a certain maturity has emerged since Ottawa has finally given up the notion of balancing its relationship with the United States through Europe. Historically Canada has been afraid of the political price for such a policy. No more.

This book, while showing a pattern of growing mutual indifference in Canada-EU relations, at the same time highlights the enduring ties that cannot be ignored. Canadian and European values and interests are more alike than those between Europe and the United States. For example, European and Canadian governments are more interventionist than their American counterparts and consequently have different approaches to public policy, welfare, labour, and social standards. Since Canadian society is more European than any other society in North America, EU officials have, in general, expressed greater affinity with Canadian positions in international and transatlantic negotiations.

But this greater European-Canadian affinity has not necessarily translated into greater influence for Canada within the North Atlantic triangle. First, Canada, in any transatlantic negotiations is overshadowed by the United States. Second, these similarities in values and structures have also been overshadowed by such controversies as the fisheries dispute and leg-hold traps. Third, words such as "sidelined," "marginalized," and "afterthought" describe how the Europeans view Canada's European role at the turn of the century. It used to be that Europeans would criticize Canada for its low per-capita contribution to NATO. One sign of Canada's growing marginalization is that the question of burden-sharing rarely arises anymore. The European view is that Canada has by and large withdrawn from Europe. In the words of a European observer, "there is a hesitation [in Ottawa] to define what Canada wants in Europe." To the Europeans' amazement, even when Canada was offered chairmanship of the OSCE in 1995, it declined.

CANADIAN NICHES IN THE FUTURE EUROPE

How will Canada project its interests in Europe in the coming years? Certainly, Canada is redefining its relations with Europe in a period of institutional flux. Where Canada asserts its interests will depend on how it defines its common security and economic interests at the end of the 20th century. As this author has argued elsewhere, Canada's best investment for the next century will be in international economic organizations rather than in international security organizations.[1] Canada has the capacity to play a much larger catalytic role on economic issues given its much larger influence in institutions such as the Quadrilateral Group and the G-7 than in security organizations such as NATO or even the UN.

One of Canada's most overlooked strengths in its transatlantic approach is its intellectual leadership on the new trade policy issues brought about by globalization. Canada has taken a proactive approach to intellectual property rights, competition policy, sustainable development, culture, and labour rights. With economic issues dominant in transatlantic affairs, trade policy cooperation will become more important.

Canada has potential to play a useful mediation role within the Triad, although it is vulnerable to being sideswiped in bilateral EU-Japan, EU-U.S., and Japan-EU conflicts. However, if the G-7 is transformed into the Group of Four (in light of the move toward EMU), then this in turn will redefine transatlanticism and have the effect of further undercutting Canadian influence.

With regard to its role in transatlantic security, Canada has, in the past, used its founding role in NATO as a basis for much of its influence in Europe. Even in the post-Cold War environment, this source of leverage should not be underrated. With the acceptance by Western Europe of the primacy of NATO in maintaining security on the continent, Canada, as an Alliance member, will continue to have a legitimate security interest on the continent. At the same time, as the intergovernmentalism of pillar three is gradually replaced by the Commission's supranational powers, a promising strategy is for Canada to pursue transatlantic cooperative security links with Brussels. And, surely, if Canada and the United States can cooperate on transnational security issues on an hemispheric basis through the Organization of American States, why would they not be able to do this on a transatlantic basis?

Traditional Canadian niches are changing, as well. For example, Canada's internationally recognized role as a peacekeeper par excellence has been smeared by the inquiry into criminal activities of Canadian soldiers while on duty in Somalia. Canada's participation in future UN peacekeeping missions is due to diminish because of a declining defence budget and the fact that the UN's demand for peacekeepers was, before the latest conflagration in Yugoslavia, projected to be down to only 10,000.[2] Moreover, as EU member states such as Britain and France take over peace enforcement duties in so-called "failed states" and other global flashpoints, Canada will be less and less able to rest on its peacekeeping laurels to gain entry into European decision making circles on questions of continental or international security.

Canada's real advantage in Europe rests on the role it can play in helping to stabilize the Eastern half of the continent. For instance, Canada has more citizens of Ukrainian descent than any West European country. This fact may lend it the moral leverage to play a mediatory role as the Ukraine adjusts itself to an expanding NATO. Canada can, therefore, increase its leverage with the Commission by promoting itself as a trade partner and political role model to the countries of Central and Eastern Europe.

Less State-driven Transatlantic Relations

A perennial concern among academic observers of Canada-EU relations has always been that too often they reflect the concerns of bureaucrats in Canada and the Commission. They have been too concerned with government-to-government institutionalization as a measurement of progress. The non-governmental community in Canada has been virtually absent from having input into policy debates on the future of transatlanticism. It is true that there are occasional conferences (e.g., the annual Canada-U.K. colloquium), and there is Canadian participation at the meetings of the Atlantik Brücke, but there is certainly no sustained discussion or research program. This is odd, to say the least, given the high level of economic interaction and political and cultural connections. For example, until 1996, there was no European Communities Studies Association in Canada. The policy networks in Canada that do exist to channel input from the non-governmental community to foreign-policy makers are predominantly oriented to the Asia Pacific region. They consist of an array of Asia Pacific Study centres at major universities, the Vancouver-headquartered and well-funded Asia Pacific Foundation, and Canadian participation at the Pacific Economic Cooperation Council. And unlike the United States, which has had considerable success in pulling top American and European business leaders into the policy process through a transatlantic "Business Dialogue," Ottawa, despite years of efforts and cajoling, has been unable to raise a similar level of interest among the Canadian business community. It is not surprising, therefore, that a Canadian version of a business dialogue is raised in the Canada-EU Action Plan. It is also worth noting that the European Parliament through a

Transatlantic Policy Network has been instrumental in prompting more activity on the future of transatlanticism by politicians, academics, and business people. Again, no such network exists in Canada.

This is certainly a rather sorry state of affairs for a country that professes to still be an Atlantic nation. There are faint rays of hope as ECSAC begins to develop organizationally. The Commission has also funded a Jean Monnet Chair in European Integration at the Université de Montréal, which has raised the profile of the EU in Quebec, but not in the rest of the country. Business leaders in Canada will, in all likelihood, continue to neglect the transatlantic policy domain unless it has a direct impact on their bottom lines.

Personal Diplomacy and Relations with Member States

One aspect of past approaches that will retain or increase its value in Canadian-European relations is the capacity of prime ministers to engage in personal diplomacy to ensure that Canada's voice is heard. In the absence of a values-driven security alliance, formalized personal access through the TAD and the Action Plan will prove invaluable. In the current global context and given an understanding of the dominant actors in the Canadian foreign policy process, personal diplomacy should not be underestimated.[3] This practice is made easier by the communications revolution and the fact that Canadian leaders meet frequently with their West European counterparts in an increasing number of forums.

Canada-EU relations past, present, and future can only be understood in the wider context of Canada's bilateral relations with the member states, both major and minor, and the participation of both Canada and the member states in various multilateral forums, whether security-related as in NATO and the OSCE or economic as in NAFO, the G-7, and the WTO.

The notion of Canada having a single postbox in Europe by virtue of its relationship with EU is overplayed; bilateral relations with the member states will still be very important. Canada will not be able to lessen its attention to the particular foreign policy perspectives of the individual member states when consulting with the EU through the CFSP framework. As Allen and Smith have suggested, by preserving the principal of consensus within the intergovernmental framework, the EU member states have, "undoubtedly chosen to accept limits on their ability to act in the world as a single entity."[4] The importance of the individual member states is underscored by the move toward an EU of 26 or 28 states by the first decade of the next century, where each new member will have a chance to influence Community policy during its six-month presidency. In terms of assets which could provide leverage in these situations, Canada could offer itself as a credible G-7 voice for the smaller EU states in return for access to EU decision making that affects its interests.

There will also be a change in Canada's relations with its historically most important European partners. Ottawa will, for example, no longer be able to rely as much on London's influence and good offices as Canada's front edge wedge in Europe.

CANADA AS *DEMANDEUR*

This book has described the future of transatlanticism as consisting of the attempt to resist the forces contributing to a drift among the three North Atlantic partners. It almost goes without saying that reversing this drift rests largely with American decision makers. Canada, for its part, can bank on the fact that it is North American rather than American. Yet, less and less do the Europeans view Canada as a useful intermediary, able to exert leverage to shift, however slightly or greatly, American positions.

Canada will never, of course, be able to drive the process of redesigning transatlanticism for the 21st century. But as noted above, it can play a number of catalytic roles. Ironically, although NATO headquarters and EU institutions are within several miles of each other in Belgium, there is very little contact between the two. Canada, as a member of NATO, can push to further contacts between the two organizations. There is also no question that it will benefit as a free-rider on some transatlantic trade negotiations between the EU and the United States.

There are a number of persistent problems and misperceptions in Canada's management of its European strategy that bear repeating. First, Ottawa, in pursuing the new transatlanticism, insists on being on the ground floor with Brussels and Washington on all such negotiations. The examinations of the negotiations leading up to the parallel TADs, the abortive attempt to create a TAFTA, and the action plans plainly show that Canada exhibits a strong me-tooism in its policy approach to transatlantic relations that leads it to attempt to trilateralize issues. While Canada is certainly more confident and no longer needs to use Europe as a counterweight to American influence, its desire to always trilateralize transatlantic issues conveys a lingering lack of maturity in relation to its American and European partners. In the words of one European Canada-watcher, "There does not seem to be a habit in Ottawa for Canada to build on its competitive edges in transatlantic affairs through bilateral means."

The Europeans, with the exception of their performance during the Helms-Burton negotiations, are willing to support this trilateralization; but the Americans reject this as seriously impractical and prefer the old dumb-bell approach to transatlanticism. As the historical record shows, the Europeans ultimately defer to Washington's preferences on the number of participants in such a dialogue.

Finally, while Canada may have trouble making its voice heard in Atlantic corridors and in achieving certain goals such as TAFTA, this should not deter it from pursuing a more cooperative transatlantic agenda. It may be that because of the more mature nature of the Canada-EU-U.S. triangle, the pressure to create a free trade zone was not as acute as in Latin America and Asia. Nonetheless, if Canada's contributions to transatlantic cooperation in the form of niche roles assists in the resolution of global problems in the security and economic domains, then so much the better.

But even such promising forecasts deserve more critical scrutiny. Canadian officials in Ottawa seem to believe that a selective, low-cost policy approach to Europe that concentrates on cooperative security will extract proportionally greater influence for Canada. The Europeans have, in fact, asked for less intellectual leadership, or software, on Atlantic issues and more hardware. Since the end of the Cold War, Canada has not been prepared to provide much more of the latter, however.

FIVE OPTIONS FOR CANADA'S FUTURE ROLE IN TRANSATLANTICISM

In light of this study's analysis, it would appear that there are five directions for transatlanticism.[5]

- *Continued fine-tuning*:
  No major treaty initiatives or official declarations, but more dialogue, coordinated policy, and common action.

- *A renewed emphasis on transatlantic security institutions*:
  The focus would be on military cooperation, humanitarian intervention, and crisis management, but it would ignore the horizontality (money laundering linked to drug trafficking, which in turn is linked to illegal migration) and transnational nature of the new security problems. Alliances would still be based on traditional conceptions of security.
- *Increased economic integration*:
  There would be an emphasis on securing a bloc-to-bloc free trade agreement between the EU and NAFTA to replace the sector-by-sector agreements that have been negotiated between Canada and the EU and the EU and the United States.
- *A coordinated response to global and regional challenges*:
  There would be a recognition of the inter-linkages among global problems such as sustainable development, migration, international criminal networks, etc. The idea is that greater transatlantic cooperation on these issues can be the incubator for best practices for the rest of the world.
- *A New Atlantic Treaty on Economic Relations and Security*:
  This would be a return to the Pearsonian vision of an Atlantic Alliance that encompasses both economic and defence cooperation.

The most likely direction will be increased coordination on global challenges as well as continued fine-tuning on the economic front. But whatever the new directions in Ottawa's European policy framework as it shifts its emphasis within the three pillars from NATO and the OSCE to the EU, what is not in doubt is that Canada, despite its eventual success with the TAD and the Action Plan, is today more than ever a *demandeur* in transatlantic relations.

At the end of the 1990s, the observer searching for a "grand design" in transatlantic relations would be disappointed. As with all such designs, perceptions lag behind reality, especially in Canada, which continues to be riven by the debate over national unity. For most Canadians, the traditional Europe with national parliaments, flags, and anthems is still the most visible. Meanwhile, the Europe beneath the surface—that of an integrating giant—is being transformed. It is to this Europe that Canada must now adjust, to a European Union that is becoming the "first pillar" in Canada's European policy approach.

NOTES

1. Evan H. Potter, "Niche Diplomacy as Canadian Foreign Policy," *International Journal* 52, 1 (Winter 1996/97): 34-35; and see also, "Redesigning Canadian Diplomacy in an Age of Fiscal Austerity," in Fen Osler Hampson and Maureen Appel Molot, eds., *Canada Among Nations, 1996: Big Enough to be Heard* (Ottawa: Carleton University Press, 1996), 23-56.
2. In 1994, UN total peacekeeping was 84,000; in 1997 it was 23,000, not including Bosnia.
3. Michel Duval, Director, West European Relations Division, EAITC, 17 July 1993.
4. David Allen and Michael Smith, "The European Community in the New Europe: Bearing the Burden of Change," *International Journal* 47 (Winter 1991/92): 11.
5. As described in "Perspectives on Transatlantic Relations," a background report initiated by the Forward Studies Unit of the European Commission, November 1995.

APPENDIX 1

INTERVIEWS

De Montigny Marchand, Under Secretary of State at the Department of External Affairs and International Trade (EAITC), (1986-1990).

John Weekes, Chief Negotiator of the North American Free Trade Agreement, Government of Canada (1989-1992).

William Dymond, Minister Counsellor, Canadian Embassy in Washington (1987-1992).

Gilles Landry, Director, West European Relations Division (RWR) at EAITC (1991-1993). He was a drafter of the EC-Canada-Transatlantic Declaration when he was a Desk Officer in RWR.

Michel Duval, Director, West European Relations Division at EAITC (Jan. 1992-1995).

Charles Court, Deputy Director, West European Relations Division (RWR) at EAITC (1989-1992).

John Klassen, Director, European Community Relations Division (RWM) EAITC (1991-1994).

Sean Boyd, Desk Officer, European Community Relations Division (RWM) EAITC (1991-1993).

Daniel Molgat, Canadian Ambassador to the European Communities (1988-1992).

Steve Brereton, Desk Officer, Canadian Delegation to the European Communities (Brussels), (1992-present).

Keith Aird, Desk Officer (forestry specialist), Canadian Delegation to the European Communities (Brussels), (1989-1993).

Gail Tyerman, Counsellor, Canadian Embassy in Washington, DC, (1988-1992).

Michael Hart, Director, Economic Planning, Policy Planning Staff at EAITC (1990-1992).

Sandy Bryce, Director, Economic Planning, Policy Planning Staff at EAITC (1988-1990).

Stuart Carre, Desk Officer, Policy Planning Staff at EAITC.

Thomas Delworth, Canadian Ambassador to Germany.

Mark Moher, former Director General, Policy Planning Staff at EAITC.

Bob Mercer, Counsellor Commercial, Canadian High Commission in London, U.K.

Cecil Latour, Counsellor (Economic), Canadian High Commission in London, U.K.

James Hyndman, retired, formerly senior official at EAITC.

Diane Thompson, Executive Director, Canadian Standards Association.

Jock Finlayson, Vice President, Policy and Research, Business Council on National Issues, Ottawa (1984-1993).

Timothy I. Page, Senior Vice President (International), Canadian Chamber of Commerce.

Jim More, Vice President (Policy), Canadian Exporter's Association.

Frank Deeg, Economic Counsellor, Delegation of the European Communities (Ottawa). He was the EC official in Canada responsible for monitoring and negotiating all bilateral agreements (Science and Technology, Fisheries, Competition, Customs).

Jacques Lecomte, Ambassador of the EC to Canada (1988-1994).

Mave Doran, Deputy Director (Canada/U.S.), Directorate General for External Affairs Relations (DGI), European Commission.

Jérome Vignon, Chief Advisor, Forward Studies Unit, European Commission.

Jeoffrey Lowe, Bureau of Economic Analysis, U.S. Department of Commerce.

APPENDIX 2

TABLE 6.2: TOP 30 CANADIAN FIRMS' INVESTMENTS IN THE EU (AS OF 1993)

Company Name	Industry	Sales, ($US millions)	Country	Pre-1986 Investments	Post-1986 Investment: Description
BCE Inc. (see also, Northern Telecom)	Communications	17,200	U.K.		BCE took 30% interest in London-based Videotron Corp. In 1992 BCE created BCE Telecom International, to manage all its transnational interests.
Royal Bank of Canada	Depositary Institution	12,414	U.K., The Netherlands, Greece, Germany, France, Belgium, Spain	Subsidiaries in U.K., Netherlands, Greece, Germany, France, and Belgium; branches in U.K. and Spain; and representative office in Italy	In 1992 Royal Bank closed its branch network in continental Europe.
George Weston Ltd.	Wholesale Trade	9,316	U.K. subsidiary		
Canadian Imperial Bank of Commerce	Depositary Institution	9,176	U.K., Italy, Holland, Germany, France	Subsidiaries	
Bank of Montreal	Depositary Institution	8,816	U.K., Germany, The Netherlands	Two branches and a subsidiary called First Canadian Financial Corp. BV (The Netherlands)	
Canadian Pacific (see also, Laidlaw Inc.)	Conglomerate: Transportation, resources, real estate, waste management, hotels	8,711	U.K., Germany, France, The Netherlands	Subsidiaries include CP hotels (Nederland); CP Steamships Ltd. U.K.); as well as affiliates in other EC countries	CP Forest Products Ltd., as a subsidiary, sells a wide range of forest products in EC.

Company Name	Industry	Sales, ($US millions)	Country	Pre-1986 Investments	Post-1986 Investment: Description
The Bank of Nova Scotia	Depositary Institution	8,287	Ireland, U.K., Germany	Subsidiary in U.K., Scotiabank (U.K.) Ltd.	In 1989 the bank established a subsidiary, NDS International (Ireland) Ltd., to handle off-shore lending. It also has an interest in First Southern Bank Ltd. (Ireland). As of 1992, it planned to expand its branch network in Greece.
Northern Telecom (see Table 6.3)	Communications Equipment	8,182			
Brascan Ltd. (see also, Noranda and Macmillan Bloedel)	Mining	7,979	The Netherlands	Brascan International BV	
Alcan Aluminum	Primary Metals	7,748	U.K., Belgium, France, Germany	Alumaier, Technal SA, and Alumines de Provence (France); PALCO (Spain)	In 1988 Alcan made significant investment in Ireland at Aughnish Alumina Ltd. In June 1990 it signed joint venture with then Eastern German producers. In June 1991 it formed a strategic alliance between its U.K. subsidiary and Japan's largest aluminum producer, Nippon Light Metal Co. (in which Alcan holds 44.3% interest).
Noranda Inc. (as unit of Brascan, see also, MacMillan Bloedel)	Lumber and Wood	7,118	U.K., Germany, The Netherlands	Sales subsidiary in London; commodity broker, Rudolf Wolff and Co. in U.K. and Germany; Highland Waferboard Mill (Scotland)	

Company Name	Industry	Sales, ($US millions)	Country	Pre-1986 Investments	Post-1986 Investment: Description
Sun Life Assurance Co. of Canada	Insurance	6,856	U.K., Ireland	Subsidiaries: Sun Life Assurance Co. of Britain with branches in 60 U.K. towns; subsidiary in Dublin, Ireland	
Abitibi-Price	Newsprint	n.a.	U.K.	Subsidiary/Abitibi-Price Sales	In 1990 Abitibi acquired a 50% stake in North British Newsprint Ltd. valued at C$400 million.
Banque Nationale du Canada	Depositary Institution	n.a.	U.K., France	Branches	In 1989 BNC made a joint venture with Banque Régionale d'Escompte et Dépots (France) to serve French-speaking Belgium, Luxembourg, Switzerland, and North Africa. In 1991 it announced a similar agreement with Caixa Galicia in Spain.
Bombardier Inc.	Transportation	3,400	Belgium, Ireland, France, U.K.		In 1986 Bombardier first acquired Belgian subsidiary BN. In 1989 it acquired Short Bros. PLC, and also purchased ANF Industrie SA of France for $C22 million. In 1990 it purchased Procor Engineering Ltd. of U.K. In 1991 it announced the consolidation of its European subsidiaries into Bombardier Eurorail SA (Belgium). This made Bombardier the fourth-largest firm in the European mass-transit sector. In 1992 Bombardier formed strategic links with Transmanche consortium and Aérospatiale in France.
CAE Industries Ltd.	Aerospace	n.a.	Germany	CAE Electronics GmbH	In 1991 CAE announced that its subsidiary was joining Lufthansa Commercial Holding GmbH.

Company Name	Industry	Sales, ($US millions)	Country	Pre-1986 Investments	Post-1986 Investment: Description
Inco Ltd.	Primary Metals	2,100	U.K., France, Germany, Italy, Belgium	Subsidiaries: Inco Europe Ltd., Inco Engineering Products, Greengrove Welding Wires, Doncasters, Incoform Bramah, Turbo Products, Renston Engineering, Inco Alloys Int'l (U.K.); Wiggin Steel and Alloys, SETTAS SA (Belgium)	
Lawson Mardon Group	Packaging	n.a.	U.K., France, Germany, Ireland, Italy	Lawson Mardon Group (Europe) Ltd., Trentesaux-Toulemond and Manelco (France); LMG Rotopac and Hammans Packaging (Germany); Superior Packaging (Ireland); Fibrenyle, Iridon, Thermoplastics, Smith Bros., Cellogals, Lloyds, Mardon, Pazo, and William Thyne (U.K.)	In 1988 LMG entered a joint venture with MB Group (U.K.) to manufacture plastic beverage containers. In 1989 they acquired the packagingdivision of U.K. candy maker, Rowntree-MacIntosh. In 1990 their London- based subsidiary purchased two German manufacturers in a move to position the firm for opportunities in Eastern Europe. Lawson Mardon further expanded in 1990 with the purchase of two U.K. firms, Jeyes Ltd. and Kooters (Liverpool) Ltd.
MacMillan Bloedel Ltd. (see also, Brascan)	Forest Products	n.a.	U.K., Belgium, Germany, The Netherlands	Macmillan Smurfit SCA Ltd. (U.K.), 50% interest in U.K. Corrugated PLC. Its European subsidiaries are MacMillan Bloedel (Europe) BV and MacMillan Bloedel (Limburg) BV (The Netherlands); MacMillan Bloedel Holdings (U.K.) Ltd., and Mercator Chartering Ltd. (U.K.)	In 1989 it invested an additional C$50 million in Dutch coated paper manufacturer KNP BV, gaining an interest in operations in The Netherlands, Belgium, and Germany.

Company Name	Industry	Sales, ($US millions)	Country	Pre-1986 Investments	Post-1986 Investment: Description
McCain Foods Ltd.	Food Processing	n.a.	U.K., France, Belgium, The Netherlands	Subsidiaries: Scarborough (U.K.); McCain Foods Europe NV (The Netherlands); McCain Alimentaire SARL (France); Frima (Belgium)	In 1986 McCain acquired Beau Marais (France). In 1990 it purchased Dutch potato producer H.A. van Tuyl BV. Europe is its fastest growing market, representing 45% of annual sales.
Molson Companies	Brewer and Retailer	n.a.	U.K., Ireland, The Netherlands	Molson Breweries (U.K.) Ltd. and Molson Financial Ltd. (U.K.); brewery in Cork (Ireland); Panlice BV and TMCL Int'l Holdings BV (The Netherlands)	
Moore	Business Forms	n.a.	Italy, Germany, licensing only in Greece	Decoflex Ltd. and Delphan Ltd. (U.K.); Carbonia BV (The Netherlands); Lampar SARL (France)	Acquired Belgian business forms firm (Lithorex). Moore has new continental head office in Switzerland, opened in 1989, to give it a continent-wide market. In 1991 it entered into joint venture with Atel (Italy), opened a sales office in Germany, and engaged in licensing agreement with a Greek firm. It is also targetting Spain.
Power Corporation of Canada	Conglomerate	n.a.	France, Belgium	Groupe Bruxelles Lambert SA (Belgium)	In 1991 Power Corp. opened an office in Paris to coordinate its European operations.
Seagram Company Ltd.	Distiller	6,242	France, U.K.		In 1988 Seagram purchased French Cognac-maker, Martell for US$925 million, and Champagne giant, Mumm & Cie.
Stelco	Steel	n.a.	The Netherlands	Stow Int'l (The Netherlands)	

Company Name	Industry	Sales, ($US millions)	Country	Pre-1986 Investments	Post-1986 Investment: Description
Toronto-Dominion Bank	Depositary Institution	n.a.	U.K.	U.K. subsidiary	In 1991 TD Securities announced a cooperative arrangement with Hambros Bank of London in the field of corporate finance, and global M&A.
John Labatts Ltd.	Food and Beverage	n.a.	U.K., Italy, Ireland	BCL Finance (Ireland)	Between 1985-87, a U.K. subsidiary, Labatt Breweries of Europe was set up. In 1989 Labatt's purchased Italy's Birra Morett Spa and Prinz Brau.
Royal Trust Co.	Depositary Institution	n.a.	U.K., Germany	Royal Trust Bank	Royal Trust began its European expansion in 1985, with European assets in 1991 totalling C$8 billion. In 1989 it bought 25% of Gries & Heissel, a German bank. In 1993 due to significant nonperforming loans outside of Canada, Royal Trust was sold to the Royal Bank.
Laidlaw Inc. (see, Canadian Pacific)	Transportation and Waste Management	n.a.	U.K.		In 1989 Laidlaw acquired a 29% interest in Atwoods PLC. It also has a 28.8% stake in British auction and security services firm, ADT PLC.
Hollinger Inc.	Newspaper Publishing	5,800	U.K.	Controllling shareholder (82%) of *Daily Telegraph* PLC and 9% of United Newspapers PLC.	In 1990 Hollinger acquired a 10% interest in Trinity Int'l PLC in Liverpool.

Source: Data compiled from survey of top Canadian firms active in Europe; Knubley, Legault, and Rao, "Multinationals and FDI," in Eden, *Multinationals in North America*, 166; Company Annual Reports; and *Business Week*, July 11, 1994, 62.

TABLE 6.3: INVESTMENTS OF NORTHERN TELECOM, 1983-93

Date	Type of Investment	Name of Company	Host Country	Financial Detail	Description	Industrial Activity
May 1993	Acquisition (Greenfield)	NETAS-Northern Electric Telekom-munikayson AS	Turkey	51%	Increased participation from 31% to 51%	
1993	Acquisition	Lagardère Groupe SCA	France	C$45M		
Jan. 1993	Partnership	Bell Atlantic Meridian Systems	U.S.		Association with Bell	Marketing, sales and services for communi-cations equipment
July 1992	Acquisition of minority stake	Matra SA	France	20% C$140M		
April 1992	Acquisition	Novatel	Alberta			
March 1992	Joint Venture	Northern Telecom de Espana	Spain	50%	Joint venture with Agroman Inversiones SA (37.5%) and Radio-tronica SA (12.5%)	
Feb. 1992	Joint Venture	Motorola-Nortel	U.S.		Joint venture with Motorola	Sales of tele-phone service in Canada, the Antilles, Central and South America, and the U.S.
Feb. 1992	Joint Venture	Northern Telecom Elwro	Poland		Joint venture with Elwro of Poland	Manufacturing of communica-tions equip-ment

Date	Type of Investment	Name of Company	Host Country	Financial Detail	Description	Industrial Activity
1991	Divestiture	Subsidiary of STC	U.K.	US$335M		
Feb. 1991	New Investment	Northern Telecom/ Asia Pacific	Asia			Sales and services
Feb. 1991	New investment	Northern Telecom Europe	Europe			
Nov. 1990	Acquisition	STC PLC	U.K.	US$ 2560M	Purchase of all shares	
1989	Joint Venture	Microtel (branch of BC Tel)	Canada	51%	Joint venture with BC Tel	
1989	Acquisition	AWA-Norel PTY		40%		
1988	Divestiture	Northern Telecom PLC	U.K.	C$70M	Sold to STC PLC	
1987	New Investment	NT Meridien SA	France			Installation and manufac-turing and R&D
Oct. 1987	Acquisition	STL PLC	U.K.	24% $US 728M	Interest accruing at 27.5%	
1986	New Investment	Northern Telecom Europe Ltd.	Europe		Manage-ment services in the Middle East, and Europe	
July 1985	New Investment	Northern Telecom Pacific	Asia			
1983	New Investment	Subsidiary of Bell-Northern Reseach	U.K.			Laboratory
1983	Joint Investment	Research in U.K./ Northern Telecom PLC	U.K.			

Source: Amesse, Séguin-Dulude, and Stanley, "Northern Telecom," in Globerman, *Canadian-Based Multinationals*, 432-34, Table 3.

APPENDIX 3

TABLE 7.1: CANADIAN EXPORTS TO THE EUROPEAN UNION, 1958-96 (C$ millions)

Country	1958	1960	1965	1970	1972
France	40	50	96	158	251
Germany	103	127	210	370	513
The Netherlands	27	32	56	79	92
Belgium/Luxembourg	36	41	72	52	90
Italy	32	43	80	145	204
U.K.*	—	—	—	—	—
Spain*	—	—	—	—	—
Portugal*	—	—	—	—	—
Greece*	—	—	—	—	—
Denmark*	—	—	—	—	—
Ireland*	—	—	—	—	—
Total Canadian Exports to EC	**237**	**293**	**514**	**805**	**1,149**
Total Canadian Exports	5,050	5,491	8,633	13,952	18,669
Exports to EU as % of total	4.7	5.3	5.9	5.8	6.1
Exports to U.S.	3,460	3,693	6,045	9,917	12,878
Exports to U.S. as % of total	68.5	67.2	70	71	69
Exports to Japan	70	110	230	582	1,071
Exports to Japan as % of total	1.4	2	2.7	4.2	5.7

Country	1975	1978	1980	1982	1984
France	350	479	1,017	754	736
Germany	609	792	1,668	1,284	1,225
The Netherlands	481	574	1,442	1,058	1,088
Belgium/Luxembourg	381	486	1,002	791	701
Italy	479	486	1,004	702	600
U.K.	1,789	1,898	3,245	2,725	2,535
Spain*	—	—	—	—	—
Portugal*	—	—	—	—	—
Greece*	—	—	—	77	50
Denmark	28	64	89	87	98
Ireland	18	31	116	99	99
Total Canadian Exports to EU	**4,135**	**4,810**	**9,583**	**7,577**	**7,132**
Total Canadian Exports	33,103	52,842	76,159	84,535	112,383
Exports to EU as % of total	12.5	9.1	12.6	9.0	6.3
Exports to U.S.	21,653	37,175	48,172	57,679	84,928
Exports to U.S. as % of total	65.4	70.4	63.3	68.2	75.6
Exports to Japan	2,122	3,062	4,374	4,594	5,666
Exports to Japan as % of total	6.4	5.8	5.8	5.4	5.0

* Figures are not provided for years prior to a country's membership in the EU.

Country	1986	1988	1990	1992	1993	1996
France	1,012	1,227	1,304	1,422	1,284	1,751
Germany	1,309	1,778	2,323	2,308	2,489	3,336
The Netherlands	1,009	1,437	1,649	1,500	1,354	1,653
Belgium/Luxembourg	845	1,335	1,252	1,094	919	1,530
Italy	711	1,034	1,188	1,175	952	1,363
U.K.	2,731	3,607	3,541	3,127	2,925	4,036
Spain	140	245	387	452	335	523
Portugal	154	169	180	166	105	100
Greece	66	61	97	74	91	121
Denmark	111	136	138	150	118	123
Ireland	91	217	139	92	93	241
Austria	—	—	—	—	—	424
Finland	—	—	—	—	—	207
Sweden	—	—	—	—	—	282
Total Canadian Exports to EU	**8,179**	**11,243**	**12,198**	**11,560**	**10,665**	**15,708**
Total Canadian Exports	120,669	138,498	148,979	162,596	186,682	275,921
Exports to EU as % of total	6.8	8.1	8.2	7.1	5.7	5.7
Exports to U.S.	93,237	100,886	111,599	125,725	150,636	223,479
Exports to U.S. as % of total	77.3	72.8	74.9	77.3	80.7	80.9
Exports to Japan	5,967	8,813	8,230	7,485	8,459	11,160
Exports to Japan as % of total	4.9	6.4	5.5	4.6	4.5	4.0

Country	1986	1988	1990	1992	1993	1996
Exports to EFTA					1,906	1,810
Exports to EFTA as % of total					1.0	.65

Source: Statistics Canada, *Exports: Merchandise Trade*, cat. 65-202, 1992, annual 1984-92, and cat. 65-006, Dec. 1993, monthly, and other catalogues prior to 1984.
Note: Figures may not be strictly comparable.

TABLE 7.2: CANADIAN IMPORTS FROM THE EUROPEAN UNION, 1958-96
(C$ millions)

Country	1975	1978	1980	1982	1984
France	487	684	773	887	1,256
Germany	795	1,244	1,455	1,384	2,249
The Netherlands	159	227	264	267	509
Belgium/Luxembourg	143	202	251	264	444
Italy	380	525	611	725	1,172
U.K.	1,222	1,600	1,974	1,904	2,474
Spain*	—	—	—	—	—
Portugal*	—	—	—	—	—
Greece*	—	—	—	30	42
Denmark	78	97	120	129	206
Ireland	32	57	101	129	157
Total Canadian Imports from EU	**3,296**	**4,636**	**5,549**	**5,709**	**8,509**
Total Canadian Imports	34,636	49,938	69,274	67,926	95,459
Imports from EU as % of total	9.5	9.3	8.0	8.4	8.9
Imports from U.S.	23,559	35,246	48,614	47,917	66,466
Imports from U.S. as % of total	68.0	70.6	70.2	70.5	69.7
Imports from Japan	1,205	2,268	2,796	3,536	6,171
Imports from Japan as % of total	3.8	4.5	4.0	5.2	6.5

* Figures are not provided for years prior to a country's membership in the EU.

Country	1986	1988	1990	1992	1993	1996
France	1,664	2,884	2,448	2,689	2,260	3,400
Germany	3,572	3,841	3,835	3,532	3,504	4,821
The Netherlands	664	762	719	599	666	931
Belgium/Luxembourg	569	608	566	448	530	818
Italy	1,750	1,954	1,954	1,747	1,934	2,719
U.K.	3,573	4,629	4,898	4,095	4,429	5,909
Spain	495	713	496	436	501	687
Portugal	82	119	171	185	179	177
Greece	73	68	71	64	58	68
Denmark	244	258	248	243	233	354
Ireland	173	216	257	393	431	591
Austria	—	—	—	—	—	607
Finland	—	—	—	—	—	418
Sweden	—	—	—	—	—	1,201
Total Canadian Imports from EU	**12,859**	**16,052**	**15,663**	**14,431**	**14,725**	**22,737**

Country	1986	1988	1990	1992	1993	1996
Total Canadian Imports	112,511	131,245	136,245	147,994	169,460	233,114
Imports from EC as % of total	11.4	12.2	11.5	9.8	8.7	9.7
Imports from U.S.	75,227	86,020	87,875	95,514	113,602	157,494
Imports from U.S. as % of total	66.9	65.6	64.5	65.2	67.0	67.5
Imports from Japan	8,367	9,267	9,525	10,762	10,690	10,444
Imports from Japan as % of total	7.4	7.1	7.0	7.3	6.3	4.5

Country	1986	1988	1990	1992	1993	1996
Imports from EFTA					3,180	3,846
Imports from EFTA as % of total					1.9	1.65

Source: Statistics Canada, *Exports: Merchandise Trade*, cat. 65-203, 1992, annual 1984-92, and cat. 65-007, Dec. 1993, monthly, and other catalogues prior to 1984.
Note: Figures may not be strictly comparable.

APPENDIX 4

TABLE 7.3: TRADE FLOWS IN CANADA-EU BUSINESS SERVICES, 1986-96
(C$ millions)

Area	Receipts						
	1986	1988	1989	1990	1991	1992	1996
EU	977	1,295	1,374	1,487	1,514	1,514	2,670
U.K.	324	518	518	560	582	6429	1,042
Belgium	39	67	42	54	73	54	70
France	179	200	202	227	236	184	234
Germany*	149	205	239	243	242	279	568
Italy	71	92	89	93	72	125	99
The Netherlands	96	118	160	169	159	85	88
U.S.	3,362	4,420	4,582	4,895	5,238	7,052	12,138
All countries	5,882	7,559	8,023	8,322	8,827	11,080	19,519
EU as % of All	16.6	17.1	17.1	17.9	17.1	13.7	13.8

Area	Payments						
	1986	1988	1989	1990	1991	1992	1996
EU	1,612	1,823	1,960	1,849	2,111	1,844	2,658
U.K.	1,067	1,027	1,120	978	1,259	998	1,287
Belgium	41	43	39	40	52	36	45
France	172	294	320	284	264	290	319
Germany*	148	167	172	208	211	235	585
Italy	72	92	101	126	115	20	71
The Netherlands	90	160	154	154	151	140	123
U.S.	6,687	7,591	8,426	8,812	8,882	10,031	16,348
All countries	9,484	11,036	11,952	12,370	12,957	14,050	22,497
EU as % of All	17.0	16.5	16.4	14.9	16.3	13.1	11.8

*Prior to 1991, refers only to West Germany

Sources: Statistics Canada, *Canada's International Transactions in Services, 1988-89.* cat. 67-203 (Ottawa: 1990); *Canada's International Transactions in Services, 1989-90.* cat. 67-203 (Ottawa: 1991); *Canada's International Transactions in Services, 1991-92.* cat. 67-203 (Ottawa: 1992); *Canada's International Transactions in Services, 1997.* cat. 67-203 (Ottawa: 1992); *Canada's International Transactions in Services, 1997.*

Note: Figures were not available for Luxembourg, Spain, Portugal, and Greece.

BIBLIOGRAPHY

Abshire, David, 1990. "The Nature of American Global Economic Leadership in the 1990s." In *The Global Economy: America's Role in the Decade Ahead*, eds. W. Brock and R. Hormats. New York: Norton, for the American Assembly.

Alexandroff, Alan S. 1994. "The Global Economy and Canada: Meeting and Managing Change." Draft report for Canada 21 Council's *Canada and Common Security in the Twenty-First Century.* Toronto: Centre for International Studies.

———. 1994. "Global Economic Change: Fashioning Our Own Way." In *Canada Among Nations 1994: A Part of the Peace*, eds. Maureen A. Molot and Harald von Riekhoff. Ottawa: Carleton University Press, 27-52.

Allen, David, and Michael Smith. 1991-92. "The European Community in the New Europe: Bearing the Burden of Change." *International Journal*, 47 (Winter): 1-28.

Allison, Graham T. 1971. *Essence of Decision: Explaining the Cuba Missile Crisis.* Boston: Little Brown.

———, and Morton H. Halperin. 1972. "Bureaucratic Politics: A Paradigm and Some Policy Implications." In *Theory and Policy in International Relations*, eds. Raymond Tanter and Richard A. Ullman. Princeton, NJ: Princeton University Press.

Amesse, Fernand, Louise Seguin-Dulude, and Guy Stanley. 1994. "Northern Telecom: A Case Study in the Management of Technology." In *Canadian-Based Multinationals*, ed. Steven Globerman. Calgary, AB: University of Calgary Press and Industry Canada.

Andrew, Arthur. 1993. *The Decline of a Middle Power: Canadian Diplomacy from King to Mulroney.* Halifax, NS: James Lorimer.

Anstis, Christopher. 1992. "CSCE Mark II: Back to Helsinki from Paris via Berlin and Prague." *Nato Review*, 2 (April): 18-23.

Aucoin, Peter. 1994. "Prime Ministerial Leadership: Position, Power, and Politics." In *Leaders and Leadership in Canada*, eds. M. Mancuso, R. Price, and R. Wagenberg. Toronto: Oxford University Press.

Axelrod, Robert, and Robert O. Keohane. 1986. "Achieving Cooperation Under Anarchy: Strategies and Institutions." In *Cooperation Under Anarchy*, ed. Kenneth A. Oye. Princeton, NJ: Princeton University Press.

Axworthy, Lloyd, and Christine Stewart. May 1993. *Liberal Foreign Policy Handbook.* Ottawa: Liberal Party of Canada.

Bakvis, Herman. 1994. "Cabinet Ministers: Leaders or Followers?" In *Leaders and Leadership in Canada*, eds. M. Mancuso, R. Price, and R. Wagenberg. Toronto: Oxford University Press.

Baldwin, Robert. 1986. *Issues in U.S.-EC Trade Relations.* Chicago: University of Chicago Press.

———. "The Growth Effects of 1992." *Economic Policy*, 2.

Barry, Donald. 1975. "Interest Groups and the Foreign Policy Process." In *Pressure Group Behaviour in Canadian Politics*, ed. A. Paul Pross. Toronto: McGraw-Hill Ryerson.

Barry, Donald. 1980. "The United States and the Development of the Canada-European Community Contractual Link Relationship." *American Review of Canadian Studies*, 10 (Spring): 63-74.

———, Mark O. Dickerson, and James D. Gaisford, eds. 1995. *Toward a North American Community? Canada, the United States and Mexico.* Boulder, CO: Westview Press.

Bedeski, Robert, and James Bayer. 1993. *Multilateralism in the Asia Pacific Region and Canada's Possible Role.* Draft made available to the author.

Benoit, E. 1961. *Europe at Sixes and Sevens: The Common Market, the Free Trade Area, and the United States.* New York: Columbia University Press.

Black, David R. and Heather A. Smith. 1993. "Directions in Canadian Foreign Policy Literature." *Canadian Journal of Political Science*, 26, 4 (December): 745-74.

Blanchette, Arthur E., ed. 1994. *Canadian Foreign Policy, 1977-1992: Selected Speeches and Documents.* Ottawa: Carleton University Press.

Boardman, Robert. 1979a. "European Responses to Canada's Third Option Policy." In *The European Community and Canada-EC Relations*, ed. Marie Fleming. Ottawa: European Politics Group.

———. 1979b. "Initiatives and Outcomes: The European Community and Canada's 'Third Option.'" *Journal of European Integration*, 3, 1: 5-28.

———. *et al.* 1984. *The Canada-European Communities Framework Agreement: A Canadian Perspective.* Saskatoon, SK: Canadian Council for European Affairs.

———. 1992. "The Singular Case of the Disappearing Link: The Economics of Change and the Politics of Survival in Canada-U.K. Relations." In *Britain and Canada in the 1990s: Proceedings of a U.K./Canada Colloquium*, ed. D.K. Adams. Aldershot, U.K.: Dartmouth Publishing and Institute for Research on Public Policy.

Boyd, James. 1992. "Canada and the European Community," Master's thesis, Carleton University, Ottawa.

Brebner, John Bartlett. 1966. *North Atlantic Triangle: The Interplay of Canada, the United States and Great Britain.* Toronto: McClelland & Stewart.

Brown, Douglas M. 1993. "The Evolving Role of the Provinces in Canada-U.S. Trade Relations." In *States and Provinces in the International Political Economy*, eds. Douglas M. Brown and Earl H. Fry. Berkeley, CA: Institute of Governmental Studies Press, University of California.

Brzezinski, Zbigniew. 1991/92. "The Consequences of the End of the Cold War for International Security." In *New Dimensions in International Security, Part I.* Adelphi Papers no. 265. London: Brassey's for the International Institute for Strategic Studies, 3-17.

Bush, George. May 21, 1989. Boston University Commencement Address.

Buteux, Paul. April 30-May 2, 1988. "Political Neglect of European Markets," *The Financial Post.*

Calingaert, Michael. 1988 *The 1992 Challenge from Europe.* Washington DC: National Planning Association.

———. 1992. "The European Community's Emerging Political Dimension." *SAIS Review* 12, 1 (Winter/Spring): 58-70.

Canada. Department of External Affairs. 1965. Study Group on Europe, "Eurocan: A Policy Planning Paper on Relations Between Canada and Europe." Ottawa: Department of External Affairs.

———. 1969. *STAFEUR Report.* Ottawa: Department of External Affairs.

———. 1970. *Foreign Policy for Canadians.* Ottawa: Supply and Services.

———. July 7, 1976. *Framework Agreement for Commercial and Economic Co-operation between Canada and the European Communities.* Ottawa.

———. 1983. *A Review of Canadian Trade Policy: A Background Document to Canadian Trade Policy for the 1980s.* Ottawa: Supply and Services.

———. 1983. Senior Officials' Meeting on Canada's Relations with Western Europe: Policy Analysis Group. Summary of Proceedings.

———. 1983. *The Third Option: Retrospect and Prospect.* Ottawa: Department of External Affairs.

———. 1983. *Canadian Trade Policy for the 1980s.* Ottawa: Supply and Services.

———. 1985. *Competitiveness and Security: Directions for Canada's International Relations.* Ottawa: Supply and Services.

———. April 1989. *1992: Implications of a Single Market.* Part I, Ottawa: EAITC.

———. Sept. 1989. *The European Community: A Canadian Perspective.* Ottawa: EAITC.

———. 1989. *Europe 1992: Your Business Opportunity.* Ottawa: EAITC.

———. 1989. *Going Global, Guide to Programs and Services.* Ottawa: EAITC.

———. 1989. *The European Economic Community: A Guide for Canadian Exporters.* Ottawa: EAITC.

———. 1990. *Statements and Speeches.* Ottawa: EAITC.

———. 1991. *Moving Into Europe.* Ottawa: EAITC.

———. 1991. *Link '92: The Experience of Successful Canadian Companies in Europe, United Kingdom, France, Germany, the Netherlands.* Ottawa: EAITC.

———. 1991. *Foreign Policy Framework, 1991: Managing Interdependence* [known publicly as "Foreign Policy Update"]. Ottawa: EAITC, Policy Planning Staff.

Canada. Department of External Affairs and International Trade. 1994. *1994-1995 Estimates, Expenditure Plan.* Ottawa: Supply and Services.

Canada. Government of Canada. Nov. 22, 1990. "Canada-European Community Agree on Transatlantic Declaration." News Release.

———. May 21-22, 1991. *Report on the Meeting of Canadian Forest Products Commercial Officers in Western Europe.* Brussels: Government of Canada.

———. June 30, 1992. *Canadian Science and Technology: Moving Forward to Cooperate with the Research and Technological Development Framework Programs of the European Community.* Ottawa: Government of Canada.

———. August 1992. *North American Free Trade Agreement: An Overview and Description.* Ottawa: EAITC.

Canada. House of Commons. June 1992. Standing Committee on External Affairs and International Trade. Sub-Committee on International Trade. *Canada's Relations with the New Europe.* Ottawa: Queen's Printer.

Canada. Industry Canada, Micro-Economic Policy Analysis Staff. May 1994. "Formal and Informal Investment Barriers in the G-7 Countries: The Country Chapters." *Occasional Paper* 1, 1: 286-89.

Canada. Industry Canada. July 1994. "Canadian-Based Multinationals: An Analysis of Activities and Performance." *Working Paper Series,* no. 2.

———. July 1994. Appendix 2, "List of Top Outwardly-Oriented Canadian-Based Firms." In "Canadian-Based Multinationals: An Analysis of Activities and Performance." *Working Paper Series,* no. 2. Ottawa: Industry Canada.

Canada. Department of National Defence. 1987. *Challenge and Commitment.* Cat. No. D2-73/1987E. Ottawa: Supply and Services.

Canada. Royal Commission on the Economic Union and Development Prospects for Canada, 1985. *Final Report.* Ottawa: Supply and Services.

Canada. Senate Standing Committee on Foreign Affairs. July 1973. *Canadian Relations with the European Community.* Ottawa.

———. 1982. *Canada's Trade Relations with the United States.* Ottawa: Senate of Canada.

———. Report, July 1996. *European Integration: The Implications for Canada.* Ottawa.

Canada. Report of the Special Joint Committee on Canada's International Relations. June 1986. *Independence and Internationalism.* Ottawa: Parliament of Canada.

Canada. Report of the Special Joint Committee Reviewing Canada's Foreign Policy. Nov. 1994. *Canada's Foreign Policy: Principles and Priorities for the Future.* Ottawa: Parliament of Canada.

Canada. Statistics Canada. 1992. *Canada's International Trade in Services, 1991-92.* Ottawa.

Canada. Statistics Canada. 1993. *Canada's International Investment Position: Historical Statistics, 1926-1991*, cat. 67-202. Ottawa.

———. *Exports: Merchandise Trade, 1984-92*, cat. 65-202 (1992), 65-203 (1992); cat. 65-006 (Dec. 1993), 65-007 (Dec. 1993).

Canadian Manufacturers' Association. 1992. *The Aggressive Economy*. Toronto: Canadian Manufacturers' Association.

Canada 21 Council. 1994. *Canada and Common Security in the Twenty-First Century*. Toronto: Centre for International Studies, University of Toronto.

Cantwell, J. 1989. *Technological Innovation and Multinational Corporation*. Oxford: Blackwell.

Caves, R.E. 1959. "Europe's Unification and Canada's Trade." *Canadian Journal of Economics and Political Science*, 25, 3 (August): 249-58.

Cecchini, Paolo, Michel Catinat, Alexis Jacquemin. 1988. *The European Challenge 1992: The Benefits of a Single Market*. Aldershot, U.K.: Gower.

Christie, Keith. 1993. "Different Strokes: Regionalism and Canada's Economic Diplomacy." *Policy Planning Staff Paper*. Ottawa: External Affairs and International Trade.

———. Jan. 1994. "The Day After: An Agenda for Diversifying Free Trade." *Policy Staff Paper*, no. 94/04. Ottawa: Department of Foreign Affairs and International Trade.

Clarkson, Stephen. December 13, 1976. *Globe and Mail*.

Clement, Wallace. 1977. *Continental Corporate Power: Economic Elite Linkages between Canada and the United States*. Toronto: McClelland & Stewart.

Cline, William. 1989. *United States External Adjustments and the World Economy*. Washington, DC: Institute for International Economics.

Coffey, Peter. 1976. *The External Economic Relations of the EEC*. London: Macmillan.

Commission of the European Communities, Canadian Delegation. 1990. "Declaration on European Community-Canada Relations." *European Community News*. Ottawa: NR(90) 9, November 22, 1990.

Commission of the European Communities. 1988a. *Completing the Internal Market: An Area Without Internal Frontiers*. Brussels: COM.

———. 1988b. *Europe 1992: Europe World Partner*. Information Memo P-117, October 19, 1988.

Cooper, Andrew F. 1993. "Questions of Sovereignty: Canada and the Widening International Agenda." In *Behind the Headlines*, 50, 3. Toronto: Canadian Institute of International Affairs.

———, and Richard A. Higgott. 1991. "Middle Power Leadership in the International Order: A Reformulated Theory for the 1990s." Paper presented at the 1991 International Studies Association Conference in Vancouver, Canada.

Cooper, Andrew F., and Kim Richard Nossal. 1991. "Bound to Follow? Leadership and Followership in the Gulf Conflict." *Political Science Quarterly*, 106, 3: 391-410.

———, Higgott, Richard A., and Kim Richard Nossal. 1993. *Relocating Middle Powers: Australia and Canada in a Changing World Order.* Vancouver: University of British Columbia Press.

Cox, David. 1994. "Canada and the United Nations: Pursuing Common Security." *Canadian Foreign Policy*, 2, 1: 29-38.

Crane, David. August 2-5, 1986. "Canada's Threatened Identity," *Toronto Star.*

———. June 8-12, 1985. "Free-Trade: Salvation or Sell-Out?" *Toronto Star.*

Cunningham, W.B., ed. 1962. *Canada, the Commonwealth, and the Common Market.* Montreal: McGill University Press.

Cutler, A. Claire. 1993-94. "Review of The Development of Postwar Canadian Trade Policy: The Failure of the Anglo-European Option." *International Journal*, 49, 1 (Winter): 160-61.

———, and Mark W. Zacher. 1992. "Introduction," in *Canadian Foreign Policy and International Economic Regimes*, eds. A. Claire Cutler and Mark W. Zacher. Vancouver: University of British Columbia Press.

Danchev, Alex. 1991. "Taking the Pledge: Oliver Franks and the Negotiation of the North Atlantic Treaty." *Diplomatic History*, 15, 2 (Spring): 199-220.

Davenport, M.W., and S. Page. 1991. *Europe: 1992 and the Developing World.* London: Overseas Development Institute.

Day, Shannon. June 30, 1993. "Canada Risks Sideswipe in U.S.-EC Telecom Spat." *Globe and Mail.*

de Clerq, Willy. August 2, 1988. "The European Community in a Changing World." Speech, Fundacion Jorge Esteban Roulet, Buenos Aires.

Demers, Michel, and Fanny Demers. 1992. "Europe 1992: Implications for North America." In *Canada Among Nations, 1992-93: A New World Order?*, eds. Fen O. Hampson and Christopher Maule. Ottawa: Carleton University Press, 191-216.

Deutsch, Karl W. 1957/1968. *Political Community and the North Atlantic Area.* Princeton, NJ: Princeton University Press.

Devuyst, Y. 1990. "European Community Integration and the United States: Toward a New Transatlantic Relationship." *Journal of European Integration*, 14, 1: 5-30.

Dewitt, David, and David Leyton-Brown, eds. 1995. *Canada's International Security Policy.* Scarborough, ON: Prentice-Hall.

———, and John Kirton. 1983. *Canada as a Principal Power: A Study in Foreign Policy and International Relations.* Toronto: John Wiley.

Dobell, Peter C. 1972. *Canada's Search for New Roles: Foreign Policy in the Trudeau Era.* Oxford: Oxford University Press.

———. 1985. *Canada in World Affairs, Vol. 17, 1971-1973.* Toronto: Canadian Institute of International Affairs.

Doern, G. Bruce, and Brian W. Tomlin. 1991. *Faith and Fear: The Free Trade Story.* Toronto: Stoddart.

Donneur, A.P., and P. Soldatos, eds. 1992. *Le Canada à l'ére de l'après-Guerre Froide et des blocs régionaux.* Toronto: Captus Press.

Dorscht, A., *et al.* 1986. "Canada's International Role and Realism." *International Perspectives,* Sept./Oct.: 6-9.

Drohan, Madelaine. July 10, 1993. "Home Alone." *Globe and Mail.*

Dunning, J.H. 1982. *Multinational Enterprise and Economic Analysis.* Cambridge: Cambridge University Press.

———. 1994. "MNE Activity: Comparing the NAFTA and the EC." In *Multinationals in North America,* ed. Lorraine Eden. Calgary, AB: University of Calgary Press and Industry Canada.

Easson, A.J., ed. 1979. *Canada and the European Communities: Selected Materials.* Kingston, ON: Queen's University Press.

Eayrs, James. 1960. *The Art of the Possible: Government and Foreign Policy in Canada.* Toronto: University of Toronto Press.

Economic Council of Canada. 1975. *Looking Outward.* Ottawa: Queen's Printer.

Eden, Lorraine. 1993. "Bringing the Firm Back In: Multinationals in International Political Economy." In *Multinationals in the Global Political Economy,* eds. Lorraine Eden and Evan H. Potter. London: Macmillan.

———. 1994. "Foreign Direct Investment in Canada: Charting a New Policy Direction." *Canadian Foreign Policy,* 2, 3 (Winter): 43-60.

———, ed. 1994. *Multinationals in North America.* Calgary, AB: University of Calgary Press and Industry Canada.

———, and Evan H. Potter, eds. 1993. *Multinationals in the Global Political Economy.* London: Macmillan.

Edwards, Geoffrey. 1992-93. "The European Community and Canada." *Behind the Headlines.* 50, 2 (Winter). Toronto: Canadian Institute of International Affairs: 18-23.

———, and Elfried Regelsberger. 1990. *Europe's Global Links.* London: Pinter.

El-Agraa, Ali M. 1989. *The Theory and Measurement of International Economic Integration.* London: Macmillan.

———. 1990. *The Economics of the European Community.* 3/e. Hemel Hampstead: Simon and Schuster.

———. 1993. "Japan's Reaction to the Single Internal Market." In *The External Relations of the European Community: International Responses to 1992,* ed. John Redmond. London: Macmillan, 12-30.

Emerson, Michael *et al.* March 1988. "The Economics of 1992: An Assessment of the Potential Economic Effects of Completing the Internal Market of the European Community," *European Economy,* no. 35. Luxembourg: European Communities Directorate General for Economic and Financial Affairs, Official Publications.

English, Edward H., ed. 1961. *Canada and the New International Economy.* Toronto: University of Toronto Press.

———. 1968. *Transatlantic Economic Community: Canadian Perspectives.* Toronto: University of Toronto Press.

English, John. 1992. *The Worldly Years: The Life of Lester Pearson, Volume 2: 1949-1972.* Toronto: Alfred A. Knopf.

European Commission. April 1993. *1993 Report on U.S. Barriers to Trade and Investment.* Brussels: Commission of the European Communities.

Evans, Paul. 1993. "Canada's Relations with China Emergent." *Canadian Foreign Policy,* 1, 2 (Spring): 13-28.

Farrell, Barry R. 1969. *The Making of Canadian Foreign Policy.* Scarborough, ON: Prentice-Hall.

Fielding, Leslie. 1991. *Europe as Global Partner: The External Relations of the European Community.* London: University Association for Contemporary European Studies.

Finlayson, Jock. 1993. "Directions for Canadian Trade Policy: A Private Sector View." *Canadian Foreign Policy,* 1, 3 (Fall): 113-22.

Foreign Policy Advisors Group. 1983. *The Third Option: Retrospect and Prospect.* Ottawa: Department of External Affairs.

Fowler, R.M. 1962. "Canada's Present Economic Position." In *Canada, the Commonwealth, and the Common Market,* ed. W.B. Cunningham. Montreal: McGill University Press.

Franklin, Michael, and Mark Wilke. 1990. *Britain in the European Community.* London: Royal Institute of International Affairs.

Galbraith, William J. 1988. "EUREKA: What Implications for Canada-EC Technology Relations?" *Journal of European Integration,* 11, 2-3 (Winter/Summer): 141-61.

Gelber, Lionel. 1968. *World Politics and Free Trade: Britain, USA, and the West.* London: Atlantic Trade Study.

Gilpin, Robert. 1972. "The Politics of Transnational Economic Relations." In *Transnational Relations and World Politics,* eds. R.O. Keohane and J.S. Nye. Cambridge, MA: Harvard University Press.

———. 1981. *War and Change in World Politics.* Cambridge: Cambridge University Press, ch.2.

Ginsberg, Roy H. 1989a. *Foreign Policy Actions of the European Community: The Politics of Scale.* Boulder, CO: Lynne Rienner.

———. 1989b. "U.S.-EC Relations." In *The European Community and the Challenge of the Future,* ed. Juliet Lodge. London: Pinter, 256-78.

Globerman, Steven. 1993. *CDIA: The Private and Public Interest.* Vancouver: Simon Fraser University, monograph.

———. 1994. *Canadian-Based Multinationals.* Calgary, AB: University of Calgary Press and Industry Canada.

———, *et al.* 1992. "Canada and the Movement Towards Liberalization of the International Telecommunications Regime." In *Canadian Foreign*

Policy and International Economic Regimes, eds. Claire Cutler and Mark W. Zacher. Vancouver: University of British Columbia Press.

Goodman, Elliot. 1975. *The Fate of the Atlantic Community.* New York: Praeger.

Gotlieb, Alan, and Jeremy Kinsman. 1981. "Reviving the Third Option." *International Perspectives* (Jan./Feb.): 2-5.

Graham, E.M. 1993. "Canadian Outward Direct Investment: Possible Effects on the Home Economy." Washington, DC: Institute for International Economics, mimeo.

Granatstein, J.L., ed. 1970. *Canadian Foreign Policy since 1945: Middle Power or Satellite?* Toronto: Copp Clark.

———, ed. 1986. *Canadian Foreign Policy: Historical Readings.* Toronto: Copp Clark Pitman.

———, and Robert Bothwell. 1990. *Pirouette: Pierre Trudeau and Canadian Foreign Policy.* Toronto: University of Toronto Press.

Griffith, Andrew. 1992/93. "Straight Talk on Why Canada Needs to Reform its Trade Development System." *Canadian Foreign Policy*, 1, 1 (Winter): 61-86.

———. 1992. "From a Trading Nation to a Nation of Traders: A Second Century of Canadian Trade Development." *Policy Planning Staff Paper.* Ottawa: External Affairs and International Trade Canada.

Hadwen, John. "Whither the Canadian Foreign Service?" *Bout de papier* 9, 1: 19-22.

Haftendorn, Helga, and Christian Tuschhoff, eds. 1993. *America and Europe in an Era of Change.* Boulder, CO: Westview.

Haglund, David. 1991. *Alliance Within the Alliance? Franco-German Military Cooperation and the European Pillar of Defense.* Boulder, CO: Westview.

Hahn, Walter F., and Robert L. Pfaltzgraff, Jr., eds. 1975. *Atlantic Community in Crisis: A Redefinition of the Transatlantic Relationship.* Elmsford, NY: Pergamon Press.

Halperin, Morton. 1974. *Bureaucratic Politics and American Foreign Policy.* Washington, DC: Brookings Institute.

Halstead, John. 1988 "Trudeau and Europe: Reflections of a Foreign Policy Adviser." *Journal of European Integration*, 12, 1 (Fall): 37-50.

———. 1993. "Atlantic Community or Continental Drift?" *Journal of European Integration*, 16, 2 (Spring): 151-64.

———. 1994. "International Security Institutions: NATO and the CSCE." *Canadian Foreign Policy*, 2, 1 (Spring): 45-62.

———, Panayotis Soldatos, and Hans J. Michelmann. 1988. *Doing Business with Europe: Canadian Trade with the European Community in a Changing World Economy.* Toronto: Canadian Scholars' Press.

Harris, Richard G., and David Cox. 1983. *Trade, Industrial Policy and Canadian Manufacturing.* Toronto: Ontario Economic Council.

Hart, Michael. 1991. "Canada Discovers its Vocation as a Nation of the Americas." In *Canada Among Nations 1990-91: After the Cold War*, eds. Fen Osler Hampson and Christopher J. Maule. Ottawa: Carleton University Press, 83-108.

———. 1992a. "Multilateralism and Professionalism." Unpublished manuscript.

———. 1992b. *Trade—Why Bother?* Ottawa: Centre for Trade Policy and Law, Carleton University.

Hart, Michael, with Bill Dymond and Colin Robertson. 1992. "Reconcilable Differences: The Rise and Triumph of Free Trade." Manuscript.

Hart, Michael. 1994. *Decision at Midnight: Inside the Canada-U.S. Free Trade Negotiations.* Vancouver: University of British Columbia Press.

Hartley, Livingston. 1965. *Atlantic Challenge.* Dobbs Ferry, NY: Oceana Publications.

Hawes, Michael K. 1984. *Principal Power, Middle Power, or Satellite?* North York, ON: York Research Programme in Strategic Studies.

Henderson, Stewart. 1992-93. "Zone of Uncertainty: Canada and the Security Architecture of Asia Pacific." *Canadian Foreign Policy*, 1, 1 (Winter): 103-20.

Henrikson, Alan K. 1993. "The New Atlanticism: Western Partnership for Global Leadership." *Journal of European Integration*, 16, 2 (Spring): 165-92.

Herter, Christian A. 1963. *Toward an Atlantic Community.* New York: Harper and Row.

Higgott, Richard A. 1991. "Towards a Non-Hegemonic International Political Economy." In *The New International Political Economy*, eds. C. Murphy and R. Tooze. Boulder, CO: Lynne Reiner.

Hill, Christopher. 1989. "A Theoretical Introduction." In *Foreign Policy Making in Western Europe*, eds. William Wallace and William Parsons. London: Pinter.

———. 1992. "The Foreign Policy of the European Community: Dream or Reality?" In *Foreign Policy in World Politics*, ed. Roy Macidris. Englewood Cliff, NJ: Prentice-Hall.

Hitchins, Diddy. 1991. *Canadian Trade Promotion Policies in Comparative Perspective.* Anchorage, AK: University of Alaska. November draft.

Hodges, Michael. 1975. "Canada and the European Communities: Problems in the Management of the North Atlantic Interdependence." In *Les Relations extérieures de la Communauté Européene: le Cas particulière du Canada.* Montréal: Université de Montréal.

Hogan, M.J. 1987. *The Marshall Plan: America, Britain, and the Reconstruction of Western Europe, 1947-1952.* Cambridge: Cambridge University Press.

Hollis, M., and M. Smith. 1986. "Roles and Reasons in Foreign Policy Decision Making." *British Journal of Political Science*, 16, 3 (July): 269-86.

Holmes, John W. 1966. "Is There a Future for Middlepowermanship?" In *Canada's Role as a Middle Power*, ed. Gordon J. King. Toronto: Canadian Institute of International Affairs.

———. 1970. *The Better Part of Valour: Essays on Canadian Diplomacy.* Toronto: McClelland & Stewart.

———. 1976. *Canada: A Middle-Aged Power.* Toronto: McClelland & Stewart.

Holmes, John W. 1982. *The Shaping of Peace: Canada and the Search for World Order, Volume 2, 1943-1957.* Toronto: University of Toronto Press.

Holst, Johan. 1975. "NATO, the European Community and the Transatlantic Order." In *The New Atlantic Challenge*, ed. Richard Mayne. New York: John Wiley.

Hufbauer, Gary. 1990. *Europe 1992: An American Perspective.* Washington, DC: Institute for International Economics.

———. 1989-90. "Beyond GATT," *Foreign Policy*, 77: 64-76.

Jackson, Robert J., Doreen Jackson, and Tom Keating. 1988. *Contemporary Canadian Politics.* Scarborough, ON: Prentice-Hall.

Jervis, Robert. 1976. *Perception and Misperception in International Politics.* Princeton, NJ: Princeton University Press.

Job, Brian L. and Frank Langdon. 1993. "Canada and the Pacific." In *Canada Among Nations 1993-94: Global Jeopardy*, eds. Fen Osler Hampson and Christopher J. Maule, Ottawa: Carleton University Press.

Johnson, Harry G. 1969. *New Trade Strategy for the World Economy.* Toronto: University of Toronto Press.

Keating, Tom. 1993. *Canada and the World Order: The Multilateralist Tradition in Canadian Foreign Policy.* Toronto: McClelland and Stewart.

Keohane, Robert O. 1980. "The Theory of Hegemonic Stability and Changes in International Economic Regimes." In *Change in the International System*, eds. Ole R. Holsti, Randolph M. Silverson, and Alexander L. George. Boulder, CO: Westview, 131-62.

———. 1984. "The World Political Economy and the Crisis of Embedded Liberalism." In *Order and Conflict in Contemporary Capitalism*, ed. John H. Goldthorpe. Oxford: Clarendon Press.

———. 1986. "Theory of World Politics: Structural Realism and Beyond." In *Neorealism and its Critics*, ed. Robert Keohane. New York: Columbia University Press.

———. 1990. *Institutions and State Power: Essays in International Relations Theory.* Boulder, CO: Westview.

———, and Joseph Nye. 1977. *Power and Interdependence: World Politics in Transition.* Boston: Little, Brown.

Keohane, Robert O., and Joseph S. Nye, eds. 1972. *Transnational Relations and World Politics.* Cambridge, MA: Harvard University Press.

———, Joseph S. Nye, and Stanley Hoffman, eds. 1993. *After the Cold War: International Institutions and State Strategies in Europe, 1989-91.* Cambridge, MA: Harvard University Press.

Kindleberger, Charles P. 1973. *The World in Depression, 1929-1939.* Berkeley: University of California Press.

Kirton, John J. 1986a. "The Continuing Success of the Third Option: Canada's Relations with Europe and the United States in the Mulroney Period." Mimeo.

Kirton, John J. 1986b. "The Foreign Policy Decision Process." In *Canada Among Nations, 1985: The Conservative Agenda*, eds. Maureen Appel Molot and Brian W. Tomlin. Toronto: James Lorimer.

———. 1995. "The Diplomacy of Concert." *Canadian Foreign Policy*, 3, 16 (Spring): 63-83.

———, and David D. Dewitt. 1983. *Canada as a Principal Power: A Study in Foreign Policy and International Relations.* Toronto: John Wiley.

Kissinger, H.A. May 14, 1973. *The Year of Europe.* Washington, DC: Department of State Bulletin.

Knubley, John, Marc Legault, and Someshwar Rao. 1994. "Multinationals and FDI in North America." In *Multinationals in North America*, ed. Lorraine Eden. Calgary, AB: University of Calgary Press.

Koekkoek, A., A. Kuyvenhoven, and W. Molle. 1990. "Europe 1992 and the Developing Countries: An Overview." *Journal of Common Market Studies*, 29: 111-32.

Kraft, J. 1962. *The Grand Design: From Common Market to Atlantic Partnership.* New York: Harper.

Krasner, Stephen D. 1972. "Are Bureaucracies Important? (Or Allison Wonderland)." *Foreign Policy*, 7 (Summer): 159-79.

———. 1978. *Defending the National Interest: Raw Materials Investments and U.S. Foreign Policy.* Princeton, NJ: Princeton University Press.

———. 1983. "Structural Causes and Regime Consequences: Regimes as Intervening Variables." In *International Regimes*, ed. Stephen D. Krasner. Ithaca, NY: Cornell University Press.

Krause, L. 1968. *European Economic Integration and the United States.* Washington, DC: Brookings Institute.

Krenzler, Horst J., and Wolfram Kaiser. 1991. "The Transatlantic Declaration: A New Basis for Relations between the EC and the USA." *Aussenpolitik*, 42, 4: 363-72.

Lake, David. 1983. "International Economic Structures and American Foreign Economic Policy." *World Politics*, 35, 3: 517-43.

———. 1984. "Beneath the Commerce of Nations." *International Studies Quarterly*, 28: 143-70.

Lake, David. 1988. *Power, Protection and Free Trade: International Sources of U.S. Commercial Strategy, 1887-1939.* Ithaca, NY: Cornell University Press.

Lamontagne, M. 1962. "Canada and the Common Market." In *Canada, the Commonwealth, and the Common Market*, ed. W.B. Cunningham. Montreal: McGill University Press.

Latsis, Spiro J. 1976. "A Research Programme in Economics." In *Method and Appraisal in Economics*, ed. Spiro J. Latsis. Cambridge: Cambridge University Press.

Lavergne, Stephen. 1994. "China 2000: The Nature of Growth and Canada's Economic Interests." *Policy Staff Paper*, 94/10. Ottawa: Department of Foreign Affairs and International Trade.

Liberal Party of Canada. Sept. 1993. *Governing for the 1990s.* Ottawa.

Lippman, Walter. 1943. *U.S. Foreign Policy: Shield of the Republic.* New York: Pocket Books.

Lipsey, R.E., and M.Y. Weiss. 1981. "Foreign Production and Exports in Manufacturing Industries." *Review of Economics and Statistics*, 63: 488-94.

Lipsey, Richard G. and Murray G. Smith. 1985. *Taking the Initiative: Canada's Trade Options in a Turbulent World.* Toronto: C.D. Howe Institute.

———, Daniel Schwanen, and Ronald J. Wonnacott. June 1993. "Inside or Outside the NAFTA? The Consequences of Canada's Choice." *Commentary*, 48. Toronto: C.D. Howe Institute.

Lodge, Juliet. 1982. *The European Community and New Zealand.* London: Pinter.

———. 1989. *The Politics of European Integration.* London: Pinter.

———. 1992. "New Zealand, Australia and 1992." In *The External Relations of the European Community*, ed. John Redmond. London: Macmillan.

———. 1989. "European Political Cooperation: Towards the 1990s." In *The European Community and the Challenge of the Future*, ed. Juliet Lodge. London: Pinter.

———. 1989/1993. *The European Community and the Challenge of the Future.* London: Pinter.

Long, David. 1994. "Europe After Maastricht." In *Canada Among Nations 1994: A Part of the Peace*, eds. Maureen A. Molot and Harald Von Riekhoff. Ottawa: Carleton University Press.

Lyon, Peter. 1992. "Britain and Canada since the Second World War: Two Mutually Entangled Countries." In *Britain and Canada in the 1990s*, ed. D.K. Adams. Halifax, NS: The Institute for Research on Public Policy.

Lyon, Peyton V. 1970. "A Review of the Review." *Journal of Canadian Studies*, 5 (May): 34.

Lyon, Peyton V. 1973. "The Quest for Counterweight: Canada and the European Economic Community." In *The European Community and the Outsiders*, ed. Peter Stingelin. Don Mills, ON: Longman, 49-62.

MacDonald, Donald S. April 10, 1992. "Should we break our bond with Europe?" *Globe and Mail.*

Macdonald, H.I. 1960. "Canada's Foreign Economic Policy." *Behind the Headlines*, 20, 4 (Nov.) Toronto: Canadian Institute of International Affairs.

———. 1958. "The European Common Market." *Behind the Headlines*, 18, 4 (Nov.) Toronto: Canadian Institute of International Affairs.

MacDougall, Barbara. 1992/93. "Canada and the New Internationalism." *Canadian Foreign Policy*, 1, 1 (Winter): 1-6.

MacLaren, Roy. 1994. "The Road from Marrakech: The Quest for Economic Internationalism in an Age of Ambivalence." *Canadian Foreign Policy*, 2, 1 (Spring): 1-8.

Mahaney, Mark S. 1993. "The European Community as a Global Power: Implications for the United States." *SAIS Review: A Journal of International Affairs*, 14 (Winter/Spring).

Mahant, E.E. 1976. "Canada and the European Community: The New Policy." *International Affairs*, 52, 4 (Oct.): 551-64.

Martin, Keith. 1992. "Canada-Transatlantic Trade and Investment Relations: A Canadian Perspective." Paper presented to the Economic Committee of the North Atlantic Assembly. Banff, AB: Assembly Spring Session, 15 May.

Martin, Morley. 1993. "Exports and Job Creation." *Policy Planning Staff Paper*, 93/06. Ottawa: External Affairs and International Trade.

Matheson, W.A. 1976. *The Prime Minister and the Cabinet.* Toronto: Methuen.

Mathews, R.A. 1962. "Canada, Britain and the Common Market." *World Today*, 18, 2 (Feb.): 48-57.

Mathews, R.A. 1972. "Britain's Move into Europe: The Implications for Canada." *Behind the Headlines,* 31, 5-6 (Oct.) Toronto: Canadian Institute for International Affairs.

Maxwell Stamp Associates. 1967a. *The Free Trade Area Option.* London: The Atlantic Trade Study.

———. 1967b. *The Free Trade Area Option: Opportunity for Britain.* London: The Atlantic Area Study.

McNaught, Kenneth. 1968. "From Colony to Satellite." In *An Independent Foreign Policy for Canada?*, ed. Stephen Clarkson. Toronto: McClelland & Stewart.

Michalska, Anna, and Hellen Wallace. 1992. *The European Community: The Challenge of Enlargement.* London: Royal Institute of International Affairs.

Michelmann, H. 1990. *The Political Economy of Agricultural Trade and Policy: Toward a New Order for Europe and North America.* Boulder, CO: Westview.

Moens, Alexander. 1994. "A New Security Strategy for Europe." In *Canada Among Nations 1994: A Separate Peace*, eds. Maureen A. Molot and Harald von Reikhoff. Ottawa: Carleton University Press, 154-71.

Molot, Maureen Appel. 1990. "Where Do We, Should We, or Can We Sit? A Review of Canadian Foreign Policy Literature." *International Journal of Canadian Studies*, 1, 2: 77-96.

Morgan, R. 1976. *Europe and the World.* London: Europe.

Muirhead, B.W. 1992. *The Development of Postwar Canadian Trade Policy: The Failure of the Anglo-European Option.* Montreal: McGill-Queen's University Press.

Munk, Frank. 1964. *Atlantic Dilemma: Partnership of Community?* Dobbs Ferry, NY: Oceana.

Munro, Gordon. 1992. "Evolution of Canadian Fisheries Management Policy Under the New Law of the Sea." In *Canadian Foreign Policy and International Economic Regimes*, eds. Claire Cutler and Mark W. Zacher. Vancouver: University of British Columbia Press.

Mytelka, Lynn K. 1993. "Strategic Alliances." In *Canada Among Nations, 1993-94: Global Jeopardy*, eds. Fen Osler Hampson and Christopher J. Maule. Ottawa: Carleton University Press, 106-30.

Nanto, Dick K. 1986. "European Community-Japan Relations." *CRS Report* 86-166 (Washington, DC).

———. June 4, 1993. "The U.S.-EC-Japan Trade Triangle." *CRS Report 92-500 E* (Washington, DC).

National Forum on Canada's International Relations. 1994. "Final Report," *Canadian Foreign Policy*, 2, 1 (Spring): 163-75.

Nau, Henry. 1993. "Europe and America in the 1990s: No Time to Mothball the Atlantic Partnership." In *The New Europe: Politics, Government and Economy since 1945*, ed. Jonathan Story. Oxford: Blackwell.

Naumann, Klaus. 1994. "Euro-American Security Challenges: Germany's Role and Responsibility." *Transatlantic Brief*, 9 (Washington, DC: Konrad Adenauer Stiftung).

Nelson, Mark. 1993. "Transatlantic Travails." *Foreign Policy*, 92 (Fall): 75-91.

Niosi, Jorge. 1994. "Foreign Direct Investment in Canada." In *Multinationals in North America*, ed. Lorraine Eden. Calgary, AB: University of Calgary Press and Industry Canada.

Nordlinger, Eric. 1981. *On the Autonomy of the Democratic State.* Cambridge, MA: Harvard University Press.

Norman, V.D. 1989. "EFTA and the Internal European Market." *Economic Policy*, 9.

Nossal, Kim R. 1982. "Personal Diplomacy and National Behaviour: Trudeau's North-South Initiatives." *Dalhousie Review*, 62 (Summer): 278-91.

Nossal, Kim R. 1983-84. "Analyzing the Domestic Sources of Canadian Foreign Policy." *International Journal*, 39, 1 (Winter): 1-22.

———. 1985. *The Politics of Canadian Foreign Policy*. Englewood Cliffs, NJ: Prentice Hall.

———. 1988. "Mixed Motives Revisited: Canada's Interest in Development Assistance." *Canadian Journal of Political Science*, 21, 1 (March): 36-56.

———. 1989. *The Politics of Canadian Foreign Policy*. 2/e. Scarborough, ON: Prentice-Hall.

———. 1991. "A European Nation? The Life and Times of Atlanticism in Canada." Paper presented at the Conference on Canadian Foreign Policy, December 10-11.

Nossal, Kim R. 1993a. "Contending Explanations for the Amalgamation of External Affairs." In *The Canadian Foreign Service in Transition*, ed. Donald Story. Toronto: Scholars' Press.

———. 1993b. "The Impact of Provincial Governments on Canadian Foreign Policy." In *States and Provinces in the International Political Economy*, eds. Douglas M. Brown and Earl H. Fry. Berkeley: Institute of Governmental Studies Press, University of California.

———. June 13, 1994. "Dividing the Territory: Prime Minister and Foreign Minister in Canadian Foreign Policy, 1968-1994." Paper delivered on June 13th to a joint session of the Canadian Political Science Association and the Canadian Historical Association, at the Annual Learned Societies Conference, University of Calgary, Alberta.

Nuttall, Simon J. 1992. *European Political Cooperation*. Oxford: Oxford University Press.

Nye, Joseph. 1990. *Bound to Lead: The Changing Nature of American Power*. New York: Basic Books.

Painchaud, Paul. 1966. "Middlepowermanship as an Ideology." In *Canada's Role as a Middle Power*, ed. Gordon J. King. Toronto: Canadian Institute of International Affairs.

———. 1985. *From Mackenzie King to Pierre Trudeau: Forty Years of Canadian Diplomacy, 1945-1985*. St. Foy, QC: Presses de l'université Laval.

Pal, Leslie A. 1997. *Beyond Policy Analysis: Public Issue Management in Turbulent Times*. Toronto: Nelson.

Papadopolous, Nicolas G. 1986. *Canada and the European Community: An Uncomfortable Partnership?* Montreal: Institute for Research on Public Policy.

Pearson, Lester B. 1972. *Mike: The Memoirs of the Right Honourable Lester B. Pearson*. Toronto: University of Toronto Press.

———. 1973. *Mike, Volume 2, 1948-1957*. Toronto: University of Toronto Press.

Pentland, Charles. 1977. "Linkage Politics: Canada's Contract and the Development of the European Communities' External Relations." *International Journal*, 32, 2: 207-31.

Pentland, Charles. 1982. "Domestic and External Dimensions of Economic Policy: Canada's Third Option." in *Economic Issues and the Atlantic Community*, ed. Wolfram F. Hanrieder. New York: Praeger.

———. 1991. "Europe 1992 and the Canadian Response." In *Canada Among Nations, 1990-1991: After the Cold War*, eds. Fen Osler Hampson and Christopher J. Maule. Ottawa: Carleton University Press, 125-44.

———. 1993. "European Security after the Cold War." In *Building a New Global Order: Emerging Trends in International Security*, eds. D. Dewitt, D. Haglund, and J. Kirton. Toronto: Oxford University Press, 59-85.

Pijpers, Alfred, Elfriede Regelsberger, and Wolfgang Wessels, eds. 1988. *European Political Cooperation in the 1980s: Towards a Foreign Policy for Western Europe?* The Hague: Nijhoff.

Pinder, John. 1989. *European Community*. London: Royal Institute of International Affairs.

———. 1991. *The European Community and Eastern Europe*. London: Royal Institute of International Affairs.

Pitts, Gordon. 1990. *Storming the Fortress: How Canadian Business Can Conquer Europe in 1992*. Toronto: HarperCollins.

Pollock, D., and G. Manuge. 1985 "The Mulroney Doctrine." *International Perspectives* (Jan./Feb.): 5-8.

Porter, Michael E., and the Monitor Company. 1991. *Canada at the Crossroads: The Reality of a New Competitive Environment*. Ottawa: Business Council on National Issues.

Potter, Evan. 1993. "A Question of Relevance: Canadian Foreign Policy and Foreign Service." In *Canada Among Nations, 1993-94: Global Jeopardy*, eds. Christopher Maule and Fen Osler Hampson. Ottawa: Carleton University Press, 37-56.

———. 1994. "A Holistic Approach to Canadian Foreign Policy." *Policy Options*, 15, 5 (June).

———. 1995. "The Impact of European Economic Integration on North America: Adjustment versus Radical Change." In *Toward a North American Community? Canada, the United States and Mexico*, eds. Donald Barry with Mark O. Dickerson and James D. Gaisford. Boulder, CO: Westview, 241-67.

———. 1995. "The Transatlantic Relationship in Flux." In *Toward a North American Community*. New York: St. Martin's Press.

Potter, Evan H. 1996-1997. "Niche Diplomacy and Canadian Foreign Policy." *International Journal*, 52, 1 (Winter): 25-38.

———. 1996. "Redesigning Canadian Diplomacy in an Age of Fiscal Austerity." In *Canada Among Nations, 1996: Big Enough to be Heard*, eds. Fen Osler Hampson and Maureen Appel Molot. Ottawa: Carleton University Press, 23-56.

Potter, Evan H., and Murray G. Smith. July 1994. *Trade Policy and Trade Development: Making the Market Access Connection.* Ottawa: International Business Studies Division, EAITC, mimeo.

Pratt, Cranford. 1983-84. "Dominant Class Theory and Canadian Foreign Policy: The Case of the Counter-Consensus." *International Journal,* 39, 2: 100-35.

———, ed. 1990. *Middle Power Internationalism: The North-South Dimension.* Kingston & Montreal: McGill-Queen's University Press.

Puchala, Donald, and R. A. Coate. 1988. *The State of the United Nations, 1988.* Hanover, NH: Academic Council of the United Nations System.

Rao, S., M. Legault, and A. Ahmad. 1994. "Canadian-Based Multinationals: An Analysis of Activities and Performance." In *Canadian-Based Multinationals,* ed. S. Globerman. Calgary, AB: University of Calgary Press and Industry Canada.

Redmond, John, ed. 1993. *The External Relations of the European Community: International Responses to 1992.* London: Macmillan.

Reid, Escott. 1977. *Time of Fear and Hope: Making of the North Atlantic Treaty 1947-49.* Toronto: McClelland & Stewart.

Reid, Tim. 1992/93. "Improving Canada's Trade System: A Private Sector Perspective." *Canadian Foreign Policy,* 1, 1 Winter: 87-102.

Rempel, Roy. 1997. *Counterweights: The Failure of Canada's German and European Policy, 1955-1995.* Montreal & Kingston: McGill-Queen's University Press.

Riddel, Peter. Nov. 9, 1990. "US-EC Ties to be Strengthened." *Financial Times (London).*

Riddell-Dixon, Elizabeth. 1991-92. "Canada's Policies on Technology Transfers." *International Journal,* 47 (Winter): 136-59.

Ries, J., and K. Head. 1993. *Causes and Consequences of Japanese Direct Investment Abroad.* Vancouver: University of British Columbia Press, mimeo.

Robertson, David. 1968. *Scope for New Trade Strategy: Dimensions of Free Trade.* London: Atlantic Trade Study.

Robinson, H. Basil. 1989. *Diefenbaker's World: A Populist in Foreign Affairs.* Toronto: University of Toronto Press.

Rochlin, James. 1994. *Discovering the Americas: The Evolution of Canadian Foreign Policy Towards Latin America.* Vancouver, BC: University of British Columbia Press.

Rollo, J.M.C. 1990. *The New Eastern Europe: Western Responses.* London: Royal Institute of International Affairs.

Roseman, Daniel. 1983. "The Canada-EC Framework for Economic Cooperation: From Dreams to Reality." Ph.D. dissertation, Institut universitaires des hautes études internationales, University of Geneva, Switzerland.

Roseman, Daniel. 1989. "Canada-European Community Relations: An Agenda for Action." *Behind the Headlines*, 46, 3 (Spring). Toronto: Canadian Institute of International Affairs.

Rothacher, Albrecht. 1982. "Trade Policies and Economic Diplomacy between the European Community and Japan, 1959-1980." Ph.D. dissertation, London School of Economics, U.K.

Royal Bank of Canada. 1992. "Is Canada Ready for Europe 1992?" *Econoscope*, 16, 1 (Feb.).

Rugman, Alan, and Joseph D'Cruz. 1991. *Fast Forward: Improving Canada's International Competitiveness.* Toronto: Kodak Canada.

Rummel, Reinhardt. 1989. "Modernizing Transatlantic Relations." *The Washington Quarterly*, 12, 4: 83-92.

Schmidt, Gustav. 1991. "The Political and Economic Dimensions of Canada's External Relations, 1947-72." In *Canada on the Threshold of the 21st Century: European Reflections upon the Future of Canada*, eds. C.H.W. Remie and J.-M. Lacroix. Philadelphia: John Benjamins, 473-86.

Schwanen, Daniel. 1992. "Were the Optimists Wrong on Free Trade? A Canadian Perspective." *Commentary* 37. Toronto: C.D. Howe Institute.

Schwartz, Jurgen. 1989. *The External Relations of the European Community, in Particular EC-U.S. Relations.* Baden Baden: Nomos Verlagsgesellschaft for the European Policy Unit at the European University Institute.

Sens, Allen G. 1993. "Canadian Defence Policy After the Cold War." *Canadian Foreign Policy*, 1, 3 (Fall): 7-28.

Services of the Commission of the European Communities, ed. 1992. *Report on United States Trade Barriers and Unfair Practices, 1992: Problems of Doing Business with the U.S.* Brussels: European Commission.

Sharp, Mitchell. 1972. "Canada-U.S. Relations: Options for the Future." *International Perspectives* (Autumn).

———. 1994. *Which Reminds Me ...* Toronto: University of Toronto Press.

Shearer, Ronald, *et al.* 1971. *Trade Liberalization and a Regional Economy: Studies on the Impact of Free Trade on British Columbia.* Toronto: University of Toronto Press, for the Private Planning Association.

Simpson, Jeffrey. 1993. *Faultlines: Struggling for a Canadian Vision.* Toronto: HarperCollins.

Smith, Michael. 1984. *Western Europe and the United States: The Uncertain Alliance.* London: George Allen & Unwin.

———. 1992. "'The Devil You Know': The United States and a Changing European Community." *International Affairs*, 68, 1: 103-20.

———. 1992. "The United States and 1992: Responses to a Changing European Community." In *The External Relations of the European Community: The International Response to 1992*, ed. John Redmond. New York: St. Martin's Press.

Smith, Michael, and Stephen Woolcock. 1992. "The U.S. and the European Community in a Transformed World" (draft manuscript).

———. 1993. *The United States and the European Community in a Transformed World.* London: Royal Institute of International Affairs.

Soldatos, Panayotis. 1993. "En guise d'introduction: le Canada devant la diversification et le continentalisme libre-échangiste." In *Le Canada à l'ére de l'après-Guerre Froide et des blocs régionaux,* eds. A.P. Donneur and P. Soldatos. Toronto: Captus Press.

———, and John G.H. Halstead. 1990. *Doing Business with Europe in a Changing World.* Toronto: Canadian Scholars' Press.

Soldatos, Panayotis, and André Donneur. 1988. *Le Canada entre le monde et les États-Unis: un pays enquête d'une politique étrangère renouvelée.* Toronto: Captus Press.

Solomon, Hyman. Oct. 22, 1983. "Trade Thinking Recognizes U.S. Reality." *Financial Post.*

———. May 30, 1990. "Trade Deals with Europe Becoming a Major Issue." *Financial Post.*

St. Laurent, Louis. 1947. "The Foundations of Canadian Foreign Policy in World Affairs." In *Canadian Foreign Policy: Historical Readings,* ed. J. Granatstein, 1986. Toronto: Copp Clark Pitman.

Stacey, C.P. 1977, 1981. *Canada and the Age of Conflict: A History of Canadian External Policies I: 1867-1920,* and *II: 1921-1948.* Toronto: Macmillan and University of Toronto Press.

Stairs, Denis. 1974. *The Diplomacy of Constraint: Canada, the Korean War, and the United States.* Toronto: University of Toronto Press.

———, and Gilbert R. Winham, eds. 1985. *Selected Problems in Formulating Foreign Economic Policy.* Toronto: University of Toronto Press.

Stairs, Denis. 1994-95. "Will and Circumstance and the Post-War Study of Canada's Foreign Policy." *International Journal,* 50, 1 (Winter): 9-39.

Stanley, Guy. 1994. "Northern Telecom: A Case Study in the Management of Technology." In *Canadian-Based Multinationals,* ed. Steven Globerman. Calgary, AB: University of Calgary Press and Industry Canada.

Stinchcombe, Arthur L. 1987. *Constructing Social Theories.* Chicago: University of Chicago Press.

Stingelin, Peter C.F. 1973. *The European Community and the Outsiders.* Toronto: Longman.

Strange, Susan. 1970. "International Economics and International Relations: A Case of Mutual Neglect." *International Affairs,* 46, 2: 304-15.

Stranks, Robert. 1994. "Outward Direct Investment: Implications for Domestic Employment." *Commentary.* Ottawa: Policy Staff, EAITC.

Swann, Dennis. 1990. *The Economics of a Common Market.* London: Penguin Books.

Talbot, R. 1978 *The Chicken War: An International Trade Conflict between the United States and the EEC.* Ames, IA: Iowa State University Press.

Thordarson, Bruce. 1972. *Trudeau and Foreign Policy: A Study in Decision-Making.* Toronto: Oxford University Press.

Tomlin, Brian W., and Bruce Doern. 1991. *Faith and Fear: The Free Trade Story.* Don Mills, ON: Stoddart.

Tsoukalanis, P. 1989. "The Defence of the European Community." In *The Politics of European Integration,* ed. Juliet Lodge. London: Pinter.

Tsoukalis, L., ed. 1986. *Europe, America and the World Economy.* Oxford: Blackwell.

U.S. International Trade Commission. April 1992. *The Effects of Greater Economic Integration within the European Community on the United States: Fourth Followup Report.* Washington, DC: United States International Trade Commission.

von Geusau, Alting. 1991. "Between Superpowers: Challenges and Opportunities for Canadian-European Cooperation." In *Canada on the Threshold of the 21st Century: European Reflections Upon the Future of Canada,* eds. C.H.W. Remie and J.M. Lacroix. Amsterdam: John Benjamins.

von Riekhoff, Harald. 1978. "The Third Option and Canadian Foreign Policy." In *Canadian Foreign Policy: Analysis and Trends,* ed. Brian Tomlin. Toronto: Methuen.

———. 1987. "The Structure of Foreign Policy Decision Making and Management." In *Canada Among Nations, 1986: Talking Trade,* eds. Brian W. Tomlin and Maureen Appel Molot. Toronto: James Lorimer, 14-30.

Wallace, William. 1983. *Britain's Bilateral Links within Western Europe.* London: Royal Institute of International Affairs.

———. 1990. *The Transformation of Western Europe.* London: Pinter.

Waltz, Kenneth N. 1959. *Man, the State and War.* New York: Columbia University Press.

———. 1979. *Theory of International Politics.* Reading, MA: Addison-Wesley.

Wardell, M. 1962. "The Challenge to Canada: The Threat to Canadian Trade." In *Canada, the Commonwealth, and the Common Market,* ed. W.B. Cunningham. Montreal: McGill University Press.

Wendt, Alexander. 1992. "Anarchy is What States Make of It." *International Organization,* 46 (Spring): 391-425.

Williams, Glen. 1986. *Not for Export: Toward a Political Economy of Canada's Arrested Industrialization,* rev./e. Toronto: McClelland & Stewart.

Williams, James R. 1978. *The Canadian-United States Tariff and Canadian Industry: A Multisectoral Analysis.* Toronto: University of Toronto Press.

Wolfe, Robert. 1990-91. "Atlanticism Without the Wall: Transatlantic Cooperation and the Transformation of Europe." *International Journal,* 46, 2 (Winter): 137-63.

Wolfers, Arnold. 1962a. "The Actors in International Politics." In *Discord and Collaboration: Essays in International Politics*, ed. A. Wolfers. Baltimore, MD: The Johns Hopkins University Press.

———. 1962b. *Discord and Collaboration: Essays on International Politics.* Baltimore, MD: The Johns Hopkins University Press.

Wonnacott, Ronald, and Paul Wonnacott. 1967. *Free Trade Between the United States and Canada: The Potential Economic Effects.* Cambridge, MA: Harvard University Press.

Wood, Bernard. 1988. *The Middle Powers and the General Interest.* "Middle Powers in the International System" ser., no. 1. Ottawa: North-South Institute.

Woods, Lawrence. 1993. *Asia-Pacific Diplomacy: Nongovernmental Organizations and International Relations.* Vancouver: University of British Columbia Press.

Woolcock, Stephen. 1991. *Market Access Issues in EC-U.S. Relations: Trading Partners or Trading Blows?* London: Chatham House Papers, Royal Institute of International Affairs.

———, Michael Hodges, and Kristen Schrieber. 1991. *Britain, Germany, and 1992: The Limits of Deregulation.* London: Royal Institute of International Affairs.

Wright, Gerald. 1985. "Bureaucratic Politics and Canadian Foreign Economic Policy." In *Selected Problems in Formulating Foreign Economic Policy*, ed. Gilbert R. Winham and Denis Stairs. Toronto: University of Toronto Press.

Yannopoulos, G.N. 1988. *Customs Unions and Trade Conflicts.* London: Routledge.

Yearbook of International Organizations 1992/93. 1993. New York: Union of International Institutions.

Young, John. 1957. *Canadian Commercial Policy.* Ottawa: Queen's Printer.

Young, Oran. 1989. *Political Leadership and Regime Reform: The Emergence of Institutions in International Society.* Washington DC: International Studies Association.

Zysman, John. 1983. *Governments, Markets, and Growth: Financial Systems and the Politics of Industrial Change.* Ithaca and London: Cornell University Press.